From Maverick to Mainstream

Cumberland School of Law, 1847–1997

David J. Langum and Howard P. Walthall

AF754298

THE UNIVERSITY OF GEORGIA PRESS *Athens & London*

© 1997 by the University of Georgia Press
Athens, Georgia 30602
All rights reserved
Designed by Louise OFarrell
Set in Garamond by G&S Typesetters, Inc.
Printed and bound by Braun-Brumfield, Inc.
The paper in this book meets the guidelines for
permanence and durability of the Committee on
Production Guidelines for Book Longevity of the
Council on Library Resources.

Printed in the United States of America

01 00 99 98 97 C 5 4 3 2 1

01 00 99 98 97 P 5 4 3 2 1

Library of Congress Cataloging in Publication Data

Langum, David J., 1940–
From maverick to mainstream: Cumberland School of Law, 1847–1997
David J. Langum and Howard P. Walthall.
p. cm. — (Studies in the legal history of the South)
Includes bibliographical references and index.
ISBN 0-8203-1892-2 (alk. paper); ISBN 0-8203-1893-0 (pbk.: alk. paper)
1. Cumberland School of Law—History. 2. Law schools—Alabama—Birmingham—History. I. Walthall, Howard P. II. Title. III. Series.
KF292.C864L36 1997
340'.071'1761781—dc21 96-51954

British Library Cataloging in Publication Data available

To Lucille Stewart Beeson

Contents

Preface · xi

CHAPTER ONE *Antebellum Beginnings, 1847–1861* · 1

CHAPTER TWO *Curriculum and Students, 1847–1861* · 24

CHAPTER THREE *After the War, 1865–1878* · 49

CHAPTER FOUR *The Student Experience, 1878–1919* · 72

CHAPTER FIVE *Prosperity and Stagnation, 1878–1919* · 97

CHAPTER SIX *Last of the Old Guard, 1920–1947* · 118

CHAPTER SEVEN *Living and Learning in Lebanon, 1920–1947* · 143

CHAPTER EIGHT *The Final Years in Lebanon, 1947–1961* · 168

CHAPTER NINE *The Cumberland Phoenix Rises in Birmingham, 1961–1983* · 196

CHAPTER TEN *Student Life and Accomplishments, 1961–1983* · 227

EPILOGUE *Foundation for the Future, 1984–1997* · 246

Notes · 255

Index · 299

Preface

Books have been written on the institutional histories of only a small number of American law schools, perhaps two dozen. All but one or two of these are either puff pieces, claiming that all connected with the institution was and still is grand and glorious, or Whiggish histories, where the vicissitudes of the past are mere preludes to the glories of the present circumstances. Honest histories of individual law schools are almost impossible to find. Since most law school scholarship finds its way into the law reviews, it is not so surprising that there are, however, a few law review articles theorizing why there are so few real histories of law schools. There is a bit of irony here, with efforts to explain why something has not happened displacing the work needed to make it happen in fact.

Several years ago the idea emerged that it would be a fine thing to have an institutional history of Cumberland School of Law, the school where we teach, for its sesquicentennial in 1997. When we first talked over the specifics with Dean Parham H. Williams Jr., for realistically we needed funding, we were at pains to explain that we wanted to write an honest history of the school, taking an analytical, critical look at its historical development, and placing it within the context of its historical setting, social and political, and particularly within the context of legal education.

We were delighted that our dean wholeheartedly endorsed our proposal and our insistence that the work be an honest history. We spoke with Thomas E. Corts, president of Samford University, the law school's host institution, because we needed access to the trustees' minutes and presidential reports, both restricted records. We were appreciative that President Corts, too, was extremely supportive of our book being a real analytical history, not simply a paean of praise.

Therefore, while this book is a commissioned institutional history, it is unusually candid about the shortcomings as well as the strengths of the institution that did the commissioning. Whether we have accomplished the goal of writing a critical, analytical, contextual history we must leave to the judgment of our readers and critics. We can assert, however, that we have had complete editorial freedom. No one from the law school or the university has read the text, suggested appropriate themes, or anything of that kind. There may be topics discussed that some administrative personnel would rather not have been included. The only test was whether a topic or fact materially aided a critical, analytical, contextual history. If it did, into the book it went. This is *not* true for the period 1984 to the present. The epilogue covers this time, and frankly, is a celebratory chronicle. Beyond the simple prudence of not bringing our analysis down to the present, there was a serious problem of detachment. We have been active participants in every triumph, shortfall, and controversy through which the Cumberland School of Law has passed since 1984. Our own viewpoints, rather than removed historical analysis, would necessarily be in the forefront. There would be no point to that, so we opted simply for a short epilogue to bring events to date.

Although we both thought about, read about, and talked with each other (and others) about the entire history of Cumberland School of Law, we did divide up the responsibilities. David J. Langum wrote chapters 1–5 and the preface, and Howard P. Walthall wrote chapters 6–10 and the epilogue. We both have benefited greatly from the skillful editing and cite-checking of our hardworking research assistant, Donna K. Vandever. Our colleague and friend, William G. Ross, read over every chapter and made extensive and very helpful editorial suggestions. To both Ms. Vandever and Professor Ross we owe great thanks.

We have other acknowledgments. Many persons at Cumberland University in Lebanon were enthusiastic and extremely helpful, including Roger M. Karl, director of the Vise Library, and Sally Robertson, reference librarian. G. Frank Burns, the Cumberland University historian, was the most helpful. He generously shared his vast knowledge of his institution's history and pointed us in the direction of many useful sources. However, when we were only half done, the trustees of Cumberland University changed their policies regarding access to the university archives, and we were denied further access to the minutes of the Cumberland University trustees. This accounts for the extensive use of the Cumberland trustees' minutes for the discussion in chapters 1–5 and its relative paucity thereafter. Fortunately, before the change in policy, G. Frank Burns had shared his notes with us concerning the minutes in the period after 1920.

This stood in complete contrast with the openness and enthusiasm of Dean Parham H. Williams and President Thomas E. Corts, who put all the records we asked for at our disposal. We thank Elizabeth C. Wells, coordinator of Special Collections of the Davis Library, for her help when we were working through the Samford trustee minutes. Edward L. Craig Jr., reference librarian of the Beeson Law Library, located all the obscure nineteenth-century books and articles we needed, and Laurel R. Clapp, director of the Beeson Law Library, told us of some rare materials her library held.

Other thanks for various matters are owed to Patsy L. Campbell, Shirley J. Clark, Virginia C. Downes, Brenda K. Jones, Linda G. Jones, Faye P. Lovelady, and James N. Lewis Jr., all of the Cumberland staff. Leigh Mattox Dulaney helped as a research assistant in the early phases of the project.

Hardly the least of our acknowledgments and thanks must go to Frances M. Langum and Kathryn T. Walthall, our wives, for their patience and understanding. That was the greatest support of all.

Over the years Cumberland School of Law has had many heroes, persons who have been of critical importance to the survival and improvement of the school. For the twentieth century, we think of Dean Arthur A. Weeks, who saved the school from certain extinction by moving it to Birmingham in 1961, and of Dean Donald E. Corley, who brought national recognition to Cumberland through his encouragement of student activities and who also significantly increased the resources available to the law school. We should also mention Dean Parham H. Williams Jr., who was instrumental in improving the quality of the faculty at Cumberland School of Law and supportive of faculty scholarship.

But as much as we appreciate these individuals, we hoped that this book might be a way of pointing the law school toward its future, as well as viewing the past. Therefore, we individually decided, without recommendation or suggestion from any source, to dedicate this book to Lucille Stewart Beeson. Her munificent gift of an extraordinarily beautiful and efficient law library building, in which it is a joy to work, will beneficially impact the school for decades into the twenty-first century. An excellent library is the cornerstone of the evolving quality of faculty, students, and research, now central to our collegial life at the law school. Truly, Lucille Stewart Beeson has pointed Cumberland School of Law toward its future.

CHAPTER ONE

Antebellum Beginnings 1847–1861

. . . to establish, and as they think render perpetual a Law Department.

—Minutes of Board of Trustees of Cumberland University

I CALL IT AN ADVENTURE, I speak of it as an experiment." With these words Abraham Caruthers, the first professor of Cumberland School of Law, described the precarious state of the institution's beginnings in his inaugural address. Judge Caruthers delivered his remarks on a hot summer day in Lebanon, Tennessee, July 29, 1847, as a part of Cumberland University's commencement ceremonies.[1]

The tentative state of the law school's beginning was underscored when instruction began on October 1. Only seven students assembled to greet the professor on that first day of classes. No facilities had been prepared for the law students in the university's building, and the first classes met in a sixteen-by-sixteen-foot room in a brick building on West Main Street, the law office of the professor's brother, Robert L. Caruthers. It was not an auspicious beginning.[2]

By the words *adventure* and *experiment,* Abraham Caruthers meant specifically that this was the beginning of the first university-affiliated law school in Tennessee, at a time when these were few. By the end of 1847, only fifteen university law schools existed in the United States.[3] Nevertheless, with the advantage of hindsight, Cumberland University's sponsorship of a law school seems very much a part of a larger national trend, and much less experimental and venturesome than it may have appeared at the time. There was something else about the new school, however, that was profoundly venturesome and new. That unique feature was its teaching method, its instructional approach. Surprisingly, pedagogy made Cumberland's law school unique, and, as we shall see, this pedagogy stamped it with distinctive qualities. First, however, we must step back and look at legal training in America up to the 1840s, and then review the foundation of Cumberland's law school.

Until the time of the American Revolution, the only method of legal training available in America was the apprenticeship. A student would pay a fee to a practicing lawyer for the privilege of working for him. The period of the apprenticeship varied from colony to colony, but it was often long, in New York as long as seven years and in some colonies even longer. There was a great deal of criticism of the apprenticeship system. Some offices offered only dreary copying of forms and other uninspiring work. The experience varied a great deal, office to office, lawyer to lawyer, student to student. John Quincy Adams had an excellent apprenticeship, and thought the lawyer for whom he clerked (Theophilus Parsons) a great teacher, fond of answering questions, and "in himself a law library." However, John Quincy Adams's father, John Adams, was highly critical of his own instructor. Thomas Jefferson had a pleasant experience studying law in Williamsburg with George Wythe, but nevertheless later wrote that he was "of the opinion that the placing of a youth to study with an attorney was rather a prejudice than a help."[4]

Even when they were ideal lawyers, these practitioners were often too busy to explain matters to their charges carefully. Even if there were adequate time and a will to explain, the flow of office work was unsystematic. The business that came in the door—rather than a graduated system of increasing complexity—often determined the order in which fledgling students would be exposed to legal concepts.[5] Nevertheless, apprenticeship remained the dominant form of legal education throughout the entire nineteenth century. Indeed, many students attending law schools in the nineteenth century did so only after they had clerked for a year or more. Law school became a method of learning law in a more abstract and conceptual manner *after* a previous exposure in the highly concrete way of clerkship.[6]

From the time of the American Revolution to about 1820, two divergent approaches to legal education competed with apprenticeships. First was legal education sponsored by universities. Yale (1777), William and Mary (1779), Philadelphia (1790), Columbia (1794), Transylvania [Lexington, Kentucky] (1799), Harvard (1815), and Maryland (1816) either planned or opened law schools. The idea behind these early university law schools was to combine law with political science. Those who actually wanted to practice law would go on to a clerkship. The studies were based on the model of William Blackstone, who in 1753 had assumed the Vinerian Professorship at Oxford, and in a series of lectures on the Common Law had introduced English law to university studies. Blackstone wrote that "a competent knowledge of the laws of that society in which we live is the proper accomplishment of every gentleman and scholar; a highly useful . . . part of liberal and polite education."[7] James Kent echoed the sentiment in the preface to his lectures at Columbia. The course was "not designed primarily for professional students" but was to be "useful and ornamental to gentlemen in every pursuit."[8]

The early efforts to bring law studies within the universities failed, except at Transylvania and William and Mary. The studies there, however, became more oriented toward career than originally planned. The early legal program at Yale never opened. Philadelphia began its program in 1790 but abandoned it two years later because of poor attendance. Columbia likewise took two years to fail. Harvard struggled on but was really refounded in 1829 by Joseph Story as a very different school. These schools either failed or changed because student demand was for technical career training. Young men did not desire to study abstract political principles but wanted practical tools to represent clients and make a living.[9]

The alternative model was private law schools that grew as an extension of apprenticeships. Lawyers who were especially skilled at instructing their charges sometimes found themselves with so many young people desiring apprenticeships that their law offices became transformed into schools. These schools generally were small and operated as a substitute, and for most states only a partial substitute, for law study in an office. The most successful of these private trade schools was the Litchfield Law School, founded in 1784 by Tapping Reeve as an outgrowth of his law office. This Litchfield, Connecticut, school continued until 1833 and was justifiably famous. It trained 2 vice presidents, 3 justices of the United States Supreme Court, 16 justices of state supreme courts, 6 cabinet members, 101 members of the House of Representatives, and 28 United States senators.[10] If George Wythe of William and Mary was America's first law professor, Litchfield was America's first law school. Most of the private law schools were much smaller and less successful, and led shorter lives. They appeared all over the country, and Tennessee had at least two small practitioner-run schools, Haywood's in Nashville and Powell's in Blountville.[11]

Jacksonian Democracy had a leveling influence on American law. Already loose standards for entry into the profession became even more minimal. Several jurisdictions abandoned any requirement of education or apprenticeship or even judicial examination of qualifications and (temporarily) opened membership in the bar to any male of good moral character. In this anti-elitist climate the price lawyers paid for respect was to abandon all claims of being members of a political elite and present themselves to America as tradesmen, small businessmen.

American universities reentered the field of legal education in the 1820s and 1830s. Harvard's law school was refounded in 1829; Cincinnati's private law school, founded in 1833, was acquired by Cincinnati College in 1835; and in 1826, Yale founded its law school by hiring the owner and professor of a small private law school, of the Litchfield model, and listing that school's students in the Yale catalogue.

In the 1840s and 1850s, university-affiliated law schools multiplied more rapidly. Many of these were in the South. The University of North Carolina acquired a proprietary law school in 1845, and Tulane established a law school in 1847 by absorbing an existing small school. The University of Louisville's law program began in 1846, the University of Mississippi School of Law in 1854, and the University of Georgia founded its Lumpkin Law School in 1859. The South, spurred by increasing litigation arising out of the region's commercial use of slaves and its historically tangled land titles, offered a boom period for lawyers, and therefore for law schools.

Nationwide, the growth was slow, and several attempts to found law schools failed. In 1840, there were but nine university-affiliated law schools in the United States; in 1850, fifteen (including Cumberland); and by 1860, still the small number of twenty-one university law schools.[12]

In two respects university legal training was very different than its earlier appearance. First, the curriculum was shorter than in the earlier period. Of the fifteen schools in 1850, six had a one-year program, one had an eighteen-month plan, and five imposed a two-year curriculum. The program of three schools is unknown.[13] Second, the emphasis was practical. A good example is the University of Virginia. When it first planned its law school, which opened in 1826, it intended to teach political science along with law. The Board of Visitors enjoined that the professor of the law school should "pay special attention to the principles of government which shall be inculcated therein, and to provide that none shall be inculcated which are incompatible with those on which the constitutions of this state, and of the United States, are genuinely based."[14]

What happened is instructive. By 1830, the law professor wrote that the law students "are eager that the period [of instruction] shall be devoted to such instruction as may practically fit them for their profession. Their demand for the law is as for a trade—the means, the most expeditious and convenient, for their future livelihood. I found myself irresistibly compelled to labor for the satisfaction of this demand, or that the University would have no students of law."[15]

Some vestiges of the earlier Blackstonian vision of law as training for political life continued on, at least at the level of rhetoric, in several law schools throughout the 1840s and 1850s.[16] The last surviving law program dedicated primarily to public law and training for public life was that of Transylvania University. It succumbed in 1858, in part because of the more practical education offered by Cincinnati to its north and Cumberland to its south.[17] These new university law schools brought their host universities prestige, but they were often kept on the margins, sometimes literally, of their sponsors. They were seldom integrated into the universities in the manner of a modern law school.[18]

In these contexts Cumberland University's law school was born. The Cumberland Presbyterians organized the original Cumberland College in March 1826 for the purpose of educating young men who had little money, particularly those preparing for the ministry. The institution was located on a farm about a mile from Princeton, Kentucky, and was organized on the principles of what we would now call work-study. All students were required to do farm work for two hours each day, the dormitories and buildings were of the plainest kind, the food was "healthful, but plain and cheap," and all luxuries were forbidden. Although there was a modest tuition, money problems plagued the institution from the beginning. Additionally, cholera and other diseases discouraged attendance.

Morale was also a problem. The General Assembly of the Cumberland Presbyterians informed the resentful faculty and students that it wished both "to dress in home-made clothing from head to foot." As to the work requirement, a sympathetic church historian noted in the 1880s that "many of the Southern boys, reared where slaves did all the work, met the labor requirements with bad grace. . . . Difficulties between students and the overseer of the farm were very frequent."[19]

One of the basic problems was the placement of the college in a location where the Cumberland Presbyterians were not particularly strong. Efforts at fund-raising in 1840 failed, court judgments accumulated, and levies were about to be made against the property in 1842. At that point, the Cumberland Presbyterian General Assembly appointed a committee to select a different location. It was this committee, meeting in Nashville in July 1842, that responded to a petition from Lebanon, Tennessee, to establish Cumberland University there.[20] Seventy years later, great legal controversy broke out over whether the institution at Lebanon was a new creation of this committee, or whether the old Cumberland College had simply been moved to Lebanon.

That question seems entirely academic now, but for a short while, as we shall see, it threatened the very existence of the institution and the law school with it. It is not entirely clear what did happen in 1842. The president of the old Cumberland College from the date of its foundation, Franceway Ranna Cossitt, simply moved to Lebanon and became president of the newly formed, and renamed, Cumberland *University.* On the other hand, the old Cumberland College teetered on in Princeton until 1858, sixteen years after classes began in Lebanon.

Several towns competed for the new institution, but Lebanon, the county seat of Wilson County, Tennessee, possessed several advantages. It was enjoying good times; farming, silk culture, flour milling, and wool mills were flourishing. The town was founded in 1802 and took its name from Biblical Lebanon because of the red cedars in that part of Tennessee.

Located thirty miles east of Nashville, six miles south of the Cumberland River, a few miles west of the Cumberland Mountains, in 1842 it was a center of the system of post roads. It even had some history. Sam Houston had practiced law in Lebanon in the years 1818–19, before he was a congressman, governor of Tennessee, and later, president of the Republic of Texas. While he was governor of Tennessee, Houston met his wife near Lebanon.[21]

But the chief advantage to Lebanon in the competition for the university was the existence there of a great number of Cumberland Presbyterians, ably led by then United States Representative Robert L. Caruthers. Later in 1889, Nathan Green Jr., a professor in the law school and himself an insider in the university's counsels, wrote that to Robert Caruthers "more than to any other man is due the credit of establishing and perpetuating Cumberland University."[22] Robert Caruthers was a wealthy lawyer, born in 1800. He was elected state's attorney for the Lebanon Circuit in 1827, to the state legislature in 1832, to the national Congress in 1841, to the Tennessee Supreme Court in 1852, to the Confederate Congress in 1861, and to the governorship of Tennessee in 1863.[23]

The people of Lebanon pledged ten thousand dollars, a considerable sum in 1842, toward the construction of a university building for the school. Robert Caruthers, the chief donor, was selected president of the board of trustees of the university, a position he held until his death in 1882. Following the Civil War, he also became one of the law professors. Other factors that induced the committee to select Lebanon for the university's location included its reputation for a healthy climate and its good moral tone.[24]

Although Cumberland University was not a division of the Cumberland Presbyterian Church, it was very much a denominationally controlled body. All but two of the original thirteen trustees (all Lebanon residents) were Cumberland Presbyterians,[25] and early resolutions of the board of trustees provided that students preparing for the ministry "according to the Book of Discipline of the Cumberland Presbyterian Church" should be educated without tuition and also that at least eight of the thirteen members of the board should be members of that denomination.[26]

Classes began at the new institution in the fall of 1842. Work began on the new building almost immediately, but it was not ready in time for the beginning of classes, which met temporarily at the Cumberland Presbyterian Church on North Cumberland Street. The new structure was ready for occupancy in February 1844.[27] It was built on a small bluff overlooking the downtown and square, at the intersection of College and Spring Streets. The building promised to the selection committee was only two stories and one hundred feet long, but the committee reported to the General Assembly that the building actually under construction was three stories and slightly longer.[28]

The title of the new school, *university* instead of *college,* was more than a mere attempt to differentiate the school in Lebanon from the old institution in Princeton. Nearly from the beginning, the trustees showed an interest in instituting professional departments and thereby creating a true university. As a step toward the introduction of legal education, in early 1845 the board appointed Nathan Green Sr., then a justice on the Tennessee Supreme Court, as "Professor of International Law & Political Economy."[29] On May 27, 1845, the president of the school informed the board that Green declined, owning to family duties and other engagements. The board then offered the position to Abraham Caruthers, a Tennessee trial judge and the brother of Robert L. Caruthers.[30]

The establishment of a professorship in international law was not intended actually to establish a law school. In a private letter from Nathan Green Sr. to Robert L. Caruthers, Green explained that he understood the offer to be "the use of my name in the way you propose, and the occasional lecture," and he declined, reasoning that anyone teaching at the school ought to reside in Lebanon.[31] Apparently, the growing interest in legal studies was controversial within the church because a theological school had not yet been established, and church leaders feared that a law department "would divert interest, distract our forces."[32]

But the idea of legal studies soon accelerated from that of an occasional lecture on law to the establishment of an actual professional school. In January 1847, the trustees appointed a committee to consider the propriety and practicability of establishing a law department.[33] The committee reported back favorably the following month. The board wished to make the school a "University in fact as well as in name," and therefore resolved "to establish, and as they think render perpetual a Law Department." It expressed the hope that it might shortly be able to establish a theology school as well. The board appointed Abraham Caruthers the first professor of the law department, with a salary of $1,500 per year "to be paid out of the tuition fees of this department," and appointed a subcommittee to make rules and regulations for the department and to "take steps to procure a library."

Considerable internal evidence in the board's resolution indicates that everything had been arranged. First, an otherwise puzzling resolution by the board as to the teaching techniques to be used in the law school clearly indicates that Abraham Caruthers, who had strong ideas in these regards, was aware of and agreed to the prospective appointment. Second, a vague reference that the board felt authorized to establish the law school "by the assurance of one of its members" is a reference to the guarantee of the professor's salary made later that summer by Robert L. Caruthers. The only conditional provision was that the law school should be established only if fifteen students would enroll by May 15 for the opening of the fall term.[34]

In the 1840s and 1850s, it was not strange, as it would be now, to establish a law school in a small town. No demand then existed for live client clinical training or student employment with local practitioners. Other southern law schools were in small towns: University of Georgia's Lumpkin Law School in Athens and University of Mississippi School of Law in Oxford. In the North, the most famous law school of the very early nineteenth century was located in Litchfield, Connecticut, a town smaller than Lebanon, Tennessee. Additionally, in the 1840s Lebanon was an important transportation hub and commercial center and was considerably more prominent a city than later in the nineteenth century or at any time in the twentieth century.

By May 14, 1847, Abraham Caruthers had accepted the professorship and was asked to deliver an inaugural address, in which he was to refer to the experimental nature of the school on commencement day.[35] The professor-elect, Robert Caruthers's younger brother, was born in 1803. He began the practice of law in 1824 and was appointed as a judge of the circuit court, Tennessee's general trial court, in 1833. He resigned from this position to become the first professor of Cumberland School of Law.[36] The salary of a circuit judge was $1,500, which for Abraham Caruthers was a near certain income. He had been a circuit judge for fourteen years, and no one doubted his reelection. On the other hand, a new law school in a state that had never had this type of school, with a bar filled with attorneys who had not themselves been educated in law schools, was indeed a risky proposition. The doubts in the mind of Abraham Caruthers were resolved by his brother's guarantee of his salary.[37]

On August 30, 1847, Robert Caruthers submitted a written proposition that was accepted by the board. It recited that the establishment of the law school and the appointment of the professor had been done "on certain conditions and assurances" he had made but that should be put in writing. Robert Caruthers undertook to guarantee the professor's salary for the first three years; that is, he would make up any shortfall between $1,500 (the amount of the previous judicial salary, and also the new compensation set by the Cumberland board) and the tuition fees received by the new department. The guarantee also provided that if there were a surplus of income to the department, above $1,500, the professor should be entitled to the surplus to a total of $2,000 per annum; that the regulations for the department should be prescribed by the board with the "counsel & advice" of the professor; and that, although the law professor would be a member of the university faculty, nevertheless, "his attendance & participation in the ordinary duties in government shall be optional with him."[38]

The school thrived from the beginning. The seven students who met the first day's class increased to thirteen by the end of the first term.[39] By the end of the first academic year the school had twenty-five students,[40] generating tuition that exceeded the judge's former salary of $1,500. Indeed, the "great and unexpected influx of students at the commencement of the second year" made it necessary to hire additional part-time instructors.[41] Both Nathan Green Sr. of the Supreme Court of Tennessee and Bromfield L. Ridley, chancellor of the 4th Chancery Division, were recruited to teach during court vacations.[42] By the second academic year, 1848–49, the law school had fifty-six students.[43]

Once it was clear that the law school would be profitable, the Caruthers brothers changed their attitudes toward compensation. On July 26, 1848, Abraham Caruthers delivered to the trustees a rather high-handed letter:

> Circumstances render it necessary that I should derive from my own labors every possible pecuniary advantage. The institution of a law school is a new and difficult enterprise in Tennessee demanding of

> any one who undertakes it his whole attention so that he cannot attend to any other business. It will also require a variety of expenditures about which I would be embarrassed to consult any body beforehand or render an account to anyone afterwards. As the law department in C. University [sic] has cost the university nothing and is not to do so under any circumstances as I am willing to take the whole risque [sic] of its success whether it yields much or little, I ask that a contract be now entered into with me securing me all its profits for the space of eight years from its commencement. Should assistance [i.e., additional faculty] be at any time be necessary my own character and interest would require me to secure it.

The trustees' committee concerned with the law department (which included Robert Caruthers, the professor's brother) reported that it considered it "but just that he should enjoy the fruits of his labors. . . . It may be that the salary will, at turns be large, but it may at other times be small . . . in just proportion to the labor performance." Accordingly, the trustees resolved that for five years, not eight, the professor of law "may have all the profits of his department whether the same be much or little for his salary after defraying all expenses." The law department still had to pay twenty-five dollars each session for the use of the room in the college building set aside for the law department (it is not clear when it was able to move out of Robert Caruthers's office), and the board expressly provided that it would be "in no way liable for any expenses for said department," and that if additional professors needed to be hired, all salaries would be paid "out of the lecture fees."[44]

Financially, aside from minor contingency fees charged law students for the benefit of the university, the law school thereafter operated as a free-standing proprietary school. The faculty received all the income, and it paid all the expenses. Accordingly, when the law school required a second room in 1849, the university charged the law school an additional twenty-five dollars per term. Also, the law school was precluded from any benefit from such slight endowment as Cumberland University enjoyed.[45]

Much later, a church historian suggested that the purpose of this agreement was to quiet continuing opposition to the law school among churchmen by making it clear the university would not be liable for debts of the law school.[46] However, there is no evidence that this was the motivation.

Nothing in the minutes of the board of trustees indicates that anything other than the simple self-interest of Abraham Caruthers was involved.

To the modern eye, this sort of proprietary takeover of a law school by its faculty appears incredible. But actually, this arrangement was normal for antebellum law schools, even those affiliated or "owned" by universities. The only universities that compensated their law faculty by straight salaries before 1860 were Harvard, Virginia, and Michigan,[47] and Virginia's arrangement was a small salary in addition to student fees. Even state schools employed proprietary compensation arrangements. When the University of Wisconsin opened its law school in 1857, the law professors' salaries were to come from tuition only.[48]

Payment of salaries by assignment of the tuition may sometimes have been because a "weak denominational college was usually unable to provide" more than classroom space.[49] But penury certainly was not a factor in Cumberland's case, where the proprietary arrangements were not made until the law school had proven itself a success. There is nothing strange about the Cumberland faculty compensation in the 1840s based on tuition receipts. What is strange is that this system continued until the 1920s, when it had become an anachronism.

Robert Caruthers understood the practices of other schools when he proposed this compensation plan. He had taken the trouble to write Simon Greenleaf of Harvard's law school, one of the leading law professors and legal authors of the 1840s. Greenleaf wrote him back in January 1848, long before the change in compensation arrangements, enclosing a copy of the Harvard catalogue and informing Robert Caruthers that he, Greenleaf, and the other professor at the law school were paid straight salaries of three thousand dollars, fixed and independent of fees, "the professors having nothing to do with the pecuniary affairs of the University."[50] Harvard, however, was ahead of its time.

Back in 1845, before the law school was organized, Cumberland University's first choice for the part-time professorship of international law and political economy had been Nathan Green Sr. With the establishment of the law school, Robert L. Caruthers was still determined to lure Green as a part-time instructor. But in May 1847 Green turned the offer down. He was too preoccupied with his forthcoming reelection to the Tennessee Supreme Court. Green expressed his high estimation of the plan for the school and of the first professor, and advised that he had planted an anonymous letter praising the school in a Nashville newspaper under the name "an old lawyer." If there were "no serious obstacle" to his reelection he would send his son, Nathan Green Jr., to the opening of the law school in the fall.[51] And indeed, he did sent the younger Green, who was among the first seven students on October 1, 1847, and who played a dominant role in the life of the law school until his death in 1919.

The success of the school during its first academic year, and especially the large enrollment in the fall of 1848, its second year, brought new pressures to add faculty. The course, as we shall see shortly in more detail, was for two years, and at least one additional faculty member was essential. The school hired Bromfield L. Ridley to teach on a part-time basis during the second year. But Ridley was a busy equity trial judge and could devote only brief periods of time to the school.[52]

Robert L. Caruthers continued to lobby Nathan Green Sr. He suggested that Green ought to move to Lebanon, continue as a justice on the Tennessee Supreme Court, and work at the law school during the long court vacations. Green responded that his wife feared the effect of year-round employment on his health. But he thought that she and other members of his family "will become accustomed to think of this result, and next fall, they will acquiesce in it." He added that his decision not to move to Lebanon was "not at all influenced by apprehensions of the success of the school," and said that he was going to help Judge Caruthers by teaching part-time at the beginning of the next term in March 1849.[53]

In November 1848 the Cumberland board formally appointed Nathan Green Sr. as a professor of law and decided that the two professors should apportion their duties as "they think proper and most conducive to the interest of the students." Further, the board resolved not to consider the issue of compensation unless disagreement arose but urged that Green's compensation "be settled and arranged between him and the present professor out of the income of the department, as they may agree."[54]

Green began teaching the senior class in the spring term of 1849, during periods of his court's recess.[55] But the use of even two part-time instructors did not relieve the pressure on the full-time professor, as the enrollment continued to mount. Nathan Green had himself noted, in his inaugural address of February 28, 1849, that the reputation of the new law school was "second to no School of the kind West of the Alleghany [sic] mountains" and that its enrollment "already amounts to half the number in the Law Department of the celebrated University at Cambridge, Massachusetts,"[56] that is, Harvard.

The enrollment declined from fifty-six students in 1848–49 to only forty-eight the following year, because of a health scare from an outbreak of cholera in Lebanon in the summer of 1849. Enrollment soared to seventy-four for academic year 1850–51.[57] This imposed new pressure on Nathan Green Sr., this time to teach full-time. Green was a good choice. Born in Virginia in 1792, he had practiced law in Virginia and acquired "quite a fortune" but gambled it away. The patience and prayers of his wife brought about his repentance. Green experienced a religious conversion, gave up gambling, and became an elder in the Cumberland Presbyterian church.[58] He moved to Tennessee to begin a new life. In 1827 Green became chancellor of East Tennessee, and in 1831 the state legislature elected him to the Tennessee Supreme Court, where he remained until 1852.[59] Green was well-regarded and prominent for his work on the Tennessee Supreme Court and was a staunch supporter of the Cumberland Presbyterian Church.

Green was uncomfortable with the part-time arrangement, feeling that "my time is so cut up, & there are so many obstacles in the way of effective service."[60] But he continued in a part-time capacity until 1852, when an additional consideration was presented. Tennessee was in the midst of its cumbersome method of constitutional amendment. Almost certain to be adopted was a provision for the direct election of its supreme court by the citizens, as distinct from the legislature, which had before been responsible for the selection. Justices would soon have to run for office. Green pondered his options, which now included a full-time professorship at the law school. He wrote to a son in April 1852:

> It is true the law school is not endowed, and the income depends on the *patronage,* which is uncertain and may fluctuate below my minimum; but the Judgeship is also uncertain, in view of the amended Constitution,—and if I am to retire two years hence,—*perforce,*—it would be more graceful to retire *now,* voluntarily,—& thereby retain the *prestige* of my former popularity as a Judge.

Additionally, Green explained to his son, he could "safely calculate that the law school will average 30 people; sometimes we have 60 or 70." Half of the income from the tuition of 30 students would be $1,500, the equal of his judicial pay. Furthermore, he recalled that he would be sixty years old in the following month. He had heard (and believed) a theory that at his age a man ought to diminish his labors, because if he overburdened himself he was "likely soon to break down,—& in such case, he dwindles rapidly into a decrepid [sic] old age." He felt he had to give up either the judgeship or the law school; "*both* press me too heavily." The law school professorship, he reasoned, was no more onerous a labor than sitting in court, and the preparation of opinions, the "heaviest burden of the office . . . would be saved."[61]

In 1852, Green resigned from the court and became a full-time member of the faculty that fall. It was not too soon, because, though the school had Ridley's help and two full-time professors, the student enrollment continued to grow.

Cumberland University in general, and the law school in particular, were skillful at promoting themselves. Inaugural addresses of the professors and graduation addresses of prominent men were reprinted into pamphlet form and distributed to newspapers throughout the South. This provided wide publicity for Cumberland and attracted students.[62] Cumberland widely distributed Abraham Caruthers's inaugural address, and it was read with approval by many leading lawyers.[63] Visiting journalists sent favorable reports back to out-of-state newspapers,[64] and before 1856 one young man studying at the University of Virginia transferred to Cumberland.[65] By October 1848, the governor of Tennessee referred to the "rising reputation" of the university.[66]

Much of this rise in the law school's reputation was owed to the acquisition of Nathan Green Sr. as a full-time faculty member. He enjoyed a great reputation throughout Tennessee and in other southern states.[67] A teaching plan that permitted young men to enter at virtually any time of the year and with no advance preparation attracted students. The widely distributed annual catalogues constantly emphasized the high points of the law school. First were the two professors devoting their full time to the law school and the assurance of their attention that that offered students. Second were the advantages of Lebanon, a place with "a constant succession of courts, conventions, legislatures, theatrical and other exhibitions," yet also "a village destitute of those attractions which, in a city, are constantly beguiling students from their studies."[68] The general healthiness of Lebanon was emphasized in most of the early catalogues, often with acknowledgment of the cholera attack in the spring of 1849 but with assurances that one need not fear further outbreaks.

The high moral tone of the town and school was another frequent topic emphasized in the antebellum catalogues. The 1846–47 catalogue informed prospective law students and their parents that the "Bible will be studied by every student and regarded as a text-book" in both the first and second year classes, a promise presumably more honored in the breach than in the observance. Cumberland made no effort to propagate any denominational viewpoint.

The 1848–49 catalogue stated that "no student of grossly immoral habits could possibly remain long in the School. . . . In the society of the town and of the School, there is every thing to repell [*sic*] and nothing to invite a student who expects to indulge vicious propensities." The 1853–54 publication informed prospects that "the influence of the local society is very salutary. Wherever a Law School may be situated, that influence will be powerfully felt. In Lebanon it is altogether on the side of virtue. The whole weight of society is actively exerted against intemperance, gambling, and vice in every shape." These were reassuring words to parents, especially when it is recalled that law students were undergraduates. We will see later how the moral sentiments were enforced.

Above all, the early catalogues emphasized the value of the teaching methodology. Three primary advantages were generally claimed for Cumberland in these antebellum catalogues. They were contrasted with apprenticeship and to a lesser degree with law schools using ordinary lectures. All involve the distinctive Cumberland teaching methodology, discussed more completely later. The selling points included the extensive moot court competitions demanded of a Cumberland student. "After remaining here long enough to graduate, he will be at very little loss to conduct a suit of any sort successfully. . . . Is this advantage enjoyed in the lawyer's office? Every lawyer knows it is not . . . [and] how much the young attorney and his clients suffer for want of this advantage."[69]

Another advantage usually mentioned in various ways was the system of daily recitations and daily examinations. The Cumberland student "not only feels constrained every day to acquire knowledge, but he also communicates it by his answers to interrogatories. . . . In the office and lecture systems this advantage is lost. And how essential is it to a lawyer that he should be well trained in the expression of his thoughts!"[70] The third Cumberland advantage was the spirit of competitiveness aroused by being in a class. "Every day the student has to be contrasted with his class-mates. They recite together. He must be prepared for the recitation or sink ingloriously in the comparison. If he has spirit enough in him to make him a lawyer this will arouse him. Is there this advantage in an office?"[71] As we shall see, these were short descriptions of ideas generated in a more sophisticated form by Abraham Caruthers, and they constituted the core of Cumberland's claim for a distinctive place in early American legal education.

This promotion clearly paid rich dividends in admissions. Following is a listing of the number of students for the academic years 1847–48 through 1859–60. The figures include those who entered the fall term, plus new students who entered in the spring term.[72]

1847–48	25	1852–53	70	1857–58	188
1848–49	56	1853–54	87	1858–59	162
1849–50	48	1854–55	100	1859–60	180
1850–51	74	1855–56	134		
1851–52	86	1856–57	167		

Tennessee students dominated the class rolls throughout the antebellum period. But other southern states were increasingly represented, and by 1860 Cumberland had become a regional institution rather than a Tennessee institution. Some students came from considerable distance; Ohio, California, Iowa, Illinois, New York, and Massachusetts were all represented. The Cumberland Presbyterians had a mission to the Choctaw Indians, and beginning in 1853, long before law schools were generally open to Indians, a handful of Choctaw students enrolled on campus. A considerable number of students from Texas reflected the strength of the Cumberland Presbyterian Church in that state.[73] A breakdown of the student body in the largest prewar year, 1857–58, offers a representative view:[74]

Alabama	39	Kentucky	4	South Carolina	3
Arkansas	9	Louisiana	3	Tennessee	72
Choctaw Nation	1	Maryland	1	Texas	7
Florida	4	Massachusetts	1	Virginia	1
Georgia	7	Mississippi	26		
Illinois	1	Missouri	9		

Cumberland encouraged this growth in student population. In the 1854–55 catalogue Cumberland claimed that "in point of numbers, it has for four years maintained the rank of the second Law School in the United States. The three highest, as appears from the American Almanac for 1855, stand as follows, for the last year: Cambridge, 143; Lebanon, 87; Virginia University, 78. . . . Might not its friends . . . by active exertion put its numbers up to an equality with the School at Cambridge?"

The Cumberland catalogues even employed a little dark humor in the effort to drum up business. In the midst of the gathering sectional division over the "peculiar institution" of slavery, the 1855–56 catalogue pointed out that the law student enrollment had increased 34 percent over the past year. It suggested that a similar increase for yet another year would put Cumberland in first place, larger than Harvard, and dryly commented that "this would distinguish it [Cumberland] as another 'peculiar institution of the South.'" Cumberland reported in its 1856–57 catalogue that with 167 students it was the largest law school in the United States. That standing is not so clear, but it is certain that in the following year, 1857–58, with 188 students, it was the largest American law school in terms of enrollment.[75] Once again, in 1859–60, with 180 students, Cumberland was the largest school; Harvard had 166 and Virginia trailed with 131.[76]

The mounting student population exerted pressure on the faculty, even with two full-time professors. Judge Ridley still taught part-time and was listed as a faculty member until the 1856–57 catalogue, even after Nathan Green Sr. became full-time. But Ridley could devote only a small amount of time, and the law school looked for still a third faculty member. The logical choice was Green's son, Nathan Green Jr.

Nathan Green Jr. was born in Winchester, Tennessee, on February 19, 1827. He entered the first class at Cumberland University in Lebanon in 1842 and obtained his A.B. degree in 1847. He then was a member of that small group of seven students who met Abraham Caruthers on October 1, 1847, as the first law class. He graduated in 1849 and began to practice law in Lebanon in partnership.[77] Young Green had expressed an interest in teaching even before he went to law school and had been appointed a tutor, presumably in the preparatory school, in July 1845, while he was yet working on his A.B. degree.[78] His interest in Cumberland continued during his years of practice, and he was elected to the university's board of trustees in 1850. On February 15, 1856, young Green resigned from the board and was simultaneously appointed a full-time professor of law.

The board noted that the large increase in students had necessitated the appointment and that the new professor would devote his "whole time" to the duties of the office, and ordered that the exact measure of young Green's "duties and compensation be arranged between him and the present professors as they may consider just and equitable among themselves."[79] This confirmed the essentially proprietary nature of the law school. Young Green's name entered the catalogue for 1855–56, along with Caruthers, the older Green, and Ridley, but the following year Ridley was dropped permanently. The addition of faculty to the antebellum roster was not yet complete. In 1858, John Cartwright Carter graduated from Cumberland School of Law, then married Abraham Caruthers's daughter, and became a professor for 1859–60. He was probably just part-time, and in any event served only one year before moving to Memphis to practice law.[80]

In 1859–60, with 180 law students, Cumberland School of Law had three full-time professors and one part-time. Cumberland was therefore a leader in faculty as well as students. In the nineteenth century, law school faculties were largely part-time, and the typical faculty consisted of one or two practicing lawyers aided by a few lectures given by outsiders.[81] The University of Virginia Law School, founded in 1825, had only one professor until 1851, when a second was appointed.[82] In 1856, the law schools of both Cumberland and Harvard moved up to a full-time faculty of three.[83]

Throughout the 1840s, the academic departments of Cumberland University experienced severe financial problems. The annual salaries of the president and professors had been fixed in 1842 at $1,200 and $1,000, respectively, but with the proviso that these would be drawn from tuition and could not be a charge on the university's physical assets or on the trustees. In other words, the stated salaries merely constituted a sort of pro rata draw upon tuition and (theoretically) interest on endowment.[84] The gate receipts, as it were, of the school were not enough to keep the faculty going, and resignations were frequent. In September 1844 the professor of mathematics quit because "for the past two years . . . I have not received a remuneration adequate to support of my family." In October 1849 the languages professor proposed a definite salary, as distinct from the pro rata share, and was told the board could promise nothing "except the lecture fees" nor was the board prepared to make any other arrangements. The professor promptly resigned.[85] By 1847, the arrearages extended to an entire year of wages owing to the president.[86]

But this penury did not exist in the Cumberland School of Law. There, the essentially proprietary faculty was flourishing. After the faculty was augmented to three full-time members in 1856, the receipts were divvied up one quarter to Nathan Green Jr. with the remaining three-quarters evenly divided between Caruthers and the older Green.[87] A modern university historian estimates that the law faculty was soon earning about $4,000 per year with a 1990 purchasing power of $100,000.[88] That appears about right. For 1857–58, and only that year, the catalogue specifies how many students attended in each session. In the fall 157 attended, and 118 attended in the spring, considering those who dropped out and those who began in the spring term. If one ignores those who may have entered late in either term and paid the $25 apportioned tuition instead of the full $50 per session tuition, these figures would indicate academic year revenues of $3,437 for the younger Green and $5,156 apiece for the older Green and Caruthers.

This was very handsome compensation, particularly when considered alongside the exiguous state of the general university's finances. The university charged the law faculty rent for the university rooms used for law instruction and also an apportioned amount for fuel, servant hire, and repairs. In 1857 the "contingency fee" charged directly to all students was increased to $2 per term, to be used to pay for fuel, servant hire, and repairs. The law faculty apparently still paid rent to the university, which only amounted to $150 per year at its highest.[89]

Another way of looking at the law faculty compensation is to compare it with the $1,500 judicial salaries that Caruthers and the older Green had been living on just before their teaching careers. Or one might compare it with the $3,000 earned by the two professors at Harvard who were at the peak of the legal teaching profession.[90] On the other hand, when the University of Virginia added a second law professor in 1851, he was paid a $1,000 salary with the privilege of dividing the student fees with the other professor up to a maximum of $3,000 apiece.[91]

This cozy arrangement, whereby the law faculty received the gate receipts, originally had been temporary. In light of the facts that the law school was a proven moneymaker, university professors were resigning because the pittances they had been promised were not being paid, and the law salaries were more than double the compensation the professors had previously received as judges; the board of trustees might well have reallocated some of the law school income to benefit the university as a whole. But on June 15, 1852, the trustees resolved that the law professors "receive all the fees of that Department, as a permanent arrangement, as they now do."[92] Thereby, the Cumberland School of Law became a cash cow milked by its faculty, a condition that would remain until the 1920s, when the law school would become a cash cow milked by a different constituency.

Even at their most profitable, Cumberland's prospects worried Judge Green. He fretted about the newly announced University of the South planned by the Episcopalians nearby in Winchester and the possibility of a law school there. He expected a falling off in enrollment from Mississippi and Alabama because the planters there had not generally sold their cotton. He feared that Cumberland "has reached its culminating point. Judge Caruthers is getting weary, and does not give it the *earnest* attention he used to do. I am getting *old,* and must soon leave it,—vigorous as my health now is. Nathan is troubled with a pain in his side." Green thought his son might have a heart problem. Surely, he would have been relieved if he could have known that in 1858, when he expressed these concerns, his son had sixty-one more years to live. But regardless of these problems, "the truth is," Green wrote his son Robert, "neither he [that is, his son Nathan], nor Judge Caruthers, nor I, can do without the income of this school. We *must* stick to it, & try to so keep it up."[93]

Among the things that Green and his colleagues had to worry about was their embroilment in the growing sectional controversies in the 1850s. Middle Tennessee was largely nationalistic in politics. Abraham Caruthers, Nathan Green Sr., and Robert L. Caruthers were consistently opposed to secession, while also denying the right of the federal government to interfere with slavery. All expressed their views publicly and before students, although once Lincoln had called for an invasion, the three supported their region against the threat.[94] In the fiery climate of 1850s politics, extreme southern nationalists attacked the faculty of Cumberland School of Law, denounced them as traitors, and urged the young men of the South not to attend the school.

In particular, the older Green wrote a public letter in 1858 in which he expressed his belief that the federal Congress had the constitutional power to prohibit slavery within the District of Columbia. For his thoughts, Green was advised in newspaper editorials to move to the North.[95] The *Montgomery Advertiser* was one of the papers that attacked him. But Green shrugged it off. He advised his son that "the attack on me in the Alabama Advertiser was not altogether produced by any differences of opinion on the subject of slavery." A law school was opening in Montgomery, and "the paragraph in my letter on which they comment, was seized upon, as a God-send to help them out in getting pupils." Lots of other southern law schools had opened, most using part-time teachers. They all expired, "after a sickly existence for a session or two. . . . None of these have injured our school. I hope & believe the same result will follow this Alabama attempt."[96]

Actually, Cumberland was playing the sectional card as well, in appealing for southerners to send their children to southern institutions. It started out somewhat subtly in the 1852–53 catalogue:

> The dissimilarity of the manners, customs and institutions of the different sections of our vast Republic, now presents to parents the important question, whether the interest of their children does not require that they should be educated among the people with whom they will have to act their parts in life, rather than among those with whom they will have no more to do after the signing of their diplomas. It is a fact well known to all observers, that the sentiments and feelings originating during the period of collegiate life, are apt to guide in manhood.

A southern parent might well have concluded that a child sent for education to the North might end up an abolitionist. By the 1855–56 catalogue, the appeal was even more blatant. "The Trustees would do nothing to engender unkind feelings between the North and South, but they can confidently assert that there is no longer any necessity for parents and guardians to send their sons and wards to Northern institutions. All must admit that a man's success in a government like ours depends upon the adaptation of his feelings and manners to those of the people with whom he acts. Hence it behooves us to strengthen and foster *our own* seats of learning."

As the student body and faculty expanded, obviously the amount of room needed to accommodate the law school increased as well. The law school acquired a second room in the university building in March 1849,[97] and in January 1856 the law school moved into the entire third floor of the building. The 1855–56 catalogue announced that the "unprecedented increase" of the law school and the recent establishment of a theology school necessitated the addition of new large wings to the existing building and a determination to raise funds for that purpose. Although the funds had not been subscribed, the board authorized the construction of two large wings in July 1858, which greatly increased the size of the school.[98]

At the end of the antebellum period, the law school occupied four large rooms in the new west wing.[99] The new building was large and imposing, three stories, 150 feet long, with wings 50 feet deep. It was built of brick with a stone foundation, a colonnaded porch, and a tall cupola. It contained a central chapel, dormitory rooms, classrooms, and separate libraries for the three departments: literary, theology, and law. There were separate rooms for the various student societies and fraternities. The facilities accommodated six hundred students, although not all of Cumberland's students roomed in the university building. The grounds around the building contained twenty acres and featured bluegrass and a grove of shade trees, entirely enclosed by a high cedar picket fence.[100] It was a most handsome building, well suited to the favorable prospects of the growing school.

CHAPTER TWO

Curriculum and Students 1847–1861

> . . . this is a *working* school, intended and calculated to send from its halls, men who shall be working Lawyers.
> —Nathan Green Sr.

> Cumberland University is no place for topers and blacklegs; and if such do not wish to be discovered and exposed, they would do well to keep away from here.
> —Nathan Green Sr.

In his 1847 inaugural address, Abraham Caruthers, Cumberland's first law professor, vigorously expounded his pedagogical philosophy. His students would be subjected to daily examination on their assigned readings. Not only would that provide a constant monitor on their progress, but it would force the students to express their ideas. He noted that "no exercise is of so much importance to a lawyer as that of communicating his knowledge." Recitations would be coupled with a strenuous moot court program through which the student could "so learn the practice of the law, as to pass at once from his pupilage to professional independence."[1]

The speech constantly contrasted the advantages of the law school with the disadvantages of apprenticeship. The association with other young men in a class, the enlightenment gained through their own discussions, the intellectual stimulation of their competition, the possibility of future referrals—none of these could be had through office study. Law school study even offered "greater security of the morals of the student." Exactly when the apprentice is feeling "the fiery passions of youth," he is "left to roam unchecked amidst all the temptations of the town." But at Cumberland "he will be under the government of the school and called to account for improprieties of conduct."[2]

Caruthers paid some lip service to the older tradition of university legal education, suggesting the advantage of legal training "to all the vocations of life . . . and whatever may be the pursuit in which a young man expects to engage." But his focus and dominant vision was on the preparation of the practicing lawyer. Cumberland was to be a place "where the law will be studied practically; so studied I mean as to prepare the student for practice." Unlike the apprentice who must obtain practical courtroom training at the expense of clients after his office study is complete, the Cumberland graduate "will be prepared to enter at once on the duties of the profession."[3]

Cumberland's admissions plan reflected this practical spirit. From the beginning, no prerequisite studies or degrees were required for admission. Some students, such as Nathan Green Jr., already had an A.B. degree before beginning their legal studies; most did not. Therefore, both the age of the students and the nature of the degree, a bachelor of laws, reflected the primarily undergraduate character of the program.

The regular program was two years, divided into junior and senior classes. However, the "courses," more accurately the assigned portions of the treatises dealing with one subject, were studied *seriatim,* that is to say, one after another. In modern terms, this would be the equivalent of everyone in the freshman class studying, for example, Contracts and only Contracts for three or four weeks, then Torts and only Torts for a specified period, then Criminal Law and only Criminal Law for three weeks, and so forth.

This curricular method permitted students to enter at any time, not just the beginning of a term. Indeed, the 1846–47 catalogue, that is, the one announcing the program for 1847–48, and subsequent catalogues halve the charge for a portion of a term, contemplating entries during the terms. Additionally, students could enter with advanced status. It must be remembered that law schools were not the normal nineteenth-century route to obtaining a license. Many young men clerked or studied on their own, obtained a license through the notoriously lax procedure of an individual judge's approval, and only then went to a law school to obtain a more abstract understanding of their discipline. Accordingly, the original Cumberland law catalogue provided that "any gentleman who has obtained a law license . . . or who has studied the law at least one year at any other Law School, or with an Attorney or Judge, may be entitled to the said degree of Bachelor of Laws upon one year's study in this School, provided the Law Faculty are satisfied with his proficiency." Paine P. Prim, who in the spring of 1848 became the first graduate of Cumberland School of Law, had been admitted to the first class with advanced standing because he was already licensed as an attorney in Kentucky.[4]

In fact, advanced standing originally was granted automatically to anyone asking for it. However, commencing with academic year 1851–52, those who "may claim an advanced standing, will be examined on the text books, in order to decide their title to it."[5] It was even possible for a student to enter Cumberland without previous training, study for a year, leave without the degree, and present himself to a judge for licensing, or perhaps study by himself or in an office for an additional time. The 1852–53 catalogue contemplates this, advising that the course of studies at Cumberland is "arranged as to embrace in the first year such studies as will best prepare those for practice who cannot remain longer in the school." The nineteenth-century law school, in the words of one historian, "was not intended to regulate entry into the legal profession; and it was not intended to certify the professional competence of lawyers."[6]

These loose admissions practices were certainly not unique to Cumberland. The 1848–49 catalogue of the Harvard Law School provided for a two-year program but permitted students to enter at any stage of their professional studies and, indeed, in the middle of a term. In fact, the degree could be awarded after eighteen months of continuous work, and in that year of 1848–49 only three of ninety-six students were in advanced study beyond the eighteen months. While the Harvard program was nominally two years, it was in reality eighteen months. In the 1840s, Cumberland's program of two years was actually longer than Harvard's.

Like Cumberland, most law schools in mid-nineteenth century had no admission requirements, no prerequisite degrees.[7] That included Harvard, whose 1848–49 catalogue expressly stated that "no examination, and no particular course of previous study, are necessary for admission." But that is somewhat misleading. Of the ninety-three students that year seeking a first degree in law at Harvard, fifty-five already had an A.B. or A.M. While some students in the antebellum Cumberland law department had A.B. degrees, they represented a lower percentage than at Harvard.

Regardless of the possibility of early exit from Cumberland to pursue other study options, the regular two-year program at Cumberland was designed to prepare a student for practice. These two years compare well in time of study with the modern three-year program. The Cumberland academic year for 1847–48, the first year of law studies, ran from October 1 through July 30, with no break between the two terms. Although in the antebellum years the school would constantly tinker with the exact starting and terminating dates, the two terms of each year remained approximately five months apiece. The two years equaled approximately eighty-six weeks of study. This compares with the modern law school semester of fourteen weeks, which, over three years is only eighty-four weeks of study.

When Judge Abraham Caruthers met with his first seven students on October 1, 1847, he took the lesson from a slim book of forty to fifty pages, *History of a Lawsuit,* that he had just written. Caruthers called it his "primer," and as the title implies it outlined the procedure for bringing a lawsuit. The book grew under Caruthers's own hands to a work of more than six hundred pages,[8] and thereafter it became the leading treatise of Tennessee pleading and practice.

Thereafter, each fall's entering class would always begin with the *History of a Lawsuit,* using the newest and increasingly more elaborate edition. More than any other single thing, old Cumberland was identified with this book. After Abraham Caruthers died in 1862, several generations of Cumberland faculty edited the work. Professors Sam B. Gilreath and Bobby R. Aderholt published the eighth and final edition in 1963, *after* the school had moved to Birmingham. The book came early in the curriculum so that, as soon as it was mastered, the student could practice in the moot courts.

The major difference between the old Cumberland moot courts and our modern programs is that in the old program the students did everything, almost literally. All they were given was a statement of facts.[9] From that point on, the two sides to the dispute had to prepare all the documents to be introduced in the trial, frame all the quite technical nineteenth-century pleadings and attacks on the pleadings, take depositions, try the cases in front of student jurors and a faculty judge, make all the appropriate trial and post-trial motions, and take or defend an appeal. Student opponents met them at each step. Students acted as clerks and sheriffs, as well as attorneys, and prepared all the forms required at each step of the process. In an age when the equity courts were still separate from the law courts, when lawsuits were still commenced by writs, followed by declarations, pleas, and replications, and when equitable actions still demanded bills and answers, the technical difficulties to be encountered by the student lawyers were enormous. Moot court was obviously a cornerstone of a student's education, not merely an educational, enjoyable, but largely collateral, endeavor, as in today's law school.

The moot court presented a wide range of cases, themselves an education. The notebook of student Columbus Sykes for the fall of 1851 reveals great diversity of moot court actions, including trespass on the case (tort), covenant (debt), assumpsit (contract), assault and battery, fraudulent transfer to defraud a creditor, and divorce. It illustrates such varied procedural matters as cost bills, jury arguments, certificate of election of court clerk, official bonds, summons of grand jury, a demurrer, interrogatories, jury verdicts, and much more.[10] What it does not reveal, unfortunately, is the number of these actions in which Sykes was personally involved. He might have copied some papers for the purpose of building a file of forms.

Although important at the beginning, the moot courts seemed only to grow in importance and prominence in the Cumberland curriculum. In 1847, the moot courts were held "at least once in every two weeks," but by 1852 they were held weekly, with supreme court sessions at the end of each session hearing cases appealed from the trial moots. Distinguished lawyers were invited to sit with the professors in the supreme court sessions, which were open to the public.[11] By 1855, there were two moot trials held on every Monday and a supreme court session on the last Friday of every month. From 1853 onward, the public moot court session at the end of each term was usually a trial proceeding.[12]

When Nathan Green Jr. was hired to teach at Cumberland, he served first as a judge of the moot court,[13] and in the fall of 1856 was "employed exclusively in holding the Circuit and Chancery Courts, and preparing cases for them." He conducted a moot court every day, with supreme court sessions "as often as the number of appeals may require," presumably more frequently than the former once a month. The public moot court sessions at the end of each session had by now become quite popular, exciting interest "not only in the school, but in the crowded audiences that attend it."[14]

The increase in the numbers of moot court trials mirrors the increase in student enrollment. But it also reflects a growing belief by the faculty in the centrality of practical trial work to the Cumberland experience and the public identification of Cumberland with that practical training. A newspaper correspondent for the *Missouri Republican* visited Lebanon and reported back, in words that surely would have pleased the faculty:

> In this town is situated Cumberland University with its famous Law School. I have attended its Moot Court several times. . . . The greatest rivalry exists among [the students], and as much pains is [*sic*] taken in the preparation of their speeches as if the fate of the nation depended on it. It is this feeling of pride and emulation among the students that has rendered the Lebanon Law School [i.e., Cumberland] so famous and so popular throughout the South. Theory is not the only law learned here. Practicable practice is taught. The graduates of the institution are as well acquainted with the forms and proceedings of a suit as the oldest lawyers. I am glad to see so many Missourians here.[15]

Of course, there was formal training in the substantive law in addition to the moot court work. The Cumberland plan was to assign legal treatises for reading. These books were written in the florid style of the nineteenth century but are somewhat comparable to the modern hornbook. Every day, from forty to a hundred pages were assigned from the textbooks.[16] The following day, the class met for one to three hours, and each member of the class was asked questions, in the presence of the entire group, pertaining to the reading that had been assigned. In addition, the faculty offered "brief explanations, and illustrations of the text" so that "every obscurity and perplexity of the text is explained and illustrated in a familiar manner."[17]

The students did not know in advance what question or questions would be put to them, but they did know that each student would be questioned at least once each day. The advantages of this technique were thought to be twofold. First, it would force the student to study. "If anything can induce a young man to read and study a lesson thoroughly, the fact that he has to be examined on it in the presence of his classmates, will. If he has any degree of self-respect he will not suffer a degrading comparison with them if he can help it, and the only way to help it is to study his lessons." Secondly, daily recitation "habituates the student to the expression of his ideas of law . . . [and that overcomes] timidity which young lawyers experience in appearing before Courts."[18]

The texts used were standard treatises of the day. Robert L. Caruthers remarked in 1852 that the books used in Cumberland were "the same, with slight modifications, that are adopted in the Harvard Law School."[19] This was probably true, but not because Cumberland slavishly copied Harvard as a model. Indeed, Cumberland made several additions, subtractions, and substitutions in the required texts during the antebellum years. But they were mostly standard fare. The 1851–52 catalogue lists the following required books:

FIRST SESSION
Preliminary Tracts (by one of the Professors)
Blackstone's *Commentaries*
Stephen's *Pleading*
Greenleaf on Evidence

SECOND SESSION
Kent's *Commentaries*
Chitty on Contracts
Long on Sales
Story on Promissory Notes
Story on Bailments

THIRD SESSION
Story on Agency
Story on Partnership
Story's *Equity Jurisprudence*
Story's *Equity Pleading*
Angell on Limitations
Wharton's *American Criminal Law*

FOURTH SESSION
Story on Bills of Exchange
Story on Conflict of Laws
Greenleaf's *Cruise's Digest*
Williams on Executors
Clancy on Husband and Wife
Story on the Constitution

The two senior professors, Abraham Caruthers and Nathan Green Sr., had completely different teaching styles in the recitation hall. One nineteenth-century Cumberland historian emphasized Caruthers's strictness, writing that while he had the "love and confidence of his students," Caruthers was also "a strict and rigid disciplinarian."[20] A student who studied with both Caruthers and the older Green wrote a vivid recollection:

> Judge Caruthers was small of stature, small boned and light weight. He usually dressed in black or dark colors, and . . . it was evident that he gave but little attention to the cut, fit or style of his garments. In walking he stooped, with his eyes upon the ground, and moved noiselessly and quite slowly, thus presenting the picture of one in profound meditation. . . . When animated in conversation or in the class room his face became almost radiant and remarkably handsome. He was somewhat of a disciplinarian in the class room, and kept the young men constantly under his eye. He adhered rigidly to the lesson assigned for the day, examined his class thoroughly upon it, and if one came without having prepared it he was sure to wish he had done so before the recitation closed. He had the tobacco habit and both smoked and chewed. His smoking was all done at home and usually with a cob pipe and long stem. His voice was thin, though not effeminate. It arrested the attention at once, and impressed one as the voice of a man in authority and of positive views. He had an irascible temper, was easily ruffled, impatient under restraint, and fearless of opposition.

This same former student then described Nathan Green Sr.:

> Judge Green was the opposite of his associate in almost everything excepting the high qualities of intellectuality and legal lore. . . . In

> stature he stood six feet five in his stockings, was raw boned, loose jointed and ungainly. . . . His appearance was most venerable, his hair, usually worn long, was white as wool, a massive pair of gold rimmed spectacles always rested on his nose, his stride was immense, his step lumbering, and his voice the roar of a lion; impetuous, compassionate and full of charity, he loved everything from the humblest flower in his garden up to his brother man. . . . He thundered in the class room, [but] did not adhere so closely as Judge Caruthers to the lesson in hand, but grew [drew?] often on the vast store of learning that crowded his brain.[21]

Nathan Green Jr. also described his father as "tall and imposing in person, with a deep-toned and impressive voice and a most earnest and dignified manner."[22] Another nineteenth-century observer wrote that as an advocate, Green "possessed almost none of the graces. . . . Physically he lacked symmetry, but he spoke with vehemence, and it need not be said that he reasoned with power. His methods were straight-forward and direct. He was wanting in wit, humor and fancy, but never in logic."[23] The only description we have of Nathan Green Jr. for this period is as a young lawyer arguing a case in Lebanon in the late 1840s. At that time, shortly before entering the teaching profession, he was "a slender young man, six feet in height and straight as an Indian."[24]

Although Cumberland started and immediately thrived as a "practical" law school, there was at its beginning something left of the older university law school tradition that emphasized political theory. We saw its echo in Caruthers's inaugural address, and the first year's class studied "the Law of Nature and Nations, the Sciences of Government." To do this they used such texts as Vattel's *Law of Nations,* the *Federalist Papers,* and Blackstone's *Commentaries.*[25] The following year, Vattel and the *Federalist Papers* were gone, but Blackstone remained, and Caruthers had added a second booklet that he had written, "presenting a plain view of the organization of the Federal and Tennessee governments, and a brief outline of the duties of the whole official corps of both."[26]

The latter pamphlet may not have been an attempt to reintroduce political economy into the curriculum so much as elementary civics needed in an undergraduate program where many students had no previous degree. In any event, the curriculum and the school remained relentlessly practical. Nathan Green Sr. charged the law students in 1849 that they would perceive "this is a *working* school, intended and calculated to send from its halls, men who shall be working Lawyers."[27] The 1856–57 catalogue proclaimed, "we have made our course American" so that the Cumberland graduate "will understand at the end of his pupilage the greatest amount of pure, living, American law." And, indeed, by that year, Blackstone's *Commentaries* had been dispensed with. Presumably to honor the promise to present *American* law, English writers could no longer be tolerated.

But Caruthers and Green were too skilled as teachers to reject completely the theoretical moorings of their craft. In the 1855–56 catalogue they lamented over a truism well-understood by every law teacher, then and now. "In the short time that students can be induced to devote to preparation, but little more than the general outlines of the science or the art [of law] can be learned. About as much as can be accomplished in either is to learn how to learn—to get the stakes well set by which they may be guided in their future progress." They occasionally tried to do more. The 1850–51 catalogue speaks of a "collateral course" designed "for the private reading of those who are able to accomplish more than the regular course." The 1859–60 catalogue lists the readings for such a "parallel course," otherwise totally unexplained. Blackstone and other English writers are back in this list. This parallel course probably represented only the wishful thinking of the faculty and its desire to present a more theoretical dimension to law. Few students, if any, took the faculty up on this alternative to legal studies. Cumberland's vision would always be dominated by "the obvious principle that the design of a legal education is to prepare young men for the bar."[28]

Even a relentlessly functional view of the law school had no quarrel with the need for a library. The original resolution of the board of trustees establishing the law department had created a subcommittee, charged to "take steps to procure a library."[29] The 1848–49 law catalogue reported that the law library had begun with gifts of the statutes and reports of the states of Louisiana and Arkansas. It solemnly intoned that "the institution will never cease to honor the names of these first contributors to its Library." It is reasonably clear that Cumberland School of Law, as an institution, has breached that promise. To right that past wrong, it may be appropriate to record that these initial donors of books to the library of the Cumberland School of Law were David B. Greer of Arkansas and H. R. W. Hill of New Orleans.

Beginning in 1859, a new charge was imposed on students. In addition to the fifty dollars per term tuition, which went to the faculty, and the two-dollar contingent fee, which went to the university, a new charge of one dollar for a library fee was added for a library fund. This fund was designed "to increase the number of books in the Library."[30] Actually, fees charged students remained remarkably stable throughout the antebellum years. Tuition was always fifty dollars per term, or one hundred dollars per year. The contingent fee of two dollars per semester was added in the early 1850s, replacing some earlier miscellaneous small charges, such as a diploma charge. Last, the very modest library fee was added.

Cumberland made a major change in its curriculum in 1854, as announced in the 1853–54 catalogue. The course of study was reduced from two years to three terms of five months each. The reason offered for the reduction illustrates again that graduation from a law school or the obtaining of a degree was not any prerequisite for admission to the bar. The catalogue stated that "we have found by seven years experience that comparatively few will remain in the School four, or even three sessions. A much greater number will remain three sessions if they can graduate in that time, and thus the School will send to the bar a greater number more thoroughly prepared than it can do by requiring a more thorough course."

The tuition of fifty dollars per semester was not changed, so this represented a financial break for those obtaining the LL.B. degree. In 1860, students had an added incentive to remain in school. Cumberland was granted a diploma privilege,[31] which meant that admission to the Tennessee bar was automatic after graduation, without even a cursory examination.

While the change from a two-year to a year-and-a-half curriculum may seem like a retreat for Cumberland, it must be kept in perspective. We have seen that eighteen months was the de facto extent of the Harvard program. Indeed, a single year was the most common program length at the time, and the two-year program did not become common until after the Civil War.[32]

What is exemplary about the Cumberland curricular program is not so much the moot court. Other schools had such programs; Harvard had a moot court that met twice a week,[33] although it was not emphasized by that school as much as at Cumberland.[34] The University of Virginia's moot court met once a week in the 1840s.[35] What was truly different was the emphasis Cumberland put on classroom instruction that proceeded through questioning of the students.

Generally speaking, antebellum law schools instructed by straight lectures, somewhat lackadaisical at best. When the leading professor at Virginia questioned students, he preferred answers of only "yes" or "no."[36] Even at Harvard, which did make some slight effort to have student interaction, the official history concedes that in the antebellum period "neither attendance nor preparation was required for recitations or lectures, and . . . the exercise furnished no test of the work done by a student."[37] A leading New York lawyer later recalled his student days of 1857 at Harvard. He wrote that, notwithstanding occasional questions, there was "no attempt to ascertain how thoroughly a student had studied the textbooks which were supposed to be used outside the lectures."[38]

However, the entire function of the recitation at Cumberland, as a catalogue explained, was "to furnish evidence that [the textbook] has been studied. . . . It is conceived to be of primary importance that the student, as well as the professor, should know every day how he is progressing. By his recitations, by the comparison of himself with his class, he finds out whether he is spending his time profitably. This is the only certain test of proficiency."[39] This is where Cumberland made its mark. As an educational historian has explained:

> Cumberland Law School in the nineteenth century is Tennessee's only original contribution to legal education philosophy and pedagogy. Cumberland pioneered "scientific" legal education in the university setting. That is, in an era when other university-based law schools used the lecture method almost exclusively, Cumberland adopted the technique of daily recitations, designed to test the student's understanding of the "science" of law, namely the textbook law as written in treatises. But Cumberland was "practical" too. . . . A vigorous moot court system was established to train lawyers, just as the classwork was designed to produce legal minds.[40]

In the antebellum period, most of the law students were young, aged eighteen or nineteen, and the promotion for the school was primarily addressed to the parents of prospective students. Accordingly, in addition to attacking apprenticeship and lecturing as methods of legal education, it is not surprising that the catalogues continually stressed the good moral climate of Lebanon, Tennessee, and the high moral tone of the school. The 1846–47 catalogue claimed that the university "is situated in the midst of a population which, for virtue, morality, intelligence and religion, will suffer no disparagement by comparison with any portion of our country." The 1848–49 catalogue informed parents that "in the society of the town and of the School, there is every thing to repell [*sic*] and nothing to invite a student who expects to indulge vicious propensities."

The 1853–54 catalogue rendered the fullest treatment. In Lebanon, "the whole weight of society is actively exerted against intemperance, gambling, and vice in every shape. Students board in private families, and are thus brought under the constraining influence of family associations." But this was not left to chance, and the school itself gave the law students "occasional lectures, urging the study of the Bible, attendance upon the Sunday Schools," and so forth. Finally, in the event all else failed, the curriculum itself served to safeguard the young since "the plan of instruction keeps the class too busy for immoral indulgences."

In reality, the antebellum Lebanon could be quite a wild place. The recollections of one young resident, not associated with Cumberland University, give a slightly different picture of the town: "Men's differences were often settled by what was called 'fist and skull' fights. I have seen many of them in the square at Lebanon. When the fight commenced the people would run from all parts of town, yelling 'Fight! Fight!'—not to stop it but to see the fun. On one occasion I saw two men shot, but not killed. About this time there was a killing in the square, the weapon being a pair of waffle irons."[41]

It also had saloons in which any white person, apparently even of young age, could buy whiskey.[42] That Lebanon offered considerably more temptation than the school administration wanted to admit in its catalogues is also shown in the rigid rules laid down for students and the strictness of discipline imposed.

At the older Cumberland in Princeton, Kentucky, President Cossitt had written a twenty-one-page booklet of rules. These were imposed on students, including law students, in the early years in Lebanon.[43] Some of these are quaint:

> [Chapter VII] Section 5: If any student shall break open the door of another, or privately pick his lock with any instrument, he shall be admonished or expelled, as the nature of the offense may deserve. . . .
>
> Sec. 8. If any student shall play at hand or foot-ball in the College buildings, or in the College yard, or throw anything by which the College buildings may be in danger of damage, he shall be admonished, sent home, or dismissed. . . .
>
> Sec. 10. If any student shall ring the College bell, except by order of the President, a Professor or a Tutor, he shall be punished at the discretion of the Faculty. . . .
>
> Sec. 26. No student shall, without permission, go to a greater distance than two miles from the College, at any time during the continuance of the session.
>
> Sec. 27. No student shall keep, for his use or pleasure, any horse, carriage, dog or servant; except when his parents or guardians shall, with the approbation of the Faculty, allow him a horse for the purpose of healthful exercise. . . .
>
> [Chapter XIV] Section 8: Every student boarding within the town corporation, or within three-quarters of a mile of the College building, shall attend morning prayers in the College chapel at sunrising.[44]

The serious rules were for drinking and gambling. The 1850–51 catalogue explained to prospective law students and their parents that "no student, in any Department of this University, shall become intoxicated, or induce others to become so, or keep, in his room, intoxicating drinks, or frequent a tippling-house. . . . Nor shall any student be guilty of any disorder, or uproar, or of making loud noises, by night or day." This warning, written in various forms, was always repeated in the catalogues, and upon even the first offense, intoxication made one subject to dismissal.

The trustees soon became alarmed about gambling and in June 1851 prohibited students from "playing at any ten or nine pin alley,"[45] a sure sign that such play was exactly what students were doing. But the gambling "problem" persisted, and in August 1858, the trustees resolved that "any student that be convicted in court or by the Faculty to which he belongs of gambling, shall be summarily dismissed, as students now are for intoxication."[46] The following year's catalogue of 1858–59 broadcast the rule that gambling was "strictly prohibited" and warned of the "severest penalties." Prospective students were also informed then that they would "have no use for pistols and Bowie-knives. The keeping or carrying of any deadly weapon is contrary to the laws, and subjects the party to admonition, suspension, and, in some cases, to expulsion."

These stern admonitions were generally repeated at the openings of the fall session and were addressed as fully to the law students as any other. At one such occasion, in the fall of 1858, Nathan Green Sr. addressed the assembled students for two hours:

> He closed by portraying very strikingly the evils of intemperance and gambling, showing how easily young men are led away by these vices. He warned those present to "touch not, taste not, handle not." And if a young gentleman could not refrain from indulging in drinking and gaming, he had better not enter the University, for the probability was that he would be detected, and be sent away in disgrace. . . . if [a student] be convicted of *drinking* . . . he is forthwith dismissed! No student shall gamble or engage in any game of hazard; and upon conviction of such engagement . . . he is dismissed from the University. Hence it is very evident that Cumberland University is no place for topers and blacklegs; and if such do not wish to be discovered and exposed, they would do well to keep away from here.[47]

The system of enforcement was also formidable. Each faculty conducted "trials" of miscreants within its department and could admonish, inform parents, suspend, or expel, saving that actual expulsion had to be approved by the trustees. Trials were conducted not merely for the mortal sins of drinking and gambling but even for merely venal matters, "charges were preferred by the college prosecutor, and the cause tried in public."[48] Years later when Nathan Green Jr. was the chancellor of Cumberland University (he took that title instead of president), he passionately criticized these "rules" and "trials" under which he himself had endured for four years in the literary department and two years in the law department:

> When I became connected with Cumberland University as a trustee and then as a teacher, more than thirty years ago, there was a formidable code of laws in force . . . related to every possible situation and condition of the student. . . . This code was presented to the student

> immediately after his matriculation. It was itself a study, and a much more difficult and objectionable one than many of the textbooks in the regular curriculum. It provided for monitors and tutors, who had power to invade the students' rooms. It recognized a detestable system of espionage. It exacted certain marks of respect to the professors. Throughout it assumed that the professors were exalted beings and far removed from the students. . . . It prescribed hours of devotion; it regulated and restrained young men even in their liberty of locomotion. And for a violation of these and scores of other laws various penalties were affixed. The result was that the faculty found it necessary to hold a regular court one day in each week to try offenders. Saturday was state's day. Before this awful tribunal scores of culprits were formally summoned each week to appear. Absence from class, absence from prayers, tardiness three minutes and a half, walking out at the wrong time, visiting a fellow-student's room in study hours, and scores of other lighter and heavier crimes were on the trial docket. It would not be safe for me to estimate at this distance the number of lies perpetrated on such occasions, for, contrary to the rule of common law, the offender was put on the witness stand and asked to testify against himself. . . . I remember that some were required in the presence of the assembled faculty and students to make most humiliating confessions of sin and earnest promises of future good conduct, and especially begging the pardon of some particular teacher whose dignity had been offended. It is easy to imagine what a state of things all this would bring about. Resentment and spite toward the by-laws and the professors, bickerings, and hard feelings among students who were witnesses against their fellows, looseness of conscience and want of reverence for the truth, consumption of valuable time, dissatisfaction among patrons, and an eternal worry and embarrassment for the professors. It was not to be endured.[49]

Nathan Green Jr. never wrote a more passionate public statement. We must keep this in mind when we see the rules of conduct he imposed when, years later, he was in the position of authority to do so.

This complex system of trials, involving law students as much as any other, was further complicated by various procedural rules imposed from time to time by the trustees. For example, in 1857 the trustees resolved that "if it is notorious that a student is in the habit of drinking intoxicating liquors or should the Faculty receive information from reliable and undoubted authority that any student has violated the law which forbids the use of liquors as a beverage," that would be sufficient to convict. Further, "it shall not be necessary for the witness or witnesses to face the accused, unless he is on trial for expulsion."[50]

Ultimately, the decision of expulsion was up to the trustees, and here we can see the final workings of the antebellum system of discipline. The pattern was that a student would be dismissed by his faculty, usually for drinking, then would petition the trustees, promising good behavior, and would be readmitted. About two dozen students sentenced to expulsion by their faculties went through the repentance and forgiveness route in the antebellum years. But some were not forgiven. The trustees' minutes reveal that on December 6, 1845, a student convicted of assaulting a fellow student with arms, frequent intoxication, playing cards, and "using profane language" was permanently expelled.[51] A freshman student assaulted a fellow student during a mathematics class; he was expelled on May 4, 1849.

No one was immune from these procedures. William A. Caruthers, son of the law professor, Abraham Caruthers, was expelled while a literary student by the faculty of that department. His offense was considered "to be of a very serious character—a positive refusal on his part to obey a proper order from a member of the faculty, and accompanying that refusal with insulting language." He was expelled, but then restored, so that he could attend law school, upon his father's assurance that William "will in future demean himself as becomes a student . . . and will treat the members of the Faculty with the respect due from a student."[52]

Some discipline cases were amusing. What to do about a Mr. Desucckes, who after being dismissed, called upon the president, tore up his dismissal, and threw it at that august personage? The answer: nothing, as the university had no further jurisdiction over him.[53] Then there was the case of an academic student (who should have been a law student), charged with being intoxicated through drinking ale. The student defended on the grounds "that he did not know that it was possible for a man to drink [ale] in sufficient quantity to intoxicate him." Fortunately, he was among those reinstated upon the promise of "future good behavior."[54]

In many antebellum universities, law students were not subjected to the general rules and regulations of their host institutions.[55] Cumberland had no such exemption, and the trustees specifically resolved that "all the laws on the subject of good order and morality and to present & punish crimes presented for the literary students shall apply to & govern the Law Students."[56] And law students figure very prominently on the discipline rolls for the university. Perhaps disproportionate numbers of law students in the antebellum years were not serious about their studies. Nathan Green Jr. later recalled of these years before the Civil War that "many young gentlemen whose parents were planters and men to [*sic*] large means, attended the school in order to make themselves more accomplished citizens, and without intending to follow the profession as a business."[57]

Such students might be more predisposed toward getting in trouble. In any event, many law students did. In the years 1857–1859, seven law students, dismissed for drinking, promised reform and successfully petitioned for reinstatement.[58] Some law students suffered a harsher fate. William G. Brian was expelled for assaulting another law student.[59] Probably the harshest and seemingly the most unjust treatment was that given to a law student whose offense was merely to unduly celebrate his graduation. In January of 1857, W. N. Seston, a student in the senior law class who was "dismissed by faculty for intoxication on the last day of the session and whose class applied to the Board of Trustees to have him restored that he might receive his diploma came on to be heard before the board and the nature of his offense considered when it appeared to the board that it was a repetition of an offense that had escaped the punishment or penalty of the law before, and refused the application."[60]

Cumberland's paternalism was not always so harsh. Sometimes it was helpful. For example, the trustees concerned themselves with the students' boarding arrangements. During the summers, the trustees sometimes appointed committees to canvass Lebanon residents to determine who would take in student boarders and to pass that information on to incoming students.[61] The students usually dined with their host families, and in November 1852 the trustees requested that the faculty adjourn their classes at the regular hours. Householders boarding students had complained they were "put to considerable inconvenience by students being detained after the usual hours for dining."[62]

One of the very first official acts of the Cumberland trustees was to appoint a committee to look into the costs of boarding. This committee reported that students could be accommodated with "boarding, lodging, room, fuel, & candles" for two dollars per week.[63] The catalogues passed along cost estimates, which ranged from forty to forty-five dollars per session (1848–49 catalogue) to fifty dollars per semester (for the years 1851 through 1855), then up to two to three dollars per week (1855–56), and finally a boarding estimate of sixty to seventy dollars per session (1859–60 catalogue). It is unclear what caused the increase.

Another element of the university's paternalism was the effort to curtail and control student spending. Although the 1848–49 catalogue assured parents that "the habits of the village [i.e., Lebanon] present no inducements to extravagance in any respect," the trustees never acted as though they believed it. The 1846–47 catalogue cautioned parents and guardians: "Do not put much money into the pocket of your son or ward nor allow him to contract debts—select for him a Patron who shall judge of the propriety of each expenditure and check that extravagance to which young men are subject when left to themselves. Economy ought to be enforced. Extravagant young men never make good students."

But the problem persisted. Too much money apparently meant the purchase of demon rum or gambling. On June 13, 1851, the trustees appointed a committee to look into the prospects "of adopting some plan to prevent the unnecessary & extravagant expenditures of money by the students of the institution by appointing a patron for each student or otherwise to remedy what is considered a growing evil." The committee reported that if students had money, there was "great danger of such students contracting habits of extravagance, if not of dissipation." The solution proposed was the appointment of a patron, a citizen of Lebanon, bonded and whose books would be subject to inspection, to receive parental funds and hold them to be paid out as the parents ordered.[64]

Such an individual was appointed and notice was given to parents of this custodial and disbursement service in the 1850–51 catalogue. It was not required, and "may be done, or not, as parents and guardians may desire." Evidently, very few parents did so desire, no doubt responding to vigorous protests of their sons. By the end of the antebellum period, the office of the patron was discontinued. The only students for whom the patron was mandatory were the Choctaw Indians who were sent to Cumberland, including the law department, by the Board of Foreign and Domestic Missions of the Cumberland Presbyterian Church.[65]

Cumberland students demonstrated youthful exuberance through more than reckless spending on liquor and gambling. There were also pranks and practical jokes. Cumberland's first president and the author of the school's stern codes of conduct, Franceway Ranna Cossitt, was by all appearances and accounts a fairly straitlaced man. But his successor, T. C. Anderson, president of Cumberland University during all the antebellum years the law school functioned, could appreciate a reasonable prank. A much later president, Laban Rice, recounted: "One Halloween night a group of students quietly entered Dr. Anderson's back yard, wheeled his carriage out of the stable, and with the help of ropes and much boosting finally perched it on the roof of the building. Just as they were about to steal away, they were surprised to hear the jolly voice of Dr. Anderson beckoning them from the back seat of the carriage, 'Very nicely done, boys. Now take me down.'"[66]

Nathan Green Jr. recalled some bantering among the students in the prewar days. "The boys," he wrote, "had a silly fad of approaching one another, and, referring to the orifices in the nose and ears, saying 'you are perforated.' Many a boy not knowing the exact meaning of the expression, and thinking himself charged with a crime or some disease, would deny it indignantly and propose to fight."[67]

We have seen that rooms were allocated to student clubs and societies in the enlarged university building completed in 1858. Before the new construction some student organizations had asked permission from the trustees to build their own structures on the twenty-acre campus. The trustees accommodated them and granted permission for offices to be built on the campus, to be occupied by students, sold to other students, or sold to third persons if then moved off the grounds. The trustees reserved a right to order their removal, but it does not appear they ever did. Most likely, these student structures were simply destroyed during the Civil War.[68]

Eight Greek letter fraternities were founded at Cumberland University before the Civil War, including Delta Kappa Epsilon (1857), Sigma Alpha Epsilon (1860), and Chi Phi (1861).[69] Beta Theta Pi, the earliest to be founded, in 1854, was also a major fraternity at Cumberland. Its chapter appeared to draw membership primarily but probably not exclusively from the literary, or academic, students.[70] The law students were of the same age as the literary students, and there was no age barrier to their membership in the same social organizations. Another social organization for students was the YMCA. Cumberland had a branch of the Young Men's Christian Association as early as 1858. Perhaps it dates from 1856, and, if so, Cumberland's would be the oldest college branch of the YMCA.[71]

A great deal of the social activity in the old Cumberland consisted of the sharp rivalry between three student literary societies, the Amasagassean, Philomathean, and Heurethelean. The Amasagassean Society was founded at the Cumberland in Princeton, Kentucky, in 1837 and then revived in Lebanon. The Philomathean and Heurethelean Societies were founded at Lebanon about 1844.[72] These organizations were open to any Cumberland student. However, they tended to draw students from specific departments, although there was crossover membership. The Amasagassean Society drew most of its members, but not all, from the college of arts, the literary department. The Heurethelean Society's membership was composed primarily of students in the theology school and ministerial candidates in the college of arts. Although the Philomathean Society was organized before the law school, after the founding of the law department most of the Philomathean Society's members were law students.[73] Law students belonged to the Amasagassean Society as well, but they were not the majority of the membership.

The Amasagassean Society held weekly debates. The topics were announced, and then the debates were held a week later on Saturday afternoons at two o'clock. They were open to the public, and often a vote was taken as to which side carried the audience. Some of the subjects were very topical, such as that for March 13, 1847: "Is the present war with Mexico justified?" and some were both topical and thoughtful, like that of March 3, 1849: "Resolved that the California gold mines will be productive of more evil than good to this country." A few topics were just humorous, for example that of March 6, 1852: "Resolved that old bachelors after they arrive at the age of 25 [*sic*] should pay an additional tax until they marry," and occasionally there was a topic both humorous and profound, such as that of January 31, 1852: "Resolved that women are more efficient in doing good than statesmen."[74]

Meanwhile, the law students in the Philomathean Society were holding their own exercises, but their records have not been preserved. During the 1850s, the Philomathean Literary Society, to use its full name, elected all sorts of prominent people from around the country to honorary membership. Particularly in January and February of 1858, it sent a rash of letters offering honorary memberships and received letters of acceptance from, among others, Chief Justice Roger B. Taney, the author Washington Irving, and politicians Jefferson Davis, Millard Fillmore, and Andrew Johnson. Two acceptances are especially noteworthy. James Buchanan, a sitting President of the United States, accepted on December 29, 1859, writing "I accept with pleasure this mark of regard & beg you to present to the members of your Society my cordial thanks for the honor they have conferred upon me." In the light of the future Reconstruction years, the most ironic offer was to the ardent abolitionist, Senator Charles Sumner of Massachusetts. Sumner accepted, and wrote to the Cumberland law students of Philomathean on February 17, 1858: "I am always happy in association with those engaged in the cultivation of letters, & accept with gratitude the honor you have conferred in choosing me a member of the Philomathean Society of Cumberland University."[75]

Of considerable interest to young men, then as now, were young women. Although it would be decades before Cumberland University began even incremental moves toward coeducation, Cumberland was a magnet for schools for women because its six hundred young men were nearly all bachelors from prominent families. Lebanon saw the opening of several finishing schools, often called seminaries in those days, for young ladies. Most had a short life.

In 1846, a school for young ladies called the Abbe Institute appeared, probably the first after the founding of Cumberland. That was followed by the Greenwood Seminary in 1851, the Cumberland Female Seminary in 1852, and, in addition, the Corona Institute for Women operated during some of the prewar period and closed in 1871. The Cumberland Female Seminary was under the patronage of the Cumberland Presbyterian Church but had no connection with Cumberland University.[76] The Greenwood Seminary was founded by a former Cumberland professor on his estate four miles from Lebanon, operated as a selective boarding school, and drew its patronage from several southern states.[77]

Many law students married local women. Nathan Green Jr., whose family home was then in Winchester, Tennessee, graduated from the literary department in 1847 and the law school in 1849. He settled in Lebanon several years before his father resigned from the court and himself moved to Lebanon. In 1850 young Green married Betty McClain, the daughter of Josiah S. McClain, Wilson County clerk and also the secretary of the board of trustees of Cumberland University.[78] John C. Carter graduated from the law school in 1858, married a daughter of Professor Abraham Caruthers, and then joined the faculty for the 1859–60 academic year. He was killed during the Civil War.[79]

Other law students wrote homesick letters to their girlfriends miles away, as in the case of Nicholas N. Cox who wrote to his fiancée, Mary Slayden, in May 1858: "I have been quite busy during the present session and have confined myself so close to my room that at the present I am completely wearied out with books, yet I am compelled to stick close to them for a short time yet, and then I will be free from college life. I have had but little enjoyment for the last seven months and have often thought that if I was so situated so that I could converse with you that I would feel more in the enjoyment of the pleasure which I have felt while at home."

Cox persisted with his books and graduated on time in June 1858. He and Miss Slayden were married on January 6, 1859.[80]

One antebellum student, Howell Jackson, should be separately discussed, since he was one of two Cumberland graduates who served on the United States Supreme Court. Jackson was born on April 8, 1832, the son of Alexander Jackson, a well-educated medical doctor who had graduated from the University of Pennsylvania Medical School. In 1849, Howell Jackson, the son, left West Tennessee College, now Union University, after following a traditional classics curriculum. He then took a two-year graduate program at the University of Virginia. He began to read law in the office of Judge Milton Brown and A. W. O. Totten, the latter a justice on the Tennessee Supreme Court. Justice Totten recommended Cumberland School of Law to Jackson, and he enrolled in 1855, graduating the following year of 1856.[81]

While a Cumberland senior, Jackson once sat as one of the appellate judges deciding appeals from the moot trial courts. Jackson wrote the opinion of the moot appellate court, and the professor who also sat on the tribunal, Nathan Green Sr., thought so much of Jackson's opinion that he sent a copy to Jackson's father and later wrote Dr. Jackson that the opinion was "a clear and cogent statement of the questions, and analysis of the case. . . . I should be most willing to see such an opinion in a book of reports, with my name attached."[82]

Howell Jackson entered the United States Senate in 1880, and in 1886 President Cleveland appointed him to the United States Circuit Court, making him the first presiding judge of the Sixth Circuit after the creation of the Courts of Appeal. President Benjamin Harrison elevated Jackson to the United States Supreme Court in 1893.[83] An unusual aspect of that nomination was that President Harrison, a Republican and a Union general during the Civil War, appointed Jackson, a Democrat, who had spent the Civil War employed as a civilian employee of the Confederacy. Harrison intended the appointment as a gesture of conciliation.

The last of the antebellum years were a golden age for Cumberland. Nathan Green Jr. recalled that in April 1861 Cumberland's law school "was enjoying the highest degree of prosperity."[84] A photograph from the period shows the beautiful university building, which was surrounded by twenty acres of campus, with groves of trees and a picket fence. Even the town itself was a picture of prosperity: "Lebanon was at that time one of the prettiest of Tennessee's county towns, situated in a rolling limestone region with, consequently, snow-white roads and evergreen forests, and built regularly around a square, in the centre of which stood the courthouse. The business houses, law offices, doctors' offices, and hotel occupied the four sides of the square, and the dwellings faced the streets radiating therefrom. The University stood upon an eminence in the southern portion of the town."[85]

But it was not to last. On April 13, 1861, Lincoln called for volunteers to invade the South. Five days later, on April 18, a Cumberland law student wrote his father that "owing to the political excitement the school is very nearly broken up & will be entirely broken up in a week or two."[86] He was too optimistic. Nathan Green Jr. recalled that within a week after Lincoln's call to arms, just days after the student's letter, the law school "was entirely broken up and the exercises ceased. Most of the young men went to their homes at once. Some enlisted as United States soldiers to fight for the Union; but the great mass, being from the South, became Confederate soldiers."[87] The arts college continued on until the end of February 1862, when it too shut down.[88] Nathan Green Sr., the oldest of the law professors, stayed quietly at home in Lebanon throughout the war.[89] Abraham Caruthers, on the other hand, feared arrest. He fled to Marietta, Georgia, where he died May 5, 1862, in his sixtieth year.[90]

Some personal documents dating from this time carry great poignancy. In the midst of the crisis leading to the war, on April 4, 1861, a young law student named S. C. Bowers took the time to purchase a book from Scobey & Hankins, a book dealer and stationer on the west side of the Lebanon square. It was a life of Patrick Henry.[91] One wonders why he chose that moment to read a life of Patrick Henry. Was it, perhaps, to contemplate the meaning of patriotism, in yet another period of fundamental strife? Might he have thought it would furnish aid to meet the conflicting calls for loyalty from nation and state?

Student autograph books are even more telling. Each year the graduating seniors and faculty ordered small oval photographs, about two inches in height, with half-body views. They then collected these photographs from classmates and faculty members and pasted them into small blank books. Some students wrote comments, farewells, or mottoes alongside their faces.

The beginnings of the military crisis prevented the completion of the spring term of the 1860–61 year, but there were autograph books for that ill-fated class. One belonged to Joseph D. Cross, and the mottoes written by his classmates in that year illustrate their deeply divided political opinions. One student wrote "Southern Rights without Abatement" and another, "Southern Rights and Southern Ladies." More pointedly, another expressed the hope that "while battling for your country, no Northern mercenary bullet may ever pierce so noble a bosom." Yet there are contrary sentiments. One student wrote: "Be True to the Constitution and the Union."[92]

The autograph book of C. W. Robertson, c. 1860, contains not only comments of students at the time of their graduation but notations added later at the top of the pictures of his friends. These later comments read: "mortally wounded . . . at Chickamauga," "killed at Dead Angle, Ga.," "Died a Confederate prisoner at Camp Douglas, Ill.," and "mortally wounded at Columbia, Tenn."[93] Such are the human consequences of war.

They were boys when they marched off, either to fight for Lincoln's abstraction of union or, more concretely, to defend their families and homes from invasion. In either event they returned, if they returned at all, no longer boys, but men. And they came back to a very different Lebanon and a very different Cumberland University.

CHAPTER THREE

After the War
1865–1878

> The father, Judge Green, Sr., did not believe the Law School could be revived, but the son was of a contrary opinion, and . . . set to work at once.
> —Andrew Bennett Martin

THE WAR TOUCHED each member of the Cumberland faculty differently. We have seen that Nathan Green Sr. stayed quietly at home in Lebanon while Abraham Caruthers fled to Georgia, dying there in 1862. Professors John Carter and Nathan Green Jr. went off to war as Confederate officers, Carter to be killed and Green to survive. But if the destruction of the faculty was only by halves, the ruin of the Cumberland campus to which they returned was total.

Lebanon, Tennessee, was not permanently occupied during the Civil War, and control shifted back and forth. While the Union forces were in control, federal troops camped on the university's grounds and quartered in the newly finished building. The cedar picket fence and shade trees were cut down for campfire, the furnishings of the building were scattered, and the sod was destroyed by trenches and breastworks the Union forces cut through the grounds. Ultimately, in 1906, the federal government compensated the university for these losses.[1]

The government did not compensate for the most significant damage, the burning and complete destruction of the university buildings, because this was caused by Confederate forces. It is not entirely clear what happened.

In late August 1864 a Confederate raiding party under General Joseph Wheeler's command retook Lebanon. Shortly thereafter the building was burned. The best account of the traditional explanation was given by the younger Green, much later, in 1890:

> It is due to truth to say here, that although the buildings were occupied by United States negro troops, and that part of the country was in their possession, this reckless and unnecessary destruction was not committed by them. Nor, indeed, was it an accident. Several thousand Confederate cavalry were on a raid in the vicinity. A detachment was sent to Lebanon, before whom the negro troops retired to Nashville, which was the nearest strong Federal post. A Confederate Major in command of the detachment, who had been a law student in former years, affected great indignation that his Alma Mater should be made barracks for negro soldiers; so, in his wrath and in his folly, he ordered the buildings to be burned. The loss was a most serious one to all departments of the University. General Wheeler promptly placed the officer under arrest, but that did not restore the buildings.[2]

Nathan Green Jr. was nowhere in the vicinity, and his explanation is entirely hearsay. A modern historian has suggested the matter is subject to doubt.[3] But the Cumberland trustees held no doubt at the time and appointed a committee "on the subject of destroying the university building and as to the propriety of bring[ing] suit against *the party* destroying the same"[4] (emphasis added). The earliest postwar history of Cumberland, published in 1876, likewise attributes the cause of the burning to the deliberate act of a Confederate officer.[5]

The destruction of the physical plant was not the last of the university's problems. Most of the prewar endowment consisted of promissory notes, which in the circumstances of the postwar South could not be collected. Such securities as were held were largely worthless. The new roof on the building was still unpaid, and there were other debts.[6]

After the war, the Rev. W. E. Ward, an alumnus of all three departments of Cumberland University, visited the campus. Walking sadly about his school's ruins, "he took out his pencil and wrote on one of the then standing columns, 'Resurgam,' or, I will rise again. The word was taken up by others, and soon became the watchword for a new struggle."[7]

The image of Cumberland arising from the ashes like the Phoenix, the mythological bird of Greece that arose from its own burnt destruction, became the symbol of the postwar Cumberland. In July 1866, the trustees adopted a new seal, including the phrase "E Cineribus Resurgo," or, "I rise from the ashes," and the image of the Phoenix bird.[8] To this day, the Cumberland School of Law in Birmingham, Alabama, includes this phrase and the image of the Phoenix on its seal.

Although undisturbed by the armed forces, Nathan Green Sr. had contracted pneumonia in 1863 and at the end of the war was in feeble health. In light of this, and considering the many physical and economic difficulties, he opposed the reopening of the school. However, his son strongly desired to go forward. The mail service was not yet fully reestablished, and the reopening was advertised "mainly by circulars sent from hand to hand."[9] At the beginning of the session on the first Monday of September 1865, only eleven men responded to the call,[10] although the class quickly increased to about twenty. Every member of the class had fought in the war, on different sides of the conflict. The class included a Confederate general and a Union colonel. All were content to leave bygones alone, and the former foes fought only in their moot court competitions.[11]

In the spring of 1866 a second class entered, and Judge Green began to teach the advanced students. It was too much for his health, and after a few weeks he took to his bed. After a week's confinement he died at seventy-four years of age on March 30, 1866. According to his son, Judge Green's death was in the manner he had wished. It had been a "saying with him that he could not bear the idea of 'rusting out,' [and] desired to be bright and actively at work till the last." Furthermore, his son added, his father's last words were, "I trust in Jesus; all is well." Nathan Green Jr. held the school together for a few months until Henry Cooper, a comparatively young circuit judge, was chosen as a second professor.[12]

In the summer of 1866 the trustees made an ill-fated decision to purchase the house of the late Abraham Caruthers and fifty acres of surrounding land west of Lebanon for ten thousand dollars, to be used as a site for the law school.[13] Donations had been solicited, in the form of promissory notes, for rebuilding the university. When it was proposed that these funds be used to purchase a building for the law school, many subscribers refused to pay their notes. The trustees then proposed to transfer the property to the collegiate department. A large number of subscribers perceived the plan as a deliberate abandonment of the former university site east of the downtown at College and Spring Streets. This only increased their dissatisfaction. Ultimately, the Theological School purchased the property with proceeds from the sale of land it owned in Chicago, and the Caruthers house, located to the west of the present Cumberland campus, became the building subsequently called Divinity Hall. Still later, it became a boarding hall in which several law students would live. The law school itself never occupied this building. The plan for the initial purchase was probably not merely a grab for advantage by the law school, as Nathan Green Jr. personally opposed the purchase.[14] The old university site was ultimately abandoned and sold off in lots, although the 1872–73 catalogue still expressed the hope of rebuilding on the old site for the college department.

In June 1866 Robert L. Caruthers, brother of the late Abraham Caruthers and also the president of the board of trustees, became a professor of law, but his actual work in the school was only part-time, if that, until 1868.[15] In that year Henry Cooper resigned, and Robert L. Caruthers became a full-time faculty member, performing "regular duty in the Recitations and Moot Courts daily," as the 1868–69 catalogue put it.[16] Robert Caruthers became the senior professor, and he and Green (the father being deceased, the younger Green will henceforth be referred to only as Green) served as the only faculty members until 1878. In that year, Andrew B. Martin, a graduate of Cumberland's law department in 1858 and a member of the Board of Trustees since 1866, became a part-time instructor.[17]

With the former university building in ruins, both the collegiate department and the law school began a period of peregrination around Lebanon before finding permanent homes. The trustees had leased the former Campbell Academy building for a term of ninety-nine years in 1854,[18] and the former soldiers who constituted the first students of the reconstituted law school met in that "bare and dreary hall" on a stony hill to the north of town. After Robert Caruthers began teaching, his classes met sometimes in his brick office building on the grounds of his residence and at other times, depending on his health, in the library of his residence. Meanwhile, Green had moved his location from the Campbell Academy to the former Baptist Seminary, an old brick building on East Main Street.[19] As before the war, the law school paid its own expenses and retained its entire tuition, and its use of the leased property was "free of rent to the trustees," as demanded by the Board.[20]

These movings ended in 1873 when Robert L. Caruthers purchased Corona Hall, a two-story brick building on West Main Street with five or six acres of grounds. This building had formerly been a private residence, and then a college for women. The Corona Institute for Women ceased operations in 1873, and Caruthers promptly purchased the building for ten thousand dollars and donated the property to the university. It was given to house the law school, the university chapel, library, and museum, and to provide rooms for the three university societies, the Amasagassean, Philomathean, and Heurethelean. According to the trustees, in their formal commendation to Caruthers for his generosity, the gift "came unsolicited, and is another among the many noble and generous acts of the donor in which he has contributed to the prosperity of our university."[21] Now, for the first time since 1861, the law school had a permanent home, in Corona Hall. However, its wandering was still not over. As we shall see, in only five years it moved to a more magnificent location.

Although the receipt of the Corona building was a bright spot on the university's financial canvas, the overall picture was dismal throughout these years. The financial situation of the university was desperate. The old endowment had been largely "paid" by promissory notes. It was in a state of great confusion, with many notes missing, some donors claiming that they had already paid, and many simply not having the money to fulfill their promises. The trustees' minutes frequently reflected this chaos, and the trustees encouraged agents to allow compromise and accept what could be obtained.[22] Faculty salaries fell into arrears, excepting law faculty, which had no stated amounts but were entirely dependent on tuition, and the trustees recited the "difficulties the trustees have in sustaining the Institution."[23] As late as August 14, 1869, the trustees promised to rebuild on the old location, but by the next spring began to sell lots carved out of the old grounds.[24]

Actually, the irresponsibility of the trustees largely caused the university's financial embarrassment. As early as 1845 the board devised a bizarre plan to raise money by selling what it called "scholarships." For five hundred dollars a subscriber would have the right to send a student to the university each year for ten years. By the late 1850s the rights granted for the five hundred dollars were extended to fifteen years. The idea was that a subscriber could "rent" out his right to an actual student, and recoup his investment or actually make a profit. In the postwar years, however, these scholarships were rented out to students at rates much less than actual tuition charges. Students would choose to rent these scholarships instead of paying normal tuition, and this arrangement deprived the university and its impoverished faculty of desperately needed revenue.[25]

This "something for nothing" mentality continued to pervade the trustees' thinking. The next folly was an endowment program consisting of life insurance policies on donors' lives. This plan was rejected on numerous occasions by the president of the university, and was also opposed by Green. But in 1871 while the president was out of town, an agent of the St. Louis Mutual Life Insurance Company, who was also an elder in one of the stronger Cumberland Presbyterian churches, talked the board into the scheme. Several scores of persons, listed in the 1872–73 catalogue, purchased life insurance policies, when they might otherwise have made cash donations. Moreover, the headstrong board for a time would not permit any other method of endowment, refused cash contributions, and ordered the president to be quiet about his doubts. The house of cards fell, before the university had received much benefit, when the insurance company became insolvent in the national panic of 1873.[26]

Nathan Green was doing more for Cumberland University than merely giving good advice that was then ignored by the trustees. In addition to his duties in the law school, he found time to help the theological school. Prior to the war, the citizens of Lebanon had given free boarding to ministerial candidates. Financial exigency prevented this in the postwar years. A minister suggested that the students might live in a campsite with tents, arrangements with which most were familiar because they had been soldiers during the war. This plan was taken up, and Nathan Green served without pay as the superintendent and treasurer of this novel tent city.[27]

After the collapse of the insurance scheme in 1873, the president resigned. There was no money to pay the $2,500 presidential salary, and prospects were not good. Green assumed the role of president of the university, taking the title of chancellor. Green served without compensation beyond his professorship as chief executive officer of Cumberland University from 1873 until 1902.[28] Although the administrative duties of this small university were not onerous, Green's new responsibilities further burdened this busy man, who was also an elder in the local Cumberland Presbyterian Church, for thirty years a leader of the choir, and a Sunday school teacher.[29] An avid gardener, Green also found time to tend his favorite flowers, dahlias and sweet peas, in his flower garden near his home.[30]

An organized alumni body could have helped Cumberland University in its time of struggle. But alumni activities were just beginning. The first meeting of an alumni society was held on June 24, 1869,[31] and for several years thereafter an annual alumni reunion was held coincident with the collegiate graduation ceremonies.[32]

Gradually, the law school began to solicit its alumni. In the prewar years it had asked for books for the law library, but in 1870 the law school made its first direct appeal for funds. It was very low-key: "Our Alumni are rapidly taking the first positions in the profession throughout the broad land. We appeal to them, confidently, to exert themselves in behalf of the School. It is in their power to place it in a short time on a firmer and more successful basis than it ever enjoyed."[33]

But these were desultory efforts, both of the university generally and the law school specifically. The law school would continue to ask for contributions of books and cash for the law library. But the organization of a broad-based alumni society and fund-raising campaigns would not begin until the 1920s.

The law school suffered little of the university's impoverishment. Faculty salaries were the amounts taken in for tuition. Those depended on enrollment and, although law salaries did not regain their prewar levels until much later in the century, they stood well in comparison with the other departments of the university. The following list shows enrollment of law students for the academic years indicated, taken from the catalogues for these years:

1865–66	43	1870–71	86	1875–76	67
1866–67	77	1871–72	92	1876–77	51
1867–68	71	1872–73	103	1877–78	43
1868–69	82	1873–74	87		
1869–70	67	1874–75	missing		

We must be very careful with these statistics. Many students did not complete their course but dropped out midway. Then too, the catalogue figures show total student populations, including students who entered in January. To determine law school revenue, one cannot simply multiply these figures by the tuition. But we can compare these figures with the rest of the university by the use of the catalogues for these years. In 1869–70, when there were 67 students in the law school, there were a total of 85 within all classes of the four-year college, 38 in the commercial school, and 73 in the theology school. In 1877–78, with 43 law students, there were only 56 undergraduates, 9 theological students, and 136 in the preparatory school. The other departments had considerably more faculty to support.

As one would expect, in the year of reopening, almost all of the 43 law students came from Tennessee, with one from Alabama and three from Mississippi. In the years immediately following, the student population remained heavily from Tennessee but broadened its draw from other southeastern states. By 1869–70, of the 67 students, only 37 were from Tennessee, although all of the remaining students were from the South.

Although Cumberland School of Law drew many students from outside the South during the prewar years, it was not until 1870–71 that the school again had a single student from outside the region. In that year a solitary student appeared from Illinois and another came from the Choctaw Nation. In the following year, another Indian student arrived, and in 1872–73 and again in 1876–77 one student in each year managed to wander into Lebanon from California. However, only a handful attended Cumberland School of Law from outside the South for this entire period, 1865–1878. The contrast with the large numbers of students from outside the South in the prewar years underscores again how terribly the Civil War blighted Cumberland.

In 1877 Cumberland received another gift that significantly affected the law school. Only five years after donating Corona Hall, Robert L. Caruthers, in 1877, gave the lot west of his residence to the school and the first ten thousand dollars toward the construction of a building for the law school. Cumberland raised another twenty-five thousand dollars, most of it local money from Lebanon, but also including a substantial gift from a female donor in Nashville.[34] The building, named Caruthers Hall in honor of the principal donor, Judge Robert L. Caruthers,[35] was dedicated in May 1878, with law classes beginning on September 2, 1878.[36]

The new structure was enthusiastically described in the 1877–78 catalogue: "This splendid structure, built after the latest architectural style, is nearly one hundred feet from base to spire, and contains two recitation rooms for the Law Department, two Society Halls, a Library, and a chapel whose seating capacity is about seven hundred."

The library was in a large room extending across the entire back of the ground floor. A wide entrance hall was in the front of the ground floor, and at either end a winding staircase went to a corresponding landing in front of the large space described in the catalogue as a chapel.[37] But this "chapel" actually became an auditorium and would be used for plays, recitals, university and community events of all description, as well as for commencements. Apparently it had excellent acoustics and very hard seats. Whatever problems had existed with Corona Hall, where the law school was located from 1873 to 1878, are unclear from this distance. Caruthers Hall was, of course, absolutely new, and the Corona building was older. It appears that there was considerably more room in Caruthers than Corona. When Caruthers Hall was occupied by the law school, its image became a symbol for the Lebanon Law School, as the Cumberland Law Department was often informally called, for the remainder of the nineteenth century and for more than half of the twentieth.

Pedagogically, Cumberland School of Law picked up in 1865 exactly where it had left off in 1861. It taught by student reading of treatises, followed by extensive recitations of approximately two hours each morning,[38] coupled with an active and mandatory moot court program. No entrance examinations or previous education was required. The tuition in 1865 was the same, fifty dollars per session, plus a contingent fee of five dollars, which went directly to the university. Even the curious "parallel course," noted earlier in the years preceding the war, continued on for several years, without any explanation in catalogues or any evidence that any student took this "parallel course."[39]

There were minor changes in the years 1868 through 1870. The catalogues for 1867–68 and 1868–69 show that a few books had been dropped from the junior or middle course. No explanation was given, but it would seem the faculty was deliberately preparing for the major curricular change of 1871 by making that future transition easier. The 1869–70 catalogue announced the requirement of a thesis for the first-semester student. He would be required to prepare and read before the class a thesis on some legal topic and then be "subjected to a rigid quizzing on the same subject by his classmates." An interesting idea, but there is no evidence this was ever put into practice. Subsequent catalogues do not discuss the thesis.

In 1871, the faculty made a major change in the curriculum, which would become first the pride and later the shame of Cumberland. In that year, the faculty reduced the course of study to a single year, and Cumberland became a one-year law school, with two five-month semesters, the junior and senior terms. This became the most distinguishing feature of Cumberland until the 1930s. The 1870–71 catalogue was candid in stating four reasons for the new curriculum:

> 1. Most of the Law Schools in the United States have shortened the time. . . . 2. But few young men who have attended the school since the war have been able to remain longer than ten months. Nearly three-fourths of those who have entered our Junior Class [have left before becoming Seniors]. 3. The condition of the country since the late civil war seems to demand . . . a change. Our young men, for the most part, are limited in their means. They are really not able to remain here on expenses longer than is absolutely necessary. And, further, their exigencies require that they should go to work for themselves as soon as possible. This they will do whether we graduate them or not. They will apply to the Judges, who will feel bound to license them after very poor preparation. . . . [The shorter, less expensive program will] induce more of them to enter the school, where they can be thoroughly drilled . . . at least for ten months. 4. . . . It once required an apprenticeship of seven years before our English ancestors would allow the attorney to engage in the practice. . . . [But] the modern diligent student can accomplish more in one year than the ancient student could in seven.

The last explanation, the seven-to-one ratio of time, is the most interesting from the viewpoint of the history of legal education. The catalogue pays express tribute to the importance of the late eighteenth- and nineteenth-century growth and development of the legal treatise, monographs stating firmly settled legal rules and precepts, not mere commentaries on the law, nor collections of precedents with brief commentary in the manner of modern hornbooks. The growth of the treatise required a great sense of intellectual stability in the law, something difficult to conceive today.[40]

In this same fascinating 1870–71 catalogue, the Cumberland faculty acknowledged its intellectual debt precisely, thereby demonstrating its continued commitment to the precepts of Abraham Caruthers and also its full understanding of where the school stood in the stream of the historical process of legal education. They explained why the law student no longer needed to study seven years:

> Anciently the law was diffused through many books, most of which were reports [of judicial decisions]. Years of labor and observation in the office and in the Courts were necessary to give the beginners any proper notion of the law itself and the practice. But now Blackstone, Kent, Story, Greenleaf and others have collected the principles of jurisprudence from the vast number of reports, and have arranged, digested and reduced them to system, and have brought them within a small compass. They have done the work for us which the British student formerly had to do himself.

A fundamental intellectual failure of the Cumberland leaders was their subsequent inability to see that they then stood at the high point of legal formalism. The settled intellectual world that made viable the treatises and their settled sets of rules, or "system," in the faculty's language, would crumble within the fifty years following 1871. Society and the law itself became more complex and specialized. Judges increasingly used law to facilitate and change public policies. Legal education changed in response to these developments. But Nathan Green Jr., a member of Cumberland's first law class and professor from 1856 to 1919, would not acknowledge the changed times.

In fact, by 1871, the Cumberland faculty was already misreading the times. Their first reason for change was simply not true. American law schools were not generally reducing their curriculum to a single year. In 1870, only twelve American law schools had a one-year program; eighteen had two-year programs.[41] The movement was toward the longer time. As we have seen, Harvard had a stated two-year program but in actuality graduated students after eighteen months. Cumberland started out in the 1840s with stiffer standards and an actual requirement of two years. In 1871, the same year that Cumberland reduced its program to a single year, Harvard required two full years. Harvard began encouraging its law students to study for three years in 1876, and mandated a three-year program in 1899.[42]

The year 1871 was significant for the practical pedagogy of law teaching, as well as its intellectual foundations. In this year, a young academic named Christopher Columbus Langdell introduced the case method to Harvard, a technique in which students would read carefully selected cases each day, rather than treatises, and then be thoroughly questioned the next day, not just on their obvious contents but also on the cases' implications, reasoning, and consistency with other lines of cases. Over the next several decades this case method, as changed somewhat from its original conception, would remake the world of legal education. But not until the 1930s would it enter Cumberland.

In short, 1871 was a significant turning point in Cumberland's pedagogical history. The year did not matter so much institutionally and financially. As we shall see, the changes made in 1871 virtually assured the school's financial success for the next fifty years and also gave the law school a short-term boost in attendance. Yet 1871 marks a turning point where Cumberland set its face resolutely to the past and began a slow slide into a status of substandard.

There was much more truth to the faculty's explanation that financial exigencies required the reduction of the curriculum to two terms. In the antebellum years Green himself noted that many of the students were sons of wealthy planters and attended the law school to become "more accomplished citizens, and without intending to follow the profession as a business."[43] In the postwar period, students more typically came from the middle or working classes.[44] The change in curriculum allowed the Cumberland faculty to raise the per-term tuition to sixty dollars each semester, while still lowering overall costs to the student. As the faculty explained: "More law is now taught in each class than formerly, and consequently more labor is devolved on the Professor. Formerly the student paid one hundred and fifty dollars in the three sessions for tuition. Now he pays for two sessions one hundred and twenty dollars only, and saves five months boarding and other expenses."[45]

In retrospect, writing in 1890, Green thought the reduction had been made "without omitting from the course of study a single important legal topic."[46] A contemporary student agreed that the change "resulted in somewhat enlarging the courses of the Junior and Senior classes, with only a slight and unimportant reduction of the whole course in point of subjects taught. The course became more strenuous, indeed, but little if any less thorough." John A. Pitts, a member of the class of 1871, also agreed that the change allowed many men of small means to attend who otherwise could not have done so.[47]

At first, the faculty took an apologetic tone toward the change. The 1870–71 catalogue declared that "we would be glad if we could induce young men to remain at the school two years or longer, but we can not." The faculty continued to offer a second year without tuition change and conceded that the new curriculum was "very imperfect; but is so necessarily. It is impossible to become a good lawyer during the short time young men can be induced to remain in any school of Law. All that can be done is to give them a decent preparation for a license, and fit them respectably for beginning the practice."[48]

Within a few years this apologetic tone was gone completely, and self-congratulation pervaded the law school's announcements. If in 1871–72 the faculty acknowledged that "many books of importance are of course left out," by 1875–76 they would claim that "every subject likely to be encountered in practice will be found treated in the course." In the 1875–76 catalogue the Cumberland faculty gave their fullest postwar exposition of legal philosophy and its relationship to teaching. The statement is important, because it fully reflects the static view of law discussed earlier and its relationship to teaching. It is doubly important because during the next fifty years this statement of philosophy would be repeated, practically verbatim, in every Cumberland catalogue, even while the legal world around Lebanon, Tennessee, was transformed:

> The law is in the text-books. The Professor can no more make law than the student himself. It is better, therefore, that the student be required to learn a portion of the text and be subjected to an examination in the presence of his class every day. It is the business of the Professor to conduct this examination, and explain difficult passages when necessary. . . . Every subject upon which a lecture could be given has been exhausted by the ablest Professors, and printed in books, after the most careful revision by the authors. We would regard it as an imposition on students, and presumptuous on our part,

> to pretend that we could improve upon Kent, Story, Greenleaf, Parsons and others, who have given to the public, in printed form, and acceptable to all, lectures on every branch of the law. We, therefore, think it better for the student to occupy his time in learning, with our assistance, what others have written than in learning from anything we could write. If our mode of teaching is more difficult for us, it is much more profitable to the student.

With the shortening of the curriculum, Cumberland began a long process of insuring that students undertook the entire course of study. First, students were now expected to enter the term promptly, in either September or January, but at or very near to the initial day. Previously, an applicant could enter the senior class merely upon taking a test on the junior class texts. Cumberland continued to urge "all who possibly can" to enter a junior class. But, in a second reform beginning in 1876, "those who read the Junior course privately and apply for admission to the Senior Class, with a view to graduation, will be subjected to a *rigid examination*" (emphasis added). This reform was the beginning of tightening standards. The nineteenth-century law school did not certify legal competence or regulate entry into the profession in the manner of a modern law school.[49] Tying the rigidity of the examination to an applicant's desire to obtain a degree was the slow start of Cumberland's assumption of responsibility for acting as a gatekeeper for entry into the legal profession.

A student attending Cumberland in 1870–71 described the law library modestly as "a nice little law library, comprising text-books, some English reports, and United States and State reports. . . . Smith's Leading Cases and White and Tudor, the Institutes of Justinian and Peterdorf's Abridgement of the Common Law, were about all the works of [secondary reports and digests] accessible."[50] Actually, this was a period of rapid growth of the law library. In 1869 it held only six hundred volumes, but by 1878 the count stood at three thousand books.[51] Unfortunately, time stood still in this area as well, and the library did not grow again for thirty-five years.

The moot court program continued its relentlessly practical approach. Students were still required to conduct trials in accordance with the *History of a Lawsuit,* prepare all documents, and fill all court offices. John Pitts, class of 1871, noted that "Judge Green was ordinarily present to direct and keep us straight; for the Moot Court was not a rival contest, as for a prize for accuracy or ability, but an effort to illustrate, in the concrete, an actual trial, and thus give the student some insight of actual Court procedure." Students were also encouraged to attend the county courts when they were in session.[52]

Pitts recalled a considerable difference between the teaching styles of Green and Robert Caruthers. Green emphasized a thorough mastery of the fundamental principles of the law, admonished against a too strict reliance on technical rules and precedents, urged honesty and fairness in practice, and drew his students' attention to the importance of attention to the details. Green once gave a commencement address in which he dwelt on attention to details, the "little things" in law and life. He ended with the advice that the young lawyers ought to marry early. "Get you a wife," he said with a twinkle of the eye and a smile on his face, "to help you care for the little things."

Green followed the standard Cumberland format of assigning a section of the treatise, and then asking questions the next day in no fixed order. He would sometimes put hypothetical cases to the class and inquire about the applicability of a legal rule. Kind and courteous, he tried to be sure that everyone understood the discussion. He worked indirectly, using "delicate complimentary comments" and avoiding any "word of criticism or disparagement calculated to humiliate or wound the feelings of those who had answered incorrectly." He would often "add adroit palliations and excuses for erroneous answers, with the plainest and most lucid expositions of the whole subject."

John Pitts was obviously impressed by the style and personality of Nathan Green Jr.:

> May I not dwell somewhat upon the fascinating personality of Judge Green. I have no scruple or hesitation in saying that he was the best teacher, and one of the best men, I have ever known. He had the power of terse and lucid statement, and of comprehensive and exhaustive explanation and illustration—in other words, the happy faculty of imparting to the untrained mind the knowledge he possessed—to a degree that I have never observed in any other teacher; and he did this in a manner so suave, so kindly, and so courteous, as to endear himself personally to every member of his class. No student could leave his class room without both a clearer conception and

> understanding of the subject of the lesson than he could possibly obtain from his own unaided study of the text, and, at the same time, a real filial and affectionate feeling for his great teacher.

Pitts was not nearly as impressed by Robert Caruthers. He described him as of "medium height, medium flesh, erect, of dignified carriage, clean shaven, and always neatly dressed." Although he characterized Caruthers as a great man and recalled that he was "very companionable" and "the boys all liked him," Pitts noted that Caruthers was a "wholly different kind of man from Judge Green," and almost everything else he wrote about Caruthers was somewhat negative:

> He was by no means "stiff" or unapproachable, but he lacked that friendly cordiality of disposition which invites or encourages intimacy and which distinguished Judge Green; nor did he possess Judge Green's happy faculty of clear statement and lucid exposition. Aside from asking questions arising directly from the subject of the lesson, he spent the recitation period chiefly in telling stories, more or less pertinent to the lesson, arising out of his experience and observation at the bar and on the Bench, many of which were exceedingly amusing, and some of which I still remember. Occasionally he would occupy the whole of the class session with these stories, without asking the class a question.[53]

The faculty's emphasis on morality and religion continued, although there was somewhat less emphasis on it in the school's bulletins. The catalogues occasionally stated that there were several churches in Lebanon, and there was no attempt to steer students to any particular one. Green wrote that the Cumberland faculty "by their influence and example, as well as by many incidental and unobtrusive conversations, . . . have invariably taught that Jehovah is the Author of all law."[54] A contemporary historian of Cumberland, J. Berrien Lindsley, claimed that during the course of instruction, "it has been [the law faculty's] habit to impress upon the youthful mind the virtues of honesty, fidelity, and purity." He went so far as to insist that "when, in the last day, all shall meet before their Eternal Judge, many will ascribe their everlasting happiness to the influence of their [law] teachers,"[55] certainly a responsibility few faculty members would undertake today.

Notwithstanding these pronouncements, there seems to have been a lighter touch on the students in the postwar years. Most important, no one could find the old code of rules that so bedeviled the students of an earlier day. Even Green, who had hated it, tried to find a copy as a curiosity but failed. A new rule was substituted: "Semper praesens, semper paratus," always present, always prepared. To this was added the requirement that students were expected to behave as gentlemen. Behind these newer, looser rules was Green's understanding that young men "who attend class regularly and recite well when there, are not likely to be insubordinate, troublesome, or dissipated."[56]

But some specific rules lingered on for a time. The 1865–66 and 1866–67 law school catalogues warned that "no student is allowed to drink any intoxicating liquors," that "gaming is strictly prohibited," and that "students have no use for pistols and Bowie-knives." For the following two years the drinking and gambling prohibitions remained, but the admonition about deadly weapons was dropped. By 1870–71, for the first time, the "no drinking, no gambling" provisions were gone, and in the following year, the 1871–72 catalogue stated: "No code of laws is used. Each student is expected to know his lessons, and behave himself like a gentleman. Those who will not do this are not wanted here."

Obviously, with a large collection of young men, some discipline problems were bound to occur. How were they handled in the absence of the elaborate trial procedures mandated by the former prewar rules? Although the trustees had been very active in expelling students earlier, the minutes are devoid of any expulsion in these postwar years. Perhaps, in part, the students were older, returning veterans and more mature, and therefore there were far fewer expulsions. Also probable is that the power of discipline and expulsion had devolved to the faculty of the individual departments, the records of which have vanished. A note in the trustees' minutes in 1873 suggests this devolution. A new professor in the preparatory department was "to be responsible for the discipline and government in his department in the same manner and with the same powers of the teachers of the other departments of the university."[57] A remark of Green in 1890 also suggests that discipline had become both more decentralized and more informal: "Now and then it has occurred that students have been disorderly and dissipated to such an extent as to require notice. In such cases they are quietly called up, and an opportunity given for repentance and reformation, which, if they do not improve, results in their enforced retirement from the school. The reins of government are held so loosely that the governed feel no pressure, but so firmly that they can be tightened in a moment."[58]

Of course, the law students continued to carry on their high jinks, many of which would not have been approved by Caruthers or Green. One of the best practical jokes was between two law students in 1870. It involved D. L. Love, from Mississippi, "very bright, but mentally unbalanced; egotistical, but with a child-like credulity and gullibility that made him the butt of many practical jokes," and George B. Peters, of Memphis. Peters pretended to be offended by Love's alleged eavesdropping on himself and a young lady he was escorting home from church.

> There was much talk of the circumstance among the boys, who saw to it that this talk got to Love. Finally, pursuant to an understanding with everyone but Love, Peters challenged Love to a duel with pistols. Love wanted to decline and apologize, but was assured by a number of the boys . . . that the pistols should be loaded with blank cartridges, so that no hurt should come to either, and he was persuaded to accept the challenge and let the duel go on, in order to play a fine joke on Peters and have some fun. . . . the duel should be fought at ten paces, with single-barrelled "derringer" pistols, each to have one shot only.
>
> Accordingly, the combatants met at the time and place appointed, with their seconds, accompanied by quite a crowd of other boys as spectators—all but Love fully in the secret of what was to be done. Love was in a carefully suppressed jubilant state of mind, knowing that the "derringers" were loaded with blanks and believing that Peters was ignorant of that fact. Peters, on the other hand, feigned a very grave countenance, plainly indicating that he feared a fatal catastrophe, and . . . delivered a brief but very solemn little speech concluding with an affectionate message which he desired sent to his mother in case he should not survive the encounter. Finally, . . . at the word "three," the combatants fired straight at each other. Of course neither fell. As Peters, gazing through the clearing smoke, saw that Love was unhurt, he frowned savagely, and with the exclamation, "Damn it, I've missed him!" threw down his empty derringer

> and whipped from his pocket a revolver and began firing it rapidly at Love, who, thinking the revolver was loaded and that the joke had miscarried, turned on his heels and yelling "Murder! Murder!" ran like a deer, never stopping till he had reached town. Of course the revolver was also loaded with blanks, as all but Love knew, and as Love got out of hearing the crowd broke into hilarious merriment.[59]

Aside from the reduction in total tuition, students' costs remained remarkably stable during the period 1865–1878. The boarding estimates were up slightly, to $3.50-$5.00 per week, and higher than prewar estimates. In 1871, a $5 diploma fee was added to the $5 contingency fee, and in 1874 a $1 "library tax" was imposed. With the reduction of the curriculum, the cost of books dropped. In 1865, the estimated costs of treatises was $157, whereas in 1874, after the new curriculum, it was only $80.[60] Even so, this $80 is over $1,400 in 1997 purchasing power and in 1874 was two-thirds of the total tuition charge. A later tradition of book rentals had not yet begun; at least it was not yet announced in the catalogues.

As was true during the prewar years, the proximity of so many eligible bachelors in Lebanon stimulated the location of women's schools nearby. Apparently girls' finishing schools were a risky business. The Greenwood Seminary, a highly selective school located a few miles outside of Lebanon, continued on after the war but closed in 1883. The Corona Institute for Women closed in 1873, thereby making the building available for purchase by Robert Caruthers. The Lebanon Female Institute closed its doors in 1876.[61] The first female student at Cumberland University itself apparently entered in 1873,[62] although this was an irregular situation and the university was not to become coed during this period. But in the spring of 1877, the Cumberland Preparatory School, an advanced high school preparing students for college, opened a female department that would offer young ladies "the same training in languages and mathematics that the young men receive who are preparing for College."[63]

Law students continued to find their wives in Lebanon.[64] The best example is that of Horace Lurton, a member of Cumberland's first postwar class. On the graduation day in 1867, Lurton "gazed into the future wondering what fortune the life which was opening up before my hopeful soul had in store for me." But he recalled seeing little else that day, since it had been his "happy lot to have won the trusting love of a Lebanon girl whose sweet presence on that occasion seemed to fill all space." Horace Lurton, many years later, became Cumberland's second justice on the United States Supreme Court, and the "Lebanon girl" became his wife and, in Lurton's words, "at all times both an inspiration and a conscience."[65]

In his earlier years, Lurton had been an ardent supporter of the South. In 1861, he was only seventeen years old and still living with his parents in Kentucky. He desperately desired to join the Confederate army. On June 2, 1861, he wrote a friend that it was "my desire to yet strike a blow in defense of that best of causes—Southern Independence. I would go *now* if ma would only consent. . . . O! how I long to see the Stars and Bars in triumph waving!"[66] The Lurtons moved to Clarksville, Tennessee, and either "ma" relented or young Horace attained the age necessary to dispense with parental consent. He joined the 5th Tennessee Regiment and enjoyed a military career that was distinguished by being captured, released, and then captured once again.

Lurton attended Cumberland School of Law immediately following the war. Fifteen years following his graduation he began a meteoric rise as a judge. In 1883 Lurton became a Tennessee state chancery judge, won election to the state supreme court in 1886, and became its chief justice in January 1893. Only three months later, in April 1893, President Cleveland appointed Lurton to the Sixth Circuit Court of Appeals. While in this post, he became friends with another judge on that bench, William Howard Taft. Lurton's abilities on the Sixth Circuit made him a leading contender for an appointment to the United States Supreme Court in 1906, but the seat eluded him that year. In 1909, his former colleague, now President Taft, appointed Lurton to the United States Supreme Court, on which he served from 1909 until his death in 1914.

Over the years, Lurton changed his political viewpoint dramatically. Even after the war, Lurton had predicted that the South would rise up again. Yet by the end of the century his speeches show him to be a firm nationalist. The leading student of Lurton's jurisprudence writes that "it remains uncertain when and how Horace Lurton ceased to be a disaffected rebel."[67] One can speculate that at least the beginnings of that change in attitude may have been the result of his contact with the conservative former Whigs in Lebanon and specifically in Cumberland School of Law. The

Cumberland law faculty had always been nationalistic, had not desired secession, and fought for the South only after Lincoln's call for an invasion. Probably the viewpoints of the Greens and Robert Caruthers contributed considerably toward Lurton's maturing political philosophy.

Cumberland law students were still overwhelmingly undergraduates, and therefore engaged in most of the collegiate social activities. The YMCA continued its work at Cumberland during this period, and the years 1876–1880 saw the revived publication of a monthly literary magazine, *Cumberland University Monthly Magazine.*[68] Organized sports belong to the period after 1878.

The Greek letter fraternities continued at Cumberland after the war, but the literary societies were more popular, and with their debates and orations, dominated the Cumberland social scene.[69] The three societies from before the war, the Amasagassean, Philomathean, and Heurethelean societies, continued on. A new group, the R. L. Caruthers Literary Society, appeared in 1874.[70] The societies are well-described in the annual catalogues.

The purposes of the organizations were very much the same. The Amasagassean Society elected orators to deliver orations at the commencement exercises in January and June. It also elected a valedictorian and held debates, awarding a gold medal each year to the best debater. The Philomathean Society was organized for the purpose of "cultivating the powers of forensic eloquence and morals" of its members. The Heurethelean Society's exercises consisted of "orations, essays, declamations and debate. The members are stimulated to give special attention to parliamentary law and practice."[71] The purpose of the Caruthers Literary Society is not as clear, but it probably was along the same lines since it also awarded a medalist honor.[72]

The Heurethelean Society was dominated by theological students and some few undergraduates. Law students were active in all three other societies and certainly held their own in the competitions for official positions and awards. In 1871–72, the Amasagassean had law students as president for both fall and spring terms, and half of the four orators and both medalists were studying law. That same year law students were president and medalist of Philomathean. After it was organized in 1874, the Caruthers group was dominated by law students in the same manner Heurethelean was by theological students. In that same year, the president of Amasagassean was not a law student, but one of four orators was.

The Caruthers Society seemed to have some trouble getting started, and there were some years, such as 1875–76 and 1876–77, when it was not mentioned in the catalogue. When it was active it was always dominated by law students. The other two societies were split. In most years, but not always, law students were the most active in Philomathean. Amasagassean was the most evenly divided. A glimpse at 1876–77 indicates a typical year: law students were the presidents for both fall and spring terms, but all the other officers and all the winners of their medals were undergraduate or theological students.[73]

The election contests for valedictorian engaged considerable attention. There were often squabbles, considerable electioneering, and, as Green considered it, "hard feeling was sure to be engendered, and even bloodshed sometimes threatened. These student feuds became a nuisance and a stench."[74] The only qualification for membership in the societies was matriculation as a student in the university, and one sharp contest between two law students for orator of the Amasagassean Society in 1870–71 involved some amusing tactics:

> There were "stump speeches" every night for weeks on the public square, and much "electioneering," after the manner of a political campaign, and the "partisan spirit" ran high. . . . On the last night that new members could be admitted and qualified to vote . . . [one candidate] corralled and marched to the Burser's [*sic*] office about fifty of the riff-raff of the town—common laborers and boys—paid their matriculation fees, and had them enrolled as members of the Society. . . . [this tactic] outraged the friends of [the other candidate and] the members of his faction in his [Amasagassean] Society, practically all the members of our [Philomathean] Society, and many students of the University who were not members of either Society. Vigorous protests were made, impassioned speeches were delivered, and pandemonium reigned for several nights, resulting finally in a formal written protest addressed to the Faculty, signed by a hundred or more students, accompanied with the declaration that all the signers would immediately quit the University unless the names of these parvenus were at once stricken from the record as students . . . The Faculty promptly took notice of this protest, made a brief examination of the matter, and ordered the money refunded and the names of the new matriculants stricken from the record [and] thus disqualified from voting in the Society.[75]

The faculty took into its own hands the appointment of a valedictorian. But the faculty chose a speaker on the basis of who was the best student. That caused jealousy, some who were clearly not the best students relaxed their class efforts, and worst of all, as Green noted, the best student was not necessarily the best speaker. Sometimes, the faculty chose "an awkward, ungainly fellow, who mumbled his piece so as to make the whole affair rather ludicrous." At other times, the faculty found it too difficult to pick the single best student and appointed two valedictorians. Eventually, the faculty abolished the honor entirely and addresses from trustees or distinguished gentlemen from a distance were substituted.[76] But that change could not have happened until the end of this period, since in a valedictory address of January 20, 1876, the speaker, a law student, stated that he had been elected by his classmates.[77] The law school held separate commencement exercises, and perhaps the tradition of valedictorian continued on longer for the law students.

The picture that emerges from these debate and oration societies is that there were a great number of offices and prizes to be handed out. They therefore provided training for many students in leadership, public speaking, and even electioneering. As we will take up in greater detail in the following chapter, they were perfect training grounds for the small-town practice toward which most graduates of Cumberland School of Law were headed.

CHAPTER FOUR

The Student Experience 1878–1919

> No greater law teachers than Judge Nathan Green and Dr. Andrew B. Martin ever sat before a class of law students in any university in this nation.
> —Cordell Hull, U.S. Secretary of State

THE STRUCTURE OF Cumberland's law curriculum remained remarkably stable throughout the years 1878–1919. Several key elements made it unique: reading of treatises and daily two-hour quizzes; mandatory and much-emphasized moot court; the ability of students to enter at either of the two terms; a repeated, second year offered free of charge; and, of course, the one-year course of study. All of these features remained solidly in place throughout this period.[1] Such curricular changes that did take place must be seen as blips on the surface of this massive continuity. But some twists and turns, modifications here and there, are interesting.

One twist was an experiment requiring theological students to read certain law books along with the law students. As the 1896 catalogue explained, "every preacher should understand something of the formation of our government, our relations to other nations, and also, for obvious reasons, the rules of evidence."[2] They were to learn these by studying the first volume of Kent's *Commentaries* and Greenleaf's *Evidence* with Nathan Green, although the "obvious reasons" for studying the rules of evidence are unclear. The divinity students apparently became temporary members of the law class. The idea apparently worked, and limited law studies were standard fare of the Cumberland theological students for years.

In the mid-1880s the law school attempted to add a postgraduate degree to its curriculum. The trustees approved a plan in 1883 to offer a five-month course leading to a masters in law and empowered the law faculty to select an appropriate course of study.[3] The 1882–83 catalogue announced that the new program would consist of nine volumes, about six thousand pages of reading, and would require one term. The books were different from those used in the regular curriculum, although the "students in the Post Graduate Course will have all the advantages of Moot Courts, drillings, etc., that others have, and be subject to the same laws of the University,"[4] and pay the same tuition, contingent fees, and diploma fee.[5]

This program was probably the dream of Nathan Green Jr., as he was the only faculty member of the 1880s who had been a teacher during the time of the "parallel course" in the antebellum period. But the plan failed for lack of students. In the years following the initial announcement, the Cumberland catalogues never listed students as postgraduates, and there is no evidence in either the catalogues or the trustees' minutes of the award of a single LL.M. degree. With the catalogue of 1889, the listing of the postgraduate course was dropped.

Like many dreams, it died hard. Twenty years after the program was established, the bulletin for January 1904 contained a small paragraph that indicated that the law school has "courses leading to the degrees of LL.B. and LL.M." But there was no resumption of any organized postgraduate program. The bulletin for March 1910 spoke of three postgraduate law students, but there was no indication of a program for them, and this probably referred to three students who were taking advantage of the continuous offer of a second year, after graduation, at no tuition. Historically, Cumberland has been too relentlessly practical a school to attract academically inclined postgraduate students.

Much more success attended the establishment of a summer school in June 1896. Unlike the regular course, this was avowedly a lecture course, consisting of forty lectures over a period of eight weeks. From the beginning, this program was the project of Andrew B. Martin, although in the first summer or two Green lectured on real property. The summer course was not designed to "take the place of any part of the regular law course . . . but [to] prepare the student for a more thorough comprehension of that course [or] as a post-graduate review." There was no credit or advanced placement derived from the course. The charge was twenty dollars, "strictly in advance."[6] This course survived and continued intact under the care of Andrew B. Martin.

During World War I, Cumberland University participated in the Student Army Training Corps. It was not a happy experience, as "academic classes suffered severely on account of the demands of military schedules and drill. . . . with the academic work dominated by the military authorities and subordinated to the discipline and drill of the army, it was an unfortunate experience and the results were utterly unsatisfactory."[7] It is unclear how much of this disruption extended to the law school, but since the law students were undergraduates and presumably eligible to participate in this program, there must have been some difficulty.

There was also a remarkable continuity in the books studied. Some substitutions, deletions, and additions were made. Cumberland's own *History of a Lawsuit* went through several editions, and students were often enjoined to buy the latest edition of this and other books. The order of reading changed ever so slightly, and, then too, there were a few real experiments. How other than experimental could we regard the 1895 addition of *Keasley on Electric Wires,* a matter of great contemporary concern with the electrification of the country.[8] But the overwhelming impression is one of continuity. The books did not change frequently. The books required at the end of this period were as follows:[9]

JUNIOR TERM:
History of a Lawsuit
Stephens on Pleading [i.e., Stephen's]
Greenleaf on Evidence (volume I)
Clark on Corporations
Kent's *Commentaries* (volumes I, II, III)
Bigelow on Torts

SENIOR TERM:
Barton's *Suit in Equity*
Story's *Equity Jurisprudence*

Kent's *Commentaries* (volume IV)
Parsons on Contracts
Black's Constitutional Law
May's *Criminal Law*

A comparison of the books required in 1852 indicates that the following books still used in 1919 were also required in 1852: *History of a Lawsuit* (in 1852 referred to as Preliminary Tracts), Stephen's *Principles of Pleading,* Greenleaf's *Law of Evidence,* Kent's *Commentaries* (volumes 1, 2, 3), Story's *Equity Jurisprudence,* and Kent's *Commentaries* (volume 4). Approximately half of the texts used in 1919 dated back, granting new editions, to 1852.

The 1894 catalogue made the first reference to legal topics, as such, distinct from merely the books studied. It listed a large number of conventional legal subjects such as agency, partnership, bailments, sales, contracts, torts, and so forth. However, to the end of this period the curriculum continued to be organized by books to be read, rather than the modern course description by topics or subjects.

In some areas of its educational program, the years 1878–1919 saw a considerable tightening of Cumberland's standards. We have already seen that from 1876 onward, students who sought advanced standing were subjected to a rigid examination on the books of the junior term. The catalogues had often urged "upon all who possibly can, that they enter the Junior class."[10] But beginning in 1893, a rigid examination and a stern warning would no longer do. In that year and thereafter, "no one will be admitted to the Senior Class with a view to graduation, except such as have gone satisfactorily through the Junior Class here, or who have studied equivalent law in some other good law school."[11] But even that was not enough. From 1896 onward, no one would be admitted to the second term as a candidate for graduation, "except such as have gone satisfactorily through the Junior Class here."[12] The entire year was to be done at Cumberland.

Another reform concerned grading. Traditionally, Cumberland had held no examinations and issued no grades. As late as 1890, Nathan Green explained why:

> The professors do not keep marks indicating the standing of the student. It is thought the stimulus afforded by the presence of the class

> and a careful examination of every student every day are sufficient. As a rule the student who merits high grading does not need the incentive, and he who does not deserve it would do no better by reason of it. . . . As to final examinations, there are none. The daily examination of every student enables the professors to know their exact merit. . . . It is thought better . . . to form an estimate of his worth, based upon the two hundred examinations [i.e., the daily quizzes] to which he has been subjected.[13]

But pressures were building for a change in this policy. One pressure, although there is no specific evidence for it, may have come from students. Young lawyers, increasingly being drawn into urban areas and large firms, may have needed some evidence besides the possession of a degree to account for how well they had done in law school. Another pressure came from the organized bar. In the late 1880s, the Tennessee Bar Association formed a Committee on Legal Education and Admission to the Bar, and in 1892 the committee issued a report. Among other things this report recommended that law students should be examined daily, which Cumberland was doing, of course, and also that students be subjected to periodical written review examinations.[14]

Beginning in 1901, in addition to daily quizzes, Cumberland law students were required to take and pass a written examination after each book was completed. The faculty determined the student's "fitness for graduation" on the basis of these grades, the student's class recitations, and, more generally, "his earnestness and fidelity in prosecuting his studies."[15] This requirement, as well as the mandatory attendance for the entire year, continued throughout the period.

Although the earliest grade book is no longer extant, the grade book for the period 1910 through 1925 still exists. At first, grades were listed partially for books and partially for subjects. The transition toward subjects was not complete until 1925, when grades became listed only under subject headings.[16]

The grades tended to be high, mostly in the 90s, many in the 80s, and some few as low as 66 or 75. Most of those who did poorly on one book nevertheless did well in exams on other books. From 1913 onward, Criminal Law was often marked "OK." Taken as a whole, the book does not suggest rigorous grading. Unit numbers appeared for the first time in 1919–20, three units assigned for each book, excepting the first three volumes of Kent were nine units; Contracts, four; and Criminal Law, two. Someone has made slight annotations by some of the students names. One fellow, T. C. Stephenson of Texas, 1913–14, has a notation alongside, "in penitentiary 1940," whereas a page away G. W. Browning, January 1914, has the notation, "governor of Tennessee in 1937–8." Grades were given in very precise numbers, including a few fractional numbers, such as 66⅔. That fact, together with evidence that Green was able to grade his examinations on the fourth volume of Kent's *Commentaries* in a single evening, suggests that the examinations were objective, short answer or multiple choice.[17]

A final reform concerned prelaw education. None had traditionally been required. Year after year, the catalogues had recited that "no previous reading in law, or any special literary qualifications" were required for admission. The 1912 Bulletin added the words "other than the equivalent of a high school education" after the word "qualifications." This same bulletin reiterated with a vengeance the requirement that the entire course must be completed on campus, warning that "to become a graduate the student must satisfactorily accomplish the entire course prescribed by study and recitation here, in the regular order, and under the immediate direction of the Faculty. No exception to this rule will be allowed."[18]

Throughout the years 1878–1919, the faculty remained remarkably steady in composition. We have already noted that Andrew B. Martin, a graduate of the class of 1858, became a part-time instructor in 1878. Two years later, Robert L. Caruthers resigned because of ill health, and Martin became a full-time professor.[19] At that point, Nathan Green Jr. became the senior professor and Andrew B. Martin his "junior" associate.

Robert L. Caruthers had been in poor health for some time, and died in 1882. He was the first president of the Cumberland Board of Trustees in Lebanon and served continuously until his death. He had a varied career, serving in the Tennessee legislature, the national Congress, and as justice of the Tennessee Supreme Court. He was elected governor of Tennessee in 1863 but was unable to take his seat because of the federal occupation of the state capital. He was the last of the founders to die. Of course, Nathan Green Jr., a member of the first undergraduate class and the first law class, present at the founding but not himself a founder, remained very much alive. Robert Caruthers was the single largest benefactor of old Cumberland, donating, as we have seen, Corona Hall, and the land and first ten thousand dollars of construction costs toward the building of Caruthers Hall. Andrew B. Martin wrote a kind tribute:

> This institution at Lebanon is his enterprise. His influence more than any other man brought it here, and his labor and purse more than any one else's kept it alive here. The history of its secret troubles, known alone to its nearest friends, will attest how many times his hands have stretched forth to steady its shaking walls. . . . there have been many days in the history of Cumberland University, when, if Judge Caruthers had withdrawn from it his support, it would have been left without subsequent history. His labor, his money, and his personal sacrifices many times kept it alive.[20]

After Martin joined Green as a full-time professor in 1880, the full-time faculty remained fixed until Green's death in 1919. However, additional part-time instructors appeared on the roster. In 1902, Waller C. Caldwell retired from the Tennessee Supreme Court, on which he was serving as a justice, to become a part-time professor of Constitutional Law and also to instruct in Tennessee Supreme Court practice. A son-in-law of Nathan Green Jr., Caldwell was actually elected in the fall of 1900 but did not enter into his duties until 1902.[21] At the same time as Caldwell was beginning to teach, Horace H. Lurton, then a judge on the Sixth Judicial Court of Appeals in Nashville, was listed as a "university lecturer" in the university catalogue. Whatever his relationship, either to the university or the law school, it must have been brief, as he was no longer listed in the March 1904 bulletin.[22] The last part-time faculty member added in this period was Judge E. E. Beard, who was already Cumberland University treasurer and a trustee. He also had thirty years of experience at the bar. He aided the preparation of moot court cases and held trial in the moot court two days a week.[23] Beard and Caldwell continued as part-time instructors throughout the years until Green's death.

The spirit of Cumberland had always opposed lecturing. The catalogue for 1878–79 explained that "regular lectures on the law are not delivered, as they would only divert the minds of the students from their daily work." Nevertheless, even a thoroughly Socratic approach in a modern law school has to bend to the hard reality that occasionally students simply do not grasp a point, no matter how brilliant and pointed the questions. Every law teacher on occasion must set forth the law in plain language to the class, call it lecturing or not. And this need was certainly present in Cumberland in the nineteenth century.

Cumberland students were permitted to ask questions, and, indeed, the duty of the Cumberland law professor, according to the 1884 catalogue, was "to correct the errors into which [students] may fall; to dispel the darkness that hangs upon many passages—this is necessary every day, and at every step of their progress." All this implies a fair amount of straight exposition on the part of the faculty. The 1904 *Phoenix,* the university yearbook, referred without any sense of irony to "points of law that failed to impress the student in a lecture." The January 1876 valedictory address praised the faculty, saying that it had been its sad job "to drag out day after day the long and wearisome hours in the classroom in lucid exposition" of legal principles.[24] Thus, we have the ironic task of inquiring, in a nonlecture school, about the quality of the lecturing.

In the 1870s, as we have seen, Green was already regarded as a great teacher. From the little we know of his teaching methodology, his techniques seem very modern. Addressing remarks directly at his teaching colleagues, Green once wrote that "of our subjects we must be perfect masters; we must interest the minds of our students; we must teach with energy, teach with enthusiasm."[25] This was clearly good advice, and it showed in the vivid mental images and models he employed to hold his students' interest. He referred to the difficult task of teaching future interests in property, estates in land, and concurrent estates (all in the fourth volume of Kent's *Commentaries*) as leading his "boys" through the tunnel. The real property involved in any class illustration was always named "Blackacre," that fabled ground revered by all property professors for hundreds of years. Bailment issues and finding problems revolved around his "strong box," containing his treasures, as he said. At the dawn of the twentieth century, Green was already seventy-three, but full of life. He remarried in 1902, at age seventy-five, and shortly thereafter acquired a sporty red automobile. He called it his "Red Devil," and it was the basis of countless classroom illustrations,[26] a harbinger of current professor Brad Bishop's Bronco, much later in the century.

Martin was also an excellent teacher. He was fond of using irony to prod his students; often an amusing gleam in his eye accompanied his teasing.[27] The 1915 yearbook said that Martin possessed:

> a perfect knowledge of student nature and an adequate comprehension of crowd-psychology. By virtue of his incomparable gift of humor, he sustained interest that might otherwise have flagged [through] the Doctor's inimitable faculty of imparting dry detail in an interesting manner. When the mule was stolen, and it behooved us to ponder upon the legal consequences flowing from the theft, we might have failed to listen with interest and apply the point of law involved had the Doctor not confided to us that it was "Brother Cheatham" who stole the mule. Ah! Then we rejoiced in the moral obliquity of our fellow classmate and drank in the sordid details with greedy zest. When the tender, star-eyed maid was led to confide in the honeyed words of her skilled and experienced charmer, and was cruelly deceived, we were at first indifferent to her woe. But when the Doctor softly confided to us that it was Wilkerson, the smooth-tongued, unprincipled Wilkerson, who caused the maiden's plight, we followed with breathless attention the devious technicalities of that breach of promise suit![28]

Tones of abundant affection reverberated between teachers and students. Green encouraged this collegiality, noting that one problem with a large university was that the teacher "might not be as social . . . toward the students as he should be . . . and that consequently there might be no great affection between them."[29] Green demonstrated affection, in the stylized manner of the nineteenth century, and it was reciprocated. Green habitually gave receptions for the senior class upon their graduations and occasionally put on entire banquets. He wrote a school song, "Cumberland, My Cumberland," set to the tune of *Tannenbaum.* In his later years many of the senior classes gave him banquets upon his birthdays, complete with bouquets of flowers equal to his years.[30] The 1912 graduating class presented the university with life-sized portraits of both Green and Martin. They were hung on either side of the stage in Caruthers Hall,[31] and they are still extant and on display in the auditorium of Memorial Hall, Cumberland University in Lebanon, Tennessee.

Andrew B. Martin also held a warm spot in the students' hearts. Student yearbooks separated by twelve years said of Martin: "few men have touched the rank and file of the student body so intimately and so truly. The Doctor is always the boys' friend, and is ready to do anything to help them along, especially in athletics" (1903) and "the radiating geniality and ready wit of his personality won our hearts" (1915). A former student formed a lifelong impression of Martin's exalted character after he personally saw Martin face down a lynch mob on the streets of Lebanon and dissuade its members from their illegal purpose.[32]

It should not be surprising that in later life, alumni almost uniformly praised these two teachers. In 1915, Park Trammell, governor of Florida, wrote that he regarded Cumberland "as one of the very best law schools in the United States." In the same year, George Huddleston, congressman from Alabama, acknowledged that "Cumberland University, its traditions, its associations and the teachings of Judge Nathan Green and Dr. Andrew B. Martin have been a constant and powerful stimulus in my life."[33] A graduate of 1912, interviewed fifty years later, recalled the faculty as "great,"[34] and Albert Neil, who entered Cumberland Law School in 1895 and later himself became a professor, in 1964 recalled Martin as "gifted as a teacher," and Green as "one of the ablest law teachers in the South."[35]

Joseph Weldon Bailey of the class of 1883 became a congressman and served two terms as a senator from Texas. In a meeting before the Tennessee Bar Association in 1926 he remarked of his own days at Cumberland that "Nathan Green was in his prime, and I do him no more than simple justice when I say that a greater law instructor never occupied a professor's chair in these United States."[36] Perhaps the most prominent Cumberland alumnus in the twentieth century was Cordell Hull. He graduated in 1891, became a congressman and senator, and served as secretary of state under Roosevelt from 1933 to 1944. He is regarded as one of the "fathers" of the United Nations, for which work he was awarded the Nobel Peace Prize. Hull wrote of the Cumberland faculty, while serving as secretary of state: "These renowned teachers will compare favorably with those of any college, of any age, in any country. No greater law teachers than Judge Nathan Green and Dr. Andrew B. Martin ever sat before a class of law students in any university in this nation. I shall always deem it one of the rarest privileges of my life to have sat at their feet during those wonderful days in the law school at Cumberland University."[37]

The three most prominent graduates of Cumberland School of Law, Supreme Court Justices Jackson and Lurton, and Secretary of State Hull, were all intensely loyal to the school. All three returned to the campus to deliver addresses while in high office, Lurton as a Supreme Court justice and Hull as secretary of state. Hull spoke at alumni meetings and allowed his name to be used for purposes of fund-raising. Very clearly, these prominent men, as well as lesser graduates, all thought the education they had received was top rate. That praise must be recalled and matched against any criticism that can be offered now from a historical remove.

Mandatory moot court trials continued as an essential part of the Cumberland law curriculum throughout the period. In addition to the required program, from time to time the students would organize their own state moot courts. In 1911, the students from Alabama had organized an Alabama moot court competition, and the Tennessee students were talking of organizing their own. In 1912 the Mississippi students had formed a Mississippi Moot Court.[38] The student-organized moot courts convened on Wednesday afternoons; Saturday morning was the other major court time. There were separate moot equity courts under Green's supervision and moot supreme courts under Caldwell's control.[39] Beard took over much of the moot court work, at least of the circuit courts, after he joined the faculty, and his initial two courts a week soon expanded to three.[40] In the earlier days, there was every indication that students who were not participating in a particular moot trial would attend to receive the benefit of the experience and the professor's remarks. This spectator attendance seems to have diminished in the twentieth century, perhaps reflecting the greater array of extracurricular activities and athletics available to the student. In any event, articles in the student newspaper in 1902 and 1911, urging students not "to neglect" and not "to overlook" the important benefits to be obtained from attending the moot court programs, suggest that many students were not attending moot court exercises other than their own.[41]

The continued emphasis on moot court and the various extracurricular activities designed to facilitate oral communication skills presupposed a model of the nature of the practice in which Cumberland graduates would engage. It contemplated a small-town practice, in which attorneys would gain a reputation, and clients as well, by being good advocates in court, impressing a jury, and making public speeches. Potential clients would learn of a lawyer through his ability to speak in public. All this expectation was changing rapidly in the late nineteenth and early twentieth centuries.

The lawyers who were advancing to the front of their profession, those on the "cutting edge," were moving to cities, where potential clients would as often hire an attorney based on the lawyer's reputation as his ability to make a great summation to a jury. Indeed, more and more lawyers were working for law firms, which often represented business corporations. These corporate clients were not impressed with the quality of jury summary that a lawyer could provide for them; they wanted their lawyers to keep them *out* of the courtroom altogether.

Green's description, in 1890, of the typical young law graduate, revealed his assumption of small-town practice with individually garnered clients: "One must learn by long practice and experience. He [the recent graduate] is not likely to be trusted at first with more than he can accomplish. He must make mistakes and meet reverses, and these are necessary in order that he may grow. . . . Why not, then, give him a start in some good law school, grant him a license, and let him take what small cases he might be trusted with?"[42]

A curriculum guided by this thought did not adequately prepare students for the highest reaches of the profession they were entering. It had a tendency to relegate most of the school's students to the more routine tasks, and the medium reaches, of lawyering. This in turn affected the status of the school. Here is another intellectual failure of the Cumberland leadership. It did not see that the nature of legal practice was changing, and it cleaved to a curriculum that faced toward the past rather than the future.

Aside from the quality of the teaching, another feature of Cumberland that all students appreciated was its modest cost. The law faculty was well aware that most of its students were of slender means.[43] This contrasted with the antebellum period, when many of the Cumberland law students were the sons of planters. Whether it was out of kindness or because of customer resistance is unclear, but the increased tuition of sixty dollars per term instituted when the program went to a single year was rescinded in 1879 by order of the trustees "upon recommendation of the faculty." Undergraduate tuition was reduced at the same time.[44]

Like so much else of old Cumberland, the reestablished tuition of fifty dollars per term became frozen in time and continued at that same rate through the end of this period. The contingent fee of five dollars, that portion of the fees that went to the university, not the faculty, rose from five dollars in 1878 to ten dollars in 1914. There was an occasional imposition of a library fee, usually only one dollar, and a five-dollar diploma fee that was increased to ten dollars by 1919. Summer school was always twenty dollars. The only significant changes in costs from 1878 to 1919 came with room, board, and books. Actually, Cumberland's tuition was in line with national standards and a bit high for the south. For example, in 1899 the law schools at Northwestern University in Illinois and Mercer University in Georgia (both private schools) charged annual tuitions of $105 and $60, respectively (compared with $100 for two semesters at Cumberland).[45]

The estimated cost of law books in 1878–79 was $35 for the junior class and $45 for the senior class. They were on the rise, and by 1881–82 were $40 and $45. The catalogue maintained, however, that this was much less than publishers' prices and the student should remember that the books Cumberland used were "the regular text-books of the profession, and will always be needed in practice, and when once bought will last a life-time." But an alternative option of rental from local booksellers was now offered, for $12.50 per term.[46] The cost of books peaked in 1897 at $95, for both terms, and then dropped dramatically to $80, rental also decreasing to $11 per term.[47] Book costs zigged and zagged a bit for the remaining years, but in 1920 stood at $110 a year, for purchase, with a rental rate of $11 per term.[48]

In 1878–79, the school estimated boarding costs with families at $3.50 per week. Boarding in clubs, however, was lower at $8 per month.[49] This was a cooperative arrangement whereby students would form a "mess," hire a cook, and share expenses. These estimates remained stable throughout the nineteenth century and were essentially repeated in the bulletin for March 1904. There is not as much information in later years for rental arrangements with families, perhaps because the university had a dormitory to fill after 1903. But it is clear that many, if not most, law students continued to board with families and were pleased with their arrangements. In 1962, fifty years after his graduation in 1912, William F. Spencer still remembered the good food served by Mrs. Billy Wilson, who ran a boardinghouse near Caruthers Hall.[50]

There was greater choice with the building of a new four-story university dormitory in 1903. With four stories, seventy-five rooms, a dining room and kitchen (on the fourth floor), it was supplied "with every modern convenience—steam heating, electricity, baths and closets on each floor, and elevator." The initial room boarding charge was $10 per month, with room rent varying from $3 to $5, per week apparently, depending on room.[51] By 1913, law students were quoted rates at the dormitory of $102 board for the academic year and $48 rent for a single room, $38 apiece for a double. The dormitory was intended primarily for undergraduates, but law students were welcome if there were vacancies.[52] That restriction was apparently never significant in practice, and by 1919 law students were expressly invited to secure room and board upon the same conditions as undergraduates.

The boarding costs soared during the war years. Board charges at the dormitory were up to $108 per year in 1915. By 1917 it was $130, and the catalogue warned that it was impossible to state the charge for 1917–18 because of the "uncertain conditions of the markets on account of the war," but promised that it would be no more than $150. By 1919 boarding was at $180 per academic year, and even the room rents had risen to $60 for a single and $50 for a shared double.[53] Doubtless, the continued increase after the war reflected inflation.

There was one lower cost alternative. A cooperative boarding club was run at the Divinity Hall on West Main Street, during the years 1875–1916. This was the old Abraham Caruthers house that the trustees had once ill-advisedly thought to turn over to the law school. It served as the site of the theological school until the completion of Memorial Hall in 1896. Some fifty students lived there, including some from the law school, at rates lower than the dormitory or boarding with families.[54] In 1904 the rate for room and board for other than divinity students was $10 per month, or a total of $100 for the academic year. For those who were really impecunious, the rooms were free. Tillman Davis Johnson, an undergraduate but later a law graduate, explains his arrangements at Divinity Hall and illustrates as well the workings of a boarding club:

> When I was in college, I lived with a lot of preachers, because it was cheap. I got my room for nothing in Divinity Hall and I paid my board, about 6 or 7 dollars a month. . . . when I was 18 in the fall of 1876 I went to Cumberland University and found out about this

> Divinity Hall. . . . I just had enough money to stay through the first half year. I had to lose the second half of the year. I went back home . . . to make money enough to get into the Sophomore class. In Divinity Hall, if a boy was poor, even though he wasn't a Divinity student, he could get up there without obligation. There were always a number of lay students there. One year there was a fellow in the law class. In the rooms some of them had 4. The smaller rooms had 2.
>
> At divinity [*sic*] Hall we hired a Negro cook. We had a room that would accommodate all of us. The old Negro was a good cook. She knew how to cook meat, potatoes, beans and cabbage and it didn't cost more than about $7 a month. We gave one fellow in the hall his board to take care of the buying and paying. . . . At the end of the month we figured the expense and divided it by the number of us, excluding him.[55]

The law school experience, of course, was not all hard study or worrying about costs. There were pranks and high jinks, dating, extracurricular activities, and athletics. We will take them up in that order.

Some college pranks were of the harmless, perennial sort, such as slipping past the housekeeper in the men's dormitory in the middle of the night or, once again, painting the Confederate general in the middle of the town square.[56] Some pranks originated customs. A common informal name for Caruthers Hall came about through a stunt of future senator Joseph W. Bailey, class of 1883. Tradition has it that one day Bailey rode a mule up the outside steps of Caruthers Hall and into the vestibule. The mule brayed loudly. Nathan Green, from alongside his classroom door, responded "No, no, Mr. Bailey, I don't believe you have given the correct answer." The expression "law barn" was born, and throughout the operation of the law school in Lebanon, students called Caruthers Hall the law barn.[57]

In the student culture at the turn of the century, innocent compared with today's, it was easy to work up a righteous indignation over the simplest of injustices. In January 1911, an undergraduate student placed a notice in the student newspaper charging an unnamed law student with the theft of two basketball jerseys. The undergraduate refused a demand of several law students that he name the suspect. The law students living in the dormitory, where the theft apparently occurred, assembled in a mass meeting and condemned the undergraduate for publishing the notice when "common sense and manhood would have dictated the approach personally of that party [the thief] and personal settlement of the difficulty, rather than the preferment of a charge by inuendo [*sic*] against the entire Law [*sic*] department."[58]

The law students resolved to reaffirm their friendship with the student publishers, the basketball team, and even the undergraduate students, "who are not in sympathy, we understand, with the methods pursued," and then published an account of their meeting in the student newspaper.[59] The incident serves as a reminder that the law students were of the same age as undergraduates and therefore just as much affected by the ebb and flow of the politics of very minor matters.

The biggest disciplinary problem facing the Cumberland administration and faculty continued to relate to alcohol. Toward the end of the century there were nine saloons on or near the public square in Lebanon, and law students patronized them.[60] Most of the incidents arising out of law students in the saloons are amusing; a few are tragic. On the lighter side is the story of Judge Green (he preferred that title to professor, as Martin preferred doctor to professor) and his difficulty with a boy from Texas, also with the name of Green. Judge Green was a teetotaler, and the antics of some of his students embarrassed him, although he did his best to control his embarrassment. The story begins on a Saturday afternoon as Judge Green strolled about the Lebanon Public Square: "As he passed a well known saloon, who should come staggering out of it but young Green, who almost fell into the arms of his beloved Dean. The latter remonstrated by saying, 'Young man, it pains me very much to see you coming out of such a place.' The young man, assuming an attitude of great dignity and respect, replied, 'Judge, you are the last man in the world I would wish to cause any distress of mind by coming *out* of such a place. Therefore, I will go back *in*.'"[61]

Actually, in the 1880s discipline became even more relaxed than in the immediate postwar period. While Green claimed in 1891 that bad students could be "detected and sent away,"[62] he also wrote in 1889 that:

> We [the Cumberland administration] now assume that he [the student] knows as well as we do what is right and what is wrong. . . . We assume that he will do his duty. We recognize the fact, heretofore

> ignored, that students have rights as well as teachers. We meet him as a gentleman; we treat him as a gentleman both in the class-room and upon the streets. We throw upon him the responsibility of a gentleman and he rarely disappoints us. We have no spies. We never invade his private apartments except to visit him when he is sick and offer him our aid and our sympathies. We do not concern ourselves as to when or where he shall walk or ride or hunt or visit. All this is none of our business. . . . We insist upon nothing except that he shall demean himself as a gentleman, obey the laws of the land like other citizens, and that he shall be always present at his class and always prepared to recite. . . . As a rule our students have been deferential, punctual, sober, and studious; and we would not on any account return to the old method.[63]

In just a few years the rules were tightened considerably. That might have happened as a result of a very unpleasant incident in the spring of 1893 at Woolard's saloon, one of the nine saloons on the square and well patronized by law students. Joseph M. Anderson, a law graduate of 1891, had been drinking there. For no particular reason he pulled a gun from his pocket, waved it around, played with it, and innocently pointed it at Charles Crutchfield, a freshman collegiate student. Somehow in the horseplay, the gun went off, and Crutchfield fell to the floor.

Anderson pleaded with Crutchfield. "Get up, Crutch! Get up friend! You're just playing with me, aren't you?" But Crutchfield was dead. Some law students present in the saloon, including Joseph Sanders, took Anderson straight to the train depot, forbidding him the time to pack anything, and put him on a night train. Ultimately, it was said, he went to Brazil.[64]

The eventual discovery of this incident by university officials might have been the cause for a tightening of the disciplinary rules. In early 1895, the trustees promulgated new rules concerning discipline. Jurisdiction was decentralized to the faculty of the school in which the offending student was enrolled, provided that faculty punishment could not go further than a suspension for the current academic year; expulsion was solely in the trustees' power. Quite unlike the period before the Civil War, there is no evidence of a formal expulsion in the postwar years, although it might have happened informally. In the 1895 reform, the trustees also made it an offense to act riotously or to disturb any religious, literary, or educational meeting. They made "intoxication and gambling and visiting drinking and gambling houses" university offenses, but did not call for automatic suspension, but only that such an offender "may be suspended" by the appropriate faculty.[65] It was not enough to be a gentleman, as Green had written in 1889, if a gentleman could take a drink.

The next step was to make it impossible for a gentleman to take that drink, at least lawfully. The "dominant moral sentiment" of Lebanon "for many years demanded" prohibition, but was "compelled to wait on tardy legislation."[66] There was an effort in 1881 to ban the saloons by repealing the Lebanon town charter and legislating that no liquor could be sold within four miles of Cumberland University.[67] Not until 1900, however, did the effort succeed. The 1900–1901 catalogue ballyhooed that on the first day of June 1901, "the sale of intoxicating liquors in Lebanon will cease [and] the saloon will disappear forever from the town."

This effort at local prohibition apparently worked. In the separate law school bulletin of 1912, the law school proclaimed that eleven years earlier, on June 1, 1901, "the saloon disappeared forever from the town. . . . the Law School can now offer to young men who come here freedom from the baneful influence of tippling houses, a condition favorable to successful study not enjoyed by any other law school known to us. Earnest young men who desire success in life will not fail to appreciate the advantages to be derived from such conditions."

The most significant catalyst for enhanced social interaction at Cumberland came with the advent of coeducation. When it finally arrived at Cumberland, it did so quickly. The Lebanon College for Young Ladies was organized in 1886.[68] Designed to provide higher education to women and a course of study "parallel with that of the University,"[69] it was technically independent of the university. However, part of the teaching was done by the Cumberland faculty,[70] and in 1891 there was enough dependence on Cumberland that the trustees loaned the women's college ten thousand dollars.[71] In 1894, Cumberland signed a three-year contract with the women's college whereby Cumberland would run the college as an annex of Cumberland.[72] Although the Cumberland University Annex did not mix men and women together in the same classrooms or study halls, it offered "practically identical courses" and used Cumberland faculty, including Martin, who taught Political Economy.[73]

At the end of the three years, Cumberland University, having tiptoed slowly into the pool of coeducation, took a sudden plunge. It declared that by action of the faculty and trustees, "all the college classes will hereafter be open to young women."[74] The Lebanon College for Young Women became completely independent once again, and tottered on until 1909, when its building burned.[75]

These developments brought more women to the Cumberland campus but did not themselves make the law school coeducational. A tradition holds that the first female student, a Mrs. W. P. Bouton, was admitted to the law school in 1902,[76] although neither the catalogues nor the minutes of the trustees mention her matriculation.

It is difficult to be certain about the first female student, because so many students at this time identified themselves in the catalogues only by initials and last names. But 1906 saw the first graduates of Cumberland School of Law with unmistakably female names: Edith Likens, of Clarksdale, Mississippi; Claire B. Newman; and Lena K. Vaughn, of Poplar Bluff, Missouri. Additionally that year, a Miss A(lberta) Sandel is listed as a student, although she did not graduate until 1908.[77] These women were accommodated by a Tennessee statute of February 13, 1907, authorizing the admission of women to the practice of law.[78] Thereafter, in almost every year through 1919, one or two females studied law at Cumberland, most of them graduating with their classes. Although coeducation at Cumberland School of Law had begun, by the end of the period the actual number of women students was still just a small trickle.

The increased numbers of females in the literary department of the university altered the social scene. It became infinitely more varied, and one can only sketch with a light touch the social activities available to the Cumberland law students. In the 1880s there were dances at Baird's Hotel, buggy rides, picnics, whist parties, and Sunday afternoon walks to the sulphur well not far from Divinity Hall. At the end of the 1880s, White's Opera House opened on the second floor of the new West Side Hotel, and it competed with Caruthers Hall as the venue for repertory companies and their performances of melodramas, musicals, and comedies. At the end of the decade there was the bicycle craze, and cockfighting at the fairgrounds, though technically illegal, was always popular. For strictly male pleasures, there were poker games in Thompson's boardinghouse, and for the women, tennis, croquet, and wading in the local creeks were popular.[79]

In the 1890s, students enjoyed "turn outs," such activities as day trips to Andrew Jackson's home, the Hermitage, or to the river for a picnic. The men would borrow or rent a buggy, and the women would fix a picnic basket. There were fraternity dances at the West Side Hotel, with orchestras and caterers from Nashville. Students could take advantage of fourteen trains a day to Nashville, sometimes special trains as well, to take their dates to shows and operas in the metropolis.[80] Sans Souci, an organization of local unmarried young women, first appeared in 1891 and was still thriving in the early 1900s. It sponsored receptions, dinners, and other entertainments, to which the women invited the university men, including law students. They were what were later called "mixers," and the purpose was clearly to show the eligible women off to eligible men in the best style possible. In case the men might otherwise miss the point, the ladies held their most elaborate receptions on St. Valentine's Day.[81]

Lyceum shows arrived in the early 1900s, and a Cumberland law student could take his best girl to Caruthers Hall to see such entertainments as an illustrated lecture on birds, or Miss Katharine Eggleston's monologue, "When Knighthood was in Flower," or perhaps a lecture on "The American Girl."[82] Of course, many of the activities mentioned before continued on throughout this decade and the next. Caruthers Hall was extensively refurbished in 1908, with its entrance halls replastered and painted, its auditorium stage enlarged, and other amenities and improvements added. It continued to be a very popular location for community entertainments as well as university functions.[83]

The Cumberland Quartet formed in 1913, and the decade also saw the annual visits of the Chautauqua.[84] The major social feature of the 1910s was the steady growth in ownership and use of the automobile, such as Nathan Green's acquisition of his "Red Devil." Increasingly, couples had both more mobility and also considerably more privacy. But the great majority of the law students, as well as undergraduates, could not afford an automobile, so this social revolution at this point affected Cumberland students very little.

But other events in the 1910s had considerable impact on dating habits. First, the movies arrived. The Lyric Theatre opened around 1910, off the public square on South Cumberland Street, and proved to be popular with students. Then on September 28, 1912, J. L. Shannon opened his drug store at 148 Public Square, fourth from the corner and right next to the Piggly Wiggly grocery store. With its marble floor, soda fountain, marble-topped, wire-legged tables and green booths in back, Shannon's soon became a hangout for students, mostly law students, and a Cumberland tradition.[85] It was the place to go when the books became too much or the day too hot; it was the place to go with a girlfriend or boyfriend and see and be seen. More practically, it was a reliable and handy place for students to cash checks.

The number and variety of extracurricular activities increased dramatically in the late nineteenth and early twentieth centuries. There were still the Greek letter fraternities. By 1881, only one of the eight Greek fraternities from the prewar period was still active, but in that decade several were restored and still others added.[86] After Caruthers Hall was complete, the three literary societies met in that building. They operated throughout this entire period, except that the Heurethelean was discontinued after the Divinity School closed its doors in 1909, and excepting further a temporary disappearance of Amasagassean in the mid-1890s. Cordell Hull was a member of the Philomathean in 1891, and participated in their lively discussions.[87] New societies emerged for brief periods. There were briefly the Caruthers Society, the Lex Society, the Inter-Collegiate Oratorical Contest Society, and the Calliopean Literary Society. Most were dominated by law students, excepting the Amasagassean.

Although there were also written essays, and the Heurethelean Society even published a monthly literary magazine in the years 1880–1894, the literary societies emphasized the development of oral skills through public debates and speeches. These clubs also prepared students to participate in the lengthy commencement exercises. One of the highlights of these exercises, although probably not ranking as high as Nathan Green's traditional reception for the graduates and their relations, was the Law Class Day. In June 1908, there were enough law graduates selected by their societies to participate that Law Class Day extended over two days. In between musical offerings by the Young Ladies Orchestra, twenty-two law students spoke to the assembled crowd on such topics as "Descent Into Hell Is Easy," "The Morning of Our Profession," "Will Our Dreams Come True?" and "Stickability." The entire graduation exercises that year extended over five days,[88] and attendance was mandatory for the graduates.

A student yearbook, the *Phoenix,* first appeared in 1895 and was published sporadically, on average half the years, until 1923, when it was put on a regular, annual basis. Students published a newspaper, the *Cumberland Weekly,* during the years 1894–1921, excepting during the war years when it was suspended.

The YMCA continued to use "every means to lead the unsaved to Christ." It announced that by the end of the 1903 campaign "only two students in the College were unsaved."[89] The bulletin did not state how many law students remained among the damned. Coeducation brought even more souls to save, and a Young Women's Christian Association (YWCA) was organized in 1904.[90] Additionally, there was a daily university chapel service, encouraged but not compulsory.

There were many other extracurricular activities, state clubs for law students, the glee club, and, of course, athletics. In these years the law students were still essentially undergraduates, in that no previous college was required. The law students participated fully in activities that today we would regard as especially undergraduate in nature. For example, we might take a snapshot view of the law class of 1903. According to the 1903 *Phoenix,* there were thirty-six members of the law class graduating in June. Thirty-four belonged to Philomathean, sixteen joined social fraternities, six played athletics, two sang for the glee club, and five worked on the *Phoenix* yearbook. This is a high level of extracurricular activity and not unrepresentative. The 1902 *Phoenix* lists thirty-three members of the senior class. That class contributed six members of the football team and three of the baseball players.

Organized athletics at Cumberland began in the late 1880s, and by the end of that decade an Athletic Association under faculty direction had oversight of the programs. An athletic field was constructed in the northwestern portion of the campus, and field days were held there once a year in May, beginning in 1894. Memorial Hall, a major undergraduate building completed in 1896, had a back hall originally designed to be a chapel. Unfortunately, the room had poor acoustics. After covering up the elaborate ceiling, the room was adapted to basketball and gymnastics.[91] A tennis club was organized in this period.

Baseball started in 1890 and throughout the decade held the greatest student interest. Although he did not play, it is said that Cordell Hull never missed a single baseball game during his spring at Cumberland. William Bradford, a 1909 law graduate, wrote poems for the student newspaper lamenting Cumberland baseball team's losses.[92] By 1902, Cumberland was playing national opponents, such as Wisconsin, Vanderbilt, Sewanee, and Milwaukee, and was attracting national attention. In that year Cumberland lost only two games, both to the professional Milwaukee Brewers.[93] The 1904 team lost only a single game. In 1908 and 1909 the Cumberland baseball team went undefeated and was declared winner of the southern college championship by the great sports writer, Grantland Rice. In 1910, Cumberland won the southern championship again. In those years several major league teams stopped off at Cumberland to play exhibition games on their return to the north from spring training. The Detroit Tigers, with Ty Cobb, played at Cumberland in 1908; the Chicago White Sox were there in the following year. Marvin O. Bridges, a Cumberland athlete, later became a major league player.[94]

The year of 1894 also saw the beginnings of basketball at Cumberland. It had its ups and downs, even the university conceding that the 1902–3 squad was merely an "ordinary team" that won and lost about the same number of games.[95] But the 1908 team was undefeated and captured the southern championship in a tournament at Asheville, North Carolina.[96] Basketball was the only serious sport offered women. Their initial practice in 1902 began mysteriously in a closed room posted "No Men Allowed." Naturally, that drew the men's attention. Eventually, the female players arrived, modestly "robed in long black cloaks and hoods," and a reporter for the yearbook posted himself near the door's keyhole. By 1905, the women's team had done so well that the *New York Sun, Chicago World,* and *Philadelphia Times* referred to it as one of the best in the South.[97]

As we have seen before, the Cumberland law students fully participated in these sports. Some law students, then and now, seem to be able to do it all. Alexander E. Wieczorowski, a law student from Chicago in 1896–97, played left halfback on the football team in the fall and was elected captain; in spring played baseball as shortstop and was elected captain of the team; and he ran the dash in track. He also found time to be a debater with the Philomathean Society, while being elected the supreme judge of the moot court. Reputedly, he did well in poker too.[98]

The big game at Cumberland, as at so many other southern schools, was football. It was introduced in 1894, and by 1902 Cumberland already had an ambitious schedule, playing such schools as Sewanee, Vanderbilt, and the University of Mississippi. In 1903, Cumberland had an excellent season, playing eight games, tying with Vanderbilt and Clemson, losing to Sewanee, and beating five schools, including the University of Alabama (44–0) and Louisiana State University (41–0).[99] Coach John Heisman, for whom the Heisman Trophy is named, and the coach of Georgia Tech, selected both Marvin O. Bridges and his brother M. L. Bridges of the 1903 football team for all-southern honors, and declared Cumberland the southern champion for the year.[100]

Cumberland dropped football in 1906 but resumed it in 1909 with stricter faculty and financial controls. Throughout the 1910s, Cumberland intermittently dropped and resumed the game.[101] The year 1914 saw only a mixed season, 4–4–1, but sportswriter Grantland Rice selected one of the team's members, John Burns, for all-southern honors.[102]

The most famous Cumberland contribution to the history of athletics was not a triumph but an unmitigated disaster. On October 7, 1916, at Grant Field in Atlanta, the Cumberland Bulldogs lost to Georgia Tech by a score of 222–0, the worst defeat in the history of football. It came during one of the periods in which Cumberland had dismantled its football program. John W. Heisman, coach at Georgia Tech and perhaps smarting under a 22–0 baseball defeat to Cumberland the year before, challenged Cumberland to a football game to be played in Atlanta. He offered a five-hundred-dollar guarantee. George E. Allen, a law student and student athletic manager, accepted, gathered some players, practiced in secret, and took his Cumberland irregulars, most of whom were law students, down to Atlanta for the big game. It was an absolute fiasco. Not only was the score the most lopsided, but several other records were broken, all by Georgia Tech: greatest number of points after touchdown, greatest number of touchdowns from kickoff, and greatest number of yards gained.[103]

Tech gained a total of 978 yards, while Cumberland's net yardage was minus 28. Grantland Rice once wrote that "Cumberland's greatest individual play of the game occurred when fullback Allen circled right end for a 6-yard loss."[104] A teammate and fellow law student recalled that another of Allen's fabulous plays was a punt. "It was a good, hard kick, but the ball hit our own center squarely in the back of the neck and bowled him over." Neither team made a first down: Cumberland because it could not, and Georgia Tech because it need not. It scored touchdowns instead.[105] In addition to a *Reader's Digest* article, the strange events of October 7, 1916, inspired an entire book, *You Dropped It, You Pick It Up!,* with made-up conversations and a large amount of inaccuracy in the interest of a good story, but amusing reading, nonetheless.[106]

In this chapter we have looked primarily at the Cumberland law students, what they were studying, the costs they paid, the pleasures they had. In the next chapter the focus will be more on the law school as an institution. A major impression one takes from the Cumberland of this period is the depth of the affection law students held for their school. It can be summed up in a poem that William R. Bradford wrote upon his graduation from the law school in 1909:

We are taking our departure
With a long sigh of regret
From the friends who hold our heart beats
Bound securely in love's net.
Fare thee well beloved city,
And dear loved ones, all, adieu;
In the twilight of the evening
We shall dream bright dreams of you.
And when life's sunset approaches
And the mists and gloom appears,
May we reach back for your friendship
Through the gloom of vanished years—[107]

Abraham Caruthers, 1861, from *Cumberland Alumnus* (1927). (Courtesy of Vise Library, Cumberland University, Lebanon, Tennessee.)

Nathan Green Sr., 1861, from *Cumberland Alumnus* (1927). (Courtesy of Vise Library, Cumberland University, Lebanon, Tennessee.)

Nathan Green Jr., 1861, from *Cumberland Alumnus* (1927). (Courtesy, Vise Library, Cumberland University, Lebanon, Tennessee.)

Robert L. Caruthers. (Courtesy of Vise Library, Cumberland University, Lebanon, Tennessee.)

Drawing of Cumberland University building, c. 1858, showing addition of new wings, from *Green Bag* (1890). (Courtesy of Beeson Law Library, Cumberland School of Law of Samford University, Birmingham, Alabama.)

Corona Hall, home of the law school from 1873 to 1878. (Courtesy of Vise Library, Cumberland University, Lebanon, Tennessee.)

Caruthers Hall, from *Phoenix* (1903). (Courtesy of Vise Library, Cumberland University, Lebanon, Tennessee.)

One vision of Blackacre, from *Phoenix* (1897). (Courtesy of Vise Library, Cumberland University, Lebanon, Tennessee.)

Auditorium of Caruthers Hall, from *Phoenix* (1895). (Courtesy of Vise Library, Cumberland University, Lebanon, Tennessee.)

Memorial Hall, from *Phoenix* (1903). (Courtesy of Vise Library, Cumberland University, Lebanon, Tennessee.)

Informal photograph of Andrew B. Martin, c. 1910. (Courtesy of Beeson Law Library, Cumberland School of Law of Samford University, Birmingham, Alabama.)

Andrew B. Martin, from *Phoenix* (1903). (Courtesy of Vise Library, Cumberland University, Lebanon, Tennessee.)

Nathan Green Jr., c. 1905. (Courtesy of Vise Library, Cumberland University, Lebanon, Tennessee.)

Informal photograph of Nathan Green Jr., c. 1905. (Courtesy of Beeson Law Library, Cumberland School of Law of Samford University, Birmingham, Alabama.)

Law Library, from *Phoenix* (1895). (Courtesy of Vise Library, Cumberland University, Lebanon, Tennessee.)

Law Library, showing repainting and electrification, 1928. (Courtesy of Vise Library, Cumberland University, Lebanon, Tennessee.)

On a snowy, winter afternoon, probably in 1940, Judge A. B. Neil, Dean and Professor of Law, arrives in Lebanon to teach his classes, having spent the morning attending to his judicial responsibilities in Nashville. (Courtesy of John A. Jamison.)

Law Library, showing further renovation, staircase in corner, and female student, 1940. (Courtesy of Vise Library, Cumberland University, Lebanon, Tennessee.)

An interior view of Caruthers Hall in about 1940, featuring the main staircase leading from the entrance foyer to the auditorium on the second floor. (Courtesy of John A. Jamison.)

Rascal, the unofficial mascot of the law school during most of the 1930s, with mortarboard and diploma, at the time of his receipt in 1935 of an honorary degree in canine jurisprudence. (Courtesy of Samford University Library Special Collections.)

The normally quiet Lebanon public square, two blocks from Caruthers Hall, draws crowds from throughout Wilson County on a Farmers' Market Saturday in about 1940. (Courtesy of John A. Jamison.)

Cumberland students stage a mock "jail break" at the Wilson County jail as part of the enactment of a crime; the accused would ultimately be "tried" in mock proceedings in Caruthers Hall. (Courtesy of John A. Jamison.)

Professor Samuel B. Gilreath presiding over Practice Court in October 1960, a role he assumed in 1932 and continued to play even after the move to Birmingham. (Courtesy of Vise Library, Cumberland University, Lebanon, Tennessee.)

Its spirit already departed to Birmingham, historic Caruthers Hall was sold and in early 1962 demolished by its new owners to make way for a savings and loan office. (Courtesy of Samford University Library Special Collections.)

Members of the Cumberland law faculty in 1952, the year the law school won full American Bar Association approval as well as membership in the American Association of Law Schools: librarian Sara Hardison, Samuel A. Gilreath, who served as president of the university after the Baptist withdrawal in 1951, Otis J. Bouswma, Dean Arthur A. Weeks, Richard J. Demeree, and Bernard B. Bailey. (Courtesy of Vise Library, Cumberland University, Lebanon, Tennessee.)

The entire law faculty in September 1961, the first year in Birmingham: Dean Arthur A. Weeks, librarian Patricia A. Coffman, Bobby Aderholt, Wooten Pearce, Samuel B. Gilreath, and Bernard B. Bailey. (Courtesy of Samford University Library Special Collections.)

Workmen finishing the interior of the Moot Court Room, part of the newly constructed Memory Leake Robinson Hall, in late 1963. (Courtesy of Samford University Library Special Collections.)

On a snow-covered campus during the 1963–64 Christmas break, conveyor belts move the law library from temporary quarters in the main college library building to the newly constructed Memory Leake Robinson Hall, which would be the home of the law library for more than thirty years until the construction of the Lucille Stewart Beeson Law Library in 1995. (Courtesy of Samford University Library Special Collections.)

Construction nears completion on the 1977 addition to Memory Leake Robinson Hall. (Courtesy of Samford University Library Special Collections.)

The members of the Law Wives Club, composed of wives of students and faculty members, in 1969. In 1985, the Law Wives admitted its first Law Husband and eventually changed its name to the Legal Auxilary. (Courtesy of Samford University Library Special Collections.)

Having been one of the last American law schools to adopt the case method of instruction, by the 1960s Cumberland had become an ardent adherent of that method of legal instruction; here, in a classroom in Memory Leake Robinson Hall, Professor Walter D. Sowa calls on a student to stand and brief a case. (Courtesy of Samford University Library Special Collections.)

In October 1961, following the law school's move to Birmingham, Professor Samuel B. Gilreath conducts Practice Court in the courtroom of the law school's unfinished, temporary quarters—marked by unfinished cinder block walls and exposed heating ducts—on an upper floor of Howard College's main library. (Courtesy of Samford University Library Special Collections.)

In the Trial Court Room added as part of the 1977 expansion of the law building, a video camera captures a student's efforts to improve his jury argument. (Courtesy of Samford University Library Special Collections.)

Cumberland School of Law in 1996, on the eve of its sesquicentennial, with Memory Leake Robinson Hall in the foreground and, visible to the right rear, the new Lucille Stewart Beeson Law Library. (Courtesy of Samford University Information Services.)

The main reading room of Cumberland's Lucille Stewart Beeson Law Library, opened in 1995 and dedicated in 1996 by President Gerald R. Ford. (Courtesy of Samford University Information Services.)

CHAPTER FIVE

Prosperity and Stagnation 1878–1919

What the average student craves is the prestige of a degree . . . and he will resort to any short cut by which he may honorably secure it. It is the degree, and not what it stands for, that interests him most.
—W. M. Lile, law professor, University of Virginia (1914)

Cumberland, which had once marked the high point of professional education, had become a captive of its own success. Unwilling to adopt modern techniques such as the case method, or to expand and deepen its curriculum by opting for the three-year standard, Cumberland became the symbol of the democratic bar.
—Lewis L. Laska, historian (1978)

THROUGHOUT THE YEARS 1878 to 1919, Cumberland was continually challenged by new ideas and techniques of legal education. The Cumberland response, however, was almost nil. The entire structure of legal education was transformed during these years. To put it in the terms of Thomas Kuhn's *Structure of Scientific Revolutions,*[1] there was a shift in the paradigm of legal education. Yet Cumberland made no response. It would be left for a later period to create the regulatory structure that would force these changes upon Cumberland, but it was in these years that the concepts of the "correct" manner, the "appropriate" way of educating future lawyers shifted dramatically. We must examine these changes, and why Cumberland made no response, but first we should look at a few modest changes in the structure of the university in relation to the law school.

After the construction of Caruthers Hall, the board of trustees gave Nathan Green, in his capacity as chancellor, the authority to rent out the hall.[2] It soon became a popular venue for community events. The issue arose from time to time whether the law school or university ought to be charged with needed repairs and renovations. At times the law school paid for repairs, and at other times the university did, depending on what portions of the building were repaired. After the university received eight thousand dollars from the federal government in 1915 to settle its claim for the federal occupation of the buildings during the Civil War, repairs and refurbishments were made from university funds.[3]

After the death of Robert L. Caruthers in 1882, Andrew B. Martin was appointed to fill the vacancy as president of the board of trustees. He served in that capacity until his death in 1920. Thus, from the founding of Cumberland in 1842 until 1920, there were only two presidents of the board of trustees, Caruthers and Martin. During that same time there were numerous presidents of the university. Green took the title of chancellor when he assumed the office in 1873. He served without pay until 1891, when he was granted an annual salary of three hundred dollars plus all the graduation fees.[4] Green resigned as chancellor in 1900 but was prevailed upon to serve as president pro tem for 1907, 1908, and a few months of 1909.[5]

Green may not have been paid handsomely as chancellor, but he and his associate, Andrew B. Martin, were still making considerable amounts as the sharers of almost all of the law school's tuition. However, throughout this period as well as earlier times, the university itself was impoverished. But Green, individually, prospered. In 1850, Green's net worth was only about $320. By the time of the war, he was worth $20,000, but he lost almost all of his wealth because most was in slave property. However, in 1888, a shrewd observer noted that Green's "life work has been teaching law, but, unlike most bookish men, he has managed to accumulate a very pretty property, keeping him in very independent circumstances."[6] The reason, of course, was the traditional Cumberland method of compensating law faculty by the tuition paid.

Even though the university, aside from the law faculty, was impoverished, the board of trustees was still acting irresponsibly, in ways that today would be considered in breach of fiduciary obligations. One specific example illustrates several instances of insider self-dealing. We will recall the trustees' earlier purchase in 1866 of the late Abraham Caruthers's house and fifty acres of land for $10,000. Originally, the trustees proposed the house be used for the law school, but it ultimately became Divinity Hall. In 1882, the trustees sold thirty-six or forty acres of this large parcel, excluding the house itself and approximately ten acres surrounding it, for the sum of $600. Perhaps, almost all of the earlier $10,000 value was in the building. Perhaps. But it is interesting to note that the sale was to a member of the board of trustees, John D. Kirkpatrick. By modern standards there is at least the appearance of impropriety. But worse, within a year after the transaction, the board lent Kirkpatrick $2,200 on the security of the property it had sold to this fiduciary for $600.[7]

The major institutional upheaval of these years was the failed church merger. This is a complicated story. Essentially, in 1906 the Cumberland Presbyterian Church by a close vote elected to merge with the larger Presbyterian Church in the United States of America. A substantial number of Cumberland Presbyterians opposed the merger, and these "loyalists" brought suit claiming the merger was invalid. There was litigation in many states concerning the merger, and in 1909 the Tennessee Supreme Court held the merger invalid. Then the loyalists threatened suit to reclaim the university property. One issue in contention was the historical question of whether in 1842 the university had been moved to Lebanon or whether the Lebanon campus was a "new" university.

There was much ink spilled on that issue, because the old "old Cumberland" in Princeton was clearly owned by the Cumberland Presbyterians, and if it had been merely moved then it was still owned by the Cumberland Presbyterians. After years of turmoil, which only indirectly affected the law school, Cumberland University offered the Cumberland Presbyterian Church $37,500 to buy its independence. This was accepted and the storm passed, but not without damage done, as the Cumberland theological school closed in 1909, a casualty of the turmoil related to the union dispute.[8]

Caruthers Hall originally had housed the libraries of all three departments, Collegiate, Theological, and Law. After the completion of Memorial Hall, the nonlaw materials were moved to libraries there, and the

1902–3 catalogue announced that "the many volumes in law, history, politics, etc., have for the most part been retained to form the nucleus of a new Law library, which has recently been opened. The room [in Caruthers Hall] formerly occupied by the University library has been renovated and arranged to suit the purposes of the Law Department. This recently established library has some three thousand or more volumes, and this number shall be increased from year to year."

The new law library was open six days a week, Sundays excepted, and was located in a "handsomely furnished room, well lighted and heated." In addition to the law books, the library carried "a large amount of the best magazine literature . . . affording the student ample opportunity for recreation and improvement."[9] The law school charged students a modest fee, usually one dollar, for the benefit of law library, and it was spent on books. In late 1902 the trustees appointed a committee consisting of the three law professors, Beard, Green, and Martin, and authorized them to spend as much as five hundred dollars in law library acquisitions.[10]

But donations were needed as well. Students from Texas, Arkansas, and Alabama who graduated in 1903 donated codes and compiled statutes of their respective states.[11] The March 1904 Bulletin called the attention of graduates to the fact that "a law library never stops growing, that to keep abreast of the times, it must continually grow," a proposition with which modern law librarians would have little quarrel. Accordingly, the bulletin announced, "the Law School will be grateful for donations, great or small, in money or new books, from any of its many friends. During the current year about one thousand dollars' worth of new law books have been added."

These statements about the need to grow and the acquisition of one thousand dollars' worth of new books during the past year were repeated in the bulletin for the next dozen years. That must have been vain repetition, for the library certainly did not grow by one thousand dollars' worth of books per annum over the next dozen years. But it did grow. Copies of order forms of books for the law library have been pasted in the end of the school's grading book for 1910–1925. On April 23, 1915, Andrew B. Martin ordered the 27-volume set of *Ruling Case Law* published by the Lawyers Co-op Publishing Company, at $3 per volume, half the normal retail price. On June 29, 1915, he purchased the 60-volume *Corpus Juris* set for $5 per volume, knocked down from a list of $7.50 per volume, and with a credit of $100 to be given Cumberland by the American Law Book Company for the return of the older and superseded set of books.[12] Martin specifically deleted the printed provision to ship future annotations of the *Corpus Juris* set.

Only an embryonic alumni association existed until 1920 and the initial publication of the *Cumberland Alumnus.* Until then, alumni affairs were limited to reunions and banquets during commencement week. Although Nathan Green was spoken of as president of the alumni association during the early 1900s,[13] no such organization appears to have been active. In 1891, the university authorities requested that alumni organize local associations in all towns where there were at least six graduates and that the clubs correspond with Chancellor Green.[14] If this impulse had been carried into action, the school would have been greatly strengthened. But alumni organization was to await a later period.

Since the antebellum times, Cumberland had enjoyed a diploma privilege. This meant that the graduates of the Cumberland law department were eligible for automatic admission to the Tennessee Bar, without the need for examination by a judge. How that operated is illustrated by the recollections of Cordell Hull. After passing their final examinations, "according to custom, we members of the graduating class, the moment we received our diplomas, took them to the courthouse, where a district judge awaited us. He swore us in as members of the bar. I was not twenty years old."[15]

During the late nineteenth century, reformers in the Tennessee Bar Association made independent bar examinations an early objective. The Committee on Legal Education and Admission to the Bar, formed in 1883, tried for years to persuade the legislature to require examinations by a Board of Law Examiners rather than the haphazard system of allowing individual judges or law professors the power to grant licenses. Cumberland consistently opposed the proposal, and Nathan Green testified against bar examinations before the Judiciary Committee of the Tennessee General Assembly in 1901.[16]

The reformers ultimately prevailed in March 1903, when the legislature created the Board of Bar Examiners and required that all applicants to the bar had to pass its examination. A diploma mill in Nashville, an outright fraud abusing the diploma privilege, provided the final incentive.[17] The bill provided two things for Cumberland, however. Lebanon was specifically designated as one site of the examination, and the bill curiously provided that "where any graduate of a law school of this State has been licensed . . . his license to practice law may on request of the faculty of said law school be sent by the Supreme Court to said faculty for delivery [i.e., to their graduates]."[18]

Cumberland put the best interpretation on the statute, announcing it immediately in its catalogue, pointing out the requirement "that the examiners shall visit Lebanon and examine applications from this school on the ground," and urging prospects that Cumberland prepared young men "in the shortest time possible, and at the least expense for that examination."[19] Martin turned the new bar examination to advantage by urging the merits of his summer course for bar preparation: "If you wish to review your reading before submitting to an examination for license, you should take this course. It will prepare you for that ordeal."[20]

Curiously enough, the bar examination probably gave Cumberland School of Law its first dean. Before the turn of the twentieth century, the school had known only the senior professor and junior professor, and all of these individuals preferred informal titles of Judge or Doctor. There were no deans, and the title was unknown. The first reference to any sort of dean at Cumberland University came in 1893 when an office of the dean was created for the theological school.[21] Although the trustees had defined the duties of a dean in a general sense as early as 1901,[22] the law school did not use the term until August 1903, when a bulletin described Nathan Green as "Dean of Law School and Professor of Law."[23] The rules governing the bar examination, pursuant to the statute of March 1903, undoubtedly required certification to the Board of Bar Examiners by the "dean" of a law school that a particular individual had graduated and was ready to take the test. If the new rules required a *dean's* certification, then Cumberland had to have a dean. In this rather casual manner, Nathan Green, as the senior professor, became Cumberland School of Law's first dean.

Two major developments occurred in legal education in the late nineteenth and early twentieth centuries. One was the lengthening of the time required for legal education, from one year ultimately to three. The other major development was the spectacular success and spread of the case method of instruction. Cumberland School of Law resisted both these trends. Because of the lack of response to these new models of legal education, Cumberland, while once in the forefront of legal education, became a maverick by 1919. Decades would pass before Cumberland returned once again to the mainstream.

As the nineteenth century waned, law school curricula expanded in response to the increasing complexity of the law and the nature of the representation and legal matters that lawyers were called upon to handle. An increase in the length of time required to obtain a degree reflects this best. As early as 1892, in a report prepared by its Committee on Legal Education and Admission to the Bar, the Tennessee Bar Association recognized the increased need for training and recommended that the law school curriculum should require three years of reasonably hard work. However, because the financial condition of the South could not afford it, the committee was willing to settle for two years.[24] This recommendation did not have the force of law, and Cumberland continued with its one-year curriculum.

The sentiment among legal educators was running toward a longer curriculum. In 1908, a legal educator wrote that "it appears to be taken for granted among the legal educators of the country that the two-year course in law is hopelessly out of date and should be abandoned in every college where it is possible to substitute a longer course in its stead." He noted that southern schools were holding out against the change and in favor of the two-year plan but concluded that "those in authority there are anxious to hasten the day when the three-year course will prevail in Southern colleges also."[25] The cutting edge of progress was the change from a two-year curriculum to a three-year plan, but Cumberland had only a one-year program.

Cumberland tenaciously retained its one-year program while other law schools were lengthening theirs. Even most southern schools required two years. In 1870, when there were thirty-one law schools in the United States, twelve offered a one-year program, while two demanded one and a half years, and seventeen required two years. No law school required three years. By 1880, of fifty-one total law schools, thirteen had three-year programs and twenty-nine, two years. By 1890, there were sixty-one law schools; only nine held onto a one-year or eighteen-month program, thirty-seven had a two-year plan, and fifteen required more time than two years. By

1899, the nation was down to four law schools, all in the South, with a one-year curriculum and thirty-seven with a two-year plan. A law professor at the University of Virginia noted in 1914 that of eighty-eight law schools not in the South, only five had a curriculum of fewer than three years.[26] The number of schools that awarded the law degree in less than three years decreased from fifty-four in 1890 to twenty-three in 1917. By 1920–21 only one school still had a one-year program. That, of course, was Cumberland.[27]

These developments in legal education eventually became common knowledge. There needed to be some response by Cumberland to prospective students and their parents to explain Cumberland's recalcitrance. Cumberland defended its archaic program by bravely insisting that its plan was superior because it was just as comprehensive and was less expensive. The 1898–99 catalogue proclaimed that Cumberland's curriculum "covers above *ten thousand* pages of living law, and is as comprehensive as the courses requiring two years study in other law schools." Parents of prospective students must have asked, or Green and Martin must have thought they were wondering, about these two-year, and even three-year, programs. This 1899 statement was Cumberland's first response to encroaching modernity.

The May 1905 bulletin claimed that "the course which is equal to the two years' course of other law schools is accomplished here in one year. . . . The same course spread over two years costs twice as much as when it is accomplished in one year." This line of response was repeated in every bulletin, usually on the back covers of the catalogue under the banner of "Facts Worth Remembering," and with TWO YEARS and ONE YEAR in capital letters. And it continued in this manner until 1915, when Cumberland acknowledged the three-year program by changing two of its "Facts Worth Remembering" on the catalogues' back covers to "The course, which is equal to the TWO AND THREE YEAR course in other Law Schools, is accomplished in ONE YEAR" and "The same course spread over TWO OR THREE YEARS costs twice or thrice as much as when it is accomplished here in ONE YEAR."[28] It is simply untrue, of course, that the Cumberland curriculum covered the same material that other law schools did in two or three years.

The neutral observer must consider Cumberland's response to this massive shift in the model or paradigm in legal education to be minimal. Even more telling was Cumberland's lack of response to the spread of the case method of legal education. When Christopher Columbus Langdell initiated the case method of study at Harvard in 1871, his underlying view of the law was actually similar to that of the treatise writers whose efforts his case method replaced. Langdell also thought of the law as essentially fixed. The relatively few underlying principles of law, he thought, should be taught only by those few "correct" cases that had applied these principles properly. However, his associate, James Barr Ames, was more skillful at actually using the Socratic techniques involved with the case method, and applied these skills not only to the "proper" cases but to all cases, even those in which the judges had applied "incorrect" legal principles. Thus, as it developed, the case method became a useful device for learning how to parse cases, take them apart and see what makes them tick, skills that a practicing lawyer needs to distinguish and analogize cases in legal memoranda submitted to judges. The modified case method did teach the actual, living law, and it became far more than a vehicle simply to put across a "correct" and narrow number of legal principles.

This modified case method swept the law school world. At first it was combined with treatise teaching. The Tennessee Committee on Legal Education and Admission to the Bar, in its 1892 report, approved of the study of cases and casebooks but thought this method of study should be preceded by books that covered the entire field of the law, in other words, treatises.[29] Some schools used both casebooks and textbooks, as the University of Virginia was doing in 1914.[30] In a sense, this is still the modern system. Faculty may teach from casebooks, but most students supplement their casebooks by reading hornbooks or other modern treatises to survey the general principles of legal fields. But among the faculty, the case method as a teaching technique quickly began to dominate American legal education.

A sampling of schools and the dates of the introduction of the case method tells the story: Notre Dame (1889), Columbia (1891), Western Reserve (1892), Northwestern (1893), Cincinnati (1895), Cornell (1896), Wisconsin and Hastings (1890s), Chicago and Stanford (1900), Valparaiso (1907), and Oklahoma (1909). Nor was this trend confined to the northern schools. The case method was introduced and in use, and in some cases completely triumphant, in the following southern schools: Richmond (1905; a night school that claimed to be the first in the South to use the case method), Tulane (adopted in 1906), Vanderbilt and North Carolina (1910), Virginia (introduced by 1914, as seen earlier, but not triumphant until many years later), Tennessee (1915), and Washington and Lee (1916).[31]

This transformation did not happen immediately but was a process, as the concept of the case method gradually gained adherents. In 1902 a professor at Cornell conducted a survey of the spread of the case method. He surveyed ninety-four schools: thirty-four had not introduced the case method, forty-eight mixed the case method with the older textbook and lecture, and in twelve schools the case method had swept the field.[32] As of 1902, the southern schools would all have been among the thirty-four not yet even flirting with the case method. That changed rapidly, with the spread of the case method in the South following Richmond's lead in 1905.

Clearly, the case method was in the process of triumph in the years 1900 to 1910. It was becoming nearly universally regarded as the "better" method. One unbiased recognition that the case method had triumphed came in 1910 when West Publishing Company, the major commercial legal publisher, sponsored an entire series of casebooks. Prudently, it also published a second series of texts with accompanying casebooks.[33]

As we saw in earlier chapters, the basic method of instruction in antebellum law schools, North and South, was lecturing. Indeed, that Cumberland did not use lectures but asked students questions, based on texts, and employed exposition only to clear up misunderstood portions was Cumberland's pedagogical claim to fame. The dominance of the lecture in most law schools continued until the introduction and triumph of the case method, which was taught Socratically, through faculty questioning of students concerning cases. As the case method caught on, the outdated system being supplanted and overcome was clearly the "lecture method."

Cumberland, in its catalogues and announcements, had always attacked both law office study and law school lecturing as methods of obtaining a legal education. It continued to do so well into the twentieth century. But increasingly, throughout the late nineteenth and early twentieth centuries,

Cumberland also undertook to insist vigorously and repeatedly in its catalogues and advertising, "Remember this is not a *lecture school.*"[34] In its own way, this was Cumberland's response to the case method. Since the success of the case method attacked the lecture system, and the informed public knew that, it was best for Cumberland to advise the public that its own system was not that which was being supplanted by the case method. But this was to be Cumberland's only response in these years.

The advent of the case method was not without its critics. Theodore Dwight of Columbia vigorously opposed it, and his views kept Columbia from adopting the case method until as late as 1891. Although introduced in Yale as early as 1903, it did not win final victory until 1916. Virginia continued to be a holdout against its complete adoption for years. And there were those with out-of-fashion views who opposed the case method of legal instruction as late as the 1930s. John A. Pitts, a Cumberland graduate of 1871, wrote in 1930 that:

> Nothing, I think, is so much debasing, deteriorating and undermining our American system of laws as the teaching of law students from "reports of decided cases" rather than from textbooks which treat of the general and fundamental principles and analogies of the science of law. But I am perfectly aware that my feeble voice of protest will not stem this vicious tide that is gradually drifting us out into a sea of chaos. . . . The authority of precedent: Yes, of course, especially where precedent has established a "rule of property," or a fixed "rule of conduct"; but in all other cases, precedent should yield to the regal and imperative demands of reason and justice as exemplified in the fundamental principles and analogies of the law, the labored and matured product of the wisdom of ages.[35]

Whether the case method was good or bad is beside the point. By 1900, it was rapidly becoming nearly universally acclaimed as the best method of instruction. By 1910, or certainly by 1915, all of the first-class law schools had adopted the case method in whole or in part. Cumberland had done nothing and increasingly it stood alone, a maverick. Legal education has its fads and trendy ideas, as much as any other industry. A law school cannot well preserve its integrity by bobbing and weaving with each new idea in legal education that comes along. Yet where there are such massive shifts in the way business is conducted, where the very paradigm of the endeavor shifts, as it did with respect to the case method, and also the expanded curriculum requiring two and then three years, institutional survival itself may demand a school pay some heed to the dramatic events taking place about it.

Yet throughout these years, 1878–1919, Cumberland seemed to pay no heed whatsoever to these dramatic changes in the way American law schools went about their business of educating lawyers. That failure first made it a maverick, and then, in a latter period when legal education became regulated by law itself, made it a pariah to be attacked, as we shall see. One historical question that demands explanation is why this happened. Why did Green and Martin, not unintelligent men, not take steps to alter Cumberland's course? Why did they not expand Cumberland's curriculum to introduce more varied legal subjects as all the other American law schools were doing? Why did they not experiment with the case method and see for themselves whether it was effective? Why did Cumberland stand fixed in its antebellum mold for the rest of the nineteenth century and several decades into the twentieth?

One obvious answer is the too-entrenched nature of the Cumberland administration. The *junior* professor, Andrew B. Martin, born in 1836, was a graduate of the law school in 1858, became a professor in 1878 (full-time in 1880) joined the board of trustees in 1866, and became president of the board of trustees in 1882. When he died in 1920, he had been a trustee for fifty-four years and a full-time faculty member for forty years. A man with such a solid, long-term connection with an institution's administration is not likely to be receptive to new ideas and innovations, no matter how quickly they are taking over his field of endeavor.

But Nathan Green surpassed even Martin's longevity. Born in 1827, Green entered Cumberland University as an undergraduate in 1842 and graduated in 1845. He served as a tutor for two years. He was on hand for the initial law class in 1847 and graduated with the first full class. He served as a trustee between 1850 and 1856, although not nearly for as many years as did Martin. Green's father was the second law professor, and young Green himself joined the faculty in 1856. He served as the junior professor until 1880, and for many of those years he probably was in actual charge of the law school because of Robert L. Caruthers's poor health. Then, from

TABLE 1. Numbers of Law Students, Graduates, and Those from Outside the South, 1878–1922

Year	*Number of Law Students*	*Number of Graduates*	*Students from Outside the South*
1878–79	43	33	not available
1879–80	38	27	0
1880–81	49	32	0
1881–82	59	40	1
1882–83	58	42	3
1883–84	48	34	2
1884–85	31	19	1
1885–86	46	27	2
1886–87	55	38	8
1887–88	missing	missing	missing
1888–89	57	38	1
1889–90	66	49	5
1890–91	58	43	8
1891–92	71	52	3
1892–93	81	58	1
1893–94	74	50	2
1894–95	76	50	not available
1895–96	98	70	6
1896–97	78	53	1
1897–98	75	53	8
1898–99	62	41	2
1899–1900	69	51	3
1900–1901	68	48	5
1901–02	70	45	6
1902–03	66	48	5
1903–04	74	49	2
1904–05	85	not available	not available
1905–06	missing	missing	missing
1906–07	80	57	3
1907–08	121	87	18
1908–09	153	100	not available
1909–10	148	100	16
1910–11	161	not available	30
1911–12	195	133	28
1912–13	205	141	29

TABLE 1. (*continued*)

Year	*Number of Law Students*	*Number of Graduates*	*Students from Outside the South*
1913–14	216	130	41
1914–15	182	128	31
1915–16	176	128	11
1916–17	missing	130	missing
1917–18	76	53	17
1918–19	58	19	9
1919–20	188	not available	26
1920–21	233	not available	not available
1921–22	225	not available	not available

1880 until his death in 1919, Nathan Green was the senior law professor and in charge.[36] As if this were not fully enough, Green was also the chief administrative officer, as chancellor, of the entire university from 1873 until 1900, and the acting president in 1907 to 1909. Would it be realistic to expect such a man in, say 1900, then seventy-three years old and with this degree of entrenchment into the institution of Cumberland, to have paid much attention to trends in legal education? The Cumberland example, under the administration of Nathan Green Jr., is an eloquent argument against excessive tenure in administrative positions.

But it is not enough to attribute Cumberland's lack of response to the challenge of modernity merely to the advanced age of entrenched faculty and administrators. Judged from a commercial viewpoint, during the years 1878 to 1919, and somewhat beyond, Cumberland was a phenomenal success. The faculty, compensated by tuition, had every incentive to resist change. The one-year program proved immensely popular with applicants, as can be seen by huge increases in the numbers of students and a change in the patterns of enrollment. The figures in table 1 are taken from the Cumberland University Catalogues and Bulletins, with minor exceptions, and include both the January graduation and the June graduation.[37] They must be used with caution. The catalogues did not report the information consistently over the years. Only degree-seeking students—"regular students," as they were called—are included. Summer and other irregular students have been excluded. The "South," for the purposes of the computation of students from "outside the South," includes the states of the former Confederate States of America plus Kentucky and Missouri. The reliability is only fair for the numbers in any particular year, and these figures should be viewed primarily as illustrative of tendencies over many years.

Several things stand out from these figures. First is the huge surge in enrollment, starting around 1907 and continuing through the early 1920s, excepting only 1917–1919, the years during and immediately after U.S. participation in World War I. The enrollments surpassed even those of the antebellum years. Second is the striking increase in the number of nonsouthern students attending Cumberland School of Law, also beginning around 1907. The vast majority of the students from outside the South were from other states. However, the law school also drew students from such faraway places as Syria, India, China, and Japan. A third point of interest is that by no means did all the law students graduate. In 1882, Cumberland estimated that approximately two thousand or more men had attended the school, and more than one thousand had graduated.[38] It appears that this proportion, 50 percent of students actually graduating, increased over the years, but the dropout rate was always high.

What cannot be seen from these law school statistics is how large they loom in relation to the rest of the university. The law school had not only larger enrollments than the other departments but a much higher proportion that remained throughout the entire course. This pattern was true throughout the later nineteenth and early twentieth centuries.

The undergraduate school had relatively large freshman enrollments but then suffered an enormous dropout after the first and second years, much larger than the law school's attrition. Only a handful of the freshmen made their way to graduation. For example, figures from the catalogues show in 1890–91 there were forty-three law graduates. That year there were only fifteen graduates in the arts and sciences and twenty-one in divinity. In 1902, there were seven arts and sciences degrees and eleven divinity degrees, compared with forty-five law degrees. In 1909, with one hundred law graduates, the arts and sciences, including a new music course, had eleven and divinity had five. Another way of looking at the undergraduate attrition problem is the profile of students by class. For example, in 1914–15, the undergraduate division had forty-nine freshmen but only ten seniors.

We need not search far for an explanation of the large increase in the law school enrollments. Cumberland offered low cost and speed, and this attracted students. We have some solid evidence of that attraction. When a future Florida governor, LeRoy Collins, decided to attend a law school, he had to save up money first, and then in 1930 he traveled from Florida to attend Cumberland. As Collins's biographer wrote, Cumberland lacked the glamour and reputation of an Ivy League school, and even the prestige of the University of Florida. Yet "its faculty was sound, and it offered the crucial advantage of saving time and money for a young man who lacked much of either."[39]

For the same reasons, Carl Hatch, later to become Senator Hatch, author of the federal Hatch Act, came to Cumberland from Oklahoma, to which he returned immediately upon obtaining his degree, in 1912. He also needed to earn money for his education, and Cumberland offered a speedy and inexpensive alternative.[40] One Illinois resident chose to attend Cumberland School of Law in 1921. His son explained why: "Dad chose Cumberland for his legal education. Here he could study law, receive the LL.B. degree, take the Tennessee bar exam, and receive his license to practice law, all within the course of a single year. For whatever the academically inclined might think of this compressed program . . . it had a certain practical appeal to a twenty-six year old man who wanted to get on with his life."[41]

In 1907, when enrollments began to soar, Cumberland was either the only place or fast becoming the only place in the country where an eager and energetic young man could obtain a law degree in only one year. What was academically a weakness became an economic advantage as students flocked in from within and without the South. Smart and aggressive young men seized the fast track. Indeed, until 1893, when the junior class was required to be completed in residence at Cumberland, a student could study at home or while working in an attorney's office and skip the first half of the single year by taking an examination. Therefore, until 1893, Cumberland was undoubtedly the only place in the country where one could obtain a law degree in *half* of a year's academic study.

Cordell Hull did just that in 1891, when he entered the senior class at Cumberland after taking what he described as a "very stiff entrance examination." Hull, the most famous of Cumberland's twentieth-century graduates, actually spent only five months of the senior term in Lebanon.[42] However, Hull was proud of his degree from Cumberland. He talked before alumni groups and lent his name for fund-raising purposes. In 1934, while speaking to an alumni group in Washington, D.C., Hull went so far as to claim of Cumberland that "if this historical institution had been located in any other section of the country instead of having been an unpretentious school and in [an] unpretentious locality, its wonderful work would be as widely known and recognized as that of any educational institution of like age in any part of America."[43]

Yet, when Hull wrote his memoirs in 1948, he referred to Cumberland School of Law much more realistically and wrote that it was "a famous institution which had turned out many Senators and Congressmen—in fact, one of the greatest second-category schools in the country."[44]

For whatever reason, be it the excellence of the faculty's teaching or the quality of the students attracted by the fast-track option to a degree, it is certainly true that Cumberland produced an outstanding group of graduates. When Cordell Hull arrived in Washington in 1907 to begin his congressional service, he found as fellow alumni in Congress four United States senators and fifteen congressmen.[45] Cumberland University gathered biographical data on its alumni in 1904. At that time, the university had graduated forty-five congressmen, twenty-six state supreme court justices, and eight governors.[46] By 1928, Cumberland School of Law had educated two justices of the United States Supreme Court, three federal circuit judges, seven federal district judges, seven United States senators, fifty-five congressmen, eight state governors, and thirty-six justices of state supreme courts. To these should be added several law professors, at Alabama, Indiana, and Vanderbilt, among others, and a dean of the Columbia University Law School.[47] It is an amazing record.

It is understandable but tragic that Green and Martin had no interest in changing a system that seemed to be working so well. As Green grew older he became a kind of legend in his own time. In 1913, a multivolume history of Tennessee stated that Green was "the oldest teacher in the State of Tennessee and has the distinction and honor of having taught more law students than any other living man."[48] He was mentally active until the end, and just a few days before his death the *Nashville Banner* published a communication from him concerning the legal aspects of a bill then pending before the legislature.[49] Nevertheless, in the spring of 1919 Green was growing old, in his ninety-second year, and becoming tired.

He told his colleague Martin that he felt sure his work was almost finished, but he thought he would be able to last long enough to finish the fourth volume of Kent's *Commentaries,* covering estates in land, future interests, and concurrent estates, and therefore one of the most difficult books in the curriculum. "I know," he told Martin, "that when I am gone the whole burden of the school will, for a time, fall upon your shoulders, and I want to get that book out of your way." He finished his class's readings in that book, gave his examinations and graded them, then went home and died that same night, February 18, 1919.[50] The ninety-two red roses that students had purchased to present Green the following day on the occasion of his ninety-second birthday instead adorned his coffin.[51]

Green received numerous tributes. His colleague Andrew Martin wrote that Green

> in physique, was a rugged man. He had none of the lines of physical beauty. His voice was a deep bass, and his gait ungainly and lumbering. . . . These outward signs did not suggest the delicacy of feeling, gentleness of speech and esthetic taste, which were among his most marked characteristics. The proprieties of social life were as strictly observed by him as by the most cultured of women. He was a peacemaker, a comforter to the sorrowing, and a lover of music and flowers. He was a man of wide learning, a profound lawyer.[52]

The *Nashville Banner* wrote that Green was a "rare old man of great personal charm, strongly endeared not only to his immediate friends and neighbors, but to many throughout the country who felt the obligation of his valuable and painstaking tutelage in their early lives."[53] This was undoubtedly the way Nathan Green would have wanted to be regarded, as strongly endeared to his students.

In respect to Cumberland University and its law school, Green was, at the trustees' tribute noted, "the last of those great men who were in at its birth."[54] And yet, curiously, Green's death gave the school one more opportunity to look toward the past rather than the future.

Two years before Green's death, a prospective candidate for the presidency of the institution, Edward P. Childs, raised the issue of the anomalous relationship of the law school to the university, its quasi-independence, and its retention of all its large earnings. He expressed his concerns in a letter to the trustees, with conditions precedent to his acceptance of the board's offer of the presidency:

> I understand that there has been some discussion of the relationship of the Law School to the University and that it is intended to provide for a definite policy in regard to adjustments that will in no way interfere with the present management and its freedom of action as at present understood. May I be assured that this matter will be definitely considered by the Board and a policy determined after a thorough canvass of conditions? This will involve either a definite ultimate separation of the two schools, or an actual union by which the Law School will become an organic part of the University in work and management. It is of course understood that this suggestion is not to be interpreted as affecting in any way the present management of the Law School . . . but that it will insure a definite adjustment, where necessary in the future.[55]

But the board, with law professor Martin as president, was unwilling to give up the comfortable arrangement whereby the law faculty retained all the tuition as compensation and paid nothing to the university of which it was a part. The board responded to Childs:

> we not[e] what you say concerning the law school, and say in reply, this Board will interpose no objection to a separate incorporation of that department. We do not now think it would be the best course for either the college or the law school to bring about a complete union of the two schools. In the early history, the university refused to be responsible for the law school, and provided that it should never share in the endowment of the college, and it never has. The policy then established and adhered to, to this date was, to set the law school upon its own feet, and let it row its own boat. We think this policy should be continued, and further emphasized, if any change is to be made, by procuring a separate charter for that department.[56]

Unfortunately, Childs accepted the board's position and took the presidency. Green's death offered another opportunity to modernize the school. The board could have offered the vacant professorship to an outsider who could have brought in modern thinking. It could have used the situation to integrate the law school more closely within the university, to give it the benefit of modern educational thinking, especially in regard to an expanded curriculum and the case method. But Cumberland chose to look to the past by offering the professorship to an existing part-time professor, Edward E. Beard. But that was not all. In taking the job, Beard wanted to make sure he would reap the lucrative rewards of the professorship and that Cumberland, on his watch, would continue to look to the past.

Beard appeared personally before the board and informed it that he would accept the position only if the law school were to remain self-supporting, paying its own bills and keeping its revenues for itself. In response to this, the board reaffirmed its policy that the law school "is not to share, in any way, in the endowment of this University, or in its income from any source." On the other hand, the university "is not to share in the income earned or otherwise received by the law school." The Board declared that this was the "true policy" and that the future success of the law school demanded that there be no departure from it. This matter being out of the way, Beard accepted the professorship.[57]

By 1919, the concept of a proprietary school, which this arrangement had effectively rendered Cumberland, was anachronistic. Increasingly, law schools were integrated into universities, receiving the many benefits of the association, including a network that told them quite clearly what was going on in the rest of the educational world. For this, law schools paid a fair share of costs. At few other places in the country, if any, did the law faculty simply keep the tuition, as had, indeed, once been a common practice.

A few years before Green's death, the *Literary Digest* called attention to Judge Green and claimed he was the "oldest man in the world actively employed in the manner of work in which he is engaged. That is quite a unique distinction and places the judge among the remarkable men of his time."[58] It would seem a mixed blessing so far as the school was concerned. Notwithstanding Green's revered status, the law school would have been far better served if someone younger and more attuned to modern trends in legal education had replaced him years earlier. It would have been far easier to make the needed adjustments at a point when profits were plentiful than to wait until they would be forced upon Cumberland by regulation and at a time when the law school would be impoverished.

In a 1962 interview, William F. Spencer, of the class of 1912, recalled his time in Lebanon as the "Golden Age" of Cumberland School of Law.[59] But he was wrong. The true Golden Age of Cumberland School of Law was in the antebellum period, when it truly was an innovator and leader in American legal education. If there was anything golden about Cumberland School of Law in the first decades of the twentieth century, it was only in a Hellenistic sense, as an afterglow of true glory half a century earlier.

CHAPTER SIX

Last of the Old Guard 1920–1947

The lack of money has been the institution's great handicap.
—Editorial, *Cumberland Alumnus* (1922)

One of our greatest problems will be, in some future day, and in some way, to raise the standards of the law school.
—Ernest L. Stockton, Inaugural Address as President of Cumberland University (1928)

I am not a modernist. . . . I am among the last of the "old guard" at Cumberland.
—Dean A. B. Neil (1938)

THREE ELEMENTS defined Cumberland School of Law's institutional history during the years 1920–1947. First, the organized bar and mainstream legal academics pressed for mandatory accreditation, a uniform three-year curriculum, and the case method of instruction. Second, the conservative Cumberland faculty preferred to maintain its traditional ways. Third, the Cumberland central administration, strapped for funds to pay for undergraduate education, diverted most of the law school's revenue.

With these factors combined, the law school lacked leadership disposed to respond effectively to the outside pressure and, because tuition revenue was diverted to the university, lacked the funds to implement a modern curriculum, even had its leaders been so disposed. Nationally, legal education became increasingly standardized throughout this period, but Cumberland not only fell behind the national institutions it once had led, it slipped behind regional schools as well.

On Nathan Green's death in 1919, Andrew Martin became dean and also continued to serve as president of the board of trustees. As we have seen, Edward E. Beard took over Green's classroom responsibilities and, on Martin's death scarcely a year later, became dean.[1]

Experience at the bar or on the bench constituted the principal criterion for selecting law faculty and administrators for most of the nineteenth century. A combination of such experience with prominence in the profession produced the perfect candidate, whether or not that person could devote full time to the law school. The outstanding example of what one educational historian calls "the Great Lawyer tradition" was Justice Joseph Story, who accepted the Dane Professorship at Harvard Law School faculty while retaining his seat on the United States Supreme Court.[2]

Harvard's 1873 appointment of James Barr Ames as assistant professor of law marked the beginning of a shift to the selection of young men as law teachers who had little or no experience in law practice but who would devote their entire careers to teaching and scholarship. Ames had received his law degree from Harvard in 1872 and had spent the intervening year pursuing additional legal studies at Harvard. While at the time the appointment seemed almost bizarre, Ames enjoyed a brilliant academic career. He succeeded Langdell as dean of Harvard in 1895 and served until shortly before his death in 1910.[3]

At the University of Virginia law school, the Great Lawyer model had never dominated,[4] and Emory in 1916 had appointed two young Yale law graduates as full-time law professors along with a distinguished but part-time dean.[5] In the years after World War I, other schools in the South, such as North Carolina,[6] Vanderbilt,[7] and Tennessee,[8] sought law teachers and administrators who exemplified the Ames model of the desirable law faculty member. During the same period, Cumberland adhered to the older tradition. It sought law teachers and deans with long experience as lawyers or judges, particularly those with established ties to Cumberland or Lebanon.

The appointment of Edward E. Beard as professor illustrates this. To fill the vacancy left by Green's death, the board turned to one of its own longtime members, Edward E. Beard, a man whose personal and family connections to the university, the law school, and Lebanon were pronounced. Beard was a distinguished local lawyer whose life was entwined with Cumberland University and Lebanon almost from the beginning. Born in 1850, the son of Dr. Richard Beard, then president of Cumberland College in Kentucky, young Beard moved to Lebanon with his family in 1854 when his father became the first professor of theology of Cumberland University in Lebanon.[9]

Beard received his bachelor's degree from Cumberland in 1870 and his law degree in 1874. He began practicing law in Lebanon and two years later received an appointment to the Cumberland University board of trustees, serving until his death in 1923. Beard became treasurer of the board in 1880, retaining that position until 1920. Active in Presbyterian circles, he himself was moderator of the Cumberland Presbyterian General Assembly in 1891 and held other significant positions. Beard also was mayor of Lebanon for at least two terms.[10]

Edward Beard's two brothers were also well-regarded lawyers. One, Richard, practiced in nearby Murphreesboro. The other, W. D. Beard, won appointment to the Tennessee Supreme Court in 1890 and became chief justice in 1903.[11] Edward Beard never held judicial office but was frequently referred to as "Judge" Beard, perhaps in recognition of his service from 1910 as the trial judge of the Cumberland moot court.

Scarcely more than a year after Chancellor Green's death, Andrew B. Martin fell ill and then died, on May 19, 1920. Members of the law school senior class served as the active pallbearers at his funeral.[12] Upon first becoming ill, in April 1920, Martin requested a Nashville trial judge and former student, Albert B. Neil, to teach his classes for a few days. When it became clear that Martin would not return to the classroom, Judge Neil agreed to complete Martin's classes for the year,[13] and Beard assumed the role of dean, a post he retained until his own death. Over the summer, the school hired William R. Chambers as a permanent replacement for Martin. Chambers remained on the law school faculty until 1934.

Chambers earned his bachelor's degree from Cumberland in 1877. He then attended Vanderbilt's law department, graduating in 1881 at a time when Vanderbilt had no full-time law teachers and the course of instruction was similar to Cumberland's.[14] Chambers had served in the legislature and as a special judge on the Tennessee Court of Appeals.[15] As with Beard, the selection of Chambers reflected Cumberland's preference for experienced practitioners rather than young academics. The length of Chambers's experience in practice was almost as great as that of Beard. With Chambers on the faculty, the law catalogue for 1921–22 boasted of "two regular teachers who have had a combined experience of 85 years in actual general practice of law, one having practiced 45 years and the other 40 years."

Beard became ill in August 1923. Though he commenced his classes that September, he could not complete the semester. The board chose a younger man to replace Beard, again one with connections to Cumberland. Albert Williams began teaching in October 1923 and continued until appointed to the criminal court bench in April 1925. Born in 1899, Williams received his law degree from Cumberland in 1917 and was a rising star in Tennessee state government. In 1923, not yet twenty-five years of age, he had already served in a variety of state offices.[16] After his elevation to the bench in 1925, Williams continued to maintain a connection to Cumberland. The catalogues for 1926–27 through 1929–30 all list Williams as "Special Lecturer" or "Judge of Moot Court" or both. Perhaps plans were made for him to return full-time to the faculty in 1930; the catalogue for the 1930–31 school year listed him as a professor. However, as will be seen, it became necessary in July 1930 to prevail upon A. B. Neil to rejoin the faculty.[17] Williams practiced law in Nashville from 1929 until he returned briefly as professor and acting dean during 1933 and 1934.[18]

Governor Austin Peay's appointment of Williams to the bench in 1925 created a faculty vacancy for the 1925–26 school term. Curiously, Cumberland chose a man in the Ames model. Julian K. Faxon earned his law degree in 1924 from the University of Chicago law school. A native of Illinois, he also had received bachelor's and master's degrees from Chicago. Faxon remained at Cumberland until 1930 and infused some of the features of the case method into the curriculum.[19] In January 1926, Cumberland introduced the case method through a second year of study but without altering the historic "regular" or "one year course." The law school catalogue for March 1926 described a new "graduate course" to be taught by Faxon:

> The authorities of Cumberland University are thoroughly convinced that the best method of acquiring the basis of a legal education is the study of text-books, and that an attempt to discard the text-books and substitute the study of cases, many of which involve collateral matter, tends often to confuse the beginner. However, for the benefit of those who have completed our one-year course, there has been added a graduate course based upon a collection of leading cases and textbooks. The object of this course is thoroughly to familiarize the student with the skillful use of a law library and the interpretation of judicial decisions, and at the same time to furnish him a thorough review of the principles already learned from the text-books.

The course required one year, in which the student would study agency, partnership, corporations, trusts, code pleading, negotiable instruments, insurance, bankruptcy, property, evidence, "and other essential courses." Students would have studied many of these topics by the textbook method in the first year. Tuition for the entire second year was sixty-five dollars while, at the same time, tuition for the regular one-year course was increased from fifty to sixty-five dollars per semester. The catalogue for the following year contained no reference to a second year or graduate course. Nevertheless, Cumberland had introduced a model for the introduction of a second year of law school. A decade later, it added a new second year that also followed the same pattern of teaching several first-year subjects, using casebooks instead of textbooks.[20] Resistance to the case method may have discouraged Faxon and led to his 1930 resignation. Perhaps he simply received an offer of a better position, and one report claims he went into business in Texas.[21]

The law school catalogue for 1928–29 for the first time listed Sara Hardison as the law librarian. University catalogues, however, had shown her in that post since 1921. Hardison received her law degree from Cumberland in 1923, apparently while also serving as librarian. In later law school catalogues she is sometimes listed as Law Librarian, sometimes as Secretary of the Law School, and sometimes as Professor of Legal Bibliography. She remained with the law school until it moved in 1961.

The catalogue for 1930–31 lists Albert Williams as professor of law as well as judge of the moot court. However, by July the board realized that Williams was not coming back and that it needed someone to fill the vacancy left by Faxon's departure. Someone in Lebanon must have recalled the creditable job Judge A. B. Neil had done in completing Andrew Martin's classes in 1920. Neil, who had taken his law degree in 1896 under Green and Martin, by 1930 had accumulated twenty years of experience as a trial court judge in Nashville. For a school that preferred teachers with practical experience and an attachment to Cumberland, Neil was a natural choice.

John J. Hooker, a member of the Board of Trustees, telephoned Neil on a July afternoon while the judge was vacationing at Tonka Bay, Minnesota, and offered Neil the job. Years later Neil, an avid fisherman and outdoor artist, recalled how restful Tonka Bay, on the shores of Lake Minnetonka, had been that July. Nevertheless, Neil cut short his vacation and immediately returned to Tennessee to discuss the position.

Judge Chambers, who had become dean on Beard's death, urged Neil to resign his position as a trial judge and devote himself full-time to law teaching. Neil was reluctant to do this but agreed to accept Cumberland's offer on a temporary basis while retaining his judgeship. For the next ten years Neil, first as a law teacher and from 1935 as dean also, held court in Nashville from 9 until 1, then drove to Lebanon where he would teach from 2 until 4, often returning on Saturdays for moot court. In bad weather, he took the bus. No wonder he would later look back wistfully on how pleasant the sky-blue waters of Lake Minnetonka had seemed that July day in 1930.[22]

As the 1931–32 school year began, the faculty of the law school consisted only of Chambers and Neil, with Hardison as librarian. However, two additional faculty positions were about to be added and filled by intelligent, energetic young men.

In June 1932, the trustees appointed Samuel B. Gilreath to the faculty.[23] Gilreath entered the law school as a student in September 1924 and graduated in June 1925. He studied at Cumberland just before more modern treatises replaced Kent's *Commentaries.* Chambers and Williams were Gilreath's two principal instructors in his year as a student. Whatever adulteration of the Cumberland experience may have occurred the following year when Faxon introduced elements of the case method did not affect Gilreath's legal education.[24]

Gilreath later prepared the sixth, seventh, and eighth editions of *History of a Lawsuit,* and thereby placed himself in an intellectual line that ran back through Martin to Abraham Caruthers and the first little group of students who gathered in Robert Caruthers's law office in 1847. Like many other Cumberland law students, young Gilreath married a Lebanon woman. Gilreath's bride was the daughter of Winston P. Bone, former president of Cumberland University, secretary of the Cumberland alumni association, and author of *A History of Cumberland University*.[25] At a time when other southern law schools were hiring law teachers committed to curricular reform, Cumberland also acquired a scholarly young man, but one committed to Cumberland's educational traditions rather than reform.

In January 1933, Albert Williams resumed teaching at the law school. Hired to fill a breach in the curriculum caused by increased bar requirements, Williams taught conflict of laws, chancery pleading, and legal form writing, and participated in the moot court program. An editorial in the student newspaper congratulated the Board of Trustees on the selection of Williams:

> The administration has acted very wisely in appointing to the law faculty a man who has had personal experience, as a lawyer, in those subjects that he will teach. . . .
>
> The administration being well aware of the many changes in legal training and requirements for admission to the bar, has made this first step toward reorganization and development of the law school. These improvements in the curriculum and instruction are showing that the lawyer of today must be master of his craft to succeed in his profession.[26]

With the appointment of Gilreath and the reappointment of Williams, the law school had added two new faculty positions in as many years. No doubt it seemed to be an especially propitious time to increase the size of the faculty. In 1933–34 the law school enjoyed the largest enrollment in its history.[27] With Williams's return, the faculty now included four strong individuals, each of whom would at some time serve as dean or acting dean: Chambers, Neil, Gilreath, and Williams. While Neil continued to serve as a trial court judge in Nashville and Gilreath had a law office in Lebanon,[28] Williams, who is listed in the 1933–34 and 1934–35 law school catalogues as acting dean, and Chambers, who is designated as dean emeritus, apparently devoted their energies entirely to the law school.

As the *Cumberland Collegian* editorial indicates, the university was putting in place a "reorganization plan" that would enable the law school at last to respond to changes in legal training and bar requirements. In 1932, the Tennessee Supreme Court increased the requirement for taking the Tennessee bar exam from one year of law study to two, effective for those taking the exam after June 1, 1934.[29] In May 1933, the university announced that the law school would extend its program to two years of instruction beginning with the 1934–35 academic year.[30] The faculty probably planned case method instruction for the second year.[31] However, the board of trustees almost immediately voted to continue the one-year program for the next academic year.[32] In fact, the Great Depression prevented the university from implementing the two-year plan until September 1938.[33]

The Depression caused other problems. In December 1934, both Chambers and Williams resigned, along with three undergraduate teachers, when the university asked faculty members to accept 30 percent of their salaries in cash with the balance represented by a letter of obligation.[34] Cumberland's modestly ambitious plan to standardize its curriculum had in one sense come too late: what might have been feasible in the mid-1920s could not be implemented in the mid-1930s when most of the law school's tuition revenue had to be diverted to prevent the financial collapse of the entire university. In another sense, the plan had come too early: only later when an unflattering report of an inspection by an American Bar Association team surveying law schools in Tennessee forced its hand would Cumberland become the last of approximately 190 schools listed in the Annual Review of Legal Education in the United States to extend its program to two years.[35]

Two elements other than the faculty shaped the institutional story of Cumberland law school during this period: the university administration and the organized bar's efforts to increase legal education requirements. We must shortly look more closely at each.

Neil became dean upon the departure of Williams and Chambers. A lawyer named Currell Vance covered the spring 1935 courses of the two who had resigned but remained only for that semester.[36] In September 1935, Frank T. Fancher became a member of the faculty and served for two years. He returned as law professor in September 1939 and in September 1941 became dean when Neil, perhaps anticipating his elevation to the Tennessee Supreme Court in 1942, resigned from the faculty and the deanship.[37] Once Fancher became dean, the following description set forth his claims in the "Great Lawyer tradition": "He graduated from this law school under the teaching of Judge Green and Dr. Martin and has had vast experience in the practice of law in Tennessee and Florida. In 1915–16, again in 1937 and in 1940–41 he served by appointment of three different Governors as a Special Judge on the Supreme Court of Tennessee. For over twelve years he was a member of the Board of Law Examiners of Tennessee."[38]

In the 1937–38 school year Lewis Cassidy appeared, a professor who, like Faxon nearly a decade earlier, was an individual in the Ames model. In addition to his basic law degree, Cassidy also held an LL.M., a Ph.D., and an S.J.D.[39] By September 1939, the returning Fancher had replaced him. During the 1938–40 period, John J. Hooker, a prominent alumnus, taught law, as did Edward L. McNeilly, from September 1938 until his death in August 1939.[40] This left Fancher as dean and Gilreath as professor, both of whom carried forward the traditions of the Old Guard.

Fancher retired in 1942, and Gilreath entered military service. Judge Allison B. Humphreys Jr., serving as acting dean, and Thomas B. Finley continued the wartime program. Humphreys, who later would become solicitor general of Tennessee and a member of its Supreme Court, graduated from Cumberland School of Law in January 1929. He taught the second-year course, while Finley conducted the first year. A Cumberland student during the war years described Finley as "an experienced trial lawyer."[41] Thus to the end of this period, Cumberland continued to be staffed by the experienced lawyer model.

In modern law schools, faculty members are valued more for their academic achievements than for their experience on the bench or at the bar, and they are tightly linked to the larger university in other ways as well. At other southern institutions, university administrators rather than law teachers tended to initiate the modernization of their law schools and sustained them through budget deficits that attended the transitions. Vanderbilt University, located in Nashville, Tennessee, only thirty miles west of Lebanon, offers an example.

Until 1900, the Vanderbilt Law School had been operated by a group of Nashville lawyers who held a twenty-five-year lease from the university entitling them to classroom space in which to conduct Vanderbilt's law department. The "lessees," all lawyers in active practice, constituted the faculty of the department and received the student tuition fees.[42]

The expiration of the lease in 1900 provided the university's young chancellor, James H. Kirkland, an opportunity to reorganize the law department and bring it under university control. Kirkland made Vanderbilt a two-year school in reality as well as name, publicly urged adoption of a three-year course of study employing the case method, returned the law school to the main Vanderbilt campus, and oversaw the hiring of the law school's first full-time administrator and first full-time faculty member. All this resulted in budget deficits that ran as high as 25 percent annually; still, Kirkland stuck to his guns. By 1921, the Vanderbilt Law School had three full-time faculty members, all law teachers with experience at other reputable schools. In the early 1920s, high enrollment generated a surplus that the law school retained in endowment.[43]

Nevertheless, Kirkland's problems continued. The Association of American Law Schools (AALS) admitted Vanderbilt to membership in 1910. However, the 1920s saw a militancy in the AALS, with new standards asserted and old standards applied with a fresh rigor. In 1926, following a visit from a tough examiner from the University of Iowa named H. Claude Horack, the AALS excluded Vanderbilt from membership. Kirkland returned to the struggle, for a time taking direct charge of the law school. He tightened admissions standards and secured approval of readmission of Vanderbilt to membership in the AALS by promising to appoint a full-time dean. He chose Earl C. Arnold, a graduate of Northwestern with wide experience in legal education and a respected record of scholarship. In addition the Vanderbilt Board of Trustees dedicated $265,000 of university endowment to the use of the law school. With the arrival of Dean Arnold in 1930, Chancellor Kirkland concluded thirty years of leadership of what was now indisputably a standard law school on the modern, national model but one that the university (in part because of the less expensive alternative available in Lebanon) would be forced to continue to underwrite for most of the Depression years.[44]

The University of Tennessee Law School, at Knoxville, 150 miles east of Lebanon, furnishes a similar story of leadership by the central university administration. There, Brown Ayres, the university president, took charge. Beginning with the 1907–8 school year, the university assumed control of law school finances, receiving all fees paid by law students, but also guaranteeing payment of law faculty salaries.[45] A vacancy in the deanship in

1920 provided the university administration an opportunity to hire a Harvard-trained lawyer, committed to the case method of instruction.[46]

At Vanderbilt and Tennessee, Kirkland and Ayres, dealing only with part-time deans and underpaid faculty members, faced little if any resistance to integrating the law school into the financial and administrative structure of the university. At Cumberland, Green, Martin, and Beard were full-time teachers with a vested financial interest in maintaining their autonomy. Additionally, not only were Green and Martin teachers of legendary stature, all three occupied positions in the university—Green as chancellor (until 1900), Martin and Beard as chairman and treasurer of the board of trustees—unimaginable to modern law school teachers and administrators. Ironically, the very weakness of the law school leadership at Vanderbilt and Tennessee made possible the integration of the law school into the university at those schools, while at Cumberland the strength of the law faculty delayed this step until Green and Martin were gone, the board of trustees had been reorganized with Beard no longer a member, and a new president, John Royal Harris, had taken charge.

In the summer of 1920, Cumberland University amended its charter to change the method of selection for its fifteen board members. Previously the board had been self-perpetuating, with the general assembly of Presbyterian Church, U.S.A. (prior to 1906, the general assembly of the Cumberland Presbyterian Church) having apparently never exercised veto power. The old self-perpetuation system of selection generally created a board dominated by residents of Lebanon. The board consisted of eleven members and four vacancies immediately prior to the charter amendment. Seven were from Lebanon; all were from Tennessee. Under the amended charter, the synod of Tennessee of the Presbyterian Church, U.S.A., chose nine members, and the synods of Alabama and Mississippi each chose three. The amendment spread geographical representation on the board beyond the borders of Tennessee. The Tennessee synod did not include Judge Beard in its quota of nine; for the first time since the 1850s, no member of the law school faculty held a position on the board of trustees. Only four members of the new board resided in Lebanon and of these only one, Amzi Waddell Hooker, was a graduate of the law school; three other law alumni were selected, including Judge James E. Horton of Athens, Alabama. A decade later Horton distinguished himself as perhaps the most courageous of Cumberland's many jurists when, presiding over one of the racially inflamed Scottsboro rape cases, he found no credible evidence of guilt of the defendant Haywood Patterson and annulled the jury's conviction. Elected to office without opposition before the trial, Horton was easily defeated in the next election.[47]

As discussed in the preceding chapter, the board under the old charter had refused to accede to then-prospective president Childs's demand either that there be "a definite ultimate separation" of the law school from the university or that it become "an organic part of the university in work and management," and, in appointing Beard upon Green's death, the board had agreed to his condition that "the law school was to be self supporting . . . and retain all its income."[48]

On June 1, 1920, at the last annual meeting of the unreconstituted board, President Childs submitted a number of far-reaching recommendations. Among them was the following: "That when a successor for Dr. Martin be chosen as Prof. of Law and Dean of the Law Dept. there shall be a full understanding with him of an intention on the part of the Trustees to establish the Law Department on a two year basis, with definite scholastic requirements of admission to and graduation from the course and such reorganization be put into effect not later than Sept. 1921. That a Com. of the Trustees be appointed to arrange definite plans in connection with such a change of policy in the department."

The minute book of the board of trustees carries the notation "No Action" next to this recommendation.[49] Probably the board discussed it, but, absent a consensus, no motion was made. The board's failure to act was undoubtedly one reason for Childs's resignation, only a little over a week later.

Upon Martin's death, the board initially selected Grafton Green, the son of Nathan Green Jr., to fill Martin's position. Grafton Green declined the position, although he agreed to help on a part-time basis. Thereafter, on July 13, the board employed Chambers as a law professor for one year. Notwithstanding Childs's recommendations, the old board continued the long-established compensation arrangements and resolved that Chambers would receive half of the net income of the law school as compensation, with Beard receiving the other half, the work of teaching to be divided among them "as they shall agree."[50]

When the reconstituted board held its first meeting in November 1920, it took the first tentative steps toward seizing control of the law school finances. First, it "asked" the law school to contribute not less than five hundred dollars each year toward the general expenses of the university "to be appropriated by said Dept. out of its tuition, diploma and contingent fees." Then it required the law school treasurer to provide the board with an annual report giving detailed statement of all receipts, expenditures, and general financial condition of the school.[51]

Previously, the law school had handled its own money and kept its own books through its own treasurer. However, the treasurer of the law department was W. J. Baird, a local banker, who in that day of casual intermingling of offices in the Cumberland hierarchy, also served as a member and secretary of the university board. As the law school treasurer he was required to submit a financial statement to the board's treasurer, A. W. Hooker, who would then submit it for inclusion in the board's minutes by the secretary of the board, the same W. J. Baird.[52]

Initially the new board, more tightly linked to the Presbyterian church than to Lebanon, concerned itself about law school student behavior more than law school finances or curriculum. Laban L. Rice, in declining election to the university presidency in July 1921, drew the board's attention to a problem with disciplinary control in the law school. "This is a time for plain understanding," Rice told the board.[53]

At its meeting on November 15, 1921, the board determined to investigate the exact relationship of the law department to the university. Apparently concerned about the behavior of law students, the board decided to use the law faculty as an instrument of social control. It adopted the following resolution, which, though stated in general terms, is almost certainly directed at the law school: "In each case where recommendation is made for the granting of a degree, that said petition shall be accompanied by a specific recommendation from the faculty of each department certifying that the personal life, studiousness, industry, and moral life of the candidate has been during his or her school terms such as reflect credit upon an institution of the character of this University, directed as it is by a great denomination of the Christian Church."[54]

It fell to John Royal Harris, who with much fanfare was inaugurated as president in June 1922, to assert full university control over law school finances.

Harris's inauguration seemed an auspicious moment in the life of Cumberland University. Born in nearby Murphreesboro, Harris graduated from Cumberland in 1894. Though a Presbyterian minister who had occupied pulpits in Tennessee and Pennsylvania, Harris had not pursued the quiet life of passive piety. Instead, he acquired considerable political and administrative skills in the prohibition movement, first as a leader of the Anti-Saloon League in Tennessee and then as a leader of the Dry Federation in Pennsylvania. Now, after the Eighteenth Amendment had established Prohibition, Cumberland welcomed Harris home to place those skills at the service of his alma mater.[55]

Harris got right to work. By the time the board convened for its next annual meeting in June of 1923, Harris had ready for the board's approval an agreement with the law school faculty. The agreement established fixed salaries for the law school faculty. In phasing in the new arrangements, for two years the law faculty received half the revenue of the law school over and above their salaries; thereafter net revenues after salaries and expenses would go to the university.[56]

Harris undoubtedly had been willing to agree to generous salaries for the law faculty to obtain their acquiescence in the new arrangements. University records from April 1924 indicate a salary level for law professors of $5,000 for the year, while professors in the college were making $1,200.[57]

This $5,000 a year equaled or exceeded the compensation for law teachers at other institutions, though it was less than what deans received. In 1920 Dean James Hoskins of the University of Tennessee, preparing to recruit a new dean, had sought information regarding salary levels. The president of the Association of American Law Schools advised that deans received between $5,000 and $10,000, full professors from $4,000 to $5,000, and younger professors from $2,500 to $3,500. The dean at Yale shared the information that professors at the University of Kentucky received about $3,000, while the dean at Harvard suggested that the salary scale at the University of West Virginia, where full professors were paid a top salary of $4,200 and the dean $4,700, would be an appropriate benchmark.[58] In November 1923, the president of the University of North Carolina visited

Harvard, Columbia, and the University of Chicago law schools and reported to his board that law professors would have to be compensated "a maximum of at least $5,000."[59]

The 1920 decanal search at the University of Tennessee resulted in the appointment of Malcolm McDermott at a salary of $5,000.[60] It is possible that the amount of McDermott's salary was known in Lebanon and played a role in fixing the salaries of the Cumberland law teachers at the same figure. In any event, by June 1923, Harris had established a new structural relationship with the law school: law teachers received a fixed salary, with the university capturing any excess of income over salaries and other expenses. With that structure in place, so long as law faculty salaries could be held steady or even reduced, increases in law student tuition revenue could be applied to general university purposes.

Even after the new structure was in place, the law school took in its own money and controlled the books that determined how much would be left for the university at the end of the year. Perhaps the law faculty had hoped to exercise that control to carve out additional compensation by charging fees in addition to their salaries. If so, those hopes were soon dashed. The board's minutes of November 6, 1923, signal that any such ploy would not work. Those minutes contain a declaration that "hereafter the law professors will be expected to grade all papers in their department without extra compensation."[61]

Harris acted to assure that the university obtained operational control of law school finances, including initial receipt of law student fees and tuition. The law school catalogue for January 1925, and for several years previously, directed new students arriving in Lebanon to report to the "Law Department's Treasurer," who would give them information and advice, and collect their tuition. However, beginning with the March 1926 catalogue, arriving students were directed to report to Memorial Hall where they would register through the university administrative structure and pay their tuition directly to the university. The catalogues contain no further reference to the law school treasurer, and the position disappeared. Instead, a new university official, the university secretary, appeared, in a man appropriately named A. J. Cash. President Harris appointed Cash as "college and university accountant" in March 1925, during the last months of his administration. As university secretary, Cash took control, in a contemporary's words, "of all fees and any money from any source due to the University or to any of its departments." The university secretary also maintained all books of account and prepared the financial reports of all university departments.[62] A law school treasurer no longer prepared and submitted reports to the board's treasurer, nor transmitted a mere share of the law school's revenues. With the appointment of Cash, the university had complete control over law school finances.

Traditionally, and continuing through 1923, the law faculty enjoyed almost total autonomy from university financial control, and the faculty bore the responsibility for the failure of the law school to modernize its program. After the university obtained financial and administrative control of the law school in 1923, institutional responsibility for modernizing and standardizing the law school program lay with the university administration.

At other institutions, the establishment of administrative and financial control over the law school foreshadowed initiatives to standardize the law school program by extending its duration, pushing the case method of instruction, appointing more academically oriented faculty and deans, or all of these. The history of law school standardization under the leadership of university administrators at Vanderbilt and Tennessee illustrates this. At Cumberland as well, the university administrators in Memorial Hall understood as well or better than the lawyers in Caruthers Hall the movement to standardize legal education, and supported that movement.

Just prior to his resignation, President Childs had recommended that a two-year program be adopted. Harris died in September 1926, not long after completing the administrative and financial integration of the law school into the university. The appointment in 1925 of a young University of Chicago graduate, Kenneth Faxon, to the law school faculty suggests that if Harris had lived, he might have followed the lead of other central administrators to standardize his law school.

Ernest Looney Stockton Sr. succeeded Harris. Stockton, formerly dean of arts and sciences and professor of English, became acting president when the board granted Harris a leave of absence shortly before his death. Stockton served as acting president during that school year, and on May 31, 1927, the board elected him president. Stockton received both bachelor's and master's degrees from Cumberland and during his first year as English professor completed the law course and received his LL.B.[63]

From the start, Stockton's paramount goal was membership in the regional accrediting body, the Southern Association of Schools and Colleges. In 1920, the Southern Association of Colleges and Schools had adopted standards required of member institutions. Stockton quickly identified several deficiencies that prevented accreditation, including salary level of undergraduate teachers, endowment, library, and the nonstandard status of the law school. The law school was a major problem because the Southern Association required that professional schools of member institutions meet national standards.[64]

Stockton's formal inauguration took place on January 20, 1928. Though the leaves were gone from the trees, the sun shone brightly on the capped and gowned dignitaries ready for the procession across campus to Caruthers Hall, where Stockton gave his inaugural address. To the gathered assemblage of Cumberland faculty, students, trustees, and representatives from other colleges and universities in Tennessee and across the South, Stockton set forth the two related goals of his administration: increased endowment and standardization of program that would permit Cumberland to become a member of the Southern Association of Colleges and Schools.

Because he recognized that under the Southern Association's 1920 standards, Cumberland University could never qualify for membership unless its law department met national standards for law schools, Stockton devoted most of his address to the subject of legal education. The young president had been doing his homework as to the national standards for law schools. In 1921, Alfred Z. Reed, a researcher for the Carnegie Foundation, published *Training for the Public Profession of the Law,* a study of legal education in the United States. In his address, Stockton referred repeatedly to Reed's work. Drawing on Reed, Stockton pointed out that, with one glaring exception, the length of study required for graduation had become virtually uniform with 159 of the 167 schools requiring three years of study, seven requiring two years, and one requiring one year. Here Stockton paused to note, "We presume that school is Cumberland."

Drawing on Reed's account of the history of American legal education, Stockton declared that "according to this good authority . . . we may be justified in our slowness to make too radical changes." But, he left no doubt as to the appropriate direction: "We are not opposed . . . to needed and constructive standardization." Although Stockton recognized that changing the law school posed a difficult challenge and could not occur immediately, he declared that "one of our greatest problems will be, in some future day, and in some way, to raise the standards of the law school."[65]

For the law school to meet national standards would require a complete reworking of its program. But what the undergraduate program needed in order for the institution to qualify for Southern Association membership could be stated in one word: money. Money was needed for teacher salaries, endowment, library, and physical plant. Lack of money prevented Stockton from following in the footsteps of university leaders like Kirkland and Ayres. Instead of being able to provide university resources to aid the law school in making the transition to a two- or three-year case method school, Stockton was forced to use the law school to generate resources to sustain the rest of the university. By 1937, approximately two-thirds of law school revenue was being used for general university purposes.[66] In the end, tentative steps toward modernizing the law school's program resulted only from the activities of persons external to the school. It is to that part of the story that we now turn.[67]

Since the turn of the century, law schools ambitious for national recognition aspired to the Langdellian ideal—one or two years of college before law school and three years of law study under a full-time faculty of scholar-teachers employing the case method—even if they sometimes fell short. Beginning in 1905, the American Association of Law Schools, the law school elite, required that its member schools grant a degree only after three years of law study. The University of Tennessee, forced to withdraw from membership because it offered only a two-year program, did so regretfully and endeavored to regain membership as quickly as possible.[68] Trinity (Duke after 1924) maintained membership and paid homage to the ideal by formally requiring three years for a diploma while actually conducting a two-year program capped with the award of a certificate.[69] However, the Reed report of 1921 revealed that, notwithstanding the acceptance of the Langdellian ideal among AALS members and aspirants, much of the legal education law students received in the United States was at law schools that fell short of the ideal.[70]

In 1920, the American Bar Association Section on Legal Education appointed a blue ribbon committee, chaired by former ABA President Elihu Root, to recommend what could be done "to create conditions which will tend to strengthen the character and improve the efficiency of persons admitted to the practice of law." Behind their concern lay a fear that the influx into the bar of immigrants and their children, particularly those from eastern European countries and specifically Jews and Roman Catholics, had lowered both the caliber and moral character of the bar. Those nativist attitudes were turned to the service of the campaign for higher standards in legal education.[71] The Root committee concluded that the best means to improve the character and efficiency of lawyers was to "purify the stream at its source by causing a proper system of training to be established and to be required," and recommended the establishment of law school standards.[72]

Specifically the committee recommended that no one be admitted to practice law without graduation from a law school that required at least two years of college before admission and three years of legal study, provided an adequate library, and employed a "sufficient number" of full-time teachers "to insure actual personal acquaintance and influence with the whole student body." In essence, the committee's recommendation would limit bar admission to graduates of law schools organized on the Langdellian model. An additional recommendation called for the publication of a list of schools complying with the stated standards. On Root's motion, seconded by Chief Justice William Howard Taft, the ABA Section adopted the committee's recommendations.[73]

While the ABA could recommend, it had no actual jurisdiction over bar admissions in any state. To encourage state and local support for the ABA recommendations, the National Conference of Bar Associations, an organization of state and local bar association representatives that the ABA formed in 1915, sponsored a conference on legal education in Washington in February 1922. Its sessions presided over by such luminaries as Taft, the Washington conference endorsed the ABA standards.[74]

Adoption of the 1921 standards vitalized the work of the legal education section. Extending the reach of compliance with the standards became the section's mission. Each year's meeting of the ABA became an occasion for rejoicing at the number of schools added to the approved list (initiated in 1923) as well as the number of local jurisdictions whose bar association or judiciary had adopted all or some of the standards locally.[75]

In Tennessee, those favoring adoption of the ABA standards made little progress in the 1920s. Tennesseans may not have shared the concern over the admission of the sons of immigrants from eastern and southern Europe. When Tennesseans thought of a young potential lawyer who might be barred by high standards, they thought not of a boy from the tenements but of a youngster from the farm.[76] However, by the 1930s, as the Depression deepened, concern over "overcrowding" of the bar came to be the reason given for increasing the standards of legal education. Economic concerns had as much potency in Tennessee as elsewhere and began to increase local interest in higher standards of legal education.[77]

The Depression had another effect as well: for a time, it helped sustain high enrollments at Cumberland. For prospective lawyers with limited resources, the ability to complete the Cumberland program in only one year gave Cumberland a significant advantage over schools that required three years for a degree. As long as graduates of Cumberland's one-year program could gain admission to the bar in Tennessee and other southern states, the economically rational choice was Cumberland. As a result Cumberland enrollment stayed high, while ABA and AALS accredited schools such as Tennessee and Vanderbilt faced declining enrollments. Naturally those at Tennessee and Vanderbilt looked for a way to do something about this.[78]

As early as 1919, the Tennessee legislature had empowered the Tennessee Supreme Court to establish standards for admission to practice law in Tennessee. For over a decade, the Tennessee Supreme Court (of which Grafton Green, son and grandson of Nathan Green Jr. and Sr., was chief justice) declined to exercise the power to require higher educational standards. However, in 1931, the court adopted rules increasing the requirement of law study from one year to two years for candidates taking the bar exam after June 1, 1934.[79]

That rule prompted Cumberland to increase the size of its faculty in 1932 and 1933 from two to four teachers and to announce in May 1933 an intention to require two years for graduation beginning with the September 1933 class. Both moves also served President Stockton's aspirations to standardize the law school.

Straitened finances, however, prevented him from being able to sustain these initiatives. By January 1935, Albert Williams, whose appointment the student newspaper had hailed as a "first step toward reorganization and development of the law school"[80] had resigned, along with Dean Chambers, in response to the university's plan to pay faculty members only 30 percent of their salaries in cash and the rest in promissory notes.

The May 1933 announcement of a requirement of two years of study for a degree was quickly superseded by one delaying the two-year requirement until 1935 and then a decision to continue awarding a degree after only one year.[81] On January 10, 1934, President Stockton, comparing the economic conditions of 1934 to those of Reconstruction that had first led to the shortening of the degree program to one year, announced that the board of trustees had decided to continue the one-year degree "until economic recovery makes possible the raising of more adequate finances for equipment and standardization." Stockton promised that as economic conditions improved, he would continue the campaign for endowment and would begin standardization.[82] Stockton's announcement added that an optional second-year course would be continued (it had begun in September 1933) to accommodate students from states, including Tennessee, that required two years of legal study as a prerequisite to admission to practice.[83] Nevertheless, as a result of his 1934 announcement and contrary to the high hopes Stockton had voiced in his inaugural address, Cumberland retained the distinction of being the only school in the country to offer a law degree after only one year of study.

The American Bar Association first directly entered into Cumberland's history in 1937. Earlier, in 1928, William Draper Lewis, the chairman of the Section of Legal Education, suggested that the American Bar Association could enlist local bar support for higher standards by providing state surveys of legal education. Lewis argued that the ABA and his section should "place itself in the position to help any state or local bar association, or organization, court, judicial council, or bar examiners to ascertain local legal educational conditions, and especially the efficiency and needs of the local schools." His section would respond favorably to a request for a statewide study of law schools.[84]

To carry out such surveys, as well as work with schools and state and local bar associations in other ways, the Section on Legal Education in 1927 had obtained an appropriation from the ABA Executive Committee that allowed it to hire an "Advisor on Legal Education," a full-time, professional employee. One law professor later called this "the most important and effective single step taken by the [ABA]" other than the adoption of the 1921 standards.[85] A law professor at Iowa named H. Claude Horack became the first advisor, to be succeeded two years later by a Denver attorney, Will D. Shafroth.[86]

In 1933, California took advantage of the ABA plan, and Shafroth, as advisor to the section, together with Horack, the former advisor by then with Duke Law School, conducted a survey of the law schools of that state.[87] In 1937, the Tennessee Bar Association decided that Tennessee as well should avail itself of the ABA section's offer. It requested the American Bar Association to make a disinterested "survey of the Law Schools in Tennessee, without expense to [this] Association," but with its wholehearted cooperation.[88] In due course, Shafroth and Horack conducted the survey, with the assistance of a team of Tennessee Bar members. An educational historian has called the result—*The Law Schools of Tennessee Report of the Survey Committee,* which appeared in 1938—"the most important document in twentieth century legal education in Tennessee."[89]

H. Claude Horack had taken his law degree from Iowa, a law school that was one of first to follow Harvard's example in converting to the case method.[90] At the time of his appointment as advisor, he also served as secretary-treasurer of the AALS.[91] The AALS had already instituted the practice of inspection visits to member schools and to those applying for memberships; Horack made these visits as AALS secretary. Horack had already acquired the range of techniques of that art form peculiar to modern higher education known as the accreditation visit, from informing, suggesting, listening, requiring information, recommending, cajoling, expressing concern, and ultimately to demanding compliance. During the two years Horack held the post of advisor, he also became president of the AALS. Thus, Horack knew elite legal education well. He had served as president of the Iowa Bar Association and knew the practicing bar's support would be important to obtaining compliance with the standards.

Horack held the position of full-time advisor for the AALS for two years and then returned to full-time teaching at Iowa. Duke University Law School soon lured Horack to Durham, first as a faculty member, later to become dean. Will Shafroth succeeded Horack as advisor. Shafroth started a powerful new organization, the National Conference of Bar Examiners, with the active assistance of the ABA Section on Legal Education. Through that organization, the American Bar Association ultimately achieved the goal of limiting the right to take the bar exam in most states to students who had graduated from ABA-approved schools. It was later said of Shafroth: "If one man can be singled out as the most effective person in the struggle to secure approval for and adoption of the A.B.A. standards, that man is Will Shafroth. When he became adviser, 15 states had accepted the recommended minimum and at the end of his service 42 states were on that list. The number of approved schools had grown from 75 to 106, but that fails to tell the whole story, for many of the schools had sought his advice and accepted his counsel to achieve a higher quality in the work being offered."[92]

Shafroth and Horack visited Cumberland in November 1937. They did not like what they found. Their report listed a number of specific complaints: Cumberland had the only one-year course in the country; it not only used the textbook method, it used outdated textbooks; part-time instructors taught the traditional, one-year, first-year course; the optional second-year course, taught by the case method, frequently repeated the first-year subjects; and the school admitted students with only a high school education. Also, the library was inadequate, Caruthers Hall poorly maintained, and standards of scholarship were low. Furthermore, no one seemed to be in charge, as the dean, Judge Neil, was part-time.[93]

However, the most important criticism was that two-thirds of the law school's revenue was diverted to general university purposes. Neil, in a published reply to the report, agreed that this was true, and, in his only point of agreement with the study, concurred in condemning this practice.[94]

The report's analysis suggested that the diversion of two-thirds of Cumberland's law school revenues caused the other shortcomings. As a result of lack of funding, Caruthers Hall was not well maintained, and in two years the library had added only 270 volumes. Funds prohibited the division of the first-year class into smaller groups where students could receive more personal attention. On the other hand, absence of a full-time dean helped account for the existing financial arrangement: "The fact that the revenues of the Law School have for years gone largely into the general University funds indicates the lack of a firm stand on the needs of the Law School, which a full-time Dean would inevitably realize."[95]

The report's criticism of Cumberland contrasted with its praise of Vanderbilt and Tennessee, the two other full-time Tennessee schools. Those law schools each required three years for a degree and two years of college for admission and employed six full-time faculty members. Each was on the ABA list of approved schools. Yet the report noted that Cumberland's income was large when compared to those schools.[96] As indicated earlier, university leadership with the desire to appoint deans and faculty of the scholar-teacher model, aided by resources to help the law schools make the transition, made those changes possible for Tennessee and Vanderbilt. At Cumberland, President Stockton had the desire to standardize the law school. But the needs of the undergraduate school required that he divert law school revenue. And the faculty appointments on his watch—primarily Albert Neil and Sam Gilreath—reflected an allegiance to the practitioner-jurist tradition in faculty recruitment, rather than that of scholar-teacher, as well as a preference for part-timers who no doubt would be more willing to tolerate the diversion of law school revenue. Though many factors probably play a part, the reason Cumberland failed to keep pace with the other two schools comes down to the thinness of the university's resources. Even during the Depression, Stockton labored mightily to build endowment, but with little success. In 1941, Stockton resigned to assume a government position, never having achieved his goal of standardization.[97]

Despite Stockton's failure to revamp the law school, the ABA report had an impact. Beginning with the class entering in September 1938, the law school required two years of study for a degree.[98] War was eminent by the time the second two-year class graduated in 1941. Stockton's successor, Laban L. Rice, a star pitcher as a Cumberland undergraduate, had been a contemporary of Cordell Hull, now secretary of state, and they had remained friends. The university laid plans for a fund-raising campaign using Hull's name to expand the law school library, but Pearl Harbor put those plans on hold.[99]

Law school instruction employing the two-year program continued during the war years. A lawyer named Thomas B. Finley taught the traditional one-year course as the first year, while Judge Allison B. Humphreys Jr., who whittled a shaft of red cedar as he conducted class, taught the second year. G. Frank Burns, later the author of the sesquicentennial history of Cumberland University, attended law school during World War II and recalls that with the small enrollment, the number of times each student was called on increased proportionately. However, in an observation that Horack and Shafroth might find surprising, Burns states that: "Fortunately, the second-year course was case law and there was not as much direct interrogation as in the first-year class."[100]

By war's end, control of Cumberland University had been transferred to a Baptist denomination. An entirely new administration had been installed, with a fresh vision for the future of the university, including standardization of the law school. Before turning to that story, however, the next chapter looks at the life of Cumberland law students during 1920–1947, in the classroom and out.

CHAPTER SEVEN

Living and Learning in Lebanon 1920–1947

The national character of the student body of the Cumberland Law School is probably largely due to its one-year course.
—The Law Schools of Tennessee Report of the Survey Committee, *Tennessee Law Review*

Lack of cooperation between the law and literary schools is another deplorable condition. The former consider the latter a bunch of farmers, while the "lits" consider the lawyers a bunch of wise guys and big shots.
—"A Senior Lawyer" in the *Cumberland Collegian,* May 14, 1937

As a result of World War I, enrollment plunged at Cumberland Law School. The 1914–15 school year had seen a total enrollment of 184 students with 128 receiving their LL.B. degrees.[1] By 1917–18 the total law school enrollment dropped to 76, with 53 receiving degrees.[2] In the following year, the effect of the war was even sharper. During 1918–19 the law school enrollment fell to 58 and the school awarded only 19 degrees, 6 in January 1919 and 13 in June.[3] But with the war's end, enrollment soared. The following chart shows the total law school enrollment for the academic years 1919–20 through 1933–34, taken from the law school and general catalogues:

1919–20	188	1926–27	334
1920–21	not available; 120 law degrees conferred in 1921.	1927–28	355
		1928–29	348
1921–22	233	1929–30	342
1922–23	not available; 105 law degrees conferred in 1923.	1930–31	318
		1931–32	303
1923–24	225	1932–33	377
1924–25	245	1933–34	304
1925–26	283		

At the beginning of this period most students arrived by rail, disembarking at the Lebanon station, a couple of blocks from Caruthers Hall, and made their way to the Union Bank and Trust Company on the Square. There, W. J. Baird, a bank officer who doubled as law school treasurer, received tuition payments and provided information on the beginning of classes and such mundane subjects as lodging.[4] At the end of their year in Lebanon, graduates generally left by train as well. G. Frank Burns, the Cumberland University historian who grew up in Lebanon during the twenties and thirties, recalls that on graduation day the young lawyers were always anxious that the morning ceremonies be concluded in time to catch the 12:45 train out of town.[5] With the mass marketing of the automobile, the growth of motorbus transportation, and the paving of southern roads,[6] throughout the 1920s many more came by car or bus.[7] For example, in the late summer of 1924, Mr. and Mrs. Parham H. Williams, a young Mississippi couple and parents of the future Cumberland dean, drove a Model T Ford from Pickens, Mississippi, to Lebanon. With the lack of both money and motels, they camped out along the way. After both received their law degrees, they returned to Mississippi by the same method.[8] Clifford E. Sanders of the class of 1933 hitchhiked to Lebanon from his home in Oklahoma.[9] The Nashville-Lebanon Pike, which eventually became U.S. 70, then ran directly in front of Caruthers Hall, permitting a student to step off the bus directly across from the law building. A sign for those approaching from Nashville directed students to the law school on the north side of the highway or to the undergraduate campus, which lay a block to the south.

Whether they came by rail or highway, Cumberland continued to draw students from afar. Law students who enrolled for 1927–28, in which Cumberland enjoyed its second highest enrollment for the years 1920–1947, hailed from thirty-one states and two foreign countries. The catalogue records one came from Liverpool, England, and another from Montreal, Canada, and the remainder from the following states:

Tennessee	77	Kentucky	11	Pennsylvania	3
Texas	56	New York	9	Colorado	2
Oklahoma	48	Louisiana	7	Nebraska	2
Florida	45	West Virginia	4	North Carolina	2
Mississippi	16	Georgia	3	North Dakota	2
Arkansas	14	Illinois	3	Virginia	2
Missouri	14	Iowa	3		
Alabama	11	Maryland	3		

California, Connecticut, Delaware, Maine, Massachusetts, Michigan, South Carolina, and the state of Washington accounted for one each.

This pattern continued into the thirties. In October 1933 the law school student body included representatives from 28 states, Canada, and the District of Columbia. Tennessee dominated with 87, followed by Texas with 38, and Oklahoma with 24. The student newspaper boasted that the law school drew "men from all walks of life; men from over half the states of the Union; men professing religions and creeds of many kinds."[10] The Report of the Survey of Tennessee Law Schools conducted in 1937 noted that during 1934–37 Tennessee accounted for only 30 percent of the student body. As to the rest: "Texas, Oklahoma, Kentucky, and Arkansas seem to be best represented, but there are also students from states from Maine to California, and in fact from all parts of the country."[11]

Though Cumberland did not impose any prelaw college requirement until 1938, many earlier law students had attended college, and some had received undergraduate degrees. For years a law school organization for "wandering Greeks" sustained fraternity men whose undergraduate fraternity did not have a Cumberland chapter.[12] A few individual examples give a snapshot of the law students' backgrounds.

James V. Allred, class of 1921, who became attorney general and then governor of Texas, had attended Rice Institute (now Rice University) in

Houston for one term.[13] Margaret Peters, class of 1931, graduated from Monmouth College in Monmouth, Illinois, with majors in English and Latin.[14] Leroy Collins, also class of 1931 and later governor of Florida, had attended one year at a business college before a Cumberland graduate persuaded him to further his education in Lebanon.[15] Clifford E. Sanders attended Southwestern State University in Weatherford, Oklahoma, before hitchhiking his way to Lebanon. Harry Phillips, from the nearby community of Watertown, Tennessee, and later chief judge of the United States Court of Appeals for the Sixth Circuit, took his law degree in 1933 after completing an illustrious career the previous year as a Cumberland undergraduate: editor-in-chief of the yearbook, captain of the debate team, and winner of the state oratorical contest.[16] However, significant college work was more the exception than the rule.

Women had attended the law school well before this period. To put this into perspective, Harvard Law School did not admit women until 1950. Beginning in 1922, the law school catalogue added a statement whose bold print made it clear that they were welcome, whether or not they intended to practice law: " *Women are admitted* to the same classes with men as students. The course, being thoroughly practical, prepares the student either to practice law, or to conduct other business according to law."

Margaret Peters recalled that there were several women in her class of 1931, although she was the only married woman. Sara Hardison, who later became the law librarian and instructor in legal bibliography, was the only woman in the class that graduated in January 1923, but there were other women enrolled in the larger classes before and after hers.[17]

However they traveled to Lebanon, wherever they hailed from, whatever educational attainments they brought with them, and whatever their gender, Cumberland law students of this era were all in a hurry. They wanted and often needed to finish school, get their law license, find employment or start a practice, as cheaply and quickly as possible. Professor Chambers spoke to the entering students on their first day. He told them, "I know why you are here. You are probably unable to attend a three-year law school, either because of money or because you are pursuing this degree late in life."[18]

Leroy Collins offers an example. When he failed to receive an Annapolis appointment, a state supreme court justice suggested that Collins try law school. Collins wasn't sure he wanted to practice law, or that he could afford three more years of education. Justice Glenn Terrell, a Cumberland graduate, assured Collins of a law degree's utility and pointed out that Cumberland offered a law degree in only one year.[19] Probably the advice of Terrell was repeated numerous times during the twenties and thirties, and throughout the South.

Richard Peters and his wife Margaret came to Cumberland because his employer laid him off. McGraw Edison of Chicago had sent Richard, originally from Missouri, to Chattanooga in 1929. Margaret then moved south and they were married, but within a year Richard was without a job. The couple had not heard of Cumberland before moving to Chattanooga, but Richard thought a law degree would help him in business. Probably he thought that Cumberland offered the chance to obtain a degree quickly while the economy was in a brief lull and before his company recalled him. When Margaret could not find a teaching job in Lebanon, she decided to go to law school as well under an unusual "family plan" that allowed a spouse to attend for one-third the regular tuition. Here again, Cumberland facilitated the education of women, years ahead of most other schools.

Cumberland students may have lacked money, but they did have plenty of determination. Clifford Sanders is a good example. Born in 1912, Sanders grew up on a poor farm near Colter, Oklahoma. Though his parents had only a third-grade education, they emphasized the importance of education to their children. The rural school in Colter offered only primary education. The nearest high school was in distant Elk City. Sanders was forced to move there, get a job, and work his way through high school. Sanders decided to become a lawyer and thought of attending the University of Oklahoma. But his brother had somehow heard of Cumberland, possibly through one of the many advertisements Cumberland published in various newspapers and magazines.[20] Sanders had no money for either tuition or room and board, but Cumberland offered him employment as janitor in Caruthers Hall in exchange for tuition, an elderly Lebanon lady gave him a room in exchange for helping around the house, and a tea room fed him in exchange for waiting tables. Working those three jobs, Sanders graduated from law school in 1933, went into practice, and later became judge on the Tennessee Court of Appeals.

During the year he and Margaret attended Cumberland, Dick Peters also worked as a manufacturer's representative for a company that sold then-new electric hot water heaters. Dick would catch a train out of Nashville on Friday night, call on a power company purchasing agent, his chief customers, and be back in Lebanon on Sunday. The company paid him twenty-five dollars for each weekend he worked.

Sara Hardison served as law librarian while attending classes.[21] Later, John A. Jamison, class of 1941, worked for her as evening attendant at the library and also, like Sanders before him, fired the ancient furnace in Caruthers. Jamison also served as university photographer to help defray his tuition.[22]

The tuition and fees remained low. Through 1925, students paid $50 tuition per semester plus a contingent fee or university fee of $10 per term and a library fee of $10 per term. Seniors paid an additional $10 diploma fee.[23] By 1928, with enrollments booming, tuition for the one-year course had increased to $100 per semester and the library fee from $10 to $12.50 per term. In 1933, the law school increased its tuition to $107.50 but dropped the separate library fee. In that year it also raised the tuition for the optional second-year course to $105.00 per semester, plus the usual additional fees. After declining during the mid and late 1930s, tuition and fees for the second year increased slightly to $70 per term in 1940–41. Beginning in June 1942, the law school operated on a quarter rather than a semester system and charged $80 tuition and fees per quarter for the three quarters of the first year and $60 per quarter in the second year. In 1920, law students paid a total of $140 per year in tuition and fees ($50 tuition and $20 in fees per semester); by 1947 the amount paid had increased to $240 per year ($80 in tuition and fees per quarter). Considering inflation, that is not a large increase. The big difference was that the 1920 students faced tuition and fees for one year, while their 1946 counterparts remained for two years, and thereafter for three years.

Students in the twenties and thirties came to Cumberland for the one-year course. For those who had always dreamed of being a lawyer, like Clifford Sanders, Cumberland offered the possibility of passing the bar and starting practice more quickly than this could be accomplished by any other route. Until the mid-1930s, Tennessee allowed a candidate with one year of law school study to sit for the bar. However, Cumberland students were not doing well on the Tennessee bar exam in these years. For the years

1933–1937, Cumberland had a pass rate of only 45 percent for first-time takers, compared with 88 percent for the University of Tennessee and 78 percent for Vanderbilt.[24] Other states, particularly in the South, either allowed students to take their bar exam after one year of study or recognized the Tennessee license earned after one year.

For those without plans to practice law, particularly those who were not college graduates, Cumberland also offered the prestige of a university degree in only one year. The long list of distinguished alumni in Cumberland's catalogue gave credibility to its program, and the widely dispersed Cumberland alumni provided a mechanism for spreading the word of the availability of Cumberland's one-year program. So long as Cumberland was permitted to hold unswervingly to its one-year program, it enjoyed record enrollments.

The 1938–39 Cumberland Law School Catalogue announced that effective September 1938, two years of law study would be required for the Cumberland degree. The Cumberland class that entered in September 1938 became the first for whom a two-year course of study was required for a degree. Though the final decision to adopt a two-year requirement may have been spurred by the visit of the ABA survey team in November 1937, the implementation of a two-year program had long been anticipated. In 1932 the Tennessee Supreme Court announced an increase of the requirement for taking the Tennessee bar exam from one year of law study to two, effective for those taking the exam after June 1, 1934.[25] Subsequently, the court agreed to extend the effective date of the new rule to January 1935.[26] While offering the option of a second year of study, Cumberland did not adopt a requirement of two years of study to earn the LL.B. until December 1937, when that requirement was imposed for the class entering in September 1938. The court's rule and the likelihood that two years would eventually be required for a degree, perhaps exacerbated by the deepening of the Depression, had an immediate impact on enrollment, beginning in September 1934. The 1933–34 academic year had seen the largest enrollment in Cumberland's history. The following year saw a modest decrease in enrollment, which then plunged in 1938 with the imposition of the two-year degree requirement.

The trend is clearly seen by comparing the number of graduates with the numbers in the second-year classes for the years when the second year was not required for graduation. Table 2 shows both the drop in enrollment and the very few who enrolled in the second year while it was optional.

TABLE 2. Numbers of Graduates and Second-Year Students, 1920–1942

Year	*January graduates*	*June graduates*	*Total graduates*	*Nondegree, 2d-year, or special class*	*Total*
1920–21			120		120
1921–22			147		147
1922–23			105		105
1923–24	34	149	183		183
1924–25	52	158	210		210
1925–26	50	179	229		229
1926–27	54	176 plus 3 in Aug. '27	223		223
1927–28	49	156	205		205
1928–29	58	166 plus 3 in Aug. '29	227	7	234
1929–30	44	157	201		201
1930–31	52	156	208		208
1931–32	43	186	229		229
1932–33	55	217	272		272
1933–34	59	217	276		276
1934–35	28	115	143	12	155
1935–36	31	137	168	25	193
1936–37	30	127	157	17	174
1937–38	33	123	156	2 years now required for LL.B.	156
1938–39	49	7	56		56
1939–40	none	48	48		48
1940–41	11	38	49		49
1941–42	5	N/A	N/A		N/A

Separate law catalogues were not published during the war. However, a transcript of the general university catalogue published as the law catalogue for 1942–43 indicates that in that year there were a total of 50 law students—31 juniors and 19 seniors.

Even allowing for other factors—the deepening of the Depression in the mid-thirties, the anticipation of war in the later thirties and early forties—it is apparent that the lengthening of the course of study blunted an important competitive advantage Cumberland enjoyed with its one-year degree program. In September 1934, with Tennessee's two-year law study soon to take effect, the 183 Cumberland undergraduates exceeded the 153 law students, the first such tilt at Cumberland in decades.[27]

Like so many other institutions of higher education, Cumberland Law School's enrollment surged when the veterans returned after World War II. In July 1946, Cumberland finally adopted a three-year curriculum. Students enrolled on July 10, 1946, could continue under the two-year program then in effect. The 1946–47 general university catalogue reported 152 seniors (that is, students who would graduate in June 1947), 167 juniors (those who would graduate in June 1948), and 5 special students.

Whether enrolled in the one-year course or later in the second-year course, the program of study followed by Cumberland students in the period 1920–1947 varied from that followed by law students today. Even the nomenclature was different. Today we most commonly use the word "course" to refer to separate self-contained units of instruction dealing with a specific subject; we speak of the "contracts course" or the "civil procedure course." Cumberland catalogues of this period use "course" to mean the entire program of instruction, from start to finish, as in "regular one year course" and later "two year course." Because each subject was taught from a separate book (sometimes a multivolume treatise) Cumberland students and faculty sometimes used "book" to refer to separate subjects within "the course." A class proceeded through the course, one book at a time, beginning with the first book in the course, Caruthers's *History of a Lawsuit,* an introduction to Tennessee practice and pleading.

Students could rent the books, but the catalogue recommended their purchase. Because these were books used by practicing lawyers, a student could leave Cumberland with the nucleus of a law library. In the regular one-year course, later the first year of the two-year course, students read only treatises.

The 1920–21 law school catalogue listed the books studied and the sequence of their study:

FOR THE JUNIOR CLASS	FOR THE SENIOR CLASS
History of a Lawsuit	Barton's *Suit in Equity*
Stephens on Pleading	Story's *Equity Jurisprudence*
Greenleaf on Evidence (vol. 1)	Kent's *Commentaries* (vol. 4)
Clark on Corporations	*Parsons on Contracts*
Kent's *Commentaries* (vols. 1–3)	Black's *Constitutional Law*
Bigelow on Torts	May's *Criminal Law*

Some of the texts listed (*Stephens on Pleading, Greenleaf on Evidence,* the four volumes of Kent's *Commentaries,* the two volumes of Story's *Equity Jurisprudence,* and the three volumes of *Parsons on Contracts*) were among the classics of the nineteenth-century legal canon, still alive in Cumberland well into the twentieth century. These were extended works of great analytical and theoretical weight. Other books on this list were of the type West Publishing Company popularized in its "Hornbook" series, elementary one-volume treatises, featuring concise "black-letter" statements of legal principles, followed by slightly more extended analysis, and authored by contemporary law professors. In the 1920s, and still today, law students, not practitioners, make most frequent use of them, and the students read them as supplemental study aides to casebook courses.

The ever-growing popularity of the Socratic, casebook method, with its insistence on analysis rather than answers, prompted a "cottage industry" of books designed to help the case method student find out "what is the law." These books were often written by the very instructors who assiduously dodged all classroom efforts by students to force them to state clearly "what is the law." Changes in Cumberland's prescribed textbook list during the decade of the 1920s took the form of substituting a treatise of the hornbook type for one of the nineteenth-century classics.

In 1922, the venerable *Stephens on Pleading,* actually an American edition of the work originally authored by Serjeant Stephens of the English bar, disappeared from the junior class list, and a hornbook, *Hughes on Federal Procedure,* entered the senior class course.[28] The following year, another hornbook by the same author, *Hughes on Evidence,* supplanted the sixteenth edition of *Greenleaf on Evidence.*[29]

The four volumes of *Commentaries* authored in 1826–30 by James Kent, the "American Blackstone," disappeared from the list in 1925. One-volume treatises of the genre previously described, *Peck's Domestic Relations* (1920), *Childs on Personal Property* (1914), and *Rood on Wills,* replaced the first three volumes of Kent on the junior class list, while *Tiffany on Real Property* (1903) took the place of Kent's fourth volume for the seniors. The same year of 1925 also saw the addition of a book on legal ethics: *Warvelle's Legal Ethics* (1920).[30]

Joseph Story doubtless would be pleased to know that he outlasted James Kent in the Cumberland course, if only for one year. In 1926, however, the school dropped Story's two-volume *Equity Jurisprudence* in favor of *Bispham's Equity Jurisprudence.* On law student bookshelves in Lebanon, from 1926 forward, only one of the nineteenth-century classics, the three volumes of *Parsons on Contracts,* shared space with the hornbook-type treatises that now dominated the Cumberland course. Perhaps because of criticism of the continued use of Parsons in the 1937 Report of the American Bar Association team surveying legal education in Tennessee,[31] Cumberland substituted Williston's more modern book in September 1938.[32] Almost immediately, however, Parsons was back in its place. Jamison, who entered the two-year program in 1939, recalls studying contracts from the three volumes of Parsons, and this classic continued to be used at least until adoption of the three-year curriculum in 1946.[33]

With the exception of Parsons, by the late 1920s the texts used in the one-year course were of the black-letter, hornbook genre, lacking both the intellectual and the physical weight of Kent or Story. This had two consequences. On the one hand, it undermined the philosophical basis for the textbook method, which was deference to the authority of the great textbook authors, a deference earned by their learning and by the wide acceptance of their work. Justifying the study of textbooks over lectures by the individual professors, the 1920 Cumberland law catalog reasserted, in repetition of decades of practice: "The law is in the textbook. The professor can no more make the law than the student himself. Every subject upon which a lecture could be given has been exhausted by the ablest professors and printed in books after the most careful revision by the authors. We would regard it as an imposition on students and as presumptuous on our part to pretend that we could improve upon Kent, Story, Greenleaf, Parsons, and others who have given to the public, in printed form and acceptable to all, lectures on every branch of the law."

As the statement implies, the strength of the textbook method's claim to superiority rested upon the authority of the textbook authors. When Cumberland substituted texts that were concise and purely descriptive, less analytical and theoretical, for those of writers such as Kent and Story, it undercut much of its own claim for the superiority of reading texts over parsing cases.

On the other hand, while the student-oriented texts of the hornbook variety lacked the intellectual vigor of the nineteenth-century treatises, their substitution in one sense benefited the Cumberland students in the one-year course. The black-letter books often discussed the leading cases featured in the casebooks they served to supplement, and the topics included corresponded to the coverage in the leading casebooks. This often improved the course content, as many topics of the nineteenth-century treatises were archaic. Adoption of the modern study aids meant that Cumberland students in the one-year course studied essentially the same topics as students in the modern casebook schools, albeit through radically different classroom methodology.

Cumberland students approved of the textbook approach. Judge Clifford E. Sanders, class of 1933, still expresses a preference for the textbook method, observing that textbooks condense the principles involved and that individual case decisions frequently fail to state the applicable rule as clearly as text writers. Russell Grant, as valedictorian in 1935 of Cumberland's first nondegree second-year class, editorialized on the merits of the case and text methods. He found cases more interesting, though sometimes baffling to the student. Textbooks, he thought, laid a better foundation, and he approved of Cumberland's continued use of textbooks in the first year.[34] John A. Jamison, class of 1941, who like Grant studied from textbooks in the first year and switched to casebooks in the second year, still today endorses the use of textbooks in the first year.

Though the Cumberland catalogue firmly maintained in bold print that Cumberland was "NOT A LECTURE SCHOOL," classes in fact consisted of a combination of lecture and question and answer, known as recitation. An alumnus of the years 1870–71, addressing the weekly university assembly in 1935, recalled that the question-and-answer method used when he attended Cumberland was "well nigh perfect," and was pleased to learn it was still used.[35] Margaret Peters, a member of the class of 1931, recalls that Chambers, who was the "senior judge" at the time she attended, sat behind a desk on a platform in front of the student seats and lectured, while the students took notes. Though Chambers was a serious person who intimidated some of the students, Peters recalls that he had quite a sense of humor, and like students today, the class soon learned to laugh at the teacher's pet jokes. Chambers was born in 1859, and Sanders recalls that by the early 1930s, he had begun to appear feeble, an appearance that was accentuated by a palsy when he stroked his long beard. Classes were not entirely lecture, however. Students were also required to recite, that is, to answer questions asked by the instructor on the basis of the assigned text. In Sanders's recollection, the question-and-answer approach predominated. He recalls that Sara Hardison, who served as Chambers's secretary in addition to her librarian duties, sat beside him in the classroom. Chambers read a question, and Hardison called the name of the next student to answer the question. Jamison recalls that the professor had a student assistant sitting next to him with cards, each bearing the name of a student. When the professor asked a question, the assistant shuffled the cards and drew one at random, selecting the student who would be required to attempt an answer. A student who was unprepared could respond "check."[36] Class attendance was expected, with apparently a maximum of eighteen cuts allowed per year.[37]

While the question-and-answer process was interactive and avoided the dullness of a straight lecture, it fell short of the ideal Socratic dialogue, in which the law teacher invites the student to express a view as to the facts, issue, or underlying principle of a case and then, gradually, question by question, leads the student to a self-realization of the incompleteness or internal inconsistency of the view the student expressed. Ultimately, if not by the end of the hour, then by the end of the term, the student is led to a more complete or more coherent view, a result that itself is less important than the training the student has received in careful, logical thinking. Of course, those undertaking to teach Socratically often fall somewhat short of this ideal goal.

The Cumberland questions and answers were less ambitious. Their fundamental purpose was to test whether the student had done the reading.

The American Bar Association's Survey Committee that visited Cumberland classes in November 1937 raised doubt that the level of questioning accomplished even the minimal goal of forcing students to prepare. The committee reported that for many of the questions asked, "the answer is indicated by the question itself or is so simple that it could be given by a good guesser."[38]

The recollections of Judge Clifford Sanders, class of 1933, give a flavor of the classroom dialogue with Judge Chambers, indicating that there were often follow-up questions that asked for a more elaborate response: "I think generally . . . maybe he would say, 'Mr. Sanders, you define a tort for us.' Or he might give you an example . . . say: 'If somebody wrongfully sues you in a lawsuit, do you have a right to sue them for damages?' and then maybe the next question—you may say 'Well, yes, you, do'—'What must you prove in order to be able to recover against him?'"[39]

Jamison also recalls that instructors' questions called for more than yes or no answers. Instead, the question called for a short discussion by the student, or the teacher would pose a hypothetical case that the student attempted to resolve.

Judge Chambers typed out the questions he planned to ask in class, along with the correct answers, and read the questions from the typescript as he conducted class. The questions were generally straightforward and quite specific, calling for responses drawn from the reading. Common types of questions asked for a definition ("What is a contract?"), the supplying of a legal term ("At common law, what kind of contract was it that was called a specialty?"), the statement of a rule ("What was the rule at common law as to whether or not the consideration could be inquired into; so as to show whether or not the contract was void because not supported by a valuable consideration"), or the elements of some legal concept ("What are the essentials of a legal contract?").[40] They are not particularly thought-provoking, but neither could they be answered with a yes or no, nor could the answers be easily surmised from the questions themselves, as the ABA Survey Committee concluded about the questions and answers in Neil's torts class. To be prepared to answer Chambers's questions, the student had to have done the reading, although he need not have spent much time thinking about what he had read.

Through 1937, students took examinations in the second-floor auditorium of Caruthers Hall, following the completion of each book studied.

The examinations were as straightforward as the questions asked in class. When the ABA Survey team visited Cumberland in November 1937, the juniors in the one-year curriculum had just finished the three-week segment on corporations; that is, they had just finished the third book in the semester. The examination consisted, in toto, of twelve straightforward questions of the type asked in class, suggesting that the examinations often consisted of selected, perhaps reworded, classroom questions. Some examples of the corporations questions are: "(3) How is membership acquired in a stock corporation? In a nonstock corporation? (6) What three things are essential to the existence of a de facto corporation? (8) Out of what only may a dividend lawfully be declared? (10) At a stockholders meeting what members must attend to constitute a quorum?"[41] Another example of final examinations is Chambers's 1926 Legal Ethics Exam. The questions were all drawn from the twenty-four questions Chambers had prepared for classroom use.[42]

If the purpose of classroom questions was to assure that students had done the reading, the purpose of examination questions was to assure that they had not only done the reading but had paid attention in class. Cumberland students must have done so, because grades on the exams were generally good. For example, exactly 150 first-year law students took the November 1937 corporations test described above. Fifty-nine of them received a grade of 90 or better on a scale of 100.

The practice of testing at the end of each book must have ceased with the adoption of the two-year program in 1938. Jamison recalls that in 1939–41, though subjects were still taught one book at a time, there was no exam when a book was completed. Instead, the faculty tested students in two days at the end of each semester through examinations that covered each of the semester's subjects. Jamison recalls that this required burning "a lot of midnight oil" because of the necessity of reviewing all the subjects for the semester, but found, as many law students still do, that the "subjects would sort of tie themselves together" and "you would see the relationship of one legal subject to another."

A formal moot court program paralleled the classroom work. By beginning with *History of a Lawsuit,* followed by the book on evidence, students became equipped to participate fully in the practice courts. According to a 1933 story in the *Cumberland Collegian,* the moot court "has all the earmarks of a regular court with the officers and clerks doing the duties that are becoming to an official of the law."[43] Even from the first day students could participate by serving as jurors.[44] Each "party"—that is, role-playing law student—was represented by three lawyers, typically a senior with two junior lawyers.[45]

At the beginning of the spring semester in 1933, Judge Gilreath presided over the opening of the moot court, which fined "Sheriff" Sherman for not being present to perform the ceremonial offices of the sheriff in opening court. The case tried that day resulted in a $40 verdict for the plaintiff, and "each of the attorneys showed good preparation in his argument, with Lawyer Templeton showing exceptional oratorical ability for the plaintiff." The student newspaper reported the names of all the lawyers and witnesses and commented that they "told good stories on the direct examination." Later that term the newspaper reported a hung jury in a case tried before Gilreath and promised that the "cow case" of John Otho vs. Silas Wilson would be tried later in the week, if time permitted after the trial of the regular case set for that day.[46]

When Judge Albert Williams returned to the law faculty in 1933, he expanded the moot court program. His moot court met at 4 o'clock every afternoon. Williams presided and also delivered lectures on practice and pleading. The *Cumberland Collegian* regularly reported the docket of his trials, including the names of the fictitious parties, the names of the attorneys, and the nature of the cases. Civil cases included claims for fraud, malicious prosecution, negligence, and the inevitable dog bite; the only case on the criminal docket was a charge of embezzlement.[47]

Meanwhile, Gilreath continued to preside over moot court at 1 o'clock on Tuesdays. A February 1933 issue of the *Cumberland Collegian* noted that the case of a Lebanon mule buyer, Thomas Lewis against Richard Brown, father of a minor who had injured Lewis in an accident, had been held before Judge Gilreath and a packed house. While the plaintiff, supported by testimony from his doctor, also played by a law student, testified effectively as to the excruciating pain he had endured since the accident, a failure to establish the elements of the family purpose doctrine resulted in the court granting preemptory instructions on behalf of the defendant dad. The article also promised that "the famous cow case" was definitely set for the following week.[48] Unfortunately no report of this mysterious case has been preserved.

The student newspaper provided an extended account of the case of John Fine vs. George Wilburn, a case involving the contractual incapacity of Fine, a minor. It vividly described the testimony of the witnesses, the cross-examination of "resonant-voiced Barrister Gibbs" and the "impressive and master" jury argument of Counselor Copeland. It set the mood for the trial with a description of the "dimly lighted" courtroom, jammed with a "throng of spectators," who attended the proceedings "despite the Turkish-bath atmosphere."[49]

Judge Williams, on his return to the law school in 1933, kept an oversize, red leatherbound minute book of the proceedings of the Cumberland Moot Court. The professor had sat as a trial judge in Lebanon, and the moot court minute book was similar to those used by county clerks for docket entries. Handwritten entries mirrored the trial of moot cases before Williams, Gilreath, Fancher, MacFarland, and others through the end of 1947. A few exhibits—a check drawn on a Lebanon bank; a Tennessee Central Railroad baggage claim, bearing authentic stamps and handwritten notations—remain tucked in the minute book.[50]

By the period 1939–41 student energy and imagination had carried moot court proceedings beyond the walls of Caruthers Hall, into the community. Students not only conducted the trials but also staged the crimes and all ancillary proceedings. The local sheriff, chief of police, and undertaker played themselves in these theatrical productions, staged at Lebanon jail and the local funeral parlor, culminating in the trial in the courtroom of Caruthers Hall. Jamison recalls one "jail break" in which some fifteen students broke into the Lebanon jail, using a telephone pole as a battering ram, to free the accused in a murder case (the sheriff actually let the accused out the back door, and no public property was injured). In the same case, the victim was "embalmed" by the local mortician because, as Jamison said, "none of us knew anything about embalming." The faculty barely tolerated these elaborate spoofs. While they permitted the use of the courtroom for the "trial," none of the faculty members wanted to preside, and the students were forced to obtain a local attorney to serve as judge.

Some students participated only minimally in the moot court program,[51] but for those who were active in moot court, it offered an effective counterpoint to the regular curriculum. The student studying law through the textbook method of instruction saw little factual context underlying the legal principles. One advantage of the casebook method is the importance laid on an understanding of the facts of the case. Moot courts provided Cumberland students with hands-on experience based on concrete (if imagined) facts and on the workaday functioning of the trial courts. The moot court program thus complemented textbook instruction in the way that the lab component of a chemistry course complements the classroom lectures.

The elite three-year schools that employed rigorous Socratic casebook instruction served law students seeking employment with the large corporate law firms that had emerged in New York, other major urban areas, and even the larger cities of the south. One commentator has observed that the Harvard curriculum served as a sorting mechanism, certifying to the intelligence, mental discipline, and capacity for hard work of those who survived its rigors.[52] But few Cumberland students of the 1920s and 1930s sought employment in such large firms. Most returned to small county seat towns or headed for southern cities, where they found employment at meager wages in an office of one or two lawyers, or hung out a shingle for themselves.[53] Success, in the form of a prosperous practice or public office, depended upon becoming known in the community through church, lodge, civic, or political activities.

Cumberland offered the opportunity to acquire the skills useful to such a career. Public speaking was one of those skills. Whether appearing in court, speaking to church or civic groups, or delivering a political address, Cumberland students needed to know how to make a speech. Each semester several law students took advantage of a course in public speaking offered by Mrs. Mary Gregory Rousseau, a public speaking instructor in the Lit School.[54] For the convenience of law students, the course met in Caruthers Hall. Under Rousseau's tutelage, students debated Roosevelt's Court packing plan and gave prepared and extemporaneous talks to the class and, once a semester, to visitors. Those expecting a political career benefited from the "Heckler's Day."[55]

Longstanding debating and literary societies provided other opportunities for aspiring orators. The oldest, the Amasagassean Society that traced its history back to the Kentucky Cumberland University, continued on in the 1930s, as did the Philomathean Society. The Philomathean Society appears to have been composed exclusively of law students, while the

Amasagassean Society included undergraduates, including members of the undergraduate debating teams.[56] In 1921, several members of the Philomathean recognized a need for more than one organization in the law school devoted to the training of orators, and revived the Caruthers Literary Society.[57] The revival was brief; by the 1930s, Caruthers Literary Society had disappeared from the scene, while a new law school public speaking group, "The Circle," emerged. The Philomathean was huge, with a membership that was almost coextensive with that of the student body, but the Circle limited the number of members to twenty "in order that each person may speak at least once a week."[58] The Philomathean Society met each week and awarded the degree of "Bachelor of Oratory" to members who attended regularly and took part in a prescribed number of programs.[59] Another group, the Barristers Club, emphasized after-dinner speaking. In 1939, the Barristers contrived a fake murder when the speaker lost patience with a "heckler," drew a gun and "shot" him; the "murder" was then followed by a trial that tested the powers of observation and recall of the members and guests.[60]

Cumberland law students were aware that many important political leaders had emerged from Caruthers Hall. With the Roosevelt victory in 1932, Cordell Hull, '91, one of the many Cumberland alumni prominent in public life, became United States secretary of state. The dignified Hull enjoyed widespread public support and might well have received the Democratic nomination in 1940 had Roosevelt not decided to seek an unprecedented third term.[61] A photograph taken by a member of the class of 1941 shows a group of Hull-for-president law students on the steps of Caruthers Hall. James Allred, '21, won the governorship of Texas in 1935, while still not much older than many law students. The pages of the *Cumberland Collegian* often featured Cumberland alumni who held political or judicial office or carried stories noting the large number of Cumberland alumni on the bench or in high political office.

While law students at Harvard or Chicago struggled for the credentials that would win access to corporate law firms—law review membership and top grades—law students at Cumberland polished the skills of political organizing and maneuvering that might lead to political success. Political energies focused on class elections. As the student newspaper observed, with some hyperbole, a law class election "has always meant to the students and town-folk of Lebanon riots, cracked heads and excitement." The February 1933 election of senior class officers had been preceded by "meetings, conferences, whisperings of 'cliques,' 'machines,' 'rail-roading,' and stuffing of ballot boxes, a meeting of the Amasagassean Society came very close to ending in riot." Faculty members did not absent themselves from these affrays. Instead, they actually assumed a mentoring role; through offering mature advice and chairing some of the meetings, they attempted to assure a minimal semblance of order. Probably the faculty enjoyed the exuberance of the electoral process almost as much as the students.[62]

The most coveted class office was that of president. Other positions were vice president, secretary-treasurer, orator, corresponding secretary, student council representative, and reporter.[63] Occasionally a woman aspired to one of the lesser offices, and Margaret Peters was elected secretary-treasurer of the class of 1931. The most visible function of the class president was to speak at the commencement ceremony. In June 1931, the class president had to return to Texas and the vice president to Indiana immediately following final exams, and neither could stay for commencement. In their absence, the duty of speaking on behalf of the class fell on Mrs. Peters. She recalls that some friends of her husband, Richard, urged him to persuade her to step aside. To his credit, Richard refused to do so but urged her to spend plenty of time in preparing the speech. Her remarks received President Stockton's compliments, and she recalls that they even attracted grudging respect from her male classmates, who admitted that they hated to have her do it but conceded in all seriousness that she had done almost as well as they could.

America is a nation of joiners, and Cumberland law students had plenty of opportunity to practice the arts of joining, belonging, meeting, organizing, and socializing. Today, in 1997, law students seldom participate in extracurricular activities outside the law school. However, in the 1920s and 1930s, while Cumberland students engaged in various law-school-related activities, they also rushed national social fraternities, played on intercollegiate athletic teams, wrote for the student newspaper, and edited the college yearbook.

In 1931, along with a local chapter of a national law school fraternity, Sigma Delta Kappa (which had a chapter house near the law school), and a national legal sorority, Iota Tau Tau (for which Sara Hardison provided leadership),[64] there were chapters of three national social fraternities, Sigma Alpha Epsilon (members that year included future Governor Collins and future Judge Phillips), Lambda Chi Alpha (future governor Allred had been active when he attended Cumberland in 1920–21); and the newest, Delta Kappa Phi. The SAE and Lambda Chi had chapter houses on West Main Street near the law school and included law students in their membership. Some students had joined these fraternities during prelaw years at Cumberland or at other universities, but others pledged while in law school.[65]

Law students continued to play intercollegiate football until World War II. The 1935 squad that won the Smoky Mountain Conference included second-year law student Wilson West, who was named all-conference center.[66] The Glee Club claimed both law and literary choristers.[67] Despite the availability of opportunities to participate in university-wide activities, most law students, like today, found themselves too busy to take advantage of the opportunities.[68] Many no doubt felt a sense of condescension toward the undergraduates and avoided activities involving them. While many law students boarded in the town, the fourth floor of the men's dormitory on the main campus was reserved for law students. John Jamison, who lived in the dorm, recalls that the law students were unhappy to eat breakfast, lunch, and dinner with the "kids" from the lit school.

Organizations existed in sufficient variety to provide an opportunity for everyone. Law students organized a number of state specific clubs. In 1932, these included clubs for Florida, Mississippi, Tennessee, Texas, Alabama, and Virginia,[69] most still extant today. Students with particular interests formed clubs. The Square and Compass Club served faculty and students who were Masons, and the Reserve Officers Club sought former officers, apparently numerous in the law school.[70] Gilreath led the university Sunday school class, a nondenominational class that met in Caruthers Hall each Sunday morning. The class was open to all Cumberland students, but doubtless law students comprised the majority. The Sunday school elected officers, including a student council representative, and sponsored picnics and other social events.[71] Sometimes a mongrel dog named Rascal, of whom more will be said later, attended Gilreath's Sunday morning Bible study.

Though Cumberland law students attended Gilreath's Bible study class on Sunday morning, some engaged in quite different activities the night before. During Prohibition no legal alcohol was available, but Cumberland students knew about the Nashville speakeasies and could get there by bus.[72] With the repeal of Prohibition, the university reiterated its policy of total abstinence. In April 1933, shortly after repeal, the *Cumberland Collegian* published an open letter from President Stockton stating Cumberland's stand on the vexing question of beer: "It is uncompromising. In our minds, beer is still in the same category with all intoxicants, which are forbidden as far as humanly possible on the campus of Cumberland."[73]

Because many law students were older and came from campuses with different policies on alcohol, predictable conflict ensued. Ultimately, the law school dean was the man who addressed that conflict in concrete terms. In his memoirs, Judge Neil recalled: "In later years, after I became Dean, the matter of discipline of students became my problem. It was no real problem, although President Stockton differed with me about it. The main problem was the over indulgence in drinking whiskey by a few students. Stockton always urged me to expel them from school summarily, yet I demurred from taking such drastic action. It was my insistence that we were not dealing with adolescents, but with young men who had passed that age and who must learn to exercise self discipline."[74]

From the earliest days, when Cumberland was affiliated with the Cumberland Presbyterians, down to the present, when Cumberland School of Law is a part of Baptist-related Samford University, alcohol has divided law students, who insist on their right to drink if and when they choose, and university administrators, who insist that no alcohol be permitted at any university event, including social events of student organizations. Now, as under Judge Neil, it falls to the dean to mediate the conflict.

Not all law students found the restrictive Cumberland University social environment to their liking. The May 14, 1937, issue of the *Cumberland Collegian,* devoted to the senior law class, carried a strong editorial from a man signing himself simply "A Senior Lawyer." The writer announced his intention to offer a view of Cumberland different from the glowing tributes that had appeared in previous senior class issues, "lest anyone be deceived into thinking this is the one Utopian College in the United States." His comments offer a clue as to why, twenty years later in the 1950s,

Cumberland alumni did not come forward with the contributions that would have allowed the school to continue in Lebanon.

Lack of social life topped the list of problems at Cumberland, according to "A Senior Lawyer": "Probably the largest problem here in our school life this year has been our social life, or rather, the lack of it. I should say that this hypothetical thing, Cumberland's Social Life, has consisted mainly of playing pingpong, attending church, holding our dances, balls and proms at a two by four tea room."

Moving right to the heart of the matter, "A Senior Lawyer" took exception to the restrictions placed on the female students at Cumberland University, a major source of dates for law students.

> The reform school restrictions on those unfortunates imprisoned in the girls' dormitories are another detriment to our social life in Cumberland. I realize that many co-eds in other colleges are even more restricted, if that be possible, but I am certain that the circumstances are somewhat different. Normal girls of college age cannot possibly be happy under such conditions as we have here. And as long as such rules exist, such rules will be broken which makes things twice as deplorable. It is disgusting to see girls having to sneak and lie to even get a minimum of pleasure out of life. It is true that too much liberty might be detrimental and if the girls were given an inch they might take a mile. Still, there is such a thing as a happy medium and reasonable treatment.
>
> From my knowledge of the facts, I should say that the three women supervising them, although no doubt fine women, are lacking in understanding of modern girls and times. The dean and matrons are probably doing their utmost and what they think is right to preserve our girls' character. Unfortunately their ideas are out of mode, having been correct during approximately, the gay '90's.

"A Senior Lawyer" saw other difficulties in the attitudes of the lawyers and the lits toward each other:

> Lack of cooperation between the law and literary schools is another deplorable condition. The former consider the latter a bunch of farmers, while the "lits" consider the lawyers a bunch of wise guys and big shots. I'm sure that the two schools in work, character, management, former life, age and temperament of the students themselves

> are entirely too foreign to ever promote harmony. As for the lawyers they put the money into our school and carry on the tradition. I met one student this year who lives fifteen miles from Lebanon and he did not know there was a literary school in Cumberland.[75]

As "A Senior Lawyer's" remark about the lawyers putting money into the school indicates, law students realized that their tuition dollars subsidized the undergraduate school. Perhaps they were aware that the Report of the Survey of Law Schools in Tennessee had verified that two-thirds of law school tuition revenue went to support the undergraduate division, or perhaps they simply made an educated guess based on respective enrollments and number of faculty. In either event, alumni who sense that they have already paid more than the cost of their education (rather than having received, as is often the case at well-endowed or state supported schools, an education that cost more than tuition) are unlikely to respond to appeals that they give more. With some justification, law students who are paying more than the cost of their education may feel that the university should adapt to standards of social behavior in accord with their views, rather than vice versa. Furthermore, if "A Senior Lawyer's" views reflect those of his fellows, the law students felt little pride in the university itself. When he wrote that the law students "carry on the tradition" of Cumberland's glory, he probably had in mind such law graduates as Cordell Hull, Howell Jackson, or Horace Lurton, who had achieved national renown. The undergraduate school, on the other hand, with a less cosmopolitan student body, was less well known outside of Tennessee. Notwithstanding the views of "A Senior Lawyer," many law students not only felt that Cumberland provided a sound legal education, but also enjoyed their stay in Lebanon.[76]

One creature who attended Cumberland Law School in the late thirties complained infrequently, at least as long as the law students bought him ice cream cones from Shannon's drug store. That creature was a white dog who answered to the name of "Rascal," or sometimes, more formally, "Rascality." Rascal belonged to a family who lived near the law school. From 1933, when he was about a year old, until his death in 1940, Rascal served as informal mascot to the law school. Beginning in about 1933, Rascal commenced regular attendance of law classes. Trotting into each class every day, he mounted the rostrum alongside the professor and student assistant where he listened as the young lawyers attempted to respond to the professor's questions. Rascal's law school attendance was unique among Cumberland students in that he never "checked," that is, passed when called on.[77] Despite the pressures of attending law school, Rascal did not ignore the need for religious instruction; each Sunday found him back in Caruthers Hall for Gilreath's Sunday School Class. Nor did he skip the required Friday assemblies of law and lit students in Caruthers court room, where his barks and gymnastics showed his appreciation of the speakers.[78] In 1935, more regular in his attendance than many of the graduating students, Rascal was officially awarded the degree of canine jurisprudence and made an honorary member of the class of 1935.[79]

This honor did not meet with universal approbation. One Lebanon resident, whose dog had apparently suffered the worst of it in an encounter with Rascal, wrote a heated letter to the editor, complaining that Rascal was nothing but a "bully." The editor acceded to the writer's request to withhold the name of the writer who feared "the displeasure of the student body."[80] Law students always suspected that Rascal harbored a hostility to lit students but was too much the gentlemen to display this aversion.[81]

Even though he received his degree in 1935, Rascal continued to attend law school, putting his long experience and profound knowledge of the law to good use by coaching the newer students on the answers they should give. It seems clear that Rascal preferred the old one-year course; after the optional second-year class was initiated Rascal remarked in an article in the *Cumberland Collegian,* "The second year class drives me frantic. They get so involved in hypothetical questions that even a dog has a hard time keeping his mind clear."[82] Whether Horack and Shafroth considered the views of Rascal in their condemnation of the simple "yes or no" questions they found marked first-year courses at Cumberland is unclear.

One quiet August evening in 1940, three weeks before the beginning of school, a heart attack claimed Rascal as he rested on the front porch of a neighbor's home. He was laid to rest in the shadow of Caruthers Hall. The students on their return conducted an appropriate memorial service in his honor, John A. Jamison, '41, officiating. In 1961, when the law school was moved to Birmingham, Rascal's remains were exhumed and reburied on Samford University's campus, next to the law building. Every spring, law day celebrations include a Rascal memorial service, and many law students bring their own pets. Jamison, the original officiant and now a retired judge, still presides over many of these ceremonies.

CHAPTER EIGHT

The Final Years in Lebanon 1947–1961

> The situation can be summarized in a sentence. It is a school recently reorganized which is working with excellent spirit and with all its might.
> —Elliott E. Cheatham, professor of law, Columbia University, in "The Law Schools of Tennessee, 1949," *Tennessee Law Review*

> Part of the decline [in enrollment] was accounted for by the ruinous effect of extending the law course to three years. Even though Cumberland University School of Law received full approval of the American Bar Association in February, 1949, the law school simply bled to death, slowly.
> —Frank Burns, *Phoenix Rising: The Sesquicentennial History of Cumberland University, 1842–1992*

In July 1947, Arthur Weeks, a thirty-two-year-old army veteran practicing law in Birmingham, Alabama, received a telephone call from Edwin Preston, the recently installed president of Cumberland University. Preston invited Weeks and his wife to visit Lebanon to explore the possibility of assuming leadership of Cumberland Law School. Preston was forthright: he told Weeks that he had already contacted two attorneys, and both had turned him down. Perhaps Weeks, who only a short time before had been exercising considerable responsibility as the chief American legal officer for the Bremen Enclave in occupied Germany, was a bit bored with the routine divorces and debtors court petitions that constituted the case load of a sole practitioner attempting to reopen a practice. In any event, he accepted Preston's invitation to visit Lebanon.[1]

In 1945 the New York City–based Board of Christian Education of the Presbyterian Church, U.S.A. (the denomination that absorbed the Cumberland Presbyterian Church in the 1906 merger), notified Cumberland that the board would no longer make the small annual financial contributions received in the past. Instead, the board intended to concentrate its support of Presbyterian higher education in Tennessee on Maryville College near Knoxville.[2] The Presbyterian Church, U.S.A., had sponsored Maryville since its founding in the nineteenth century.[3] Probably the leaders of the denomination had a greater affinity for Maryville than for Cumberland, affiliated until 1906 with a separate denomination with its own general assembly, the Cumberland Presbyterian Church.

The amount provided by the board was not large, and Cumberland probably welcomed the opportunity to seek sponsorship elsewhere. While Scotch-Irish settlers had made Presbyterianism the largest denomination in Tennessee at the time of Cumberland's founding in 1842, a century later that was no longer the case.[4] Cumberland's centennial catalogue included a table of the religious affiliations of enrolled students; Methodists and Baptists each ranked ahead of Presbyterians.[5] The opportunity to affiliate with a denomination with a larger membership in Tennessee and other southern states probably seemed like a stroke of good luck. In December 1945 the executive board of the Tennessee Baptist Convention accepted a proposal of Cumberland's Board of Trustees to transfer its campus and the sponsorship of its programs to the Tennessee Baptist Convention. In January 1946, Cumberland consummated the transfer, the old Cumberland board resigned, and the Tennessee Baptist Convention replaced it with a new board. W. Edwin Richardson, a Baptist minister, became chairman of the new board, which called Preston as president of the university.[6]

The new Baptist administration moved quickly to standardize the law school. All students entering after July 10, 1946, enrolled in a new three-year program of concurrent (rather than sequential) courses, using casebooks rather than texts. Admission required a minimum of two years of college. By the time Weeks visited Lebanon in the summer of 1947, the process of phasing out the old two-year program of sequential courses and first-year textbooks was well under way. Samuel Gilreath, who had returned from the war to the law school as its only full-time instructor, served as acting dean and taught the students completing the two-year program. A separate cadre of practitioners from Nashville and Lebanon, all part-time, taught the courses in the separate three-year program.[7]

Preston saw Cumberland University as well positioned to become the outstanding Baptist university in the Southern Baptist Convention. Cumberland was the only Baptist college in middle Tennessee. Prior to the acquisition of Cumberland, the Baptists had sponsored Tennessee Women's College in nearby Murphreesboro, but that institution was merged into Cumberland and its campus closed. Of the other two colleges sponsored by the Tennessee Baptist convention, Carson-Newman was located in Johnson City in the eastern tip of the state and Union University was in Jackson in the west. Like Cumberland they were located in small towns, but unlike Cumberland each was a considerable distance from any metropolitan area. Proximity to Nashville provided Cumberland with an advantage over these institutions.

Moreover, Nashville was the headquarters of the Southern Baptist Convention's Sunday School Board, one of the strongest institutions in the Southern Baptist denomination. Drawing its leadership from administrators and faculty members of Baptist colleges and universities, the Sunday School Board was a center for some of the brightest and best connected individuals in the Baptist higher education network. Preston foresaw an informal linkage of the Sunday School Board with Cumberland and believed that the Sunday School Board's prestige combined with Cumberland's long tradition provided the foundation for a great institution.

Preston relied on a major fund-raising drive, the Second Century Campaign, to fulfill this vision. Full accreditation of the law school might convince alumni that the school was worthy of their financial support, and Preston sought a dean who could accomplish that. Weeks must have seemed a good choice to Preston. Weeks was a Baptist, and while his law degree was from the University of Alabama, both Weeks and his wife received their undergraduate degrees from Howard College, later Samford University, the largest Baptist-supported institution in Alabama. Preston may also have known that Weeks's father-in-law, a Birmingham supporter of

Howard, had helped raise the funds that had kept Howard afloat during the Depression. Today the selection of a law school dean is usually the result of an elaborate search process involving faculty, alumni, and bar representatives, but the procedure was simpler in 1947. Preston offered a salary that Weeks considered comparable with other deans' compensation, and he accepted the offer. Weeks and his wife, simultaneously appointed as a part-time music teacher, moved to Lebanon for the 1947 fall term.[8]

However, Preston retained Gilreath as acting dean during 1947–48 and told Weeks that this was a matter of good public relations with the Tennessee bar and with the alumni. The law school celebrated its centennial in 1947 with a two-day convocation in October, shortly after the beginning of the fall term. While Preston wanted the new and permanent dean present for that event, it seemed politic to have Gilreath in the dean's chair in the centennial year as a symbol of continuity. Indeed, Gilreath's formal role on the centennial program was to present a historical sketch.[9]

Before he met Gilreath, Weeks thought that the retention of Gilreath as acting dean was to sooth Gilreath's ruffled sensibilities. After meeting Gilreath, Weeks realized that Gilreath was not at all sensitive about titles and positions. There was a reason other than alumni relations that Preston kept Gilreath as acting dean for the 1947–48 school year. Preston emphasized to Weeks that in the transition to a three-year program, the new program had been kept entirely separate from the old two-year program. Preston wanted the three-year program to be evaluated by the American Bar Association strictly on its own, with no linkage to the two-year program. Therefore, Weeks taught exclusively in the new program in 1947–48, while Gilreath had sole charge of the remaining students in the two-year program. By retaining Gilreath as acting dean, Weeks was spared any association with the two-year unapproved program, even to the extent of having served as dean of a law school that included an unapproved program. With the 1948–49 school year, Weeks was officially designated as dean.[10]

Cumberland enrolled its first students in the three-year program in the fall of 1946, and they were scheduled to graduate in the spring of 1949. Preston's goal was to have the school on the ABA-approved list by the time of their graduation. That was important. Since the 1920s, the ABA Section of Legal Education had recommended that eligibility to sit for state bar examinations be limited to persons who had graduated from a law school on the ABA-approved list.[11] By 1948, many states, including several southern states that supplied Cumberland with numerous students, had adopted rules that required bar exam applicants to have graduated from an ABA-approved law school.

For the first graduates of the three-year program to be assured of being permitted to sit for the bar in any state, ABA approval was required. Moreover, for the future, unless its graduates were to be restricted to taking the bar in states like Georgia and Mississippi, which imposed no legal study requirements, or in Tennessee, where Cumberland might expect to continue to be approved by the State Board of Bar Examiners, ABA approval was vital. Since Cumberland expected to continue to draw students from a wide array of states—the first class in the three-year program numbered only twenty-five but included individuals from nine states other than Tennessee—ABA approval was essential. In 1947–48, while Gilreath remained acting dean, Weeks put in place the changes that would allow the school to apply for ABA approval in 1948–49.

It was a propitious time to seek ABA approval. The legal education establishment, now confident that the standards it had long espoused were firmly established, seemed content to make peace with the wayward schools that had fought those standards in the 1920s and 1930s. For their part, the schools that once had resisted strenuously the drive for standardization had by now acquiesced. For example, at the quite unpleasant 1929 meeting of the ABA Section of Legal Education, the deans of John Marshall Law School in Chicago and Suffolk Law School in Boston carried the banner of opposition to the section's program of raising standards. Yet by 1951 John Marshall sought and received provisional approval, as did Suffolk in 1953.[12]

In addition, though the standards for ABA approval soon began to be tightened, year after year, in 1948 they remained light. The standards in 1948 required two years of pre-law-school college[13] and a three-year course of full-time law school work or four years part-time study. Approval required an "adequate library," interpreted as a minimum of "seventy-five hundred well-selected, usable" volumes, and no less than three full-time instructors. An approved school could not be "operated as a commercial enterprise" and compensation of faculty or administrators could not "depend on the number of students or on the fees received," Cumberland's traditional compensation practice that had been eliminated in the 1920s. A final requirement for accreditation was the judgment of the Council of Legal Education and Admissions to the Bar, a division of the ABA, that the school possessed "reasonably adequate facilities and maintains a sound educational policy."

The law library required improvement. Now designated the "Cordell Hull Law Library," it contained a sufficient number of books to meet the minimum volume count of 7,500 volumes.[14] However, the ABA's interpretation that an "adequate library" required the volumes be "well selected" posed a problem. The existing Cumberland library had been assembled to provide materials for supplemental state-specific research by students studying law by the textbook method. Dean Neil had insisted in his 1938 response to the ABA Survey Report that, in teaching from treatises, the instructor called attention to the illustrative or minority cases that occupied the lower portion of every treatise page.[15] While the likelihood was low that students went to the library and read those cases, the library had been assembled to facilitate that possibility. Weeks was pleasantly surprised to find that Cumberland had a very adequate case law collection. In addition to a complete set of the National Reporter System reporting cases from all states and from the federal courts, Cumberland's holdings also included each state's books of cases that predated the 1879 beginning of the National Court Reporter System.[16] Cumberland also had complete runs of various encyclopedias and annotations, such as *Corpus Juris Secundum, American Jurisprudence, Ruling Case Law,* and *American Law Reports,* used to research the case reporters. Nor were statutes neglected: the Cordell Hull Library boasted sets of codes from every state.[17]

Ironically for a school that for a century had based classroom instruction on the use of treatises or textbooks, beyond extra copies of those used in classes, the library contained few treatises. Apparently, the law school administration had thought that additional treatises would be merely redundant to those studied in class and add little value.[18]

Under the textbook method of teaching, law reviews also served little purpose.[19] When Weeks asked to see the periodical section, his guide responded, "What's that?" While individual faculty members received the *Tennessee Law Review,* the only law reviews held by the library were reprints of the first fifty volumes, through 1937, of the *Harvard Law Review.* Weeks built up the periodical collection by subscribing to numerous law reviews. A number of law schools were just commencing law reviews in the years after World War II, so he obtained a complete run of those with a few back issues. The library also began the longer-term task of completing the sets of better established journals, such as the *Yale Law Journal*.[20]

In the late 1940s, a law school needed only a minimum of three full-time faculty members to apply for ABA approval. All of the faculty used in the three-year program prior to the addition of Weeks were part-time. Weeks himself satisfied one of the required full-time positions, and Bernard B. Bailey, who had a J.D. from the University of Chicago, was hired to fill a second. With the phasing out of the two-year program, Gilreath was available to teach in the new three-year program as a full-time faculty member. However, Preston opposed retaining Gilreath, fearing he would be a liability when the school applied for ABA approval. Gilreath had not attended college and was a graduate of an unapproved law school—Cumberland under the old one-year program. Perhaps Gilreath's connection to the pre-1946 Cumberland University administration, as former president Bone's son-in-law, also troubled Preston. Nevertheless, Weeks thought Gilreath was both an effective teacher and well connected with alumni and the bar, and insisted that he be retained. Gilreath constituted the third full-time faculty member, satisfying the ABA minimum. In 1947–48, Weeks, as the only full-time teacher in the new three-year program, had carried a class load of twelve hours per term. This exceeded the ABA maximum, and Weeks knew that the ABA would insist that class loads be reduced to nine hours per term, which he accomplished in 1948.[21]

Accreditation required some changes in the facilities as well. ABA Standard 1(f) demanded that the school possess "reasonably adequate facilities," and an interpretation of Standard 1(c) required that a school be "adequately . . . housed so as to make possible efficient work on the part of both students and faculty." The law library was enlarged by cutting through eighteen-inch brick walls into an adjoining room. The motivation was probably not to accommodate book acquisitions but to provide student seating and work areas. In 1937, the ABA report on Cumberland had noted that there were only thirty to forty seats in the library.[22] The upstairs auditorium, which had pew-type seats similar to a church with no writing surfaces for the audience,[23] was renovated to serve as a classroom. The large auditorium was seldom used for that purpose, but with two classrooms downstairs and a courtroom that could also serve as a classroom, the law school held a total of four classrooms. A place was needed for a student lounge, but none seemed to be available until a student suggested the landing on the huge staircase going up to the second floor. A soft drink machine and some chairs were installed on the landing, and Caruthers Hall had its first student lounge.[24]

Cumberland implemented a standard case method curriculum in the fall of 1946 for the twenty-five students who enrolled in the new three-year program. The ABA Standards did not in so many words require that instruction adhere to the Langdellian case method, but that was implicit in Standard 1(f)'s requirement that an approved law school be one that, in the judgment of the ABA Council of Legal Education, "maintains a sound educational policy." The new curriculum, the first year of which was taught entirely by a cadre of bright young part-time faculty, represented a total restructuring of the traditional Cumberland curriculum. Two traditions endured from the past. Law 101 was called Introduction to Legal Procedure, but the words "Pleading & Pr" along with "(Hist/Ls)" handwritten alongside it in a copy of the 1946–47 catalogue retained in the law school archives suggests that Caruthers's *History of a Lawsuit* still introduced Cumberland students to the study of law. Another tradition was the continued importance assigned to Practice Court, which consumed six required quarter credit hours in each of three years.

The 1946–47 Special Announcement Cumberland University Catalogue published the three-year course of study. All courses were required, and there were no electives.

This curriculum was no doubt drawn from other schools and was a standard course of study. In many respects it remains so today, except that it required far more unit hours than are common now. At Cumberland and elsewhere in 1997, Procedure, Torts, Contracts, Property and Criminal Law remain the first-year building-block courses. A few of the 1946 courses, such as Bailments and Carriers, Suretyship, and Negotiable Instruments and Banking, are now incorporated into Uniform Commercial Code courses. However, generally speaking, Cumberland's 1946–47 curriculum bears a closer resemblance to the curriculum of the 1990s than to that of the 1930s. By 1946–47, Cumberland had modernized its curriculum.

TABLE 3. Curriculum for the Three-Year Course, 1946–47

FIRST YEAR			
	Hrs.		*Hrs.*
Introduction to Legal Procedure	4	Contracts	6
Torts	4	Personal Property	4
Agency	3	Real Property	4
Bailments and Carriers	3	Domestic Relations	4
Legislation	3	Criminal Law	4
Legal Bibliography	3	Practice (Moot) Court	6
SECOND YEAR			
	Hrs.		*Hrs.*
Evidence	4	Landlord and Tenant	3
Damages	3	Titles and Abstracts	4
Insurance	3	Negotiable Instruments	
Equity	4	and Banking	4
Bankruptcy Procedure	3	Procedure in Appellate Courts	2
Trusts	3	Pleading	3
Quasi-Contracts	3	Practice (Moot) Court	6
Partnership	3		
THIRD YEAR			
	Hrs.		*Hrs.*
Municipal Corporations	3	Conflict of Laws	4
Constitutional Law	4	Labor Legislation	2
Taxation	3	Practice	3
Suretyship	2	Procedure in Federal Legal Courts	4
Administrative Law	4	Wills and Administrations	
Research and Writing	4	of Estates	5
Legal Ethics	2	Practice (Moot) Court	6
Private Corporations	3		

ABA approval involved an application by the school followed by an on-site visit by a team of ABA inspectors. Weeks officially became dean in the summer of 1948 and in the fall of that year filed the school's application with the ABA. That same fall, eleven years after the scornful visit of Shafroth and Horack, an inspection team consisting of John Hervey, then advisor on legal education of the ABA, and Elliott Cheatham, a Columbia University law professor, inspected the school.

In November 1937 the school had only one full-time faculty member and required only one year to graduate. In the fall of 1948 Cumberland had three full-time faculty members, counting the full-time dean, and required three years to graduate. Furthermore, the 1948 curriculum was a standard case method program of study. While in 1937 two-thirds of law school tuition revenue was diverted to the support of other departments, in 1948 the law school retained virtually all of its revenue and dedicated the net proceeds toward the law school's improvement. Hervey and Cheatham were much more pleased with what they found in 1948 than Shafroth and Horack had been in 1937.

The inspectors were impressed with the quality of classroom instruction. They were very impressed with Gilreath, who had the enviable gift of inventing hypothetical questions that were both realistic and challenging. Weeks taught the course on conflicts of laws and used Cheatham's casebook on the subject. Cheatham visited the class. No doubt, Weeks had warned the class of what was at stake and told them to be on their best behavior, hoping that they would be well prepared and serious. Naturally, there was a cut-up in the class. That person insisted, contrary to the legal rule that a person can have only one domicile, that a person could have different domiciles for different purposes, even a "fishing domicile." Weeks, fearing embarrassment in Cheatham's presence, pushed the student hard with sharp questions about the implications of his argument. Perhaps a little to Weeks's surprise, Cheatham, impressed, roared with laughter at the whole colloquy. He thought it was one of the funniest things he had ever heard.

Preston had been reluctant to retain Gilreath, but Hervey formed a very favorable impression of him. It resulted from an incident when Weeks and Gilreath took Hervey to visit Andrew Jackson's home, the Hermitage, only a few miles from Lebanon. As they visited Jackson's gravesite in the gardens, Hervey was reminded of Themistocles, the Athenian military leader and democratic politician responsible for the Greeks' victory over the Persians at the Battle of Salamis. He quoted a line of Greek poetry about the ancient soldier-statesman. Gilreath, quite cultured despite the lack of a college education, immediately followed with the next line. Hervey retorted with the next line, and Gilreath followed again. Hervey later told colleagues throughout the country that the finest law teacher in the nation was to be found, not at Harvard or Yale, but at little Cumberland in middle Tennessee, in the person of Sam Gilreath.[25] Cheatham published a report in the *Tennessee Law Review* of a 1949 survey of law schools in Tennessee. His discussion of Cumberland probably reflects views developed in the course of the 1948 inspection visit:

> The situation can be summarized in a sentence. It is a school recently reorganized which is working with excellent spirit and with all its might. Its attitude was well expressed in a report to the Survey:
>
> "We are dissatisfied with the present state of (several matters dealt with in the questionnaire). We are not dissatisfied, however, with the progress we have made since June, 1946 and the progress we are now making. We want full approval by all those interested in the highest standards of legal education."[26]

Cumberland received provisional approval from the ABA in February 1949, during Weeks's first year of deanship and prior to graduation of the first class in the three-year program. Its graduates would now be able to sit for the bar exam in any state. The next step would be to obtain full approval from the ABA and membership in the American Association of Law Schools. That ultimately came in 1952, but by that time dramatic institutional changes resulted in Cumberland Law School becoming a freestanding institution.

With the effort to obtain provisional approval successfully concluded, Weeks took a one-year unpaid leave of absence to use his G.I. bill benefits. He spent the 1949–50 academic year at Duke, where he earned an LL.M. degree. Gilreath served again as acting dean, and Weeks stayed in contact with the school by mail and telephone.[27]

While the push for ABA approval was successful, the Second Century fund-raising campaign was not, probably because the new administration of Cumberland had not yet gained the confidence of the alumni. Although

Gilreath was named to the Nathan Green Chair of Law,[28] the endowment behind the chair, a goal of the drive, was weak. Years later, in 1961, the endowment of the Green Chair amounted to only $3,058.32.[29] The drive's failure led to Preston's resignation effective August 31, 1949. Edwin Richardson, chairman of the board of trustees and acting president when the Baptists first acquired control of Cumberland, replaced him.[30]

In 1951 the Tennessee Baptist Convention acquired the Nashville campus of Ward-Belmont, once a posh women's finishing school and college that had fallen on hard times. Charles W. Pope, the executive secretary of the convention who had presided over the convention's acquisition of Cumberland in 1946 and of the merger of Tennessee Women's College into Cumberland, now saw the Belmont campus as providing the superior location for Baptist higher education efforts in middle Tennessee. Pope planned to move Cumberland to the Belmont campus, creating "Cumberland-Belmont University." The Lebanon campus would be sold.[31]

Cumberland University catalogues since 1946 observed that in that year the Tennessee Baptist Convention received the institution "from the friendly hands of its trustees."[32] When Pope's plan surfaced, those once friendly hands balled into a suit-threatening fist. Pope probably hoped the merger could be quietly approved by the executive committee of the convention and the new Cumberland board, which had been appointed by the convention. The chairman of the Cumberland board of trustees, however, was Harry Phillips, a young Wilson County lawyer who had been an outstanding student both as a Cumberland undergraduate and as a law student, and who later serve as chief judge for the United States Court of Appeals. Although appointed by the convention, Phillips's sympathies were with the Lebanon location. He alerted many of the former trustees, most of whom were Lebanon business and civic leaders, to the planned move. The former trustees threatened suit, apparently on the grounds that the 1946 transfer agreement required that Cumberland operate under its existing charter, which provided for its location in Lebanon.[33]

Pope met with Weeks, Gilreath, Richardson, and an attorney for the convention to negotiate a compromise. At the end of the morning, it appeared an acceptable agreement had been reached under which a satellite campus of "Cumberland-Belmont" would remain in Lebanon. Richardson would serve as president of the Lebanon campus, which would be home to the law school and perhaps a junior college or nondegree adult education program. Weeks, Gilreath, and Richardson went off to a celebratory lunch, but when they met with Pope again later in the afternoon, he declared the retention of a campus in Lebanon to be a temporary expedient pending ultimate decisions, and that the Lebanon group would not have a voice in those decisions.[34]

Once Pope staked out that position, the negotiations took another turn. Ultimately, the Baptists agreed to withdraw from Cumberland, taking with them most of the assets associated with the arts and sciences division, including the library. Cumberland retained its campus, the law school, and the small endowment, about $125,000, that predated the Baptists. With the 1951 graduation, the undergraduate faculty of Cumberland was dissolved and all undergraduate programs terminated. With the withdrawal of the Baptists, the former trustees reassumed control but without any denominational affiliation. After more than a century of existence as a church-related school, first affiliated with the Cumberland Presbyterian Church, then the Presbyterian Church, U.S.A., then the Tennessee Baptist Convention, Cumberland University became a nonsectarian, independent institution.[35]

Since the law school was the university's only educational program, as of the fall 1951 semester, the law school became a freestanding institution. Gilreath became acting president, and Weeks remained as dean, to demonstrate continuity of leadership as the law school sought full approval from the ABA and membership in the Association of American Law Schools, or AALS.[36] In agreeing to remain, Weeks extracted two promises from the trustees. The first was that all of Cumberland's resources would be devoted to the law school, that is, Cumberland would not itself undertake an undergraduate program. The other was that if an established institution or denomination could not be persuaded to undergird or sponsor the entire university, then the trustees would allow Weeks to move the law school by affiliation with another college or university. With those understandings, Weeks continued to work toward full ABA approval and membership in the AALS, because achieving those goals would be important in obtaining new sponsorship or to effect a move.[37]

To obtain provisional ABA approval in 1949, Weeks had promised the ABA inspectors to add two additional faculty positions. Before he left to earn his LL.M. at Duke during the 1949–50 school year Weeks added two additional teachers, both of whom had already earned LL.M.s from Duke. One of these left after one year, and, in 1951, Weeks replaced him with a law teacher from Emory who had gone through a rancorous divorce and was forced to leave that Methodist university. At the beginning of the 1951 school year, the first academic year after the Baptist withdrawal, the law faculty consisted of Weeks, Gilreath, Bailey, Alfred T. Adams, William J. Stanford, and Richard J. Demeree.[38]

To obtain full approval from the ABA and membership in the AALS, the law school needed more space than was available in Caruthers Hall. For one thing, the new faculty needed offices. For another, the library's collection had significantly increased and by 1950 numbered more than 14,000 volumes.[39] To alleviate the constricted space, the law school moved from the historic Caruthers Hall, or "law barn," to Memorial Hall, the principal building of the main campus. The move was effected in an inexpensive and casual manner. Weeks himself went around to grocery stores and gathered up boxes; then he recruited some student volunteers, and, with the use of the school's truck, they moved the library several blocks to Memorial Hall. Adequate shelving was already in place, as Memorial Hall had housed the arts and sciences library, now gone to Belmont.[40]

In addition to raising the full-time faculty to five, increasing the size of the library to more than 14,000 volumes, and moving to more adequate space, the school also increased its prelaw requirements in September 1952, from two years of college to three years.[41] With those improvements, and a reinspection of the school by Hervey, the law school received full ABA approval in September 1952.[42]

That December, Cumberland's application for membership came up for consideration before the AALS. Weeks appeared before the committee to answer questions. Sheldon Elliott, formerly dean of the University of Southern California School of Law, chaired the committee. During the war, Elliott had been an army colonel, and Weeks was attached to his unit. When the vote was taken, the members of the committee were evenly divided, with those opposed concerned about the thinness of Cumberland's resources. It fell to Elliott to break the tie, one way or the other. Elliott agreed that the resources were pretty thin but observed that if Weeks remained with the school, he believed AALS standards would continue to be met. Apparently as a matter of personal confidence in Weeks, he voted to admit Cumberland to AALS membership.[43]

Within a little more than a year of losing denominational sponsorship and witnessing the suspension of all undergraduate operations, Cumberland had at last obtained full ABA approval and AALS membership. It was a standard law school at last. The problem it faced was that of maintaining enrollments sufficient to support the more costly standard law school program. In the 1920s and 1930s, by offering students the ability to obtain a law degree in only one year, Cumberland had enjoyed a competitive advantage over three-year schools, and enrollments at Cumberland had been strong while those at schools like Vanderbilt and the University of Tennessee had languished. By the late 1950s and 1960s, rising bar eligibility requirements forced Cumberland to forgo its earlier advantage. Continued success would depend on its ability to attract students. However, its primary competitive offering for many years had been its speed. Now, Cumberland could no longer offer a one-year course or even a two-year course and would have to compete directly with Vanderbilt and the University of Tennessee as a three-year school on issues such as cost, quality, and prestige.

Indications from the first few years of the three-year program were encouraging. In the years immediately following World War II, the return of veterans, coupled with the continued availability of the two-year program for students who enrolled prior to July 1946, had once again given Cumberland large enrollments. In 1946, there was a total of 350 students enrolled in the law school, though only 26 were enrolled in the nascent three-year program, then in its first year.[44] By the spring term of 1948, when the last of the students in the two-year program completed their studies, there were 70 students enrolled in that program, 53 in the three-year program, and two special students, for a total law school enrollment of 125.[45] The following year, 1948–49, was the first year in which there were no longer any students enrolled in the two-year program, and also the first in which students were enrolled in each of the three classes—freshman, junior, and senior—of the new program. The fall term of the 1948–49 school year saw 71 freshman students enroll at Cumberland, with overall enrollment totaling 113.[46] Fall enrollment figures for the following three years showed a slow decline: 116 for 1949–50; 107 for 1950–51; and 102 for 1951–52.[47] They soon slipped further.

Tuition and fees were $115 per quarter in 1951–52, up from $85 per quarter in 1946–47 to $100 per quarter in 1947–48 and then to the $115 level in 1949–50.[48] If one assumes an average enrollment of 100 in each quarter, that number multiplied by $115 per quarter tuition and fees equals $11,500 per quarter, or $34,500 for three quarters. Cumberland's 1951–52 catalogue indicated a total of ten scholarships in the law school, which probably consisted simply of tuition remission, so the foregoing calculation probably yields a figure higher than the actual tuition revenue. On the other hand, Cumberland offered a summer quarter that was well attended, drawing a total of 83 students in the 1951 summer session.[49] Total annual revenues of about $40,000 are a reasonable approximation, not too far below the $45,000 level that was noted for 1937 in the ABA survey report.

Though the foregoing enrollment and tuition income figures are very low compared to those all law schools enjoy in the 1990s, in 1951–52 Cumberland employed only five full-time faculty members, including the dean.[50] The median salary of all American law school professors in 1948–49 was only about $5,000,[51] and Cumberland almost certainly fell below the median. The revenues of the school covered the salaries of five full-time teachers and a librarian (Sara Hardison), paid for library continuations and acquisitions (ABA standards required a minimum average expenditure of $3,000 per year, with a minimum in any particular year of $2,000),[52] and maintained the physical plant, with enough remaining for incidental costs such as publication of the catalogue and other miscellaneous expenditures. But there was little room for slippage. Unless external support could be obtained, any decline in enrollments or increase in expenditures would spell disaster.

Following World War II, the number and the purposefulness of the returning veterans, the merger with Tennessee Women's College, and the enthusiasm of the new Baptist sponsors energized the Cumberland campus. Intercollegiate sports returned, with the Cumberland football team achieving a 6–0 victory over Florida State in 1947.[53] The 1948 *Phoenix* included features on the football, basketball, and baseball teams.[54] Intercollegiate social fraternities, such as SAE and Lambda Chi, which had included law students and had been an important part of prewar social life, did not reappear after the war. None are present in the 1948 *Phoenix.* The

Philomathean Literary Society was revived. However, while law students had predominated in the prewar Philomathean, by 1948 it became an exclusively undergraduate organization, as was a new literary society, the Ionian.[55] Probably the absence of chapter houses of undergraduate fraternities, in which law students had participated prior to the war, stimulated the establishment of two law school fraternities. The 1948–49 university catalogue indicated that a local chapter of Delta Theta Phi had been established at Cumberland, with the local chapter given the name of the Green Senate. By the following year Phi Alpha Delta established its Cordell Hull chapter.[56] When law school operations were moved from Caruthers Hall to Memorial Hall after the suspension of the undergraduate program, a room was set aside for each of the two fraternities.[57] Judge Gilreath continued the Sunday School class that had been a feature of prewar Cumberland. The Gilreath class would continue throughout the balance of the years in Lebanon, and indeed Judge Gilreath would conduct the class in Birmingham after the move in 1961.[58]

Occasionally law students participated in undergraduate activities. For example, in 1948, Hal Forrester, a second-year law student, served as an officer of the yearbook, the *Phoenix*.[59] Generally however, far more than before the war, law students left sports, campus newspapers, and a cappella choirs to the undergraduates. However, sports events, concerts, and plays, presented in Caruthers auditorium, offered law students inexpensive entertainment and a sense of university life. For single men in the predominately male law school student body, the presence of undergraduate coeds, particularly after the merger with Tennessee College for Women, offered the possibility of a social life.

Law students served on the campus-wide student council and were selected along with undergraduates for Blue Key, a scholastic honor society, and for Who's Who in American Colleges.[60] With the suspension of the undergraduate program, the student council became, in the now freestanding law school, the student bar association (SBA), with the responsibility for overcoming "any difficulties that arise concerning the students" and appointing "heads of the various publications and intramurals."[61] After the restoration of the undergraduate program, the SBA retained its separate existence and soon undertook sponsorship of Law Day, an annual day of celebrating the benefits of the legal system through speakers and banquets.[62]

With the removal to Birmingham in 1961, the SBA continued as a central feature of law school life and continued the sponsorship of Law Day, which eventually would grow to Law Week.

With the termination of the Baptist connection at Cumberland and the suspension of all undergraduate programs, the institution had limited choices of direction in which it could go. One was to continue as a freestanding law school. As a freestanding law school, law school revenue would not be used to support undergraduate programs. On the other hand, a solid undergraduate school could serve as a feeder of students as well as providing activities that would be of interest to law students and faculty. In any event, that approach was unattractive to the Lebanon-oriented men who dominated the reconstituted board of trustees.[63] For them, a local undergraduate college provided an opportunity for students from the local region to obtain a college education without going too far from home. A college program also served as a badge of civic pride and introduced into the community a cadre of teachers who raised the tone of church and civic life. For the Lebanon residents on the board, reinstituting an undergraduate program seemed the natural step.

Weeks, however, was opposed to reinstituting an undergraduate program without significant external sponsorship. He knew that the undergraduate programs prior to the Baptist interregnum had not been self-supporting for years and, in the absence of denominational support, this had led to a massive diversion of law school tuition to cover undergraduate deficits.

Accordingly, Weeks favored one of two possible approaches. One was to buttress the law school, either by transferring an established undergraduate institution with solid denominational support to the Lebanon campus, or by inducing a church denomination with significant membership and resources to sponsor the reinstitution of Cumberland's undergraduate program. Another alternative for Weeks was moving the law school to a more advantageous location than Lebanon, preferably by affiliation with an established college or university. These preferences were the bases for the promises Weeks extracted from the Cumberland board, discussed earlier, that the university would devote all its resources to the law school and would permit the relocation of the law school if he found a suitable affiliation.

With those understandings, Weeks and the board began to explore possible connections to undergird the law school. The first overture came from representatives of the Roman Catholic Church and was initiated even before the law school moved from Caruthers to Memorial Hall. At that time, there was no Catholic church and only a few Roman Catholics in Wilson County, although one was a member of the Cumberland board. Both the Cumberland board and Weeks were enthusiastic about the interest expressed by the Catholic Church. They gave the church representatives access to information about the school and sold them a tract of land on the edge of the Cumberland campus to build the first Catholic church in Wilson County. However, to the disappointment of Cumberland, the Catholic Church officials decided that it was probably unwise to undertake sponsorship of a college in an area with few Catholic parishioners and dropped their interest.[64]

A second possibility was to merge with Martin College, a Methodist junior college in Pulaski, Tennessee, a small community just north of the Tennessee-Alabama line. Dr. Joe Quillian, Martin's president, contacted Cumberland in 1953. He had prominent lawyers as relatives, so presiding over a university that included a law school probably appealed to him. Moreover, while Vanderbilt retained loose connections to Methodism, in 1914 it won the right to elect its own trustees. There seemed to be opportunity in middle Tennessee for a Methodist-related school tied more closely to the church. The move to Lebanon would allow Martin to jump from junior college to university in a single leap. Cumberland would become a Methodist institution. Although Martin's president was enthusiastic about the move, his board of trustees rejected the plan, and the president's sponsorship of it cost him his job.[65]

Major Harwell G. Davis, president of Weeks's own alma mater, Howard College (now Samford University), occasionally visited in Lebanon where one of his daughters lived. Weeks talked with him, but Davis made it plain that Howard was not then in a position to acquire a law school. Prophetically, Davis indicated that in the future there might be an interest.[66]

However, David A. Lockmiller, president of the University of Chattanooga, invited Weeks to his Chattanooga campus to discuss the possibility of a move. Lockmiller had earned a law degree at Cumberland but had abandoned practice to pursue an academic career. After teaching history at

North Carolina State and authoring a biography of William Blackstone, Lockmiller entered university administration and became president of the University of Chattanooga, then a Methodist-related school though later it became part of the state university system.[67]

Lockmiller told Weeks that a spare building on the Chattanooga campus could be the home of Cumberland law school, but only if the initiative for the move came from Cumberland and its trustees. Lockmiller stated that he and the University of Chattanooga in no way wanted it to appear that they were trying to steal the school from Lebanon. Weeks presented the possibility to the Cumberland trustees, who stated that they were not interested.[68]

Nor were they interested in a move to Memphis, where either Memphis State University or Southwestern University, a small Presbyterian school later renamed Rhodes College, seemed possible host institutions for the law school. Weeks undertook to introduce the possibility of a move to Memphis by addressing the West Tennessee Bar's midyear meeting on the subject of "Conditions of Legal Education in Tennessee." To show the need for an ABA-approved law school in Memphis, he pointed out that in Memphis there were more students attending unapproved schools than the number of students at Cumberland, Vanderbilt, and the University of Tennessee combined. But the Cumberland trustees did not want to move, and nothing came of it.[69]

Weeks made one last attempt to move the law school by connecting with a denomination that would support an undergraduate school on the Lebanon campus. The Free Will Baptists, a small southern sect of about 200,000 members,[70] operated the Free Will Baptist Bible College in Nashville. It was housed in rented quarters, a circumstance that would make moving the school to Lebanon much simpler. The Free Will Baptists envisioned instituting a Sunday School Board that would be housed in Lebanon, like that of the larger Southern Baptists in Nashville, so that Lebanon would become the headquarters for their denomination. They even had Weeks draw up corporate papers for the board. However, they did not want a law school, and Weeks would be free to move the law school to a larger city.[71]

The Cumberland trustees, however, had no enthusiasm for the plan. Partly the opposition was to any scheme that involved moving the law school, and partly they found the Free Will Baptists, who practiced foot washing, too far removed from mainstream religious groups. However, the nearly desperate search among various denominations for an affiliation for the law school does demonstrate that the Cumberland board, generally speaking, had far fewer religious concerns than secular ones, specifically, the local interest in retaining the law school in Lebanon. One trustee, Athens Clay Pullias, a graduate of the law school and president of Nashville's David Lipscomb College, a Church of Christ school, was particularly forceful in opposing the Free Will Baptist plan, proposing instead that Cumberland start a junior college itself. Pullias prevailed, and the board decided to begin a junior college program.[72]

For Weeks, this was the last straw. Not only did it violate the understanding he had with the board that all of the school's resources would be placed behind the law school, but it also made clear that the board would continue to resist all efforts to move the law school. Weeks resigned in 1954 and returned to Birmingham to reopen his law office.[73]

In advocating moving the law school, Weeks displayed sound instincts as to how to increase the school's enrollment. This can be seen by comparing the enrollment experience of the law schools of two other southern universities, Stetson and Wake Forest. In the fall of 1952, with the end of the enrollment surge created by the return of World War II veterans, the enrollments at both these Baptist-related law schools were comparable to that at Cumberland. The fall 1952 enrollment statistics at the three law schools were Cumberland with 83; Stetson with 90; and Wake Forest with 81.[74]

Cumberland's enrollment during the subsequent years in Lebanon never reached 100.[75] Stetson's enrollment, however, while sinking to 67 in the fall of 1953,[76] rebounded to 94 in 1954,[77] 138 in 1955,[78] and by 1959 was up to 246.[79] The reason is not hard to find. In September 1954, Stetson's law school, which was operating at a deficit and faced threats of loss of accreditation, moved from the small community of Deland, Florida, where the main Stetson campus was located, to booming St. Petersburg, Florida. Though the Stetson Law School continued to face financial problems in its new location, the sharp upsurge in enrollment provided a basis for solving them.[80]

In the case of Wake Forest, the entire university moved in 1956 from Wake Forest, North Carolina, the tiny community that had given the university its name, to the thriving tobacco city of Winston-Salem, North Carolina. Though the enrollment growth enjoyed by Wake Forest in its new setting was not as dramatic as that at Stetson, the pattern was the same. From 89 law students in 1955,[81] law enrollment at Wake Forest went to 118 in 1956[82] and 132 in 1957.[83]

Cumberland catalogues, perhaps making a virtue of necessity, had earlier extolled the advantages of studying law in a small town isolated from the temptations presented by larger cities. For the years 1955–1957, the catalogue returned to the theme of Cumberland's advantageous location in Lebanon, trumpeting the happy combination of "the quiet, leisurely paced environment of a small town for undisturbed study and relaxation" with proximity to Nashville. However, in the 1950s it was clear that law students preferred the social and professional advantages of attending law school in a larger community. A city offered the possibility of part-time clerkships during law school and full-time employment after graduation. For married students, a larger community offered more opportunities for their spouses to find jobs, and for both single and married students, a greater range of recreational choices. For the school itself, the local bench and bar of a growing city supplied a source of adjunct faculty and financial support.

Based on the experience of Stetson and Wake Forest, Weeks's early recognition of the advantages of moving the law school to a larger community appears farsighted. But after the severance of the Baptist connection, the members of Cumberland's board were individuals who held retention of Cumberland in Lebanon uppermost. Weeks later recalled a conversation he once had with William D. Baird, who, as an alumnus of both the undergraduate school and the law school and as mayor of Lebanon, had led the fight against the Baptist attempt to move the school to Nashville. After that was prevented, Baird became a member of the board and was one of those most opposed to Weeks's plans to move the law school. Baird demonstrated his devotion to the institution at his death, after the law school had moved to Birmingham, by leaving his entire estate of more than $2 million to Cumberland University. Before that move, Baird once asked Weeks what would happen if the board did not let Weeks move the law school to Memphis, Chattanooga, Birmingham, or a similar city. Weeks replied that the school ultimately would have to close. Baird then asked, if the board permitted the move, would not the school be closed as far as Lebanon was concerned? Weeks had to concede that from the point of view of the Lebanon community, a move to a distant city differed little from simply closing the institution. That reality made it very difficult for a board dominated by persons attached to Lebanon to consider seriously any proposal to move the school.[84]

Not surprisingly, the plans to move Stetson's law school as well as the move of Wake Forest University to Winston-Salem also provoked local resistance. In the case of Stetson, the Deland newspaper editorialized against the move, which cost the university some local supporters.[85] Wake Forest required litigation to establish the legality of its move.[86] The board members of those institutions, however, were drawn from a broad area, and local considerations were subordinated to considerations of what was best for the institution. In the case of Cumberland, the board of trustees was dominated by individuals with strong attachments to Lebanon. Recognizing that the board would not permit a move until the situation became truly dire, Weeks returned to Birmingham, but he maintained his friendship with Gilreath and with others in Lebanon. Perhaps as he left Lebanon in 1954 he knew that a move to a larger community could only be a matter of time.

With the decision to institute a junior college program, Cumberland appointed a new president in April 1955. Charles B. Havens had been dean at Martin College in Pulaski, Tennessee.[87] Doubtless Cumberland became acquainted with Havens and he with Cumberland during the discussions of a possible merger of Cumberland and Martin. After Weeks's departure, Bailey served as acting dean of the law school. In 1955, Grissim H. Walker, who had been appointed to the law school faculty in 1953, was elevated to the office of dean. Walker had his law degree from Harvard, but his undergraduate degree was from Cumberland.[88] Probably Walker appeared to combine an understanding of the highest standards of legal education with an appreciation of the importance of remaining in Lebanon.

At thirty-two years of age, Havens at the time of his appointment may well have been the youngest college or university president in the country. As he later admitted with respect to his first appearance at an alumni meeting in June 1955, he was "a very scared boy, indeed"[89] and well he should have been: he and Dean Walker faced a challenge that would have been daunting to much more seasoned educational administrators. Insofar as the law school was concerned, the nub of their problem was the bleak enrollment picture. In the fall of 1951, the first year the law school was freestanding, enrollment still hovered above 100, but then went steadily down, from 102 in fall 1951, to 83 in fall 1952, 65 in 1953, to only 40 enrolled students in 1954.[90]

With an enrollment of only 40, the law school operated at a deficit. In a report to alumni in June 1956, President Havens noted that the deficit for the fiscal year of September 1, 1954–August 31, 1955, totaled $22,700. Havens and Walker attempted to staunch the hemorrhaging of enrollments. In the summer of 1955, Havens personally visited more than forty colleges and universities in Kentucky, Tennessee, and Virginia, attempting to recruit law students. Perhaps as a result of that effort, the law school enrollment in fall 1955 crept up to 52. During the 1955–56 school year Havens and Walker visited and revisited schools in those states, as well as a dozen more in Florida and Alabama. Meanwhile, bulletin board holders, containing preaddressed inquiry cards, were mailed to several hundred colleges in the South.[91]

With the slight increase in enrollment in the fall of 1955 and with various other belt-tightening moves, including the elimination of nonsubsidized scholarships, Havens and Walker managed to reduce the operating law school deficit for 1955–56 to $8,500. However, the institution faced significant nonoperational expenses that year. Plans were made to return law school operations to Caruthers Hall and to an adjacent building on West Main Street that the university would purchase, thereby making way for the opening of a two-year undergraduate college in Memorial Hall. No money was available to carry out the purpose. An alumni solicitation drive was undertaken and letters mailed to 4,200 law graduates in November 1955. Some 800 were returned undelivered, an indication of the law school's lack of attention to alumni affairs. The law school requested only modest gifts, and when the Law School Moving Fund drive was completed, a little more than $3,000 had been collected.[92]

With the aid of the contributed funds, on January 2, 1956, law school operations were returned to Caruthers Hall, creating space for a cafeteria in Memorial Hall. Though law school enrollment was less than it was prior to World War II, Caruthers Hall lacked capacity to accommodate the larger faculty and library mandated by ABA and AALS standards. Accordingly a large Victorian residence next to Caruthers Hall was acquired, christened the Cordell Hull Building, and converted to faculty and administrative office space.[93]

In an attempt to solve the problem of the operating deficit, tuition and fees were increased to a total of $140 per quarter in 1956. In 1957, a single inclusive fee of $155 per quarter was charged. That amount remained in effect through the final term in Lebanon.[94]

Total law enrollment for fall 1956 rose to an encouraging 69.[95] Then, despite the personal efforts of Havens and Walker, and even though the opening of the two-year college and the move back to Caruthers brought a spark of college life back to the campus, enrollment dipped again in fall 1957, to 49.[96] The enrollment figures for the fall terms for the period from 1956 through 1960 were as follows:[97]

1956	69	1958	49	1960	67
1957	49	1959	64		

Though enrollment was down, the law school continued to employ five full-time faculty members, as required by AALS and ABA standards. There could be little if any increase in compensation, so naturally there was turnover in the faculty. One significant addition in 1957 was Claude E. Bankester, who took a leave of absence in 1960–61, but later rejoined the law faculty in Birmingham.[98]

Even though the financial situation was bleak and enrollments poor, the law faculty made many very principled decisions during the troubled years from 1954 to 1960. Specifically, it refused admission to several applicants who were ill-prepared or had prior academic problems, and it dismissed several students who had experienced academic difficulties while at Cumberland.[99] Curiously enough, discipline problems continued. On November 5, 1957, and in response to both an incident and a letter from President Havens,[100] the law faculty resolved that "Drinking of intoxicating beverages by students is disapproved by the Law Faculty of Cumberland University and may be considered by the law faculty as sufficient ground for the suspension or expulsion of any student."[101]

Thereafter, the president again wrote the law faculty, complaining of gambling among students in the dormitory. At its March 4, 1958, meeting, the law faculty adopted a policy that gambling was also disapproved by the law faculty and would be grounds for suspension or expulsion. How little had changed in one hundred years of futile attempts to control student behavior.

To provide a supplement to the law school's tuition, Havens, realizing that substantial alumni contributions were unrealistic, devised a modest fund-raising mechanism called the "Buck-A-Month" club. The school sent preaddressed return envelopes to alumni and asked them to mail in at least a dollar bill. The next month they mailed another envelope and requested the contributors to repeat the exercise. The program was instituted in March 1956. By the time Havens addressed the alumni banquet in June of that year, the program had yielded about $2,500, and Havens expressed the hope that it might yield an annual return of about $8,000 to $9,000, which would just about have covered the deficit in the year ending August 31, 1956.[102]

But with enrollment continuing at a low level, more substantial financial resources were needed than those generated by the Buck-A-Month Club. Law schools are reinspected by the accrediting bodies at least once every seven years. Beginning with a 1955 report by ABA Legal Education advisor John Hervey on his inspection of the school, ABA and AALS reports hammered away at the school's financial problems. Hervey's report noted that the school's deficits for the past several years had been financed by a bank loan in the amount of $47,000. Hervey questioned how long the school's finances would allow it to continue to function.[103] A 1956 inspection by Dean A. E. Papale of Loyola of New Orleans found that in 1955–56 the law school had total revenues of $49,229.63 but expenditures of $55,468.12, including a modest university overhead charge of $1,012.50. Papale referred to the law school as largely a "boot strap" operation and recommended that it be given not less than two and no more than five years to get its financial house in order.[104]

Slightly more than two years later, the school received another inspector, this time Page Keeton, dean of the University of Texas Law School. Though a bequest of Texas attorney and Cumberland law alumnus Robert L. Carlock Sr. had supposedly eliminated the law school's indebtedness in 1957,[105] Keeton found in 1959 that the university's indebtedness had grown to $160,000, largely, in Keeton's view, a product of law school deficits. Keeton agreed with Weeks's earlier assessment that Lebanon was a poor location for a law school, and he saw a move, perhaps to Memphis, as the ultimate solution to its financial problems. Nevertheless, he recommended that the school be given one year to show "substantial progress" by raising $500,000 in endowment. Pursuant to Keeton's recommendation, the school was notified in July 1959 that it had one year to show progress toward three goals: (1) a $500,000 endowment; (2) increased faculty pay scale; and (3) a new library.[106]

Even before Keeton's inspection, in 1958 Cumberland had launched an ambitious development program, with a total goal of $2,000,000, including $150,000 earmarked for a new law library, $75,000 to renovate Caruthers Hall, and $1,000,000 in endowment.[107] In April 1958, the board, no doubt in an attempt to find leadership that could more effectively lead the campaign, replaced Havens with a man whose name was familiar to most Cumberland alumni, Ernest L. Stockton Jr., whose father had been president of Cumberland from 1926 to 1941.[108]

The campaign continued for a number of years and funded several important capital improvements on the main campus,[109] but it failed to raise the funds necessary to solve the law school's financial problems by the summer of 1960, the ABA's deadline. As a temporary expedient, reminiscent of the endowment equivalency program in the 1920s, Cumberland proposed to the ABA that in lieu of $500,000 law school endowment, its accreditation be continued based on pledges of amounts equal to the income from such an endowment.[110] The ABA, which, like Weeks, probably saw a move of the law school as the only realistic alternative to closing it, rejected that expedient. After several extensions, in May 1961 the school still had failed to satisfy the requirements set for it in 1959. The ABA stood ready to suspend Cumberland's approval, and the AALS its membership.

Like his father before him, the younger President Stockton's primary objective was to obtain accreditation for the undergraduate program from the Southern Association of Schools and Colleges. Under the Southern Association's standards, accreditation was impossible if the law school did not enjoy approval by its professional accrediting agency, the ABA. The law school's unapproved status had been one of the obstacles that had prevented the elder Stockton from achieving the goal of Southern Association accreditation. Now if the law school lost ABA approval the younger Stockton's efforts would also be doomed to fail. In order to achieve accreditation of the undergraduate program by the Southern Association (which was in fact achieved in 1962), Cumberland's leadership at last agreed to negotiate a move of the law school. Upon assurances that negotiations for the transfer of the school were being undertaken, and that the school would not continue to operate in Lebanon after the 1961 summer quarter, the ABA and the AALS in May 1961 deferred action on Cumberland's suspension.[111] The scene was now set for the reentry of Arthur Weeks onto the Cumberland stage.

CHAPTER NINE

The Cumberland Phoenix Rises in Birmingham 1961–1983

Cumberland's board of trustees had few precedents to go by in unloading a law school, lock, stock, and alumni.
—"Change of Venue," *Newsweek,* August 14, 1961

Howard College . . . agrees . . . [t]hat it will henceforth and forever continue to use the name "Cumberland" in the name of the School of Law of Howard College.
—Provision in agreement and bill of sale between Cumberland University and Howard College, dated June 27, 1961, under which Cumberland Law School was acquired by Howard College.

IMPATIENT WITH Cumberland's progress in returning to the mainstream of American legal education, the American Bar Association and the American Association of Law Schools continued to insist that Cumberland accelerate its pace of improvement. In 1959, they imposed a requirement that Cumberland raise $500,000 in endowment, as well as build a new library, renovate Caruthers Hall, add to library holdings, and increase faculty salaries. The Cumberland leadership had endeavored to raise the necessary sums but, despite several extensions from the AALS and the

ABA, had failed to do so. Cumberland was granted a final extension to May 17, 1961, the date of a meeting of the AALS Executive Committee in Washington, D.C. It was clear that Cumberland would not be able to report success. Accordingly, the sword would likely fall unless, by that date, some other plan, such as a merger with an approved institution, was well underway.[1]

Knowing that Weeks, while dean, had wanted to move the school, Sam Gilreath met with him when Weeks returned to Lebanon for Law Day celebrations in spring 1961. Gilreath asked him to find a college or university to which the law school could be moved. Gilreath indicated that he thought the law school could be acquired for about $100,000, which would be applied to the law school's accumulated deficit. Despite the close attachment he and his wife had to Lebanon, Gilreath assured Weeks that he would teach on the faculty in the new location for one year. He also assured Weeks that he need not limit his search to Tennessee.[2]

Returning to Birmingham, Weeks did not have to look far to identify a college that might be interested. Weeks and his wife were graduates of Howard College, which only four years earlier had moved from a smaller campus in an older residential section of Birmingham to a more spacious suburban campus. Weeks promptly advised Howard College president Leslie S. Wright and chancellor (and former president) Harwell G. Davis of the possibility of acquiring Cumberland's law school. To discuss the possibility, Weeks and Davis, himself a lawyer who at one time had served as attorney general of Alabama, called on Memory Leake Robinson, chairman of the Executive Committee of the Howard College Board of Trustees and a senior partner in a well-established local law firm, Lange, Simpson, Robinson and Somerville.

Much to their disappointment, Robinson was cool to the idea of acquiring the struggling Lebanon school, and Weeks left the meeting with Robinson doubtful that Howard College would be interested in the project. Then a fortuitous event occurred that altered Robinson's thinking and made him one of the leading proponents of the acquisition. A day or so after Weeks and Davis called on Robinson, John Hooker, a Nashville attorney, came to Birmingham to talk with Robinson about a case. Robinson told Hooker of the visit only a day or two earlier and the discussion about a small law school in Lebanon. Hooker had grown up in Lebanon, graduated from Cumberland, taught moot court at the school for a while, and remained a member of its board of trustees.

Hooker seems to have had a gift for appearing on the scene at critical moments: it was Hooker who, thirty years earlier, had phoned Judge A. B. Neil while the latter was vacationing at Lake Minnetonka to persuade Neil to cut short his vacation to come home and fill the vacancy on Cumberland's faculty. There probably could have been no better emissary to convince the skeptical Robinson of Howard College's good fortune in being presented with the opportunity to acquire a law school with Cumberland's tradition and heritage.

By the time Hooker left, Robinson had become an enthusiastic supporter of Howard College's acquisition of Cumberland School of Law. A few days later, Wright called a meeting of the Howard College Board of Trustees Executive Committee, of which Robinson was chairman. The executive committee unanimously endorsed Wright's recommendation that Howard College explore the possibility of acquiring the law school. On May 15, representatives of Howard College visited Lebanon for preliminary discussions with President Stockton and members of the Cumberland University Board of Trustees. Two days later, President Stockton and Dean Grissim Walker of Cumberland appeared before the AALS executive committee in Washington. They were able to tell the committee that serious negotiations were underway for Howard's acquisition of the law school. Weeks and Davis also appeared before the committee to provide information about Howard and as evidence of the seriousness of Howard's interest. Upon assurances by Cumberland that it would not conduct law classes in Lebanon after the end of the 1961 summer quarter and that acquisition of the school by Howard College or another established institution seemed imminent, the AALS committee agreed to defer suspension of Cumberland's accreditation.[3]

Howard was not the only suitor for Cumberland's hand. On May 4, 1961, Cecil C. Humphreys, president of Memphis State University, in Nashville to attend the meeting of the Tennessee State Board of Education, had been invited to dinner at the home of Athens Clay Pullias. Pullias, president of Nashville's David Lipscomb College, and a Cumberland alumnus and member of its board of trustees, invited Humphreys to meet with several Cumberland trustees to see if Memphis State would be interested in acquiring Cumberland School of Law. In 1954, Pullias had been the member of the Cumberland board most opposed to Weeks's efforts to move the Cumberland law school to a larger city. After several years of deficit operations and with loss of accreditation imminent, Pullias had changed his mind. Perhaps because it preferred to keep the law school in Tennessee, the Cumberland board indicated that Memphis State could acquire it by payment of only $80,000. As in the discussions with Weeks, Humphreys was assured that Gilreath would come with the school for one year.

Humphreys was excited at the prospect of acquiring the law school and quickly obtained pledges of $75,000 from Memphis sources to apply toward the acquisition. Cumberland students favored the move to Memphis State, and the Memphis State proposal received support from Cumberland alumni in Memphis and west Tennessee, and indeed from prominent Cumberland alumni elsewhere. Retired chief justice (and former dean) A. B. Neil wrote Governor Buford Ellington in support of the Memphis State proposal, and former Florida governor Leroy Collins, in an interview in the Memphis newspaper, expressed an interest in seeing the law school move to Memphis.[4]

But while Weeks had needed only a decision by the Howard College leadership, readily obtained with the fortuitous aid of Hooker, Humphreys had the bureaucratic apparatus of Tennessee higher education to deal with, in which the University of Tennessee was a powerful and turf-conscious player. Memphis State's acquisition of Cumberland's law school would require approval by the Tennessee Joint Committee on Higher Education, a committee created by Governor Ellington to coordinate programs at the state's colleges and universities. The joint committee appointed a four-member subcommittee to study the Cumberland-Memphis State issue. The four members consisted of the president of the University of Tennessee, a member of the University of Tennessee board of trustees, a prominent Memphis State alumnus, and Humphreys.

At a meeting of the subcommittee on May 24, in Ellington's office in Nashville, Humphreys found himself isolated by the unavoidable absence of the Memphis State alumnus member of the subcommittee, and completely outflanked by the University of Tennessee forces who already had developed a plan for an overall study of legal education in Tennessee and the need for a public law school in Memphis.[5] Apart from the time constraints that the situation presented, the decision to conduct such a study was quite reasonable. However, it would not be completed and submitted to the joint committee until July 17.

Cumberland had already announced that it would not operate in Lebanon after the summer quarter. Humphreys was probably aware in a general way of the negotiations with Howard College and that it was unlikely that Cumberland could wait until the completion of the study was submitted on July 17, especially without any assurance as to what the study might conclude.[6]

Humphreys probably realized at the conclusion of the May 24 meeting that the University of Tennessee had effectively blocked moving Cumberland Law School to Memphis State. Perhaps realizing that Memphis State (not to mention Cumberland) had been treated unfairly through the bureaucratic maneuverings described above, in 1962 the State Board of Education approved Memphis State's application to begin a law school. Since many Tennesseans, particularly those in the western portion of the state, blamed the University of Tennessee for the loss of Cumberland to Alabama, it was not in a position to oppose approval of the Memphis State proposal to establish a law school, eventually named for Humphreys after his retirement.[7]

The University of Tennessee itself offered $50,000 to acquire Cumberland.[8] Gilreath confirmed that to Weeks, indicating that the University of Tennessee proposed simply to integrate Cumberland's remaining students, library, and records into the Knoxville school, retaining the Cumberland name only for the building. The University of Tennessee Law School happened to be located on Cumberland Avenue in Knoxville, and Gilreath feared that if the Tennessee offer were accepted, future law students would probably think the name was derived from the location, and Cumberland School of Law's long history and tradition would soon fade away. Gilreath was particularly resentful of the University of Tennessee offer, which seemed designed to eliminate Cumberland not only from the field of competition but from history as well. No doubt other Cumberland trustees shared Gilreath's view, which made acceptance of the University of Tennessee's offer unlikely so long as any other possibility existed.[9]

In August 1961 an article in *Newsweek* describing Howard College's purchase of Cumberland Law School stated that Howard had "slipped" a venerable Tennessee institution across the state line.[10] The Cumberland trustees doubtlessly would have preferred to retain a Tennessee location. Even Weeks, while working hard on the Howard College option, probably saw Memphis as the most logical new home for the law school. If blame is to be assigned for Tennessee's loss of Cumberland Law School, that blame probably should fall on the University of Tennessee, which contrived to prevent the law school from going to its junior rival in Memphis, while itself making an insultingly low offer that, to Gilreath and no doubt to many Cumberland trustees, seemed designed to depreciate Cumberland's heritage.

At any rate, the way was clear for Howard College. On May 26, 1961, the full board of trustees of Howard College approved a motion by Robinson that authorized the executive committee to go forward with negotiations.[11] On June 3, President Wright, along with Robinson and Weeks, visited Lebanon to confer with President Stockton and members of Cumberland's board. Thereafter, Howard College made a definite offer for the acquisition of the law school that included payment of a sum of money and an agreement to retain the name of the law school. Howard would operate the summer session on the Lebanon campus (that is, be responsible for the summer quarter deficits) and accept all enrolled Cumberland students who wished to transfer with the school. Probably this initial offer was for $100,000, the sum Gilreath had mentioned earlier to Weeks and the amount the Howard board of trustees had authorized at its annual meeting. In return, Howard would receive the law library of 24,000 volumes, the name Cumberland, the goodwill of the institution, the records of the registrar's office and alumni files, all available class composites, and a portrait of Cordell Hull. Howard also would receive certain trust funds, including the relatively minuscule ($3,058.32)[12] endowment of the "Green Chair of Law."

For an institution with its back against the wall, Cumberland University proved to be a resourceful negotiator. Its trustees, who probably were best aware of what would be necessary to clear accumulated law school deficits, insisted on an increase in the amount of the cash payment. Hooker and Robinson ultimately agreed on a total payment of $125,000, and on June 22, President Wright sent the following telegram to Hooker: "Terms agreed upon by you and Mr. Memory L. Robinson for acquisition of Cumberland Law School by Howard College and set forth in your correspondence with him are acceptable. President Stockton has agreed to come to Birmingham on Tuesday, June 27. Appropriate contract will be ready for execution on that date."[13]

On Tuesday, June 27, stories appeared in the *Birmingham News* as well as in Tennessee newspapers announcing the agreement to move Cumberland Law School to Howard College.[14] The *Birmingham News* coverage included stories on the history of Cumberland.[15] On the same date, President Stockton mailed a letter to Cumberland alumni explaining the reasons for the move, while President Wright mailed each of the Cumberland alums a letter welcoming them to the Howard College community.[16] The June 1961 issue of the *Howard College Alumnus* also announced the acquisition and included a letter from the Howard College Alumni Association president, welcoming Cumberland alumni as members of the association.[17]

Whether it was added as an afterthought or had been inadvertently omitted from the agreement and bill of sale, a separately executed "Amendment to the Agreement and Bill of Sale" later would assume importance. The amendment provided:

> Howard College shall have the perpetual right to use the name "Cumberland" in connection with any law school operated at Howard College or that may be operated by any successor or assignee of Howard College, it being the purpose of this agreement to pass on with the property conveyed and assigned the exclusive right to use the name "Cumberland" in connection with the operation of a law school; and Cumberland University at Lebanon, Tennessee, agrees not to reestablish any law school at Cumberland University.

Over thirty years later, in 1993, Cumberland University, having just celebrated its sesquicentennial, sought a judicial declaration that it had the right to open a law school, notwithstanding the foregoing provision.[18] The District Court in Nashville held that Cumberland University was bound by the provision in the amendment.[19] Had that provision not been added by amendment, the world of legal education might have been graced with two Cumberland law schools, one in Birmingham and one in Lebanon.

While carrying on negotiations for the purchase of the law school, Howard College also took steps to assure the law school's continued accreditation. On May 31, John Hervey, the advisor to the ABA Section on Legal Education who had officiated over the original approval of Cumberland by the ABA in 1952, visited Howard College at Wright's request. Hervey met with the Howard College Executive Committee and with a large group of Birmingham lawyers and judges. From that visit, Hervey was able to give Howard sufficient assurances as to the prospect of retaining ABA approval. By June 3, Wright felt he could go forward with a formal offer to the Cumberland trustees.[20]

On July 20, Hervey returned, this time accompanied by two AALS representatives, Dean Page Keeton of the University of Texas Law School and president of the AALS, and Samuel D. Thurman, a Stanford law professor who was AALS president-elect. It was Keeton's 1959 report on his inspection of Cumberland that had led the AALS to require raising an endowment of $500,000 as well as making other costly improvements as a condition to continued membership. Keeton's report had also identified Cumberland's location in a small industrial community rather than an urban center as an underlying factor in its continuing low enrollments. Apparently Keeton was satisfied with the prospects for the school on Howard College's Birmingham campus. Based on the recommendations of Keeton, Thurman, and Hervey, the AALS continued Cumberland's membership.

With the purchase concluded on paper and with accreditation apparently successfully maintained, the problem of actually moving the law school to Birmingham and commencing operations remained. That required making provision in a Howard College building for classrooms, library, and faculty offices; physically moving the library books and student and alumni records from Lebanon to Birmingham; and assembling students and faculty.

A committee of the Howard board of trustees, including Robinson and District Judge H. H. Grooms, as well as Frank P. Samford and L. E. Bashinsky, was formed to oversee the plans for opening the law school on Howard's campus. Weeks, still maintaining his Birmingham law practice, visited Lebanon during the summer at the request of the committee to urge students enrolled on the Lebanon campus to make the transfer to Birmingham, and consulted on recruitment of a faculty. Patricia Coffman, who had worked in the law libraries of Mercer and Santa Clara, was hired to supervise the relocation of Cumberland's law library from Caruthers Hall to the third floor of Howard's Davis Library, which would serve as a temporary home to the law school until its own building could be constructed.

The Lebanon administration had taken no steps to admit an entering class for the fall term. However, the front-page publicity given by the Birmingham newspapers to Howard's acquisition of a law school had attracted the attention of Birmingham residents who were interested in attending law school locally. This interest was especially strong among those with a connection to Howard College: among those in the first entering class in Birmingham was Betty Davis Eshelman, one of Chancellor Davis's daughters. Weeks also obtained a file of applications that had been received in Lebanon. From these sources an entering first-year class was drawn.

At the time the agreement of purchase was executed on June 27, the summer quarter was already in progress in Lebanon. In the agreement, Howard College was to take over and operate the law school in Lebanon for the balance of the summer quarter. Because the summer program was already well underway at the time the document was signed, this primarily entailed paying all expenses (up to an agreed ceiling of $7,881) of the summer quarter. The last law school commencement exercises held in Lebanon took place June 1, 1961.[21] In anticipation of the law school's move, however, some law students pushed to complete their graduation requirements and to receive their degrees, without benefit of the pomp and circumstance of a commencement address, at the end of the summer quarter. Though Howard had assumed financial responsibility for the law school for that final summer quarter, those students, like those in the first law class that had included Nathan Green Jr., received Cumberland University degrees. The honor of receiving the last law degree issued in Lebanon went to Van Reeves Michael, a third-generation Cumberland alumnus from Sweetwater, Tennessee.[22] On Friday August 25, 1961, the summer quarter ended. The doors to old Caruthers Hall were closed forever.[23] Cumberland University sold the site, separated from the main Cumberland University campus by several blocks, and the new owners razed the law barn to construct a savings and loan office.

On Saturday, August 26, the day after the summer quarter was completed in Lebanon, Howard College announced the appointment of Arthur Weeks as acting dean.[24] Weeks, who as dean in Lebanon had presided over the transformation of Cumberland to a standard three-year law school and obtained ABA approval and AALS membership, now endeavored to coax the Cumberland law school *Phoenix* to rise from the ashes once again.

Howard College, whose campus provided the law school's new home, had been founded in 1842, by Alabama Baptists, the same year that Cumberland Presbyterians had founded Cumberland University in Lebanon (a coincidence President Stockton remarked on in his letter to Cumberland alumni announcing the law school's move).[25] Howard's founding president, Samuel Sterling Sherman, like Cumberland University's first president, Franceway Ranna Cossitt, was a graduate of Middlebury College in Vermont who had gone south to pursue a career in education.[26] Originally located in Marion, Alabama, on the edge of the cotton-growing Black Belt, Howard in 1887 had been moved to the new industrial city of Birmingham.[27]

Howard's move from Marion proved advantageous. The support of the larger Birmingham community, including that of many of Birmingham's business leaders, coupled with its connection with Alabama's largest religious denomination, allowed Howard to face successfully the financial adversities that frustrated Cumberland's development in little Lebanon. Shortly after the Southern Association of Colleges and Secondary Schools formulated standards for membership in 1920, Howard gained admission to membership, the goal that always eluded the first President Stockton at Cumberland. Howard had gained admission only through the association's agreement to waive the requirement of a minimum endowment of $500,000, and Howard, like Cumberland, was never free from financial concerns. During the Depression, Howard carried a heavy burden of debt with its own meager endowment invested in mortgages, many of which were in default. On the eve of the appointment of Davis as president, several faculty members were involuntarily "retired" for financial reasons. Though loss of association membership sometimes seemed imminent, Howard managed to emerge from the Depression and World War II a fully accredited member of the Southern Association.

In 1952, Davis obtained authority from the Alabama Baptist Convention to move Howard College from the East Lake campus, whose ancient buildings were in constant need of ever more expensive repair, to a new and more spacious campus consisting entirely of newly constructed buildings of a neo-Georgian style in the Birmingham suburb of Homewood. With the first eight buildings on the new site ready for occupancy, Davis oversaw the move to the new campus in September 1957. At the conclusion of that academic year, Davis, who was then seventy-five years of age, was elevated to the office of chancellor, with Wright succeeding him as president.

Not only was Birmingham a community more likely than Lebanon to attract law students, Howard College was a stronger, better established institution than Cumberland University. While Howard was by no means one of the country's or even the region's giants of higher education, the fact that it was a well-established institution helps account for the willingness of the ABA and the AALS to withhold suspension of the law school's accreditation. For example, at the May 17, 1961, meeting with the AALS, Hervey was impressed by the association memberships enjoyed not only by Howard but by various constituent schools, such as the music, education, and pharmacy schools.[28]

Now that the move to the new campus had been completed, Howard's leadership no doubt indulged ambitions for a larger role for the institution in the city and region, as well as within the Southern Baptist denomination. Several Baptist universities sponsored law schools. For Davis, acquisition of a law school meant that Howard, after long years of struggle, was now ready to take its place alongside Wake Forest, Baylor, Stetson, and Mercer. In meeting with the AALS Executive Committee in May, Davis evidenced an appreciation for the status a law school conferred on those institutions.[29] Indeed, in 1965, only shortly after dedication of the new law school building, Howard would claim university status for itself, changing its name to Samford University.

For Davis and Wright, a law school probably seemed a better fit with Howard's role as a denominational liberal arts college than other professional or graduate programs would have been. A group of Birmingham business and civic leaders had only recently explored with the Howard leadership the possibility of instituting an engineering school at Howard. Howard had rejected the suggestion, viewing an engineering school as requiring a disproportionate (and expensive) emphasis on the hard sciences.[30] A law school seemed a better fit with Howard's liberal arts orientation.

Birmingham civic leaders also welcomed the acquisition of the law school by Howard. In Birmingham, an organization called the Committee of 100, made up of the community's civic and financial leadership, was led by James Head, a Birmingham businessman and a member of the Howard board of trustees. Head told the *Birmingham News* that acquisition of the law school filled a need in the city for an accredited law school. Head viewed Howard's acquisition of an accredited law school as comparable to the recent opening of an engineering school by the University of Alabama in Birmingham as contributing to the array of educational opportunities available in the city. By coincidence, Howard acquired Cumberland School of Law only a few days after the infamous Mother's Day beatings of the Freedom Riders in Birmingham. For civic leaders like Head (who two years later would be a leader in the move to alter Birmingham's city government, resulting in the ouster of Eugene "Bull" Connor as police commissioner), acquisition of Cumberland School of Law probably seemed like a rare bit of positive news for the city.

In years to come the allocation of law school tuition revenue would become a recurring source of disagreement between the law school and the central administration. It is unlikely, however, that Howard in acquiring Cumberland's law school looked on it as a potential net revenue generator or "cash cow." For one thing, the law school had operated at a deficit during its last years in Lebanon. For another, Howard committed itself from the beginning to the expensive construction of a separate law school building within three years. At the dedication of the law school building in the spring of 1964, Dean Weeks recurred to the circumstances surrounding the founding of Cumberland Law School in 1847, when the Cumberland University trustees agreed to permit the law school to be established only on the assurance that they would not be called on to provide resources to support it. In contrast, Weeks observed, the Howard College trustees were under no such impression in acquiring the law school.

The years immediately following Howard's acquisition of Cumberland School of Law constituted an era of good feeling between the law school and the larger Howard community, including the Howard administration. Joining Weeks on the five-person faculty were Gilreath and Bailey, who had been on the Lebanon faculty, along with Bobby Aderholt, an Alabama native who had attended Cumberland (and who, with Gilreath, would prepare the last revision of *History of a Lawsuit*), and Wooten Pearce, a graduate of Berkeley and of Georgetown Law School. Patricia Coffman, a Cumberland law graduate who had served on the law library staffs at Mercer and at Santa Clara, served as law librarian. At its first meeting, on September 7, 1961, the law school faculty decided that "as a matter of courtesy" it would attend general college faculty meetings and certain chapel services.[31] In the second faculty meeting, they discussed a theme, under the heading "thought-of-the-month: The theme for thought was "INCONSPICUOUS INTEGRATION INTO THE COLLEGE."[32]

For baseball fans in the summer of 1961, the watchword was "61 in '61," in reference to the parallel attempt of New York Yankee sluggers Roger Maris and Mickey Mantle to break Babe Ruth's single season home run record.[33] Howard and Cumberland officials could well have adopted the same watchword with reference to the number of students they hoped to enroll that first September in Birmingham.[34] On September 17, 1961, less than a week after registration on September 11, President Wright was able to advise the executive committee of the Howard College Board that sixty students had enrolled in Cumberland School of Law, and that five more had requested permission to register late. Of the students enrolled, twenty-five were new students. In a report submitted to the ABA a few weeks later, Weeks reported a total of sixty-three students enrolled, of whom twenty-eight were first-years. Thus a total of thirty-five students had transferred from Lebanon as members of the second- and third-year classes.

At the time Howard acquired Cumberland School of Law, University of Alabama law graduates still enjoyed the diploma privilege (conferring bar membership on graduation from law school, without taking a bar exam) that had been long eliminated in Tennessee. Howard indicated that it would seek legislation to extend the diploma privilege to Cumberland graduates.[35] The American Bar Association Section on Legal Education had long opposed the diploma privilege. Rather than see the controversial principle of the diploma privilege extended, University of Alabama officials, eager to evidence their support for the ABA's position and perhaps believing that the performance of their graduates would always be superior to that of the Cumberland graduates, indicated that they would have no objection to elimination of the diploma privilege. According to Weeks, this was exactly the outcome that Howard and Cumberland had expected in proposing extension of the diploma privilege.[36] In any event, the outcome was a level playing field between Cumberland and Alabama as to requirements for admission for the Alabama bar.

At the time of the acquisition, Wright had announced that Howard anticipated constructing a separate building for the law school within three years.[37] Possibly Wright already had an informal commitment for funding the building from Frank P. Samford, then Howard's most generous benefactor. At a meeting of the executive committee of the Howard board of trustees on November 7, 1961, Wright called on Frank P. Samford to announce that an anonymous gift of $548,000 had been received for the construction of a law building on condition that it be named for Memory L. Robinson,[38] and at the annual meeting of the board on May 21, 1962, he revealed that Mr. and Mrs. Frank P. Samford were the anonymous donors. Wright stated the gift constituted "by far the largest contribution ever made to Howard College by any individual or corporation."[39]

On March 7, 1962, Howard College formed a sixteen-member law school advisory board. The various committees of the board included a law building committee. Not surprisingly, Samford was chair of this committee, which met in April 1962 and approved preliminary architectural plans.[40] Official groundbreaking took place on October 9, 1962.[41] The law school moved into the building, designed to accommodate a student body of 200 and a library of 94,000 volumes,[42] during the 1963–64 Christmas break. Dedication ceremonies were held April 17–18, 1964, with the principal address delivered by Lewis F. Powell, then president of the American Bar Association and later justice of the United States Supreme Court. Other speakers included Judge Grooms, a trustee who had been active in effecting the acquisition; Chief Judge Harry Phillips of the Sixth Circuit Court of Appeals and a Cumberland alumnus; and United States Representative George Huddleston Jr. of the Birmingham district and the son of a Cumberland law alumnus. John Hervey, the ABA Adviser on Legal Education who had presided over Cumberland Law School's initial accreditation by the ABA in 1949 and then over the retention of accreditation in connection with the move from Lebanon, received an honorary doctorate from Howard College during the ceremonies.[43]

In 1965, Howard College changed its name to Samford University. The change bore witness to the increased importance of graduate and professional education at the institution, and also recognized the longtime leadership and financial contributions of Frank P. Samford. The school of arts and sciences retained the name "Howard College."

With a total enrollment of 63 students, in the fall of 1961, its first year in Birmingham, Cumberland was the smallest member of the AALS. By the 1965–66 academic year, Cumberland had 283 students in its full-time or regular program, together with 49 in the freshman class of a newly initiated evening or extended program, for a total enrollment of 332. In his dean's report that year, Weeks could proudly proclaim that Cumberland was "now the largest Baptist law school in the nation and one of the largest law schools in the Southeast."[44]

For Cumberland, vexed with low enrollments throughout its last decade in Lebanon, an enrollment of 332 no doubt seemed a bonanza. The following year, however, total enrollment reached 381 (298 day students and 83 evening students) and in 1967–68 exceeded 400 for the first time in Cumberland's history. In that year there were 423 students enrolled (321 in the day program and 102 in the evening program). In the 1970–71 academic year enrollment totaled 404, of whom 303 were day students and 101 were evening students.[45] In large measure, the growth in enrollment at Cumberland mirrored developments in legal education generally. In the fall of 1961, total enrollment at ABA-approved law schools in the United States totaled 41,499. In the fall of 1966, total enrollment at ABA-approved schools had increased to 62,556, and by the fall of 1970 had increased to 82,499, an increase of nearly 100 percent over 1961.[46] Cumberland's enrollment increase had been proportionately greater in the same period, but its starting numbers in 1961 were particularly low.

With the possible exception of Weeks, those involved with Howard's acquisition of Cumberland envisioned that the law school would achieve a size of 200 to 300. Robinson had in mind a school of about 200, and the law building dedicated in 1964 was designed for a student body of 200 to 300 students.[47] A study of American legal education for the period 1955–1970 found that law schools at the beginning of the period fell roughly into two categories, small schools with enrollments below 250, and large schools with enrollment ranging from 250 to as many as 1,500. The small school category accounted for two-thirds of the law schools in the country, but, with an average enrollment of only about 140 students, only about one-third of the total law students enrolled. Schools in the study's large school category made up only one-third of the schools in the country but, with an average enrollment of 490 students, accounted for two-thirds of the students enrolled. Average faculty size at small schools was 8 to 10 while at large schools it was about 20. Generally the large schools enjoyed the greater prestige. By teaching basic courses in large classes, they were able to offer a richer curriculum with more electives, and their faculties were more research-oriented. At small schools faculty numbers were usually barely sufficient to cover the basic cirriculum, but smaller classes and a faculty not greatly preoccupied with research had the advantage of allowing students to enjoy more contact with a faculty.[48]

Memory Leake Robinson Hall seemed designed to place Cumberland at the upper end of the small school category. Weeks pressed unsuccessfully for a larger building with an unfinished upper floor that could accommodate further expansion in enrollment. Although the building lacked room for expansion, Weeks found a way to make greater use of the building by adding an evening division. He was thereby able to expand the student body beyond the size for which the building was designed. Besides increasing enrollment, the extended program also permitted persons in the community to enroll who might otherwise have been unable to attend law school. Donald E. Corley, who would succeed Weeks as dean, started law school at night and then switched to the regular program after his outstanding performance persuaded him to give up his day job. Thomas B. Bishop, who had made a name for himself as a debate coach at Mississippi State University, decided to attend Cumberland and to accept an appointment as Samford's debate coach after Weeks assured him that he could attend either day or evening classes as his duties as debate coach permitted. Bishop turned down an offer from the University of Mississippi, whose law dean, Parham H. Williams Jr., could not offer the same accommodation to his schedule.[49]

The law school's evening program expanded access to legal education in other ways as well, at least indirectly. In January 1967, Samford admitted its first black student, a young housewife named Audrey Lattimore Gaston who had applied to the law school's evening program. Cumberland's move to Alabama probably made integration more difficult than it would have been in Tennessee; it probably also occurred later in Alabama.

In relocating from middle Tennessee to central Alabama in 1961, the law school had moved from a border state where public opinion permitted leaders, several of whom were connected to Cumberland, to adopt a moderate stance on racial issues, to a Deep South state where the opposition to racial integration was most intransigent. In central Alabama, on the other hand, challenges to racial segregation had been met with confrontation and violence. In Birmingham, 1963 had been the year of greatest turmoil. April and May had seen the use of police dogs and fire hoses against demonstrators protesting segregated lunch counters downtown, and September had witnessed the Sunday morning bombing of the Sixteenth Street Baptist Church, in which four young girls were killed.[50]

All law schools in the South were racially segregated by state law until 1950, when the Supreme Court ruled that blacks could not constitutionally be excluded from the state-supported law school at the University of Texas.[51] That ruling did not directly affect private law schools, but in 1963 the American Bar Association had adopted a position prohibiting racial segregation by any approved law school, and a similar requirement had been adopted as a requirement of membership in the AALS.[52]

In 1967 Samford still adhered to a policy of admitting only white students, and accordingly the matter of Gaston's admission had to be resolved at the board of trustees level. No doubt Birmingham's recent history, as well as the ABA and AALS requirements, were in the mind of Wright as he laid the matter first before the executive committee on January 17, 1967, and then before a called meeting of the full board four days later. Weeks attended the meeting of the full board, as did representatives of the Alabama Baptist Convention. According to the minutes of the meeting of the full board, Wright reported that the law school had previously denied admission to academically unqualified black applications. But he pointed out that, since Gaston was academically qualified for admission, denial of her application could result in censure of the university by the AALS, as had occurred at the University of Richmond under similar circumstances. Knowledge of the application was widespread, and Wright pointed out that the applicant was the wife of a grandson of A. G. Gaston, Birmingham's wealthiest black businessman and one who had played a significant role in resolving the city's recent conflicts. A better candidate to break the institution's color barrier could scarcely be found, and a motion to admit her was "overwhelmingly carried." Three and one-half years later, in May 1970, Audrey Lattimore Gaston became the first black person to graduate from Samford University or from Cumberland School of Law.[53]

By 1968, the law school faculty had not only grown, it had also changed. Of the five who had constituted the original Birmingham faculty in 1961, only Weeks remained. Several of those on the 1968 faculty had retired from other positions. They included William Rollison, newly retired after twenty years on the Notre Dame law faculty and author of a textbook on wills and estates, who added a touch of distinction; "Commander" James Hughes and Loren Bulloch, both retired military lawyers; Walter Sowa, also an older faculty member; and Raymond Hutchens, who had served as dean at another law school. Claude Bankester, who had taught at Lebanon before the move, returned in 1962 from two years spent pursuing graduate studies at Virginia and working for a congressional committee in Washington, and in that same year a scholarly former FBI agent, Frank Donaldson, also joined the faculty. In 1965, the law school added Janie L. Shores, the first full-time female law faculty member in Alabama and the second in the Southeast. Shores had been at the top of her class at the University of Alabama Law School. Two young January 1966 graduates, Charles Cole and John Harrell, joined the faculty almost immediately following their graduation. In August 1967 Annette Dodd, Janie Shores's law school classmate, succeeded Chriss Doss, who had served as librarian while pursuing his law degree at Cumberland, and Edwin Sterne, with an LL.M. from Chicago, joined the faculty.

By 1968, Cumberland had brought together a more ambitious and energetic faculty. Shores and Dodd both pursued graduate studies at the University of Mississippi Law School, abandoning that effort only to support Shores's campaign for the Alabama Supreme Court. She ultimately became the first woman elected to the court. Cole devoted a series of summers to obtaining an LL.M. from New York University, before leaving the law school for a number of years to be involved in court reform. Harrell left law teaching and became a partner in Alabama's largest law firm. Donaldson ran for the United States Congress on the Republican ticket. His race was not successful, but he did ultimately serve as U.S. Attorney from 1981 to 1993. Overall, by 1968 the faculty had become a more self-assertive group, one that ventilated any grievances in the way that deans and university administrators all over the country have come to expect of law professors.

Grievances there were, as Weeks and the Samford administration probably were already aware. The evening program, now fully implemented, imposed a substantial burden, as faculty members often were required to teach one or more courses in the morning or early afternoon, and then either remain on campus or return in the evening. Moreover, faculty members were on a twelve-month contract that required them to teach in the summer term for no additional compensation.

Low faculty salaries added to faculty discontent. In 1968 the Faculty Relations Committee, chaired by Professor Shores, did a study that found that of church-related law schools in the South, Cumberland had the lowest salaries at every faculty level, as well as the lowest average salary. A comparison with all law schools in Florida, Georgia, Tennessee, and Alabama yielded the same result.[54]

The faculty forwarded a copy of its report to the Samford University administration. The Samford administration attempted to address the problem. On May 1, 1968, Wright requested authorization from the executive committee of the trustees to launch a $1 million endowment campaign for the law school, with appeals to be made to law alumni, Alabama law firms, foundations, and others.[55] At the annual meeting of the Samford board on May 31, 1968, Wright announced the creation of the Cumberland Law School Foundation, gifts to which could only be used for law school purposes. A prominent Atlanta alumnus of the Lebanon campus was named chairman of the fund-raising drive. In his report to the trustees two years later, Wright stressed that "faculty salaries must be increased in accordance with national norms. It is absolutely imperative that revenue sources other than tuition be developed to their fullest potential."[56]

However, the endowment campaign fizzled. After 1970, there is no further mention of it in the trustee minutes or the president's annual report. The failure of the campaign is not surprising. After all, less than ten years earlier, the Lebanon leadership had been unable to raise $500,000 in order to keep the school in Tennessee, and most graduates of the Birmingham campus had only recently begun building their practices. In any event, it seems clear that the campaign was unable to raise enough resources to deal with the problem of exceedingly low faculty salaries, as that is one of the problems identified by an ABA report after a 1971 inspection.

After the move from Lebanon, Hervey inspected the law school again for the ABA, in May 1962, at the end of its first year in Birmingham. Hervey returned in 1964, but no other inspection occurred until that of Dean Roy L. Steinheimer Jr. in 1971. The Steinheimer inspection was the first of a series of inspections and mandated self-studies and progress reports imposed by the ABA and the AALS. The law school was occupied almost continuously with accreditation difficulties for more than a decade.

Steinheimer's 1971 report identified four glaring problems: faculty salaries, which were found to be "among the lowest of all of the accredited law schools in the nation"; a student faculty ratio of over 36:1, which the report found to be too high; admission of too many students who were only marginally qualified; and a lack of scholarship funds. The report called for Cumberland to submit follow-up reports as to how it dealt with these problems in 1971–72 and 1972–73.[57]

Steinheimer's report observed that the law school building could not accommodate more than 400 students and assumed that there would be little further growth in the size of the student body. Dealing with the problem areas identified by the ABA would require additional resources, however. For Cumberland, a tuition-driven school that had just tried unsuccessfully to raise endowment through gifts, the only practicable source of resources to hire new faculty and to increase the faculty salary structure was to admit more students. A portion of the resources generated could be applied to fund scholarships for well-qualified students, thereby improving the student profile, despite taking more students. On August 29, 1971, Wright informed the executive committee that in order to address the ABA concerns, it was necessary to raise the enrollment maximum in the law school from 450 to 600.[58] That fall the law school enrolled a first-year class in the full-time division of 282 students, with total enrollment in the day division amounting to 505. In addition, enrollment in the evening division, soon to be phased out, totaled 92,[59] for a total only barely below

600.[60] By 1976, total enrollment would exceed 700,[61] and continued above 700 for the balance of the decade. In fall 1980, total enrollment was 748, and in fall 1984, 729.[62]

While the 1971 Cumberland decision to increase enrollment may have been driven by the need to increase resources in response to Steinheimer's ABA inspection report, Cumberland's growth in enrollment in the 1970s mirrored the trend in legal education generally. In the fall of 1971, law school enrollment in ABA approved law schools totaled 94,468. By 1980, total enrollment had reached 125,397, finally cresting in 1982 at 127,828. Writing in 1985, a veteran legal educator looked back at the law school world of about the time Cumberland moved to Birmingham and observed that it "seems almost a miniature."[63]

While the growth in law school enrollment in the 1960s may have been largely a reflection of the coming of age of the "baby boomers" born during or immediately after World War II, in the 1970s the most important element in the growth in enrollment was the fact that women were going to law school in unprecedented numbers. In the fall of 1971, a total of 8,914 women enrolled in American law schools. The fall of 1982 saw 47,083 women enrolled, for an increase of 38,169, or over 400 percent. Because total law school enrollment during the same period increased 33,360 (from 94,468 to 127,828), it is clear that the increase in the number of women was sufficient in and of itself to account for the overall increase in enrollment.[64] Cumberland's enrollment figures during the 1980s reflect this trend as well, though not quite to the same extent. In the fall of 1971, of the approximately 600 students enrolled at Cumberland, only 32, or about 5 percent, were women. The large entering class of 282 that matriculated that year included only eleven women.[65] By 1980, Cumberland's total enrollment of 748 students included 150 women, approximately 20 percent of the total.[66] By 1985, when overall enrollment at Cumberland had decreased to 665, enrollment of women had increased to 163, or approximately 25 percent of the total enrollment.

Cumberland made its follow-up report to the ABA at a meeting in New Orleans on February 3, 1972. President Wright, Dean Weeks, and Judge H. H. Grooms attended the meeting, along with other members of the university and law school administration. They reported that the median faculty salary had been substantially raised and that the scholarship budget had doubled. On March 29, 1972, Grooms reported to the executive committee and characterized the meeting as completely satisfactory.[67]

While the immediate concerns of the ABA might have been temporarily satisfied, the increase in enrollment had created problems of its own. Not only were additional resources needed to hire additional faculty members to hold down the student-faculty ratio, resources would also be necessary to fund an expansion of the law building to accommodate the increased enrollment. The use of classrooms for law classes in neighboring undergraduate buildings could only be a temporary expedient.[68] After the New Orleans meeting, Weeks became convinced he lacked the confidence of Wright and the board necessary to expand the law school's facilities. At the end of the 1971–72 academic year, Weeks offered his resignation. Among his suggestions for acting dean was a junior professor, Donald E. Corley, one of the three faculty members added in the fall of 1971. That summer Corley became acting dean.[69]

Corley had grown up in Linden, a small town in Alabama's black belt. He attended Auburn University, completed graduate work in accounting, and was employed by a Birmingham industrial concern, American Cast Iron Pipe Co., as a staff accountant. Corley later recalled that from the time he had watched trials in the county courthouse in Linden, his dream had been to become a lawyer. When Cumberland opened an evening division, Corley saw his opportunity. Working a full day, then attending law school at night, he developed an ulcer, which disappeared when, having performed successfully in the law school program, he decided to leave his employment and enroll in law school full-time. Interested in an academic career, upon graduation from Cumberland he accepted appointment in the business school at the University of Alabama, where he was elected "Outstanding Professor" in 1971. That fall Cumberland's increase in enrollment permitted it to add to the faculty, and Corley became a law professor. Only one year later, Corley accepted the acting dean's chair.[70]

Corley now faced the task of transforming the school into one whose facilities, library, faculty, student body, and resources met the heightened expectations of the legal education establishment (represented by the ABA and the AALS) and of the Cumberland faculty and students themselves in the 1970s and 1980s. An experienced legal educator, in comparing legal education in 1985 with 1956, noted "the enormous increase in resources now devoted to legal education."[71] With growth in the size of the law school student bodies came larger faculties, new or expanded law school buildings, greater library holdings, broader curricular offerings, including clinical programs, and overall the commitment of far greater resources to legal education than had been the case earlier.[72] Increased resource commitments were possible even for tuition-driven private schools, where increasingly tuition was financed through long-term loan programs rather than paid from savings or current income of students and their families.[73] At Cumberland, however, the increase in resources devoted to training lawyers lagged behind developments at other schools. It was under Corley's leadership that Cumberland was able to make up a substantial amount of the lost ground.

Corley had a brief time to settle in to his new position and address a variety of internal administrative problems. The school's administrative and record-keeping procedures had failed to keep pace with the increase in student body size. Corley had served as chair of the academic standards committee and had dealt with deficiencies found in the records of a number of seniors scheduled for graduation. Corley's skill in resolving that situation probably prompted Weeks to suggest him as a possibility for the deanship. The substantially larger entering class admitted in 1971, though its average entrance credentials exceeded slightly those of the previous class, found a number of its members in academic difficulty at the end of the spring term. Professor Annette Dodd, appointed to succeed Corley as chair of the academic standards committee, took up the tasks of academic dismissals and readmissions and of overseeing students' completion of academic requirements for graduation.[74] Larger classes also meant more difficulties in registration, and Corley appointed Professor Thomas B. ("Brad") Bishop, who like Corley had joined the faculty only in the fall of 1971, to handle registration for the 1972 summer term.[75] A number of Cumberland graduates failed the Alabama bar examination in the summer of 1972, and Corley assembled information for the faculty on the academic backgrounds of those students. The school was not only admitting a larger entering class, it was also receiving a larger number of applications. In the fall of 1970, Cumberland had received approximately

350 applications; for fall 1971, 650; and for fall 1972, 1,339. In numerous reports submitted to the faculty, Corley insisted on a better organized admissions process.[76]

On March 25, 1973, Wright reported to the executive committee on Corley's success in working out "certain internal problems in the Law School which have accumulated over the years . . . largely [involving] faculty relations with students, faculty committee work on the admission and retention of students, academic standards and law school budget." Wright reported that Corley had "made a number of improvements in the faculty structure and in admissions and retention policies." Earlier trustee minutes had made vague references to appointment of a search committee for a permanent dean, but with few details. At the March 25 meeting, Wright announced that Grooms would chair the search committee. Previously the committee's work was delayed "pending an opportunity to work out some of the internal problems in the law school," but, with those problems eliminated, the committee could begin its work. Wright stated that Corley had indicated an interest in the deanship and would "of course, be among those considered by the Committee."[77]

To all indications, Corley seemed about to receive the permanent appointment, but first another challenge awaited him. On February 15, 1973, Millard Ruud, Hervey's successor as ABA liaison, wrote Wright and Corley that the ABA Council on Legal Education continued to have doubts whether Cumberland had remedied the weaknesses identified in the 1971 Steinheimer report. In sharing Ruud's letter with the Cumberland faculty, Corley indicated that while there had been progress in some areas identified in the Steinheimer report, some of the weaknesses were worse than at the time of the Steinheimer inspection. Corley noted that while scholarship funds had been increased and the university had approved five new faculty members for the next academic year, there was a "drastic need" for additional classroom and office space, faculty salaries were still well below the national median (which Corley estimated at $20,000 a year, more than that of any Cumberland professor), and the student faculty ratio, which should be near 20:1, was actually near 40:1. Nevertheless, Corley was upbeat, reasoning that Ruud's visit was unlikely to result in disaccreditation and more likely would benefit the law school.[78]

Ruud visited Cumberland on April 18, 1973. His follow-up report confirmed concerns about the strength of Cumberland's program. By November, Ruud had changed jobs, taking the position of executive director of the AALS. In that capacity he wrote Wright and Corley on November 13, 1973, indicating that Steinheimer's 1971 reinspection report and Ruud's own 1973 follow-up report raised questions about Cumberland's compliance with the AALS's membership requirements. Accordingly, the AALS conducted a reinspection of the school in April 1974. The subsequent AALS report identified several areas of concern, including faculty and law library staff salaries, which "may well be the most important problem"; library acquisitions "both in volume and type"; and faculty/student ratio "requiring an increase in the size of the faculty."[79]

The report recognized that the university already had made plans for a campaign to answer the lack of classroom space and office space needed to accommodate the increased enrollment. The report noted that Samford had completed plans for an addition that would double the size of the law school building and that a $1 million challenge gift had been received toward a $3 million endowment campaign, $2 million of which would be used for the building addition. The challenge gift came from a bequest from the estate of Frank P. Samford Sr., who, together with his wife, had provided the funds for the original law school building.[80] Under the direction of a professional fund-raising consultant, the campaign, known as the "Phoenix Fund," eventually reached at least $2.5 million, including major gifts from the Samford estate and the Daniel Foundation. Construction began in March 1976, and the addition was available in time for the fall 1977 academic year with an official dedication on November 4, 1977.[81]

As to the other areas of concern, the 1974 AALS report proposed that the dean and faculty of the law school formulate for university approval a five-year program, with annual subgoals, to deal with each problem area. Corley, appointed to the permanent deanship in July 1974, appointed a committee to conduct the study, chaired by Charles Gamble, who had joined the faculty at the beginning of the 1972–73 academic year, and who would later become dean at the University of Alabama Law School.

Conducting the study and setting the nonfinancial goals to establish Cumberland as a law school of some stature proved easier than getting university approval of the annual budget goals. Samford's traditional approach had been one of comparatively low tuition, coupled with a policy of fiscal restraint with regard to recurring budget items, such as faculty salaries and library acquisitions. This approach no doubt reflected Howard College's experiences in the Depression, when the college had survived financially only by dismissing a number of faculty members. Probably the strategy also reflected the university's religious mission. Low tuition served to make the school's programs accessible to a broad range of families in the denominational constituency as well as in Birmingham and Alabama generally. Finally Samford's campus, while strikingly attractive, probably required greater maintenance expense than a more functional but less aesthetic campus would have, which decreased the availability of funds for direct instructional purposes.

The dean search process that ultimately resulted in Corley's appointment reflected the gap between Samford's low salary structure and the salary structure in legal education generally. On January 24, 1974, Judge Grooms, chair of the search committee, advised a meeting of the executive committee of Samford's board that "the task has been difficult due to the fact that the salary range at the Cumberland School of Law is considerably lower than at most law schools." In May, Grooms reported that the committee had interviewed a number of prospects, some of whom were interested in the position "but their request for compensation was far above what the University could afford to pay." Grooms advised that the only prospect who had not been eliminated was Acting Dean Corley, who had "done a splendid job as acting Dean," was "well qualified," and enjoyed "the respect and confidence of the students." Grooms correctly predicted that Corley would be selected at the next meeting of the search committee.[82]

The efforts of Gamble's committee to set five-year budget goals for the law school encountered resistance from the university administration. On March 13, 1975, the law faculty approved the self-study and the committee submitted it to the university administration. The administration then rejected those portions of the report setting budget goals and recommended its own, much lower goals. On June 18, 1975, the faculty voted to resubmit the original report to the administration without change. In August, Gamble reported that he and the chair of the budget subcommittee, Professor Kenneth R. Manning Jr., had met again with university academic vice president

Ruric Wheeler but that the administration's position was unchanged. On September 11, 1975, Gamble reported that at Wheeler's request, Corley had worked out a compromise five-year budget projection, which the faculty committee then rejected, believing that "a mediocre law school would be projected" under the compromise.

On November 10, 1975, Ruud wrote Corley requesting a copy of the completed five-year report by December 10, in order for it to be considered by the AALS accreditation committee at its meeting in late December. Perhaps prompted by the imminence of that deadline, President Wright began meeting personally with Gamble's committee. On December 2, 1975, Gamble, noting that "a breakthrough was evident," presented budget projections that included a substantial increase in tuition over five years (reporting that "the more they looked at the figures, the more they realized that the primary problem was insufficient funds—inadequate tuition") which would result in an increased library collection and meet the national median in faculty salary by 1979–80. On December 9, Corley forwarded copies of the self-study and five-year projection to Ruud.

After consideration by the AALS accreditation committee, Cumberland's report reached the AALS executive committee at its meeting in late May 1976. Despite the efforts that had gone into the self-study and the concessions made by the Samford administration, the five-year projections did not go far enough. On June 1, Ruud advised Wright and Corley that the AALS executive committee had determined that the self-study "discloses a lack of a plan to comply fully" with certain AALS member requirements and had ordered a new inspection of the school in the fall of 1977 "to consider the advisability of action pursuant to Article 7 of the Bylaws," that is, membership suspension or expulsion.[83] On October 16–19, a combined ABA and AALS team inspected Cumberland.

Their report was generally complimentary of the progress the school had made since Steinheimer's visit in 1971 and particularly praised the attractiveness of the new addition to the law building. Nevertheless, in polite but insistent tones, the report hammered on areas, such as its library, where Cumberland lagged behind national norms. While praising the work of the head law librarian, Laurel R. Clapp, an experienced law librarian hired by Corley in 1975, the report pointed out that while only 35 law schools had a larger full-time enrollment than Cumberland's, the library ranked 135th in total volumes and lacked an adequate support staff. The report also observed that "despite very marked improvement over the past several years, the faculty salary scale is very low by national and regional standards" and that "it is still one of the lowest among law schools of the entire country." As to salaries of library staff, those were "very low even by Birmingham standards." The report also found very little scholarly research and writing, in part because of a lack of financial support.

Underlying the report's finding of a poor commitment of resources to the library and faculty salaries was a concern with the proportion of law-school-generated revenue that, under Samford's budgeting process, went to indirect costs or overhead rather than to direct support of the instructional program. Indirect costs refer to the costs of various services and facilities provided by the university, which law students share with other university students, such as the costs to support the university's main library, student union, and athletic facilities, as well as such general expenses as utility costs, which had become increasingly significant in the 1970s. Samford had adopted the convention of allocating such costs among its various schools based on each school's total credit hours taught. While this method of allocating shared costs among the various units of the university had the merit of simplicity of application, it probably had the result of overcharging the law school budget in terms of actual utilization by law students of shared facilities. As the report observed: "Despite the handsome and spacious addition to the law school building, which has more than doubled its square footage and given the school much higher quality spaces, it is questionable that one-fifth of all utility costs are generated by the law school, even considering extensive use by the law school of the student service facilities such as the cafeteria and recreational space."

The issue of indirect costs is certainly not so visible a marker of the quality of a law school's program as is the size of its library collection, the credentials and scholarship of its faculty, or the quality of its student journals. Nevertheless, to the extent law student tuition dollars are used to cover indirect costs, those dollars are unavailable to support expenditures more directly related to the quality of the instructional program. The report, as the quoted language indicates, was concerned that law school tuition was covering more of such expenses than was justified. To the extent the law school's share of such expenses were reduced, resources would be available to address the various deficiencies in the law school identified by the report.

The ABA accreditation committee was the first to act on the 1977 inspection report. On June 2, 1978, James P. White, the ABA consultant, wrote Corley and Wright notifying them of the accreditation committee's finding that the law school might not be in conformance with ABA Standards. Specific accreditation committee concerns were "very high overhead costs assessed the School of Law," an underpaid library staff with insufficient clerical support and a library collection insufficient for the size of the student body and to sustain scholarly research by the faculty, low faculty salaries, an unfavorable faculty/student ratio, and insufficient support for scholarly research. Cumberland was required to show by July 1, 1978, that steps were being taken to remedy the stated deficiencies or the committee would thereafter consider whether to recommend that "proceedings be initiated to determine whether Cumberland School of Law of Samford University should be removed from the list of approved schools."[84]

Doubtlessly Wright and other members of the Samford administration thought they had been more than supportive of the law school in the past. Wright had engineered the purchase of Cumberland Law School, saving it from closing, and the construction of the law school building and its addition had been funded primarily by gifts from friends of the university, particularly the Samford family. Though faculty salaries were well below the national median, they had been substantially increased in recent years. When John Hervey inspected the law school in 1963, his report had stated that he was sure Howard College officials would not regret the law school's acquisition. By 1978, Wright might have begun to doubt Hervey's prophecy.

Nevertheless, in a letter of June 23, 1978, responding to the ABA action, Wright undertook fresh financial commitments to the law school. He agreed to revise the method of calculating indirect costs, resulting in an additional $270,000 available to the law school for the budget year 1978–79, two-thirds of which was allocated to the law library. The book budget for 1978–79 increased by 124 percent over the previous year. Addressing the problem of an unfavorable faculty/student ratio, Wright also committed to add two new faculty positions in 1979–80 and two more in 1980–81, to bring the size of the faculty to thirty, without increasing student enrollment, as well as to increase the size of the library clerical staff. Finally, Wright agreed to raise salaries of the law library staff, to achieve the national median in faculty salaries, and to establish a fund to aid faculty research. Later that summer a similar commitment was made to the AALS.

At a July 22–24 meeting, the ABA accreditation committee found that "genuine concern has been expressed and meaningful action taken by Samford University and Cumberland School of Law in initially addressing findings in the Committee's resolution of May, 1978." Follow-up reports would be required for at least three more years, along with the fine-tuning of some commitments, but with the increase in resources beginning in June 1978, Cumberland's program had taken a substantial step forward. Cumberland School of Law's budgets from 1972–73 through 1979–80 increased overall from $537,498 to $1,840,400, an increase of 242 percent, which represented progress despite the high inflation of the period. Scholarships increased from $43,000 to $160,000 (272 percent), and the book budget for the library grew from $54,000 to $279,766 (418 percent). Reflecting an increase in compensation as well as numbers, faculty salaries increased from $279,180 in 1972 to $766,400 in 1979, while the number of full-time faculty members increased from 17 to 29.[85] Ironically, these dramatic increases in the law school's resources had been achieved under the leadership of a dean who, in 1974, was the only decanal candidate willing to accept the position despite the university's low salary scale.

The careers of Weeks and Corley, contrasted with those of Green and Martin, illustrate the changes in the world of legal education in a little more than half a century. Green and Martin were masters of their own destiny. The university exercised little if any control of their conduct of the law school operations in Caruthers Hall and certainly had no say in its financial policies. Since the two of them constituted the entire regular faculty, no adjustments had to be made to conciliate disgruntled law faculty. Nor was it necessary to expend efforts or funds to comply with the mandates of the ABA or the AALS, of whose existence they gave little if any notice. After the elimination of the diploma privilege in 1903, some attention had to be given to the necessity of equipping students to take the bar examination, but other than that, their only concern was in providing a product that was satisfactory to the students, their paying customers. Weeks, and especially Corley, operated in a far different world. As dean, each mediated among a number of conflicting constituencies: central university administrators and trustees, accreditation inspection teams, and assertive faculty leaders, as well as students now paying higher tuition and imbued with a modern consumer consciousness. The 1974 inspection report captured the role of the modern dean, as well as Corley's ability in playing that role: "Dean Corley has walked a fine line, apparently with substantial success. On the one hand, he appears to have the faculty and student body behind him in his efforts to correct the School's principle [*sic*] deficiencies. On the other, he apparently is able to work effectively with the University administration in obtaining a greater understanding of the problems of the Law School, and consequently, greater financial support."

At the end of the 1982–83 academic year, Wright retired, having completed twenty-five years of service as president of Howard and of Samford. Corley served on the presidential search committee, whose efforts ultimately resulted in the board's selection of Thomas E. Corts to succeed Wright. Corts commenced his service in the summer of 1983 and was formally inaugurated on November 19, 1983. As early as the spring of 1982, Corley apparently had considered leaving the law school for a position in judicial administration[86] but announced to the law faculty in April 1982 his decision to remain.[87] Now, with a change in command in the president's office, and, on a sad note, perhaps already aware of the illness that would claim his life less than two years later, Corley tendered his resignation as dean, announcing this to the law faculty on February 6, 1984. Brad Bishop was appointed to serve as acting dean.[88]

CHAPTER TEN

Student Life and Accomplishments 1961–1983

When the school began winning legal writing contests, and the fraternities received outstanding recognition on a national basis, the spirit of accomplishment seemed to permeate the whole school.
—"Dedicated to Dean Arthur A. Weeks A Decade of Progress," *Cumberland Lawyer* (November 1971)

The law school has a wide range of co-curricular activities which seem to be thriving. The newly established law review is off to an excellent start. . . . The moot court and legal aid programs are healthy enterprises which are energetically supported by the students. . . . The student bar association is very active in all facets of the affairs of the law school.
—American Bar Association, *Report on Cumberland School of Law, Samford University, Birmingham, Alabama, March 31, April 1 and 2, 1971*

ELABORATE MOCK TRIALS and hard-fought student elections, debate societies and state-specific law clubs, intercollegiate athletics, fraternities, and Judge Gilreath's Sunday morning Bible class all marked law student life at Cumberland in Lebanon from the 1920s through 1940s. During the 1950s, with reduced law school enrollment, student activities continued, but at a more modest level. After the move to Birmingham, as law school enrollment increased from 63 students in 1961 to more than 600 students a little more than a decade later, extracurricular activities bloomed once more. Extracurricular life in the 1960s and 1970s at Cumberland in Birmingham differed, however, from that at Cumberland in Lebanon in two respects. First, in Birmingham extracurricular activity was directed not only at serving the educational and social needs of the students, but also at achieving regional and national recognition for the school. Second, Cumberland in Birmingham, now a mainstream, three-year, case method law school, emphasized those student activities, such as appellate advocacy and law review, typical of such schools and reflecting the educational philosophy underlying the three-year, case-oriented model.

At Cumberland in the 1960s and 1970s student activities assumed a new role in the life of the institution. In Lebanon extracurricular activities had provided an outlet for law student energies, an opportunity for socializing, and a chance to develop skills that would be useful in the practice of law or in politics. In Birmingham, extracurricular activities assumed the additional purpose of winning recognition for the law school and its students. For decades, Cumberland had celebrated the achievements of its alumni, including in each law school catalogue an ever-lengthening list of former Cumberland students who had achieved reknown as judges, governors, members of Congress, state legislators, and of course, in the case of Cordell Hull, cabinet members. Now trophies captured by the student bar association, legal fraternity chapters, competitive moot court teams, and student authors of prize-winning essays came to be seen as outward and visible signs of the quality of the law school's program. Cumberland in the 1960s and 1970s encouraged an array of student activities, some new and some with roots in the past, but all with a view to planting the school's flag on distant shores. In Birmingham under the deanships of Arthur A. Weeks and Donald E. Corley, student activities became a mechanism for publicizing Cumberland.

A lead article in the student-edited *Cumberland Lawyer* in November 1971, shortly after Weeks's resignation as dean, noted that under his leadership Cumberland had ceased to emphasize "purely intramural competitive" activities and instead emphasized activities that "would place Cumberland students on a working relationship with students and schools on a national basis."[1]

The activities of Cumberland legal fraternities during the 1960s afford an example of the shift in emphasis toward national involvement. In Lebanon, legal fraternities had formed a significant element in the infrastructure of student life, performing some functions, such as sponsorship of speakers, that would later be assumed by the student bar association. Judge John A. Jamison, a 1941 graduate, was a member of the Sigma Delta Kappa law fraternity, which then had an active chapter at the law school. Jamison recalls that the SDKs sponsored talks by practicing lawyers to the student body.[2] National social fraternities, such as Sigma Alpha Epsilon, whose chapter houses near the law school had once attracted many law students, were not reestablished at the law school after World War II, and this may have stimulated an increased interest in legal fraternities. In 1951, when the law school occupied Memorial Hall after the suspension of the undergraduate program, a room was set aside for each of the two legal fraternities then active, the Green Senate (chapter) of Delta Theta Phi and the Cordell Hull Chapter of Phi Alpha Delta.[3] A law sorority, Iota Tau Tau, also was active.[4]

Both Delta Theta Phi and Phi Alpha Delta continued to be active in Birmingham, where they were soon joined by the Robinson Inn of Phi Delta Phi and by a revived chapter of Jamison's fraternity, Sigma Delta Kappa,[5] along with a new legal sorority, Phi Delta Delta.[6] For the wives of law students, the Cumberland Law Wives provided a focus for social and service activities. By 1971, law fraternities were admitting women members and the law sorority had disappeared; by the mid-1980s the Law Wives, following the admission of a "law husband," had become the Legal Auxiliary.[7] The fraternities were sufficiently important that the *Cumberland Lawyer* featured a column in each issue on fraternity activities.[8]

The pattern of social activities characteristic of fraternity life, including new member rushes and parties, continued. A March 1969 *Cumberland Lawyer* article reported the ground rules followed in the spring rush that year. To be eligible to rush a fraternity, a law student was required to have completed at least ten hours of credit with at least a C grade point average. Prior to rush week, the president of the SBA met with a representative of each of the four fraternities and assigned each of them a separate night during rush week (PAD, Monday night; Delta Theta Phi, Tuesday night; and so forth) to conduct rush activities (that is, a party). Because the fraternities could also hold rush parties whenever they wished during the weekend, law students intent on pledging a fraternity probably did only minimal studying during rush week. A very unofficial ground rule in these years was that, while alcoholic beverages were absolutely banned on the campus, student groups could serve them at their off-campus functions.

Along with the parties, a new theme had appeared in law fraternity life, that of achieving national recognition for service activities. Phi Alpha Delta sponsored a high school speaker program in which members of the fraternity spoke on legal subjects in area schools, a legal research program, and a program of speakers within the law school. It enjoyed success in achieving recognition, first at the regional level where the Cumberland chapter was selected as the outstanding chapter for several years in succession, and ultimately as the outstanding chapter in the nation in 1969.[9] Meanwhile, the Grafton Green Senate was recognized by Delta Theta Phi as "The Best Chapter in the District" consisting of Alabama, Tennessee, and Mississippi, and also received the "Highest Academic Average Award" for the district.[10] By 1979, Delta Theta Phi had received that annual award a total of four times.[11] A 1975 report by two faculty members entitled "The Positive Image" noted that one fraternity sponsored a "Ride-Along" program in which law students could accompany police officers on patrol, while another operated a big brother program.[12]

During the period between the two world wars, student bar associations had begun to appear at a few law schools around the country. Apparently, the first student bar association was organized in 1929 at the University of Southern California Law School, at the suggestion of Dean Justin Miller. Two years later, Miller, by then dean at Duke, prompted the organization of a student bar association at Duke, apparently the first SBA in the South. By 1933, law school student bar associations had also been organized at the University of Colorado, New York University, and other schools. The Duke student leaders saw the association's function as training the law student in the work of bar associations (based on the organizational model of the American Bar Association, the Duke SBA was organized into sections) and developing his sense of professional responsibility. In practice, the function of the Duke SBA appears to have been primarily to sponsor a speakers' program, as well as serving as a link between the student body and the administration.[13] The Cumberland SBA would later serve both functions.

Until 1951, there had not been a student bar association at Lebanon. In the old one-year and two-year programs, the most important representatives elected by the law students had been class officers.[14] Prior to 1951 the student council drew representatives from the law classes and various law student activities. With the suspension of the undergraduate program, the student council was reorganized as the student bar association.[15] After the restoration of the undergraduate program, the SBA retained its separate existence, one of its responsibilities being the sponsorship of an annual Law Day celebration.[16]

With the removal of the law school to Birmingham, the SBA continued as a central feature of law school life and continued the sponsorship of Law Day (which eventually would expand to Law Week). At the dedication of Memory Leake Robinson Hall in April 1964, the president of the SBA, and a member of the first class to enter Cumberland after its removal to Birmingham, represented the student body in extending formal appreciation for the new building.[17] In 1964, the SBA had sponsored a used book exchange and a freshman orientation program. Under the heading of "Some Things Never Change," it is interesting to note that in November 1964 there was an SBA group "working toward a conclusion of the parking problem."[18] While Cumberland lacked a placement office, the SBA undertook the publication of a senior placement brochure, which was sent to law offices throughout Alabama and elsewhere as an aid for graduating seniors.[19] The placement brochure and the organization of freshman orientation reflected a pattern in which the SBA would perform functions, which at times included registration,[20] later taken over by law school administrative staff as staff positions expanded.

Beyond functioning as a service organization, Cumberland's SBA began to be involved in the American Law Student Association (ALSA), an organization consisting of the student bar associations from each American Bar Association-approved law school, formed under the sponsorship of the ABA in 1949.[21] ALSA was operated as a separate organization until 1967 when the ABA constitution was amended to permit law students to join the ABA before graduation, and ALSA was superceded by the Law Student Division of the American Bar Association (ABA/LSD).[22]

In line with Cumberland's emphasis on achieving national recognition, Cumberland student bar leaders began to campaign for positions as officers of ALSA or ABA/LSD, and also to promote recognition of the

Cumberland SBA itself. Their efforts resulted in a number of Cumberland students holding national office in ALSA or the later ABA / LSD, while the Cumberland SBA was named the outstanding SBA in the nation on a number of occasions.

The first Cumberland students to hold national office included a national vice president for the "Fifth Circuit" in 1965, and the chair of the ALSA Credentials Committee in 1965.[23] Following them, five Cumberland students served as Fifth Circuit vice president or, as it was later called, governor, in the years 1969–76, while another held the office of second vice president and delegate from the Law Student Division to the House of Delegates.[24] In 1974, a Cumberland student was elected first vice president, in charge of coordinating activities among the thirteen circuits of the LSD/ABA.[25] Then in August 1978, a Cumberland student became the first law student from the Deep South to be elected president of the Law Student Division of the ABA.[26] In 1982, the Cumberland SBA president became president of the National Student Bar Association.[27]

Soon the Cumberland SBA, aided by the knowledge Cumberland students had gained of ALSA and of the LSD/ABA while serving as national officers, began to focus its energies on programs that would win recognition at the national level. A steady stream of awards followed. The Law Student Division of the American Bar Association in 1971 recognized the Cumberland SBA as the outstanding SBA in the country among law schools with a student body of less than 500. At the 1972 ABA Convention the Cumberland SBA captured a total of three awards: the National Membership Achievement award (in recognition of the increase in Cumberland students belonging to LSD/ABA from 120 to 300); the Outstanding Law Day Program Award; and, once again, the award for the outstanding SBA (this time in the larger and more competitive category of schools with student bodies between 500 and 1,000). Cumberland's Law Day celebration had included sending speaker panels to other colleges and universities in the Birmingham area to address such issues as the laws relating to the sale and use of drugs, abortion, and consumer protection, as well as a program within the school that included an address by former secretary of state Dean Rusk.[28]

Much as the tension between "lawyers" and "lits" had been a feature of law student life in Lebanon, in Birmingham, law students, generally older and from more varied religious and geographical backgrounds than the undergraduate students at Howard (later Samford), did not always fit well into the larger university background. A particular source of friction was the university's mandatory chapel program, which often left law students bored and sometimes deeply resentful. For some students, the resentment continued for years. Dean Weeks recalls a Roman Catholic student who was so angered by a chapel speaker who, in the student's view, had impugned the piety of the Pope, that he told Weeks he would not attend another chapel program even if it meant his expulsion from school.[29] Actually, the exact nature of the penalty for missing chapel seems never to have been made clear. An article in the *Cumberland Lawyer* by a law student who had received a notice advising him of his delinquencies in chapel attendance noted that the letter made no mention of penalties. The student facetiously suggested that chapel attendance offenders be forced to serve time in conspicuously located stocks during chapel hours.[30]

Acting dean Donald E. Corley and the 1973–74 SBA president fashioned a solution to the mandatory chapel problem by persuading the Samford administration to allow the law school to sponsor its own speakers' forum, which, preceded by a prayer or short devotional given by a student member of the Christian Legal Society, would satisfy the chapel attendance requirement.[31] The result was "Forum '74" (eventually to be called the Cordell Hull Speakers Forum),[32] which attracted such diverse speakers as Senator Joseph Biden; Charles Morgan, national director of the American Civil Liberties Union; Morris Dees of the Southern Poverty Law Center; Ralph Nader; conservative columnists Max Rafferty and James J. Kilpatrick; ethicist Dr. Joseph Fletcher; and Peace Corps director and 1972 vice presidential candidate Sargeant Shriver. A local bank helped provide the funds to cover the expenses of the program, which also received a grant from the LSD/ABA.[33]

In August 1974, Forum '74 won the prize for outstanding SBA project in the nation. The SBA president learned that Cumberland had the best three projects in the competition. Cumberland's SBA again won the award for outstanding SBA in the nation in 1974, an honor that was repeated in 1975 as well.[34] In 1977, Cumberland's Law Day program won the ABA award for the best Law Day observance, marking the second time Cumberland had won this award and the seventh national first-place award

Cumberland had won.[35] Cumberland's 1979 Law Day celebration featured Arkansas's thirty-two-year-old governor William J. Clinton as banquet speaker, and won yet another best Law Day award,[36] as did the 1980 Law Day, featuring Oklahoma governor David Boren as banquet speaker.[37]

Indeed in 1982, the Cumberland SBA again won the Outstanding SBA award, though the award had become so routine that it only merited space on a back page of the student newspaper.[38] In 1983, the SBA repeated its record of 1972 in which it captured three national awards, winning the Outstanding SBA award once again as well as the Best SBA Project award for its orientation program, along with the Best Law Day award.[39] Thus from the pioneering efforts during Weeks's deanship through the period as Corley's deanship was nearing its close, Cumberland's SBA maintained a position of high visibility in terms of national offices and awards.

The SBA's successes could not have been accomplished without the support of the Cumberland administration, and indeed SBA leaders were quick to give credit to the administration.[40] In Lebanon, scant attention had been paid to activities beyond the law school itself. Deans Weeks and Corley, on the other hand, encouraged participation by the SBA and its leaders in the national ABA organization. In sending a delegation each year to the ABA convention where the issues of the day were debated, Weeks and Corley prevented isolation of Cumberland students from the interests of law students nationwide. For a law school in Birmingham, Alabama, a community that in the 1960s found itself isolated during the civil rights struggles, this was particularly important.

While Cumberland had a long history, in many ways it made a new beginning in Birmingham, almost as if it were a newly established law school. The successes in winning offices and awards won by the SBA and its leaders served to sustain the morale of the student body as the law school went through that process. Those successes also served to energize the SBA leaders as they went about their basic task of performing service functions for the law school. Moreover, the recognition received by the SBA established a pattern for extracurricular activities at Cumberland during this period in which the worth of extracurricular activities was measured not only by the contribution they made to the educational experience and quality of life of Cumberland students—probably the principal if not the only consideration in Lebanon—but also by the degree to which they brought external recognition to the school.

At the most basic level, differences between the structure of law student extracurricular life at Cumberland in Birmingham in the 1960s and 1970s and that at the school in Lebanon during the large enrollment years of 1920s and 1930s echo the differences between the instructional models in place during the two eras: the difference between a one-year, treatise-based course emphasizing student memorization of the law according to the treatise writers, and a three-year course in which students, working with the primary materials of actual judicial decisions and statutes, developed their analytical abilities by probing the cases and statutes for ambiguities, internal inconsistencies, and policy goals, sometimes stated and sometimes not.

Under the treatise-based program of study, the student, and indeed the classroom instructor, assumed a posture of deference to the learned treatise author. The Socratic approach of the case method of law study, in contrast, places the responsibility on the student to discover the law for himself. In place of an attitude of deference to received knowledge, the case method of instruction, which is unique to American law schools, encourages skepticism and a presumptuousness on the part of the student to seek ways to improve the law and legal institutions.

The Socratic case method of instruction is not the only unique feature of American legal education. Another, perhaps even more remarkable feature, is the importance of student-edited law reviews. In other academic disciplines, editorship of the leading scholarly journals is accorded to leading scholars in the field. To the amazement of academics in other fields, however, in modern, mainstream American law schools, the scholarly journals (with few exceptions) are under the autonomous editorship of law students who have completed only one or two years of law study.[41]

The model for modern student-edited law reviews is the *Harvard Law Review,* the first volume of which was published in 1887. With the encouragement of Ames, the *Harvard Law Review* evolved from the Langdell Society, a student club formed for the purpose of hearing presentations of papers written by members, into a journal that would permit publication and circulation of student and faculty work. As the name of their society indicates, the founding editors of the *Harvard Law Review* were enthusiasts for the case method, by 1887 firmly established at Harvard. As stated in the first issue, one purpose in publishing the review was to spread the word about the case method of instruction.[42] The founding editors included John Wigmore and Julian Mack, who later carried the case method to Northwestern University, and Joseph Beale, who would establish the case method at the University of Chicago.[43]

The case method of instruction naturally encouraged and complemented the development of student-edited journals, for the case method elevates the student to the role of critic of the most distinguished jurists, and law review enables the student to edit the work of experienced scholars and practitioners. As the case method of instruction gained a foothold at a law school, a student-edited law review generally soon followed. For example, at the University of North Carolina the first issue of the *North Carolina Law Review* was published in June 1922, through the efforts of the school's first case method instructor, who had been appointed only a year earlier.[44] Though law-school-sponsored journals at some schools—those at the University of Michigan and Northwestern University are notable examples—were at first under faculty control, most ultimately conformed to the pattern of student control.[45]

At Cumberland in Lebanon, Lewis Cassidy, a case-method-trained law professor who taught briefly at Cumberland prior to World War II, had suggested as early as 1938 that Cumberland publish a law review, but nothing came of the idea.[46] By the 1960s, a substantial number of American law schools published law reviews. Cumberland would not actually publish a law review until 1970, nearly a decade after the move to Birmingham, as Weeks's deanship neared its end. Prior to that time several harbingers of the long-awaited event had appeared, however.

After the move to Birmingham, the first student publication was a law student newspaper called the *Cumberland School of Law Student Lawyer,* first published in November 1964. The *Student Lawyer* published four issues in the 1964–65 school year and again in the 1964–66 school year. Varying in length from four to seven mimeographed or photocopied legal size pages, the *Student Lawyer* attempted nothing grander than circulating news of the school: announcements of law fraternity pledges,[47] brief faculty profiles,[48] stories on moot court teams (such as the account of Cumberland's victory in the first and last Law Day intrastate moot court competition with the University of Alabama),[49] and announcements from the administration.[50]

The following year the name was shortened to the *Cumberland Lawyer* and a magazine format was adopted. It included legal and political commentary by outside authors (with an article on third parties by Alabama governor George C. Wallace,[51] followed in the next issue by an article on civil disobedience by Alabama attorney general Richmond Flowers, Wallace's political adversary on the issue of racial integration),[52] case notes,[53] and student-authored legal commentary.[54] Like a bar association magazine, the *Cumberland Lawyer* had come to include, although sometimes in a sketchy way, some of the elements of a standard student-edited law review, a format it retained through the balance of Weeks's tenure as dean, while still providing news of the school. With the November 1972 issue, the *Cumberland Lawyer* dropped some of its earlier law-review-type features and began to function in a more focused way as an alumni newsletter, with feature articles about the school, though it was still student-edited. In 1976, with the establishment of the National Alumni Association of the Cumberland Law School, the *Cumberland Lawyer* became the official organ of the alumni association. Meanwhile a new student newspaper, *Pro Confesso,* emerged that reported law student organization news, administration announcements, and editorials on law school issues. Beginning in 1971 as a typescript publication on letter-size paper, by 1974 *Pro Confesso* had become a tabloid printed on newspaper stock, complete with a crossword puzzle prepared by a member of the faculty. Answers to the crossword were always terms associated with the law school.

Apart from the writing of the *Cumberland Lawyer,* writing contests also foreshadowed the establishment of a law review. For the school, writing contests offered the prospect of capturing more trophies, always pleasing to the administration; for the student they offered the equally appealing prospect of a cash award. While Cumberland students would continue to participate in writing contests after the establishment first of the *Cumberland Law Review* and then a second journal, the *American Journal of Trial Advocacy,* in the 1960s the law school used legal writing contests to offer the students opportunities to pursue legal scholarship without the cost of supporting a publication. "Writing contests should be pushed,"[55] exhorted the minutes of a law faculty meeting at the beginning of the 1965–66 academic year. The same faculty meeting minutes boasted that Cumberland had won awards in two national legal writing contests during the summer of 1965. Cumberland students won the ABA/ALSA legal writing contest, and also a contest sponsored by Sigma Delta Kappa Law Fraternity.[56] These successes, proudly reported by Weeks in January 1966 in his annual report to the president and board of trustees, inspired calls from the faculty for more hard work and preparation. The minutes of the December 1996 faculty meeting declared "that if we are to win [writing contests], we must start earlier."[57] Articles in the law student newspaper in October 1965 alerted students to the variety of legal writing competitions available. With the urging of the faculty, Cumberland students continued to enter legal writing contests.[58]

Though Cumberland never again enjoyed two national awards in a single year, in 1967 another student won the SDK contest and, in 1968, another became the third Cumberland student to win the award.[59] In 1983, an essay by a third-year Cumberland student, entitled "Black Women Attorneys in the Community: Advocates for Social Change," won first prize in an essay contest sponsored by the National Association of Black Women Attorneys.[60]

In 1968, thirty years after Lewis Cassidy proposed the publication of a law review, the *Cumberland-Samford Law Review* came into view.[61] The 1968 announcement, however, heralded the beginning of a two-year process of effort and organization that would ultimately lead to the publication of the first issue in 1970.[62] In addition to student casenotes and comments, the initial 1970 issue included articles by two Cumberland faculty members.[63] A second issue soon appeared with articles by a faculty member and recent graduate.[64] Thus began an annual cycle of law review boards, each taking office in the spring, succeeded by a new board the following spring. In 1975, with volume 6, the review shortened its name from *Cumberland-Samford Law Review* to *Cumberland Law Review*.[65] The review hosted the 30th National Conference of Law Reviews in spring 1984, which brought representatives of eighty member law reviews and journals to Birmingham.[66]

By the 1970s many law schools were publishing more than one law journal. In 1977, Cumberland established its second journal, the *American Journal of Trial Advocacy*. The Cumberland Trial Board organized the journal in the spring of 1977 and the first issue appeared that fall.[67]

One way in which extracurricular activities in Birmingham differed from those at Cumberland in Lebanon was the increased importance of appellate advocacy, in which students practice briefing and arguing cases to appellate courts, as contrasted with trial advocacy, in which students play the role of trial lawyers interrogating witnesses, often before a jury. At

Lebanon in the twenties and thirties mock trials were one of the most important features of a student's experience, and this emphasis continued through the last years in Lebanon.[68] However in Birmingham, during Arthur Weeks's deanship in the 1960s, appellate advocacy became the more important form of advocacy training.

In Birmingham, Cumberland wholeheartedly adhered to the case method. The first law school catalogue in Birmingham announced that the school employed the case method, warning that "students are required to study and brief all assigned cases in each of the courses and to recite in class."[69] Because, as the catalogue advised, the case method included the study of "significant opinions of the various courts of the United States and other countries," it was natural that at a case method school advocacy training would focus on the process of brief writing and appellate argument that shapes the content of appellate opinions.

In line with the pattern of seeking outside recognition seen in the activities of the fraternities, the SBA, and writing contests, participation of Cumberland teams in national appellate moot court competitions offered the possibility of prizes and publicity for the school. The first issue of the *Student Lawyer* in November 1964 carried a story that Cumberland's National Moot Court Team, having labored since August, was ready for the competition it would face in the regionals that month in Atlanta. The faculty advisor called the team's written brief, which had been placed on reserve in the library for interested students to read, a "winning brief," and Dean Weeks announced that the school would pay mileage for Cumberland students who wished to make the trek to Atlanta to provide moral support to the team.[70]

Cumberland had entered a team in the National Moot Court Competition in 1963 as well, but it had not fared well. A December 1964 *Student Lawyer* article reported that the 1964 team came in fifth in overall standings and placed third in oral argument, and noted that "this is a great deal of improvement over last year's results."[71] The article expressed the school's satisfaction in the improved standings and anticipation of the day when a Cumberland team would reach the top in overall standings. In the meantime, the administration took steps to underscore the importance of the National Moot Court Competition and to recognize the efforts of Cumberland team members. The 1966 law school catalogue carried a description of the National Moot Court Competition and an announcement that a plaque displayed prominently in the law school would bear the names of Cumberland's representatives in the competition.[72]

From Cumberland's first Law Day in Birmingham in the spring of 1962, a student moot court competition had been a feature of Cumberland's Law Day celebration.[73] Law Day 1966 saw the first and only intrastate moot court competition between a Cumberland team and a team representing the University of Alabama law school, with the chief justice of the Alabama Supreme Court presiding. The Cumberland team prevailed over a University of Alabama team.[74] The contest was not renewed in subsequent years, perhaps because of a disagreement as to how the teams were to be constituted. Cumberland, intent on improving its standing in the national competition, viewed the Law Day Competition as a preliminary springboard to the next year's national event.[75] Accordingly, it favored limiting the Law Day teams to junior law students, from whose experienced ranks the next year's national team could be drawn. Alabama's preference was apparently to permit seniors to compete.[76] After 1966, Cumberland's Law Day moot court competition resumed its character as a strictly intramural competition,[77] though in 1970 an interschool contest was held between Cumberland and the University of Mississippi teams.[78]

In 1967 Cumberland made a bold move calculated to give it an experienced team in 1968, even at the expense of a lesser showing in 1967: it fielded a team made up of two juniors, both of whom had been members of the runner-up team in the Law Day moot court competition as freshman. Cumberland borrowed this strategy from the University of Miami.[79] Coached by a former member of the 1964 Cumberland national team, the two juniors won the first round before being eliminated.[80] In 1968, though, the experience notwithstanding, the same team, burdened by a low score on its brief, lost in the first round "by a slight margin—so slight that it evoked comments from the judges on the rarity of such an occasion."[81]

Despite that disappointment, students and faculty advisors were developing a depth of experience in moot court competition that ultimately would bear fruit. It had become clear that while scores on a team's written brief counted only one-third of the overall score, very rarely could a team progress beyond the preliminary rounds without a solid brief score. In 1970, the Cumberland team learned when they arrived at the competition that their brief score was the second highest in the region, trailing only Loyola. Under a double elimination format, Cumberland faced Loyola twice, and each time Cumberland's oral advocacy score was sufficient to overcome Loyola's advantage on the brief. In the other rounds, including the finals against Tulane, Cumberland's brief score provided the margin of victory that allowed it to win its first regional championship and the chance to participate in the final rounds in New York City, where it lost to a team with a four point advantage on the brief.[82]

Dean Weeks celebrated the national moot court team's victory by creating, in January 1971, the Cumberland Moot Court Board to coordinate moot court activities.[83] In 1980, the board was renamed the Henry Upson Sims Moot Court Board, in recognition of a generous gift underwriting the board's activities and in honor of a distinguished Birmingham attorney and former president of the American Bar Association.[84]

In 1972, a Cumberland team again won the regional competition and advanced to the finals in New York City. Cumberland hosted the regional competition in 1979.[85] Perhaps inspired by that event, in 1980, Cumberland again made it to the finals in New York City, this time as runner-up in the region. Once again, the brief score made the difference. Cumberland, with the second best brief score that year, lost in the finals to the team with the best brief score, by a narrow margin, less than the difference in the two teams' brief scores.[86]

In 1968, Cumberland decided to expand its involvement in appellate advocacy competitions by entering a team in the Philip C. Jessup International Moot Court Competition. Supporting a team in the Jessup competition, named for an American lawyer who served on the International Court of Justice, did not conflict with administrative and faculty support of the national team, as the two competitions occupied different parts of the academic calendar. The National Moot Court Competition, in which Cumberland was already heavily involved, began in August with the receipt of a problem prepared by the sponsors and culminated in a regional competition in November and a national championship in December. The Jessup competition, on the other hand, began in November with regional competitions in March and national and international championship rounds in April.[87] Cumberland sent a team to the 1968 regional competition, and the results were gratifying: the team achieved a third-place finish, and one member tied for best oralist.[88]

Encouraged, the faculty advisor and interested students formed the International Law Society, with the four team members as founding officers.[89] By the next fall, the society had enlisted seventy members, applied to join the Association of Student International Law Societies,[90] and entered a team in its spring 1969 competition, losing one round to Tulane but winning a round against Texas.[91] By 1970, the application, which included the submission of information on the number of international law books in the library,[92] was approved. That year Cumberland hosted the regional Jessup competition.[93] In the fall of 1971, the International Law Society, renamed the Cordell Hull International Law Society, to honor the Cumberland graduate who became the American secretary of state, joined the fledgling Moot Court Board in cohosting the regional National Moot Court Competition and, in the spring, the regional Jessup Competition.[94]

The following year, 1971, saw a Cumberland student elected to the national office of treasurer of the Association of Student International Law Societies.[95] In 1972, with a membership of 200, Cumberland apparently had the largest international law society in the world.[96] That same year, another Cordell Hull Chapter member became national treasurer of the Association of Student International Law Societies,[97] and the following year was elected president of that body. Reportedly, this election marked only the third time in the history of the Association of Student International Law Societies that a president had been elected from a school other than Harvard or the University of Virginia.[98] In 1979, yet another Cumberland student became national treasurer.[99]

One element in the success of the Cumberland International Law Society lay in a funding mechanism that the advisor, Professor James L. Hughes developed. Hughes, a former Navy legal officer, also taught the course in admiralty. Lawyers who practice admiralty law are known as proctors. Beginning about 1970, the Cordell Hull Chapter began selling "Proctor in Admiralty" certificates, gold-lettered and suitable for framing, not only to current students who successfully completed the course but also to alumni who had taken the course in earlier years.[100] As a result, the Cordell Hull Chapter rejoiced in the fall of 1971 that "we anticipate a tremendous party at the Valley Ridge Apartments, Friday night, October, 15."[101] Little wonder the International Law Society was able to sustain its activities through a large and energetic membership.

Despite Cumberland's support for the Jessup Competition in twice hosting the regional round, no Cumberland team was able to win the regional competition until 1978. Once again, a solid score on its brief—second in the regional, and only two points behind the winning brief—coupled with an outstanding score in oral competition—thirty-five out of a possible thirty-six points—was the formula for success.[102]

Notwithstanding the emphasis placed on appellate advocacy during Weeks's deanship, Cumberland students continued to participate in mock trials, interrogating witnesses and practicing the fine art of closing jury arguments. In the 1960s, linking the Birmingham campus to Cumberland's past, Judge Gilreath continued to conduct mock trials as he had done in Caruthers Hall in Lebanon as long ago as 1932.[103]

The 1970s saw an increased emphasis on trial practice teams that competed in mock trial competitions, just as moot court teams competed in the National and the Jessup Moot Court competitions. The Clinical Trial Board appeared in 1976 on the model of the Moot Court Board. In 1974, the Young Lawyers Section of the Texas State Bar undertook the sponsorship of a National Mock Trial Competition, paralleling the National Moot Court Competition.[104] The trial board fielded two teams in the regionals of the National Mock Trial Competition held at Duke in January 1977.[105] Both teams reached the quarterfinals, and one advanced to the semifinals.[106]

Hoping to build on that success, in the spring of 1977 the Cumberland Trial Board instituted an intramural competition for juniors, designated the Donald E. Corley Mock Trial Competition,[107] while the Jefferson County Circuit Judges' Mock Trial Competition for seniors practicing under the third-year practice act entered its second year.[108] Establishment in 1977 of the Center for Advocacy and Clinical Education provided a framework for the administration of the various trial and advocacy programs, including the already anticipated *American Journal of Trial Advocacy* that appeared the next year.[109]

In 1980, the trial board hosted Cumberland's first regional round of the National Mock Trial Competition. Moreover, Cumberland's two teams did well: one team defeated Duke in the finals to advance to the national round in Houston, and the other team made its way to the semifinals, where it lost to Duke.[110]

In 1981 a Cumberland team won the National Mock Trial Championship with one member named Outstanding Oral Advocate.[111] Their advisor, Judge James O. Haley, in 1991 received the Richard S. Jacobson Award for Excellence in Teaching Trial Advocacy from the Roscoe Pound Foundation.[112]

In 1982, Cumberland won a third straight regional championship in the National Mock Trial Competition.[113] In that same year, a Cumberland team won the regional championship in client counseling, another area in which the school sponsored teams. Meanwhile a mock trial team took the regional championship in a different competition, the American Trial Lawyers Association (ATLA) Mock Trial Competition.[114]

A second team in 1983 captured the ATLA regionals, a feat that was repeated in 1984.[115] However, it was the National Mock Trial Teams that enjoyed the most remarkable success in 1984. Cumberland fielded two teams in that competition. Remarkably, they both reached the finals of the regional championship, where Cumberland faced Cumberland for the regional championship.[116] Both teams advanced to the national finals, where one claimed the national championship, one member being best advocate, while the other team finished third in the nation.[117]

Capping off an extraordinary spring for Cumberland's trial advocacy program, in May 1984 the American College of Trial Lawyers announced that Cumberland had been selected to receive the Emil Gumpert Award, given for excellence in the teaching of trial advocacy.

In February 1984, Dean Donald E. Corley announced his resignation as dean. Following the lead of Dean Weeks, Corley had encouraged law student activities that would bring recognition to the school. As Corley returned to full-time teaching, it appeared that the goals of the two men had been accomplished. Law students had certainly been active in other pursuits during the Weeks and Corley deanships. An environmental law society had been active, as had a chapter of the Christian Legal Society and the Black Law Students Association. Harking back to the state-specific clubs in Lebanon, there were organizations of students from North Carolina, Virginia, Florida, and Tennessee. Nevertheless, the emphasis had been on those organizations and activities that would bring recognition to the school. With the school SBA selected once again in 1983 as the outstanding SBA in the country, with the law review hosting the National Conference of Law Reviews in 1984, and with the victories won by the mock trial teams in 1984, it was clear, as Corley returned to full-time teaching, that he and Weeks had succeeded in promoting student activities that would win success outside the walls of the law school building.

Nevertheless, the question remained whether student awards and trial team victories would be sufficient to win for Cumberland the recognition that Weeks and Corley sought. A more lasting institutional reputation has to be built on the achievements of its faculty as teachers and scholars. Corley, who in the last years of his deanship had appointed an advisory committee to the dean on faculty development, was certainly aware of this.[118] It remained for a future administration to stimulate faculty development to parallel the efforts of Weeks and Corley in building a spirit of accomplishment in the student body.

EPILOGUE

Foundation for the Future 1984–1997

The resolution of this problem [inadequate scholarly productivity] requires, in essence, the development of a total environment in which scholarship is encouraged, required for promotion and tenure, applauded, and rewarded.

—Statement of April 9, 1986, of Cumberland Law School, Samford University, in response to ABA Accreditation Committee Report

The intent and spirit of this Statement is to serve as a vehicle for Faculty development—development of the Law School Faculty as a body and of Faculty members individually.

—Promotion and Tenure Policy, Cumberland School of Law, Samford University, adopted by 12–10 vote of the Law Faculty, March 18, 1986

DRIVING FROM Birmingham to Oxford, Mississippi, on a December Saturday in 1984, Samford President Thomas E. Corts no doubt nurtured the hope that the Samford Bulldogs could upset the University of Mississippi Rebels in that evening's basketball game. Sixty years earlier, in 1924, a young Mississippi couple, Mr. and Mrs. Parham Williams Sr., drove from Pickens, Mississippi, to Lebanon, Tennessee, where they both studied law at Cumberland School of Law. Corts's route from Birmingham to Oxford necessarily intersected that taken sixty years earlier by the Williamses. Had Corts thought of the fact that he was crossing the elder Williamses' path, he would have appreciated the irony, for Corts's visit to Oxford, Mississippi, had a purpose other than cheering for the Samford basketball squad. He was to interview Parham Williams Jr., son of the young couple who long ago had journeyed to Lebanon and now dean of Mississippi School of Law. Accompanied by a member of the Dean Search Committee, Corts had arranged his schedule to include a visit with Williams prior to the basketball game.

The trip to Oxford was a fruitful one. Though Samford lost the basketball game, Corts won a dean, first by convincing Williams to become a candidate and ultimately by selecting him. Williams assumed the deanship on July 1, 1985, and remained as dean until June 1, 1996.

In writing to the faculty on September 15, 1995, announcing his plans to retire from the deanship at the end of the 1995–96 academic year, Williams reflected on the achievements of his deanship. He claimed that "the most useful achievement of the past decade has been the creation of a nurturing environment in which law teachers are encouraged and enabled to exploit their skills and knowledge to the fullest extent possible." Publications provide the paper trail marking the developing intellectual strength of a law faculty. During the period covered by this epilogue, the Cumberland faculty's published writings increased dramatically, even to the point that one faculty member gained recognition as one of the ten most prolific law scholars in the country.

Even prior to Williams's appointment, there were signs of an increasing emphasis on faculty development. On one occasion in the 1980s, Dean Corley empaneled a faculty committee to advise the dean on recommendations for faculty promotions and tenure. However, in the absence of specific guidelines for evaluating their colleagues, the members of the committee soon ceded back to the dean exclusive responsibility for rank and tenure deliberations. Nevertheless, acting dean Brad Bishop saw the need for faculty involvement and established a rank and tenure committee as a permanent feature of the law faculty committee structure. One of Williams's first acts was to charge the committee with the development of rank and tenure procedures and standards. An AALS-ABA inspection team that visited the school in 1985 had expressed concern at the absence of a clearly enunciated rank and tenure policy.

The committee circulated a discussion draft to the faculty on November 27, 1985. Extensive meetings and revisions followed. At the regular faculty meeting on March 18, 1986, the further revised document was presented for a vote by secret ballot.

In addition to teaching and service, the proposed standards imposed a requirement as to scholarly research and writing. This was the most controversial aspect of the proposal. No specific standard as to scholarly research and writing had existed previously. The new policy required authorship of a quantifiable amount of law review writing or books as a faculty member progressed from untenured, assistant professor to the ultimate status of tenured, full professor. Though a generous grace period was provided, the new requirements applied to existing faculty members who had not yet achieved tenured, full professor status. Therefore, despite the fact that the policy statement had been discussed since December and though some changes had been made, including extensions of the grace period, substantial opposition to adoption of the policy still existed and the outcome was uncertain as the vote was taken. A tally of the secret ballots revealed, however, that the rank and tenure policy had received endorsement by a narrow margin: 12 in favor, 10 opposed, and one abstention. Hardly a landslide, but nevertheless, the faculty had now expressed a willingness to impose on itself heightened standards of performance for promotion and tenure, including a requirement of scholarly publication.

In his September 1995 letter, Williams reported that in the more than nine years since the policy was adopted, a total of fourteen faculty members had been able to meet its requirements and receive the award of tenure.

Requiring scholarship for rank and tenure is only one part of the creation, in the language of the chapter's epigram, of a "total environment in which scholarship is encouraged." Other aspects include a sabbatical leave policy, research assistants, summer research stipends, and, perhaps most important, the recruitment of faculty members with scholarly promise. Prior to 1986, during the entire quarter century that the law school had been a part of Samford, no more than one or two sabbaticals had been granted to law faculty members. Beginning in 1986, sabbatical leaves were granted on an average of two a year to faculty members whose length of service qualified them for a sabbatical and who presented a proposal for a suitable project to be advanced during sabbatical leave.

Beginning in 1986, Cumberland School of Law commenced a program of awarding summer research stipends permitting recipients to forgo teaching for the summer and concentrate on scholarly research. In the decade since 1986, faculty members have received more than thirty research stipends. The law school also instituted a policy of providing paid student research assistants to assist faculty members with their research. This policy provides the student assistant with an income supplement as well as the opportunity to work closely with a faculty member on a research project.

The development of productive faculty scholars begins with the recruitment of faculty members whose records evidence a promise of high-quality scholarly performance. Among the indicators of scholarly promise are graduation from a highly ranked law school, law review experience, and judicial clerkships.

The 1997 faculty of the Cumberland School of Law includes members, added during the years 1984–1995, with their primary law degrees from Yale, Stanford, Harvard, Vanderbilt, Chicago, Texas, and Emory, among other fine law schools, and with graduate degrees in law (LL.M. or S.J.D.) from Michigan, Stanford, Temple, and Yale.

Of the faculty hired during Parham Williams's administration almost all had been officers of their law schools' law review, and most had clerked for a federal judge upon graduation. One had been a Rhodes Scholar; several were first in their classes. In addition, distinguished former public servants and judges were recruited into full-time or part-time faculty positions: a former governor of Alabama, a senior status chief judge of a federal circuit court of appeals, and a former state supreme court justice.

The assemblage of such a strong faculty, combined with sabbaticals, research assistants, research stipends, and a compensation policy rewarding scholarship, resulted in "a rich outpouring of scholarship," in the words of Parham Williams in his September 1995 letter. Faculty productivity soared within a comparatively brief period of time.

In the academic year 1984–85 the number of books authored by the faculty was zero and the number of articles only one. In 1986–87, however, a total of three books and eleven law review articles were published;

in 1987–88, no books, but nine law review articles. The academic year 1988–89 saw one book published along with sixteen law review articles; and 1989–90, three books and twelve law review articles. As gratifying as the numbers are alone, the quality of journals is impressive and extensive. Among the books, several were published by university presses, including the prestigious Princeton University Press and University of Chicago Press. These books garnered five national book prizes, including the notable James Willard Hurst Prize awarded by the Law and Society Association.

Beginning in 1994, a number of new initiatives provided new kinds of opportunities for Cumberland faculty and students to enjoy the presentation of scholarly papers, dialogue, and informal scholarly exchange with each other and with some of the country's most distinguished legal minds. The Cumberland faculty colloquia bring scholars from around the country to the law school to present papers to a faculty audience and invited student guests, and to engage in specialized scholarly exchange. The first of these was the Cumberland Colloquium on Law, Religion, and Culture, which began in the spring of 1994. Cumberland's legal historians initiated a separate colloquium on American Legal History in 1996.

In March 1995, Cumberland launched a Distinguished Lecturer Series, featuring Yale's Akhil Reed Amar as the first principal lecturer, with commentary by panels made up of invited scholars from other schools as well as Cumberland's own faculty members. By 1996 the series had attracted the financial support of Birmingham attorney Wyatt Rushton Haskell and was christened the Ray Rushton Distinguished Lecturer Series in honor of Haskell's grandfather, an Alabama attorney and civic leader. The principal lecturer in 1996 was Anthony T. Kronman, dean of the Yale Law School.

Meanwhile, Cumberland's long-standing and award-winning Cordell Hull Speakers Forum included more academics and others engaged in the intellectual debates of the day in its list of speakers. In 1995–96, the Speakers Forum hosted Justice Clarence Thomas as well as the president of the American Civil Liberties Union, among many others. In October 1995, Cumberland joined the Birmingham Civil Rights Institute and Miles Law School of Miles College, a historically black college in Birmingham, in sponsoring a Conference Commemorating the 30th Anniversary of the Voting Rights Act of 1995.

Many other diverse activities characterized the Cumberland faculty during these years. Some faculty members wrote appellate briefs as court-appointed counsel or as friends of the court in public interest litigation. Others lectured for national bar review courses, continuing legal education programs, or as visiting lecturers. One faculty member consulted on the establishment of private legal education within the former Soviet Union. Many primarily engaged in scholarship. The composition of the faculty became more diverse in these years, as well, with many women and African-Americans joining the faculty.

The most far-reaching revision of policy undertaken by the faculty was the adoption of a new faculty governance document. Prior to 1986, Cumberland could fairly be characterized as a dean-run school. While law faculty committees provided a vehicle through which the full-time faculty participated in institutional policy making, the dean selected the committee chairs, appointed the committee members, and determined if new committees were needed. The ABA reinspection team that visited Cumberland in the spring of 1985 recommended greater faculty participation in law school governance. In response to that recommendation, a faculty committee drafted a charter for law school governance that would appropriately delineate the roles of the faculty in establishing educational policy and the role of the dean in administering that policy. As with the rank and tenure document, there was vigorous debate and revisions, but the final version was adopted by faculty vote on May 5, 1986.

With the strengthening of the faculty came the capacity to support a program of increased breadth. In 1984, the law school supported one joint degree program, a combined JD/MBA (Juris Doctor/Master of Business Administration) program offered with Samford's School of Business. By 1997, six additional joint degree programs were offered: a JD/MACC (Juris Doctor/Master of Accountancy) offered with the Samford School of Business; a JD/MAE (Juris Doctor/Masters of Art in Education) offered with the School of Education of the University of Alabama in Birmingham; a JD/MPH (Juris Doctor/Master of Public Health) offered with the School of Public Health of the University of Alabama in Birmingham; a JD/MPA (Juris Doctor/Master of Public Administration) offered with the School of Social and Behavioral Sciences of the University of Alabama in

Birmingham; a JD/MDiv (Juris Doctor/Master of Divinity) offered with the Beeson Divinity School of Samford University; and a JD/MS (Juris Doctor/Master of Science (in environmental management) offered with the graduate school of Samford University. In addition Cumberland offered a Master of Comparative Law, or MCL, in a degree program available to lawyers from other countries interested in learning more about American law and the American court system.

By 1997, Cumberland's International Law Society was no longer the largest in the country, as it once had been, but the School now enjoyed a much greater variety of international linkages. In addition to the MCL program, which brought foreign students to Cumberland, the school's offering of in-country study opportunities for American students included summer programs at the University of Durham in England, where the focus was on the European Common Market, and at the University of Victoria in British Columbia, where the focus was on the Pacific Rim.

An expanded program necessarily calls for an expanded administrative structure. Accordingly, various offices and assistant and associate deanships blossomed. The Cumberland Institute for Continuing Legal Education had originated during Corley's deanship. With the adoption of a mandatory continuing legal education rule by the Alabama State Bar, the offering of CLE activities became increasingly active, with Cumberland offering one or more programs almost every week.

Libraries have occupied an important place in Cumberland's history. In 1977, the law school's permanent Birmingham home, Memory Leake Robinson Hall, more than doubled in size, and with that came more than a doubling of the floor space available for the library. Even the expanded space proved inadequate. In 1990, the faculty's library committee undertook a study that identified the long-term library needs of the school, in light of anticipated growth of the collection. Thanks to a magnificent gift from Lucille Stewart Beeson, a longtime benefactress of Samford University, construction soon began on a new, freestanding library building to the east of Memory Leake Robinson Hall, but connected to it by a glass-enclosed breezeway.

During February 1995, the library staff organized a caravan of carts stacked with books that proceeded from the old library located in the center of the main law building to the new library and returned empty for further loads. By March 1, the library had completed its last move—or at least its last move of the school's first 150 years—and opened its doors.

The library is light, airy, and spacious, with a central atrium that gives an openness to all the upper levels. By some miracle of the architect's craft, sounds are several decibels lower in the new library than in the main law building. Entering the front foyer, patrons pass a bust of the donor, Lucille Stewart Beeson, and an etching of her words, enjoining those who use the facility to "Seek Wisdom to Temper Justice With Compassion." In the library courtyard, the theme of those words are taken up in a statue (commissioned by the donor) of Lady Justice, seated with the scales of justice in her hand, while an angel of advocacy whispers in her ear a plea for sympathy. On February 15, 1996, former President Gerald R. Ford dedicated the facility.

From its very local, Tennessee origins in 1847, Cumberland School of Law soon emerged as a premier law school with a national status. It excelled in faculty, teaching methodology, and numbers of students. Following the Civil War, Cumberland rebuilt itself and ultimately succeeded on a grand scale with its single-year curriculum. Then it became a victim of its own success, trapped within its familiar patterns even as the legal educational world changed about it. Cumberland remained frozen in time, even while other schools adopted a three-year curriculum, Socratic pedagogy, and ever stricter pre-law-school educational requirements.

By the 1920s and 1930s, external accreditation agencies and the state bar pressured for change. Cumberland had become a maverick among law schools. By this time the school and its host institution lacked the funds to institute successful reform, and the efforts made toward standardization of the curriculum and teaching methodologies failed.

Beginning with its move to Birmingham in 1961, Cumberland School of Law has struggled to reenter the mainstream of legal education. By 1997, it is fair to say that it has once more entered into the main channels of the law school world. The question now before Cumberland School of Law is whether it can regain the premier status it once held.

Notes

Chapter 1. Antebellum Beginnings, 1847–1861

1. Abraham Caruthers, "Inaugural Address of Hon. A. Caruthers . . . on the 29th of July, 1847," Banner of Peace Office, Lebanon, Tennessee.

2. Nathan Green Jr., "The Old Guard," in *Echoes from Caruthers Hall,* ed. Nathan Green Jr. (Nashville: Cumberland Presbyterian Publishing House, 1889), 215; Nathan Green Jr., "The Law School of Cumberland University," *Green Bag* 2 (February 1890): 64; "The Law School, 1847–1897," *Phoenix* (1897): 3. A complete run of the *Phoenix,* Cumberland University's yearbook, is in the Cumberland University Archives, Vise Library, Lebanon, Tennessee.

3. William R. Johnson, *Schooled Lawyers: A Study in the Clash of Professional Cultures* (New York: New York University Press, 1978), 12.

4. Robert Stevens, *Law School: Legal Education in America from the 1850s to the 1980s* (Chapel Hill: University of North Carolina Press, 1983), 10–11 n. 5.

5. Johnson, *Schooled Lawyers,* 52.

6. Ibid., xiii, 44, 48–49, 53–54.

7. Ibid., 4–5.

8. Ibid., 5–6.

9. A discussion of this failure of early university legal education on account of a demand for practical training is in Craig Evan Klafter, "The Influence of Vocational Law Schools on the Origins of American Legal Thought, 1779–1829," *American Journal of Legal History* 37 (July 1993): 313–14.

10. Marian C. McKenna, *Tapping Reeve and the Litchfield Law School* (New York: Oceana, 1986), 175.

11. Ibid., 123.

12. For 1840, Stevens, *Law School,* 8; for 1850 and 1860, Alfred Zantzinger Reed, *Training for the Public Profession of the Law* (New York: Carnegie Foundation for the Advancement of Teaching, 1921; reprint, New York: Arno Press, 1976), 171.

13. Reed, *Training for the Public Profession,* 171.

14. Quoted in John Ritchie, *The First Hundred Years: A Short History of the School of Law of the University of Virginia for the Period 1826–1916* (Charlottesville: University Press of Virginia, 1978), 7–8.

15. Quoted in Johnson, *Schooled Lawyers,* 11.

16. Stevens, *Law School,* 21.

17. Paul D. Carrington, "Teaching Law and Virtue at Transylvania University: The George Wythe Tradition in the Antebellum Years," *Mercer Law Review* 41 (Winter 1990): 698–99.

18. Stevens, *Law School,* 21.

19. Discussion of Cumberland at Princeton is drawn from Richard Beard, *Brief Biographical Sketches of Some of the Early Ministers of the Cumberland Presbyterian Church* (Nashville: Southern Methodist Publishing, 1867), 158–62, 168–73, 182; and B. W. McDonnold, *History of the Cumberland Presbyterian Church* (Nashville: Board of Publication of Cumberland Presbyterian Church, 1888), 224–28.

20. T. C. Anderson, "History of Cumberland University," *Theological Medium, and Cumberland Presbyterian Quarterly* 3 (December 1858): 191.

21. Frank Burns, *Wilson County,* Tennessee County History Series (Memphis: Memphis State University Press, 1983), vii-x, 25–27.

22. Green, *Echoes,* 201.

23. Joshua W. Caldwell, *Sketches of the Bench and Bar of Tennessee* (Knoxville: Ogden Brothers, 1898), 144.

24. McDonnold, *History of the Cumberland Presbyterian Church,* 220; Winstead Paine Bone, *A History of Cumberland University, 1842–1935* (Lebanon, Tennessee: n.p., 1935), 37, 41.

25. Bone, *History of Cumberland University,* 40.

26. Minutes of the Board of Trustees of Cumberland University, February 17, 1843 (tuition free) and January 12, 1844 (members of Cumberland Presbyterian Church). The Minutes of the Board of Trustees are on deposit in the Cumberland University Archives, Vise Library, Lebanon, Tennessee (hereinafter, Minutes of Board of Trustees).

27. Bone, *History of Cumberland University,* 37, 58.

28. McDonnold, *History of the Cumberland Presbyterian Church,* 220.

29. Minutes of Board of Trustees, February 27, 1845.

30. Ibid., May 27, 1845.

31. Letter, Nathan Green Sr. to Robert L. Caruthers, March 15, 1845, Robert L. Caruthers Collection, University of North Carolina Library, Chapel Hill.

32. McDonnold, *History of the Cumberland Presbyterian Church,* 512.

33. Minutes of Board of Trustees, January 7, 1847.

34. Ibid., February 22, 1847.

35. Ibid., May 14, 1847.

36. Green, *Echoes,* 214–15.

37. J. Berrien Lindsley, "Outline History of Cumberland University," *Theological Medium* 12 (October 1876): 427 (new series vol. 7).

38. Minutes of Board of Trustees, August 30, 1847.

39. Green, *Echoes,* 215.

40. Cumberland University Catalogue, 1847–48 (catalogues were published following the year to which they relate, e.g., that marked 1847–48 was published following the completion of that academic year). Nearly complete runs of the catalogue are on deposit with Cumberland University Archives, Vise Library, Lebanon, Tennessee and Beeson Library, Samford University, Cumberland School of Law, Birmingham, Alabama.

41. Ibid., 1856–57.

42. Ibid.; Cumberland University Law Department Catalogue, 1848–49.

43. Cumberland University Catalogue, 1857–58 (historical data in this year's catalogue).

44. Minutes of Board of Trustees, July 26, 1848.

45. Ibid., March 3, 1849.

46. McDonnold, *History of the Cumberland Presbyterian Church,* 512.

47. Johnson, *Schooled Lawyers,* 21.

48. Ibid., 13.

49. Reed, *Training for the Public Profession,* 183.

50. Letter, Simon Greenleaf to Robert L. Caruthers, January 7, 1848, Robert L. Caruthers Collection, University of North Carolina Library, Chapel Hill.

51. Letter, Nathan Green Sr. to Robert L. Caruthers, May 18, 1847, Robert L. Caruthers Collection, University of North Carolina Library, Chapel Hill.

52. Green, "The Law School of Cumberland University," 65; Caldwell, *Sketches of the Bench and Bar of Tennessee,* 148.

53. Letter, Nathan Green Sr. to Robert L. Caruthers, November 10, 1848, Robert L. Caruthers Collection, University of North Carolina Library, Chapel Hill.

54. Minutes of Board of Trustees, November 3, 1848.

55. Letter, Nathan Green Sr. to John Alexander Green (son), October 18, 1849, Cumberland University Archives, Record Group 490, Box 1, Vise Library, Lebanon, Tennessee; Green, *Echoes,* 216.

56. Nathan Green Sr., "Address of Hon. Nathan Green, Judge of the Supreme Court of Tennessee, Delivered February 28th, 1849, on entering on the duties of professor of law in Cumberland University at Lebanon, Tennessee," Banner of Peace Office, Lebanon, Tennessee.

57. Cumberland University Catalogue, 1857–58 (historical data in this year's catalogue).

58. Green, *Echoes,* 220. Nathan Green Jr. also wrote a fictional biography of his father's life up to the point of his repentance, under a pseudonym, "Over Forty," *The Tall Man of Winton and His Wife* (Nashville: Cumberland Presbyterian Board of Publication, 1872).

59. Will T. Hale and Dixon L. Merritt, *A History of Tennessee and Tennesseans,* 5 vols. (Chicago: Lewis Publishing, 1913), 3:728.

60. Letter, Nathan Green Sr. to Robert L. Caruthers, September 25, 1850, Robert L. Caruthers Collection, University of North Carolina Library, Chapel Hill.

61. Letter, Nathan Green Sr. to John Alexander Green, April 11, 1852, Cumberland University Archives, Record Group 490, Box 1, Vise Library, Lebanon, Tennessee.

62. Lewis L. Laska, "A History of Legal Education in Tennessee, 1770–1970" (Ph.D. dissertation, Vanderbilt University, Peabody College for Teachers, 1978), 128–29.

63. Letter, Nathan Green Sr. to Robert L. Caruthers, September 27, 1848, Robert L. Caruthers Collection, University of North Carolina Library, Chapel Hill; Lindsley, "Outline History of Cumberland University," 435. The pamphlet of Nathan Green's address was discussed and extensively quoted with approval in a leading legal journal published in New York City, *United States Monthly Law Magazine* 2 (September 1850): 133–44.

64. For example, see letter, in *Missouri Republican* (St. Louis), December 15, 1859, reprinted in *Cumberland Alumnus* 4 (April 1925): 9.

65. Wharton J. Green, *Recollections and Reflections: An Auto [sic] of Half a Century and More* (n.p., 1906), 107–8 (date inferred through author's reference to certain faculty member).

66. Bone, *History of Cumberland University,* 76.

67. Caldwell, *Sketches,* 141–42.

68. Cumberland University Catalogue, 1853–54.

69. Ibid., 1847–48.

70. Ibid., 1854–55.

71. Ibid., 1847–48.

72. The years 1847–48 through 1857–58 are included in Cumberland University Catalogue, 1857–58; the two following years are in Cumberland University Catalogues, 1858–59 and 1859–60.

73. G. Frank Burns, *Phoenix Rising: The Sesquicentennial History of Cumberland University, 1842–1992* (Lebanon, Tennessee: n.p., 1992), 340.

74. Cumberland University Catalogue, 1857–58.

75. Katherine B. Fuller, "A History of the Cumberland University School of Law from Its Beginning in 1847 to Its Acquisition by Howard College in 1961" (M.A. thesis, Birmingham-Southern College, 1962), 15–16; Burns, *Phoenix Rising,* 83.

76. Reed, *Training for the Public Profession,* 451.

77. Resolution of Board of Trustees of Cumberland University, in Minutes of Board of Trustees, June 3, 1919, following Green Jr.'s death; Hale and Merritt, *History of Tennessee,* 5:1354–55.

78. Minutes of Board of Trustees, July 30, 1845.

79. Ibid., February 16, 1850, and February 15, 1856.

80. Green, "Law School of Cumberland University," 65; Lindsley, "Outline History of Cumberland University," 431. For a fuller biographical study of Carter, see, Harris D. Riley Jr., "A Gallant Adopted Son of Tennessee—General John C. Carter, C.S.A.," *Tennessee Historical Quarterly* 48 (Winter 1989): 195–208.

81. Johnson, *Schooled Lawyers,* 42, 44.

82. Charles R. McManis, "The History of First Century American Legal Education: A Revisionist Perspective," *Washington University Law Quarterly* 59 (Fall 1981): 626.

83. Reed, *Training for the Public Profession,* 182.

84. Minutes of Board of Trustees, July 29, 1842.

85. Ibid., September 27, 1844, and October 3, 1849.

86. Ibid., August 30, 1847.

87. Letter, Nathan Green Sr. to Robert Green, January 16, 1858, Cumberland University Archives, Record Group 490, Box 1, Vise Library, Lebanon, Tennessee.

88. Burns, *Phoenix Rising,* 82.

89. Minutes of Board of Trustees, January 11, 1856; September 10, 1857.

90. Letter, Simon Greenleaf to Robert L. Caruthers, January 7, 1848, Robert L. Caruthers Collection, University of North Carolina Library, Chapel Hill.

91. Ritchie, *First Hundred Years,* 36.

92. Minutes of Board of Trustees, June 15, 1852.

93. Letter, Nathan Green Sr. to Robert Green, January 16, 1858, Cumberland University Archives, Record Group 490, Box 1, Vise Library, Lebanon, Tennessee.

94. Green, "Law School of Cumberland University," 66; Caldwell, *Sketches of the Bench and Bar of Tennessee,* 142; and Burns, *Phoenix Rising,* 35.

95. Philip M. Hamer, ed., *Tennessee: A History, 1673–1932* (New York: American Historical Society, 1933), 1:512.

96. Letter, Nathan Green Sr. to Thomas Green, September 25, 1858, Cumberland University Archives, Record Group 490, Box 1, Vise Library, Lebanon, Tennessee.

97. Minutes of Board of Trustees, March 3, 1849.

98. Ibid., July 2, 1858, August 30, 1858, and August 31, 1858; Anderson, "History of Cumberland University," 197.

99. Lindsley, "Outline History of Cumberland University," 437; Green ("Over Forty"), "Reminiscences of Early Days," *Phoenix* (1897): 123.

100. Most of this description is from Senate Document No. 288, 59th Congress, 1st Sess. (1906), Claim of Cumberland University before Court of Claims.

Chapter 2. Curriculum and Students, 1847–1861

1. Abraham Caruthers, "Inaugural Address of Hon. A. Caruthers . . . on the 29th of July, 1847," Banner of Peace Office, Lebanon, Tennessee, 8–9.

2. Ibid., 8–9, 18–20.

3. Ibid., 19–22.

4. License of Paine P. Prim to Practice Law in the State of Kentucky, June 26, 1847, Cumberland University Archives, Record Group 960, Box 1, Folder 24, Vise Library, Lebanon, Tennessee.

5. Cumberland University Catalogue, 1850–51.

6. William R. Johnson, *Schooled Lawyers: A Study in the Clash of Professional Cultures* (New York: New York University Press, 1978), 42.

7. Ibid., 12.

8. Joshua W. Caldwell, *Sketches of the Bench and Bar of Tennessee* (Knoxville: Ogden Brothers, 1898), 148; Nathan Green Jr., "The Law School of Cumberland University," *Green Bag* 2 (February 1890): 64.

9. Cumberland University Catalogue, 1855–56.

10. Columbus Sykes Collection, Mississippi State Archives, Jackson.

11. Cumberland University Catalogues for 1846–47 and 1851–52; Introduction of Robert L. Caruthers as president of board of trustees, August 1852, in booklet of "Baccalaureate Address Pronounced by Chancellor Ridley before the Graduating Class," Banner of Peace, Lebanon, Tennessee, iii-iv.

12. Cumberland University Catalogues, 1853–54 and 1854–55.

13. Andrew Bennett Martin, "A Colleague's Tribute to Judge Green," *Cumberland Alumnus* 1 (April 1920): 9.

14. Cumberland University Catalogue, 1855–56.

15. Salathiel, *Missouri Republican* (St. Louis), December 15, 1859, reprinted in *Cumberland Alumnus* 4 (April 1925): 9.

16. Cumberland University Catalogue, 1855–56.

17. Quotations from Cumberland University Catalogue for 1850–51 and "Address of Hon. Nathan Green . . . delivered February 28th, 1849, on entering on the duties of professor of law . . . ," Banner of Peace Office, Lebanon, Tennessee, 15. Virtually every catalogue in the antebellum period explains this teaching technique.

18. Cumberland University Catalogue, 1854–55.

19. Introduction of Robert L. Caruthers to Ridley, "Baccalaureate Address," iii-iv.

20. J. Berrien Lindsley, "Outline History of Cumberland University," *Theological Medium* 12 (October 1876): 435 (new series vol. 7).

21. "The Law School, 1847–1897," in *Phoenix* (1897): 3, 5. A complete run of the *Phoenix* is in the Cumberland University Archives, Vise Library, Lebanon, Tennessee. G. Frank Burns, the present historian of Cumberland University, believes that the author of these descriptions is Professor Andrew B. Martin.

22. Nathan Green Jr., "The Old Guard," in *Echoes from Caruthers Hall,* ed. Nathan Green Jr. (Nashville: Cumberland Presbyterian Publishing House, 1889), 221.

23. Caldwell, *Sketches of the Bench and Bar of Tennessee,* 143.

24. Martin, "Colleague's Tribute," 9.

25. Cumberland University Catalogue, 1846–47.

26. Ibid., 1847–48; Cumberland School of Law Catalogue, 1848–49.

27. Green, "Address of Hon. Nathan Green . . . delivered February 28th, 1849," 16.

28. Cumberland University Catalogue, 1854–55.

29. Minutes of Board of Trustees of Cumberland University, February 22, 1847. The Minutes of the Board of Trustees are on deposit in the Cumberland University Archives, Vise Library, Lebanon, Tennessee (hereafter Minutes of Board of Trustees).

30. Cumberland University Catalogue, 1858–59.

31. Alfred Zantzinger Reed, *Training for the Public Profession of the Law* (New York: Carnegie Foundation for the Advancement of Teaching, 1921; reprint, New York: Arno Press, 1976), 252 n. 1.

32. Charles R. McManis, "The History of First Century American Legal Education: A Revisionist Perspective," *Washington University Law Quarterly* 59 (Fall 1981): 625; Reed, *Training for the Public Profession,* 171.

33. Harvard Law School Catalogue, 1848–49.

34. Lewis L. Laska, "A History of Legal Education in Tennessee, 1770–1970" (Ph.D. dissertation, Vanderbilt University, Peabody College for Teachers, 1978), 139.

35. John Ritchie, *The First Hundred Years: A Short History of the School of Law of the University of Virginia for the Period 1826–1926* (Charlottesville: University Press of Virginia, 1978), 35.

36. Ibid., 39.

37. *The Centennial History of the Harvard Law School* (n.p., 1918), quoted in William P. LaPiana, *Logic and Experience: The Origin of Modern American Legal Education* (New York: Oxford University Press, 1994), 52. The issue of how much demand was put on Harvard students is discussed, 48–51.

38. Ibid., 51, quoting Everett P. Wheeler.

39. Cumberland University Catalogue, 1847–48.

40. Laska, "History of Legal Education in Tennessee," 757–58.

41. F. F. Johnson, *Life and Works of F. F. Johnson, M.D.* (Stonefort, Illinois: Turner Publishing, 1913), 18–19.

42. Ibid., 22.

43. B. W. McDonnold, *History of the Cumberland Presbyterian Church* (Nashville: Board of Publication of Cumberland Presbyterian Church, 1888), 225–26; Winstead Paine Bone, *A History of Cumberland University, 1842–1935* (Lebanon, Tennessee: n.p., 1935), 59–61.

44. *Phoenix* (1896): 15–6.

45. Minutes of Board of Trustees, June 27, 1851.

46. Ibid., August 30, 1858.

47. Remarks of Nathan Green Sr., printed in "Collegial," *Cumberland University Monthly Magazine* 2 (October 1858): 37–38.

48. Green, "Law School of Cumberland University," 73.

49. Nathan Green Jr., "Government," *Echoes from Caruthers Hall,* ed. Nathan Green Jr. (Nashville: Cumberland Presbyterian Publishing House, 1889), 22–23.

50. Minutes of Board of Trustees, February 20, 1857.

51. Ibid., November 1, 1845; December 6, 1845.

52. Ibid., June 1, 1848; July 5, 1848; October 2, 1848.

53. Ibid., July 5, 1848.

54. Ibid., May 24, 1854.

55. Johnson, *Schooled Lawyers,* 21–22.

56. Minutes of Board of Trustees, May 8, 1851.

57. Green, "Law School of Cumberland University," 65.

58. Minutes of Board of Trustees, February 4, 1857; February 20, 1857; May 16, 1857; February 2, 1858; May 5, 1859.

59. Minutes of Board of Trustees, February 28, 1851.

60. Ibid., January 31, 1857.

61. Ibid., July 16, 1842; August 24, 1857; September 2, 1859.

62. Ibid., November 30, 1852.

63. Ibid., July 16, 1842; July 29, 1842.

64. Ibid., June 13, 1851; June 21, 1851.

65. Ibid., February 7, 1855.

66. Katherine B. Fuller, "A History of the Cumberland School of Law from Its Beginning in 1847 to Its Acquisition by Howard College in 1961" (M.A. thesis, Birmingham-Southern College, 1962), 11 (based on conversation with Mrs. Virginia Lawlor, amateur historian of Wilson County, Tennessee, March 13, 1962).

67. Nathan Green Jr. [under pen name, "Over Forty"], "Reminiscences of Early Days," in *Phoenix* (1897): 123.

68. Minutes of Board of Trustees, November 1, 1856.

69. G. Frank Burns, *Phoenix Rising: The Sesquicentennial History of Cumberland University, 1842–1992* (Lebanon, Tennessee: n.p., 1992), 77, 158; a complete listing of Greek fraternities and their dates at Cumberland, throughout the nineteenth century, is in Bone, *History of Cumberland University,* 288.

70. Francis W. Shepardson, "Under the Stars and Bars," *Beta Theta Pi* 62 (February 1935): 357–62.

71. Bone, *History of Cumberland University,* 252–53; Burns, *Phoenix Rising,* 42.

72. *Phoenix* (1896): 16.

73. Bone, *History of Cumberland University,* 256–57.

74. *Proceedings of the Amasagassean Society,* 1846–1851, on deposit with the Cumberland University Archives (no record group indicated), Vise Library, Lebanon, Tennessee. The spelling of the Society's name on this document varies from that found everywhere else.

75. "Interesting Historical Notes from the Archives of the University," *Cumberland Alumnus* 4 (December 1924): 4–7.

76. Burns, *Phoenix Rising,* 45–47, 93.

77. James V. Drake, *An Historical Sketch of Wilson County, Tenn., From its First Settlement to the Present Time* (Nashville: Tavel, Eastman and Howell, 1879; reprint, Lebanon, Tennessee: Press of the Democrat, 1976), 13.

78. William S. Speer, *Sketches of Prominent Tennesseans* (Nashville: Albert B. Tavel, 1888), 436; Minutes of the Board of Trustees, June 3, 1919 (memorial tribute to Nathan Green Jr.).

79. Harris D. Riley Jr., "A Gallant Adopted Son of Tennessee—General John C. Carter, C.S.A.," *Tennessee Historical Quarterly* 48 (Winter 1989): 196.

80. Letter, Nicholas N. Cox to Mary Slayden, May 4, 1858, Cumberland University Archives, Record Group 960, Box 3, Folder 16, Vise Library, Lebanon, Tennessee. Date of marriage from other records in that and associated files.

81. Terry Calvani, "The Early Legal Career of Howell Jackson," *Vanderbilt Law Review* 30 (January 1977): 41–45; Burns, *Phoenix Rising*, 344.

82. Letter, Nathan Green Sr. to Alexander Jackson, March 7, 1856, Small Collection, Harding-Jackson Papers, folder 7, Tennessee State Library and Archives, Nashville; letter, Nathan Green Sr. to Alexander Jackson, March 23, 1856, Beeson Library, Samford University, Cumberland School of Law, Birmingham, Alabama. Copies of both letters are in Cumberland University Archives, Vise Library, Lebanon, Tennessee. Dr. Jackson was so well educated that he apparently wrote to Green with comments on the merits of the appeal that was the subject of his son's opinion. The later letter of Green to Dr. Jackson has extensive discussion of the merits. Green must have believed Dr. Jackson would understand.

83. Calvani, "Early Legal Career of Howell Jackson," 40.

84. Nathan Green Jr., "Law School of Cumberland University," 65.

85. John William Burgess, "A Civil War Boyhood," *Atlantic* 151 (February 1933): 201.

86. Letter, S. C. Bowers to Dear Sir [Bowers's father], April 18, 1861, Cumberland University Archives, Record Group 960, Box 1, Vise Library, Lebanon, Tennessee.

87. Green, "Law School of Cumberland University," 65.

88. Burgess, "Civil War Boyhood," 202–3; Bone, *History of Cumberland University*, 83, 86.

89. Green, "Law School of Cumberland University," 66.

90. Green, *Echoes*, 217.

91. Account of Scobey & Hankins with S. C. Bowers, 1860–1861, Cumberland University Archives, Record Group 960, Box 1, Vise Library, Lebanon, Tennessee.

92. Autograph Book of Joseph D. Cross, undated but autographs date from June 1860 through April 1861, on file with Beeson Library, Samford University, Cumberland School of Law, Birmingham, Alabama.

93. Autograph Class Book of C. W. Robertson, undated but probably 1860, Cumberland University Archives, Record Group 960, Box 1, Folder 25, Vise Library, Lebanon, Tennessee.

Chapter 3. After the War, 1865–1878

1. Senate Document No. 288, 59th Congress, 1st Sess. (1906), Claim of Cumberland University before Court of Claims.

2. Nathan Green Jr., "The Law School of Cumberland University," *Green Bag* 2 (February 1890): 67.

3. See, G. Frank Burns, *Phoenix Rising: The Sesquicentennial History of Cumberland University, 1842–1992* (Lebanon, Tennessee: n.p., 1992), 59–60.

4. Minutes of the Board of Trustees of Cumberland University, undated but doubtless in late 1864 or early 1865 (p. 220 of vol. 1 of trustees' minutes). The minutes of the Board of Trustees are on deposit in the Cumberland University Archives, Vise Library, Lebanon, Tennessee (hereinafter Minutes of Board of Trustees).

5. J. Berrien Lindsley, "Outline History of Cumberland University," *Theological Medium* 12 (October 1876): 437 (new series vol. 7).

6. Ibid., 401–2.

7. B. W. McDonnold, *History of the Cumberland Presbyterian Church* (Nashville: Board of Publication of Cumberland Presbyterian Church, 1888), 515.

8. Minutes of Board of Trustees, July 11, 1866.

9. Green, "Law School of Cumberland University," 67–68.

10. "Clarksville Pays Last Tribute to Beloved Son," *Clarksville (Tenn.) Leaf-Chronicle,* July 15, 1914, p. 1 (reporting details of Justice Horace Lurton's career).

11. Green, "Law School of Cumberland University," 68.

12. Ibid; Nathan Green Jr., "The Old Guard," in *Echoes from Caruthers Hall,* ed. Nathan Green Jr. (Nashville: Cumberland Presbyterian Publishing House, 1889), 223.

13. Minutes of Board of Trustees, undated. (The minutes for 1864–1866 are irregularly placed and some undated, but the context makes the approximate dating of the summer of 1866 reliable.)

14. Lindsley, "Outline History of Cumberland University," 404; McDonnold, *History of the Cumberland Presbyterian Church,* 516, 519–20.

15. Minutes of Board of Trustees, June 8, 1866; Cumberland University Catalogue for 1866–67.

16. Lindsley, "Outline History of Cumberland University," 440–41; Cumberland University Catalogue, 1868–69.

17. Will T. Hale and Dixon L. Merritt, *A History of Tennessee and Tennesseans,* 5 vols. (Chicago: Lewis Publishing, 1913), 5:1338; Cumberland University Catalogue, 1877–78.

18. Winstead Paine Bone, *A History of Cumberland University, 1842–1935* (Lebanon, Tennessee: n.p., 1935), 243.

19. Burns, *Phoenix Rising,* 24–26, 83–84; John A. Pitts, *Personal and Professional Reminiscences of an Old Lawyer* (Kingsport, Tennessee: Southern Publishers, 1930), 55, 354, 363.

20. Minutes of Board of Trustees, July 19, 1866.

21. Bone, *History of Cumberland University,* 116, 119–20; Burns, *Phoenix Rising,* 24–26, 36; Lindsley, "Outline History of Cumberland University," 415; Minutes of Board of Trustees, February 28, 1874.

22. Minutes of Board of Trustees, December 26, 1868; May 6, 1870.

23. Ibid., August 24, 1866.

24. Ibid., August 14, 1869; March 22, 1870.

25. Ibid., May 29, 1845; October 31, 1851; July 3, 1856; Burns, *Phoenix Rising,* 64; McDonnold, *History of the Cumberland Presbyterian Church,* 516–17.

26. Burns, *Phoenix Rising,* 66; McDonnold, *History of the Cumberland Presbyterian Church,* 520–21; Minutes of Board of Trustees, August 17, 1872.

27. McDonnold, *History of the Cumberland Presbyterian Church,* 518.

28. Burns, *Phoenix Rising,* 69; McDonnold, *History of the Cumberland Presbyterian Church,* 521; Lindsley, "Outline History of Cumberland University," 414.

29. Bone, *History of Cumberland University,* 116–17.

30. Hale and Merritt, *History of Tennessee and Tennesseans,* 5:1357.

31. William B. Bate, *An Address Delivered by Gen. Wm. B. Bate before the Alumni Society of Cumberland University* (Nashville: J. O. Griffith, 1869).

32. Cumberland University Catalogues, 1868–69 and 1875–76.

33. Catalogue of the Lebanon Law School, 1869–70 (i.e., Cumberland University Law Department; Lebanon Law School was an informal name sometimes used even by the school itself).

34. Bone, *History of Cumberland University,* 119–20; Burns, *Phoenix Rising,* 84–85; Minutes of Board of Trustees, September 24, 1877.

35. Bone, *History of Cumberland University,* 42; Cumberland University Catalogues, 1877–78 and 1878–79.

36. Burns, *Phoenix Rising,* 87.

37. Katherine B. Fuller, "A History of the Cumberland University School of Law from Its Beginning in 1847 to Its Acquisition by Howard College in 1961" (M.A. thesis, Birmingham-Southern College, 1962), 28–29.

38. Green, "Law School of Cumberland University," 74; Pitts, *Personal and Professional Reminiscences,* 354.

39. Cumberland School of Law Catalogues, 1865–66 and 1866–67.

40. For interesting insights on this, see A. W. B. Simpson, "The Rise and Fall of the Legal Treatise: Legal Principles and the Forms of Legal Literature," *University of Chicago Law Review* 48 (Summer 1981): 632–79.

41. Lewis L. Laska, "A History of Legal Education in Tennessee, 1770–1970" (Ph.D. dissertation, Vanderbilt University, Peabody College for Teachers, 1978), 136.

42. Robert Stevens, *Law School: Legal Education in America from the 1850s to the 1980s* (Chapel Hill: University of North Carolina Press, 1983), 37.

43. Green, "Law School of Cumberland University," 65.

44. Laska, "History of Legal Education in Tennessee," 126.

45. Cumberland University Catalogue, 1870–71.

46. Green, "Law School of Cumberland University," 70.

47. Pitts, *Personal and Professional Reminiscences,* 353–54.

48. Cumberland University Catalogues, 1870–71 and 1871–72.

49. William R. Johnson, *Schooled Lawyers: A Study in the Clash of Professional Cultures* (New York: New York University Press, 1978), 42.

50. Pitts, *Personal and Professional Reminiscences,* 365.

51. Laska, "History of Legal Education in Tennessee," 141.

52. Pitts, *Personal and Professional Reminiscences,* 366.

53. Ibid., 54–55, 354–58, 361–63.

54. Green, "Law School of Cumberland University," 75.

55. Lindsley, "Outline History of Cumberland University," 449.

56. Bone, *History of Cumberland University,* 108; Green, "Law School of Cumberland University," 73; Nathan Green Jr., "Government," in Green, *Echoes from Caruthers Hall,* 23–24.

57. Minutes of Board of Trustees, August 20, 1873.

58. Green, "Law School of Cumberland University," 73.

59. Pitts, *Personal and Professional Reminiscences,* 369–71.

60. Cumberland School of Law Catalogues, 1865–66 and 1866–67; Cumberland University Catalogue, 1873–74.

61. Burns, *Phoenix Rising,* 46–47.

62. Ibid.

63. Cumberland University Catalogue, 1876–77.

64. Judges Caldwell and M. M. Neil according to Pitts (a member of the 1870–71 class), *Personal and Professional Reminiscences,* 282.

65. Lurton's words quoted from Horace Lurton, Cumberland University Commencement Address, undated c. 1912, Box 1, Lurton Collection, Manuscript Division, Library of Congress, Washington, D.C.

66. David M. Tucker, "Justice Horace Harmon Lurton: The Shaping of a National Progressive," *American Journal of Legal History* 13 (July 1969): 223–24.

67. Ibid., 224–25.

68. Bone, *History of Cumberland University,* 252–53, 257–59.

69. Pitts, *Personal and Professional Reminiscences,* 367.

70. Cumberland University Catalogue, 1873–74.

71. Ibid., 1875–76.

72. Ibid., 1873–74.

73. See ibid., 1871–72, 1873–74, 1875–76, and 1876–77.

74. Green, "Law School of Cumberland University," 72.

75. Pitts, *Personal and Professional Reminiscences,* 368–69.

76. Green, "Law School of Cumberland University," 72; Lindsley, "Outline History of Cumberland University," 414.

77. Albert Norrell, Valedictory, January 20, 1876, manuscript on file with the Beeson Library, Samford University, Cumberland School of Law, Birmingham, Alabama.

Chapter 4. The Student Experience, 1878–1919

1. Cumberland University Catalogues for this entire period, ending with Cumberland University Register, 1918–1919; announcements, 1919–1920.

2. Cumberland University Catalogue for 1896 (describing 1895–96) (during certain years the format of the catalogues was changed to a single year, which would generally describe the academic year ending with the year in the catalogue and announce the academic year beginning with that same year).

3. Minutes of the Board of Trustees of Cumberland University, June 4, 1883. The Minutes of the Board of Trustees are on deposit in the Cumberland University Archives, Vise Library, Lebanon, Tennessee (hereinafter Minutes of Board of Trustees).

4. Cumberland University Catalogue, 1882–83.

5. Ibid., 1883–84.

6. Ibid., 1896.

7. Cumberland University Register, 1918–19.

8. Cumberland University Catalogue, 1895.

9. Cumberland School of Law Catalogue, 1918–19.

10. Cumberland University Catalogue, 1892.

11. Ibid., 1893.

12. Ibid., 1896.

13. Nathan Green Jr., "The Law School of Cumberland University," *Green Bag* 2 (February 1890): 72, 74.

14. Lewis L. Laska, "A History of Legal Education in Tennessee, 1770–1970" (Ph.D. dissertation, Vanderbilt University, Peabody College for Teachers, 1978), 188–89.

15. Cumberland University Catalogue, 1900–1901.

16. This material from "Grading Book," on file with the Beeson Library, Samford University, Cumberland School of Law, Birmingham, Alabama.

17. Ibid.; Andrew Bennett Martin, "A Colleague's Tribute to Judge Green," *Cumberland Alumnus* 1 (April 1920): 10.

18. Cumberland School of Law Bulletin, 1912.

19. Green, "Law School of Cumberland University," 69.

20. Andrew B. Martin, *Address upon the Life and Character of Judge Robert L. Caruthers* (Nashville: Cumberland Presbyterian Publishing House, 1883), 15.

21. Minutes of Board of Trustees, October 24, 1900; Cumberland University Quarterly, 1902–3; G. Frank Burns, *Phoenix Rising: The Sesquicentennial History of Cumberland University, 1842–1992* (Lebanon, Tennessee: n.p., 1992), 103–4; "The Law School," *Lebanon (Tenn.) Democrat,* January 23, 1908, p. 10.

22. Cumberland University Quarterly, August 1903; Cumberland University Bulletin, March 1904.

23. Bulletin of Cumberland University, March 1910.

24. Albert Norrell, Valedictory, January 20, 1876, manuscript on file with the Beeson Library, Samford University, Cumberland School of Law, Birmingham, Alabama.

25. Nathan Green Jr., "Government," in *Echoes from Caruthers Hall,* ed. Nathan Green Jr. (Nashville: Cumberland Presbyterian Publishing House, 1889), 25.

26. These conclusions are based on illustrations and drawings appearing in various issues of the *Phoenix* and the *Cumberland Alumnus.*

27. Interview with William F. Spencer, class of 1912, June 25, 1962, quoted in Katherine B. Fuller, "A History of the Cumberland University School of Law from Its Beginning in 1847 to Its Acquisition by Howard College in 1961" (M.A. thesis, Birmingham-Southern College, 1962), 41.

28. *Phoenix* (1915): 37, 99.

29. Nathan Green Jr., *Sparks from a Backlog* (Nashville: Cumberland Presbyterian Publishing House, 1891), 136.

30. As, for example, the senior class did on Green's eighty-ninth birthday in 1916, referred to in *Phoenix* (1916): 67, 69.

31. Will T. Hale and Dixon L. Merritt, *A History of Tennessee and Tennesseans,* 5 vols. (Chicago: Lewis Publishing, 1913), 5:1357.

32. Albert Bramlett Neil, "My Great World or Fifty Years on the Bench," typescript, 1964, p. 68, on deposit with Beeson Library, Samford University, Cumberland School of Law, Birmingham, Alabama.

33. *Phoenix* (1915): 99.

34. William F. Spencer, interviewed June 25, 1952, and quoted in Fuller, "History of the Cumberland University School of Law," 41.

35. Neil, "My Great World," 32.

36. Joseph Weldon Bailey, "A Tribute to the Law School of Cumberland University," *Cumberland Alumnus* 9 (November 1929): 10.

37. Cordell Hull, speech before Washington alumni of Cumberland University, May 4, 1934, quoted in "Hull Calls for Consecration," *Lebanon (Tenn.) Democrat,* May 10, 1934, p. 1.

38. *Cumberland Weekly* (student newspaper), February 14, 1911, p. 3; February 6, 1912.

39. *Phoenix* (1904): 65–66.

40. Cumberland University Bulletin, March 1915.

41. *Cumberland Weekly,* October 29, 1902, p. 3; February 14, 1911, p. 3.

42. Green, "Law School of Cumberland University," 70.

43. Ibid.

44. Minutes of Board of Trustees, April 18, 1879.

45. Henry L. Taylor, *Professional Education in the United States* (Albany, New York: University of the State of New York, 1900), 182, 179.

46. Cumberland University Catalogues, 1878–79 and 1881–82.

47. Ibid., 1897 and 1898.

48. Cumberland School of Law Bulletin, 1920.

49. Cumberland University Catalogue, 1878–79.

50. Interview with William F. Spencer, June 25, 1962, in Fuller, "History of the Cumberland School of Law," 37, 41.

51. Cumberland University Bulletin, March 1904.

52. Ibid., March 1913.
53. Ibid., March 1915 and June 1917; Cumberland School of Law Catalogue, 1918–19.
54. Winstead Paine Bone, *A History of Cumberland University, 1842–1935* (Lebanon, Tennessee: n.p., 1935), 264–65.
55. Tillman David Johnson, "Reminiscences Recorded in 1949," Cumberland University Archives, Record Group 960, Box 3, Folder 22, Vise Library, Lebanon, Tennessee.
56. *Nostalgia* (undated promotional publication of Cumberland University; internal evidence indicates post-1961) (unpaginated), copy on file with Beeson Library, Samford University, Cumberland School of Law, Birmingham, Alabama.
57. Burns, *Phoenix Rising,* 322.
58. *Cumberland Weekly,* January 31, 1911, p. 2.
59. Ibid.
60. Burns, *Phoenix Rising,* 77–78.
61. Neil, "My Great World," 126.
62. Green, *Sparks from a Backlog,* 138.
63. Green, "Government," 24–25.
64. Based on an interview with G. Frank Burns, Cumberland University historian, February 18, 1994. His source was a personal interview with a participant and witness to the events, Flavius Josephus Sanders Jr., held in 1960. The catalogues confirm the attendance of these individuals in the years indicated.
65. Minutes of Board of Trustees, March 18, 1895.
66. Cumberland University Catalogue, 1900–1901.
67. Ibid., 1881–82.
68. Bone, *History of Cumberland University,* 123.
69. Cumberland University Catalogue, 1889.
70. Ibid.
71. Minutes of Board of Trustees, January 17, 1891.
72. Ibid., February 20, 1894.
73. Cumberland University Catalogue, 1894.
74. Ibid., 1898 (for years 1897–98).
75. Bone, *History of Cumberland University,* 123, 249.
76. Burns, *Phoenix Rising,* 93.
77. Cumberland University Bulletin and General Catalogue for 1906–7 (issued March 1907); Cumberland University Bulletin and General Catalogue for 1907–8 (issued April 1908).
78. 1907 Tennessee Public Acts, ch. 69.
79. Drawn from Burns, *Phoenix Rising,* 77–78.
80. Most helpful was Fuller, "History of the Cumberland School of Law," 36–37.
81. "Sans Souci," *Phoenix* (1903): 158.

82. Cumberland University Bulletin, March 1904.

83. *Lebanon (Tenn.) Democrat,* October 1, 1908, p. 1; October 15, 1908, p. 1.

84. Burns, *Phoenix Rising,* 237.

85. Frank Burns, *Wilson County,* Tennessee County History Series (Memphis: Memphis State University Press, 1983), 71–72; *Nostalgia* (undated promotional publication of Cumberland University; internal evidence indicates post 1961) (unpaginated), copy on file with Beeson Library, Samford Universtiy, Cumberland School of Law, Birmingham, Alabama.

86. Burns, *Phoenix Rising,* 77.

87. Cordell Hull, *The Memoirs of Cordell Hull,* 2 vols. (New York: Macmillan Company, 1948), 1:26–27.

88. Cumberland University "Commencement Calendar," in Cumberland University Archives, Record Group 200, Box 4, Vise Library, Lebanon, Tennessee.

89. Cumberland University Bulletin, January 1904.

90. Bone, *History of Cumberland University,* 254, 256–59 (dates of student publications indicated).

91. Cumberland University Catalogues, 1899–1900 and 1900–1901; Bone, *History of Cumberland University,* 259; Burns, *Phoenix Rising,* 296.

92. Burns, *Phoenix Rising,* 293, 177; Bone, *History of Cumberland University,* 259; Poetry of William Robert Bradford, Samford University Special Collections, Collection Number 1089, Box 1, Folder 1, Harwell G. Davis Library, Birmingham, Alabama.

93. "Sports in Cumberland," *Cumberland Alumnus* 9 (November 1929): 9; Burns, *Phoenix Rising,* 294.

94. Burns, *Phoenix Rising,* 104–5; 293–94, 176–77.

95. Cumberland University Bulletin, January 1904.

96. Burns, *Phoenix Rising,* 296–97.

97. "Sports in Cumberland," 9.

98. Burns, *Phoenix Rising,* 292.

99. Cumberland University Bulletin, January 1904; Burns, *Phoenix Rising,* 104.

100. Ibid., 104–5, 288–91, 293.

101. Ibid., 114, 289.

102. "Sports in Cumberland," 9; Burns, *Phoenix Rising,* 290–91.

103. George E. Allen, *Presidents Who Have Known Me* (New York: Simon and Schuster, 1950), 23–25.

104. "222–0. Cumberland Can Laugh About Football Fiasco," *Nashville Tennessean,* October 7, 1981.

105. B. P. Paty, quoted in O. K. Armstrong, "The Funniest Football Game Ever Played," *Reader's Digest* (October 1955): 56–57.

106. Jim Paul, *You Dropped It, You Pick It Up!* (Baton Rouge, Louisiana: n.p., 1983).

107. Untitled poem (partial quotation), Poetry of William Robert Bradford,

Samford University Special Collections, Collection Number 1089, Box 1, Folder 1, Harwell G. Davis Library, Birmingham, Alabama.

Chapter 5. Prosperity and Stagnation, 1878–1919

1. Thomas S. Kuhn, *The Structure of Scientific Revolutions,* 2nd ed. (Chicago: University of Chicago Press, 1970).

2. Minutes of Board of Trustees, April 18, 1879.

3. Ibid., March 8, 1884; September 6, 1897; November 6, 1908; June (n.d.) 1915; September 28, 1915; Senate Document No. 288, 59th Congress, 1st Sess. (certification of findings of Court of Claims dated March 22, 1906, Claim No. 11003).

4. Minutes of Board of Trustees, January 17, 1891.

5. Ibid., March 24, 1900; January 26, 1907; April 22, 1909.

6. William S. Speer, *Sketches of Prominent Tennesseans* (Nashville: Albert B. Tavel, 1888), 436.

7. Minutes of Board of Trustees, December 6, 1882; July 21, 1883; November 9, 1883.

8. G. Frank Burns, *Phoenix Rising: The Sesquicentennial History of Cumberland University, 1842–1992* (Lebanon, Tennessee: n.p., 1992), 107–9; Minutes of Board of Trustees, June 26, 1909; April 18, 1911; May 2, 1913; July 1, 1913.

9. Cumberland University Bulletin, March 1904.

10. Minutes of Board of Trustees, November 4, 1902.

11. Cumberland University Catalogue, 1902–3.

12. "Grading Book," on file with Beeson Library, Samford University, Cumberland School of Law, Birmingham, Alabama.

13. Cumberland University Catalogue, 1902–3; Cumberland University Bulletin, March 1910; Winstead Paine Bone, *A History of Cumberland University, 1842–1935* (Lebanon, Tennessee: n.p., 1935), 267.

14. Cumberland University Catalogue, 1891.

15. Cordell Hull, *The Memoirs of Cordell Hull,* 2 vols. (New York: Macmillan, 1948), 1:26–27.

16. Katherine B. Fuller, "A History of the Cumberland School of Law from Its Beginning in 1847 to Its Acquisition by Howard College in 1961," (M.A. thesis, Birmingham Southern College, 1962), 33; Lewis L. Laska, "A History of Legal Education in Tennessee, 1770–1970," (Ph.D. dissertation, Vanderbilt University, Peabody College for Teachers, 1978), 190–212.

17. Lewis L. Laska, "Our Sordid Past: Anecdotes of Tennessee's Legal Folklore," *Tennessee Bar Journal* 31 (May/June 1995): 30.

18. 1903 Tennessee Public Acts, ch. 247.

19. Cumberland University Catalogue, 1902–3.

20. Cumberland University Bulletin, April 1908.

21. Minutes of Board of Trustees, February 17, 1893.

22. Ibid., September 18, 1901.

23. Cumberland University Quarterly, August 1903.

24. Laska, "History of Legal Education in Tennessee," 188–90.

25. Thomas A. Street, "The Two-Year Course in Southern Law Schools," *Law Student's Helper* 16 (1908): 55.

26. W. M. Lile, "Legal Education and Admission to the Bar in the Southern States," *Virginia Law Review* 2 (January 1914): 241–42.

27. Statistics, other than those attributed to the University of Virginia law professor and for 1899, are from Alfred Zantzinger Reed, *Training for the Public Profession of the Law* (New York: Carnegie Foundation for the Advancement of Teaching, 1921; reprint, Arno Press, 1976), 171, 180. Statistics for 1899 are from Henry L. Taylor, *Professional Education in the United States* (Albany, New York: University of the State of New York, 1900), 155.

28. Cumberland School of Law Catalogue, 1915.

29. Laska, "History of Legal Education in Tennessee," 189.

30. Lile, "Legal Education and Admission to the Bar in the Southern States," 245.

31. Robert Stevens, *Law School: Legal Education in America from the 1850s to the 1980s* (Chapel Hill: University of North Carolina Press, 1983), 60–63 and accompanying notes.

32. Ernest W. Huffcut, "A Decade of Progress in Legal Education," *American Lawyer* 10 (September 1902): 408.

33. Alfred S. Konefsky and John Henry Schlegel, "Mirror, Mirror on the Wall: Histories of American Law Schools," *Harvard Law Review* 95 (February 1982): 837–38.

34. Cumberland University Catalogue, 1894.

35. John A. Pitts, *Personal and Professional Reminiscences of an Old Lawyer* (Kingsport, Tennessee: Southern Publishers, 1930), 75–76, 356–57.

36. J. Berrien Lindsley, "Outline History of Cumberland University," *Theological Medium* 12 (October 1876): 421 (new series vol. 7).

37. Figures for 1913–14 and 1914–15 from the commencement weekend booklets, "Commencement Calendar," on file with Cumberland University Archives, Record Group 200, Box 1, Vise Library, Lebanon, Tennessee.

38. Cumberland University Catalogue, 1881–82.

39. Tom Wagy, *Governor LeRoy Collins of Florida* (Tuscaloosa: University of Alabama Press, 1985), 14.

40. David Porter, "Senator Carl Hatch and the Hatch Act of 1939," *New Mexico Historical Review* 48 (April 1973): 151.

41. James D. Heiple, "Legal Education and Admission to the Bar: The Illinois Experience," *Southern Illinois University Law Journal* 12 (Fall 1987): 141–42.

42. Hull, *Memoirs of Cordell Hull,* 1:26–27.

43. "Hull Calls For Consecration," *Lebanon (Tenn.) Democrat,* May 10, 1934, p. 1.

44. Hull, *Memoirs of Cordell Hull,* 1:26–27.

45. "Hull Calls for Consecration," 4.

46. Cumberland University Bulletin, January 1904.

47. "The Notable Record of Cumberland University," *Cumberland Alumnus* 8 (November 1928): 5–9.

48. Will T. Hale and Dixon L. Merritt, *A History of Tennessee and Tennesseans,* 5 vols. (Chicago: Lewis Publishing, 1913), 5:1356.

49. "Judge Nathan Green," *Nashville Banner,* January 31, 1920, quoted in *Cumberland Alumnus* 1 (April 1920): 11.

50. Andrew Bennett Martin, "A Colleague's Tribute to Judge Green," *Cumberland Alumnus* 1 (April 1920): 10.

51. Fuller, "A History of the Cumberland School of Law," 44 (based on an interview with Annie Partee, March 12, 1962).

52. Martin, "Colleague's Tribute to Judge Green," 10.

53. "Judge Nathan Green," quoted in *Cumberland Alumnus* 1 (April 1920): 11.

54. Minutes of Board of Trustees, June 3, 1919.

55. Quoted in ibid., January 30, 1917.

56. Ibid., February 15, 1917.

57. Ibid., March 15, 1919.

58. "Judge Nathan Green," quoted in *Cumberland Alumnus* 1 (April 1920): 11; *Lebanon (Tenn.) Democrat,* n.d., week following February 19, 1916.

59. Fuller, "History of the Cumberland School of Law," 41.

Chapter 6. Last of the Old Guard, 1920–1947

1. Cumberland University Law School Bulletin, 1922.

2. Lewis Lyman Laska, "A History of Legal Education in Tennessee, 1770–1970" (Ph.D. dissertation, Vanderbilt University, Peabody College for Teachers, 1978), 524–25.

3. Robert Stevens, *Law School: Legal Education in America from the 1850s to the 1980s* (Chapel Hill: University of North Carolina Press, 1983), 38–39; William P. LaPiana, *Logic and Experience: The Origin of Modern Legal Education* (New York: Oxford University Press, 1994), 15; *Centennial History of The Harvard Law School: 1817–1917* (Boston: Harvard Law School Association, 1918), 175–89.

4. John Ritchie, *The First Hundred Years: A Short History of the School of Law of the University of Virginia for the Period 1826–1926* (Charlottesville: University of Virginia Press, 1978), 30–33.

5. Henry Morton Bullock, *A History of Emory University* (Atlanta: Cherokee Publishing Company, 1972), 360–64.

6. Albert Coates, "The Story of the Law School at the University of North Carolina," *North Carolina Law Review* 47 (October 1968): 47–51.

7. Laska, "History of Legal Education in Tennessee," 531–35.

8. Ibid., 406–10.

9. Winstead Paine Bone, *A History of Cumberland University, 1842–1935* (Lebanon, Tennessee: n.p., 1935), 199, 205–7, and 227–28.

10. Ibid., 198–200.

11. Ibid., 199 and 228; 88 Tennessee Reports iii; 109 Tennessee Reports iii. (The "Tennessee Reports" is the official collection of opinions rendered by the Tennessee Supreme Court during the terms of court covered by each volume, which also lists the judges serving on various Tennessee courts during those terms. Most academic law libraries would contain a complete run of the Tennessee Reports.)

12. "The Passing of Dr. Andrew B. Martin," *Cumberland Alumnus* 1 (November 1920): 9–10.

13. Albert Bramlett Neil, "My Great World or Fifty Years on the Bench," Typescript, 1964, p. 120, on deposit with Beeson Law Library, Cumberland School of Law of Samford University, Birmingham, Alabama. (Neil incorrectly recollected 1921 as the year of Martin's death.)

14. Laska, "History of Legal Education in Tennessee," 510–15 (describing the early years of the Vanderbilt law department).

15. Bone, *History of Cumberland University,* 200–201; *Phoenix* (1923): 13.

16. Bone, *History of Cumberland University,* 201.

17. Cumberland School of Law Catalogues, 1926, 1927, 1928–29, 1929–30, and 1930–31.

18. Bone, *History of Cumberland University,* 201.

19. Ibid.

20. Cumberland School of Law Catalogue, 1934–35.

21. Bone, *History of Cumberland University,* 201.

22. Neil, "My Great World," 120–22; Bone, *History of Cumberland University,* 201–2.

23. The position Gilreath assumed had apparently been created in January 1932 and filled for one semester by an individual named Sinclair Daniel. Cumberland School of Law Catalogue, 1933–34.

24. Bone, *History of Cumberland University,* 201.

25. Interview by the authors with Arthur Weeks, former dean of the Cumberland School of Law, Birmingham, Alabama, April 10, 1990 (transcript on file with Beeson Library, Samford University, Cumberland School of Law).

26. *Cumberland Collegian,* February 10, 1933, p. 2.

27. See chapter 7 on enrollment patterns.

28. Interviews by Walthall with Judge Clifford E. Sanders, Cumberland School of Law class of 1933, Birmingham, Alabama, March 29, 1990, and Margaret Peters, Cumberland School of Law class of 1931, Birmingham, Alabama, March 31, 1990 (transcripts on file with Beeson Library, Samford University, Cumberland School of Law); "The Report of the Survey Committee of Law Schools in Tennessee, Conducted in November, 1937," *Tennessee Law Review* 15 (June 1938): 361.

29. "The College of Law," *Tennessee Bar Review* 11 (December 1932): 52; Laska, "History of Legal Education in Tennessee," 252.

30. "Two Years for LL.B. Required," *Lebanon (Tenn.) Democrat,* May 23, 1933, p. 1.

31. Cumberland School of Law Catalogue, 1933–34.

32. *Cumberland Collegian,* May 26, 1933, p. 1; Cumberland School of Law Catalogue, 1933–34.

33. Cumberland School of Law Catalogue, 1938–39.

34. *Cumberland Collegian,* 4 January 1935, p. 1; G. Frank Burns, *Phoenix Rising: The Sesquicentennial History of Cumberland University, 1842–1992* (Lebanon, Tennessee: n.p., 1992), 151. Burns interviewed Sam Stratton Bone, the university financial secretary who had the unenviable task of meeting with the faculty to persuade them to accept payment of only 30 percent of their salaries. Bone recalled that Judge Chambers walked out of the meeting and later opened his own school, which he called the "Lebanon Law School," the informal name often given to Cumberland Law School. According to Burns, it was not successful.

35. "Report of the Survey Committee of Law Schools," 358.

36. *Cumberland Collegian,* January 4, 1935, p. 1.

37. Cumberland School of Law Catalogue, 1942–43; Burns, *Phoenix Rising,* 171–73.

38. Cumberland School of Law Catalogue, 1942–43.

39. Ibid., 1938–39; "Report of the Survey Committee of Law Schools," 361 (reflecting Cassidy's presence on the faculty and characterizing him as "an experienced teacher in the case method of teaching").

40. Cumberland School of Law Catalogue, 1940–41.

41. Burns, *Phoenix Rising,* 170–73.

42. Laska, "History of Legal Education in Tennessee," 511–12; Paul K. Conkin, *Gone With the Ivy: A Biography of Vanderbilt University* (Knoxville: University of Tennessee Press, 1985), 55.

43. Laska, "History of Legal Education in Tennessee," 523–34; Conkin, *Gone With the Ivy,* 120–22, 202, and 261.

44. Conkin, *Gone With the Ivy,* 261–63, and 374; Laska, "History of Legal Education in Tennessee," 537–43.

45. Laska, "History of Legal Education in Tennessee," 396–401; James Riley Montgomery, Stanley J. Folmsbee, and Lee Seifert Greene, *To Foster Knowledge: A History of the University of Tennessee, 1794–1970* (Knoxville: University of Tennessee Press, 1984), 157.

46. Laska, "History of Legal Education in Tennessee," 404–10.

47. Dan T. Carter, *Scottsboro: A Tragedy of the American South,* rev. ed. (Baton Rouge: Louisiana State University Press, 1979), 263–73.

48. See chapter 5, notes 55, 56, and 57 and accompanying text.

49. Minutes of the Board of Trustees of Cumberland University, vol. 2, June 1, 1920. The Minutes of the Board of Trustees are on deposit in the Cumberland University Archives, Vise Library, Lebanon, Tennessee.

50. Ibid., July 13, 1920.

51. Ibid., November 20, 1920.

52. Cumberland University Catalogue, 1921–22 (identifying the various board members and university officers).

53. Minutes of Board of Trustees, July 4, 1921 (as cited in notes of G. Frank Burns prepared for *Phoenix Rising;* on file with the Beeson Library of Cumberland School of Law, Samford University, Birmingham, Alabama).

54. Ibid., November 15, 1921.

55. Bone, *History of Cumberland University,* 156–58; *Cumberland Alumnus* 2 (August 1922): 5; and *Cumberland Alumnus* 5 (October 1926): 3–4.

56. Burns, *Phoenix Rising,* 128; Minutes of Board of Trustees, June 1923 (as cited in notes of G. Frank Burns).

57. Minutes of Board of Trustees, April 3, 1924.

58. Laska, "History of Legal Education in Tennessee," 406–8.

59. Coates, "Story of the Law School," 44.

60. Laska, "History of Legal Education in Tennessee," 408–9.

61. Minutes of Board of Trustees, November 26, 1923 (as cited in notes of G. Frank Burns); Burns, *Phoenix Rising,* 128.

62. Bone, *History of Cumberland University,* 161–62.

63. *Cumberland Alumnus* 6 (June 1927): 3.

64. E. L. Stockton, "Heroism and Progress in the Past," *Cumberland Alumnus* 7 (September 1927): 4.

65. "Inaugural Address of President E. L. Stockton," *Cumberland Alumnus* 7 (February 1928): 3.

66. "Report of Survey Committee of Law Schools," 356.

67. See Stevens, *Law School,* 112–30 and 172–90.

68. Laska, "History of Legal Education in Tennessee," 397–401.

69. Earl W. Porter, *Trinity and Duke, 1892–1924: Foundations of Duke University* (Durham, North Carolina: Duke University Press, 1964), 143–44.

70. Alfred Z. Reed, *Training for the Public Profession of the Law,* Bulletin No. 15 (New York: Carnegie Foundation for the Advancement of Teaching, 1921), 44–64.

71. "Proceedings of the Section of Legal Education," *American Bar Association Journal* 6 (1920): 64–65. See discussion in Stevens, *Law School,* 176.

72. "Report of the Special Committee to the Section of Legal Education and Admissions to the Bar of the American Bar Association," *Reports of American Bar Association* 46 (1921): 681.

73. Ibid., 656–88; "Transactions of the Forty-fourth Annual Meeting of the American Bar Association," *Reports of American Bar Association* 46 (1921): 37–47 (reporting that the recommendations of the section were approved by the general assembly of the American Bar Association).

74. "Conference on Legal Education," *American Bar Association Journal* 7 (1921): 637–38; and 8 (1922): 137–57.

75. "Report of the Section on Legal Education and Admissions to the Bar," *Reports of American Bar Association* 54 (1929): 56–60, provides an example.

76. Laska, "History of Legal Education in Tennessee," 261–63.
77. Ibid., 247–51.
78. Ibid., 265–66 and 387–88.
79. Ibid., 238–52; "The College of Law," *Tennessee Bar Review* 11 (December 1932): 52.
80. *Cumberland Collegian,* February 10, 1933, p. 2.
81. *Cumberland Collegian,* May 26, 1933, p. 1; and January 19, 1934, p. 1; Cumberland School of Law Catalogues, 1933–34 through 1937–38.
82. *Cumberland Collegian,* January 19, 1934, p. 1.
83. Ibid.
84. "Proceedings of the Section of Legal Education and Admissions to the Bar," *Reports of American Bar Association* 52 (1927): 546.
85. Russell N. Sullivan, "The Professional Associations and Legal Education," *Journal of Legal Education* 4 (Summer 1952): 417.
86. 415–17.
87. "Proceedings of Fifty-sixth Annual Meeting," *Reports of American Bar Association* 58 (1933): 91.
88. "Proceedings of the Fifty-sixth Annual Session of the Bar Association of Tennessee," *Tennessee Law Review* 15 (December 1937): 18.
89. Laska, "History of Legal Education in Tennessee," 279–80.
90. Sullivan, "Professional Associations and Legal Education," 417–19.
91. Ibid.; "Proceedings of American Bar Association" *Reports of American Bar Association* 58 (1933): 91; "Proceedings of the Section of Legal Education and Admissions to the Bar," *Reports of American Bar Association* 52 (1927): 547.
92. Sullivan, "Professional Associations and Legal Education," 419.
93. "Report of Survey Committee of Law Schools," 356–61.
94. Ibid. 356–57; A. B. Neil, "Reply to the Report," *Tennessee Law Review* 15 (December 1938): 490.
95. "Report of Survey Committee of Law Schools," 356–57.
96. Ibid., 325–26.
97. Burns, *Phoenix Rising,* 144–48.
98. Cumberland School of Law Catalogue, 1938–39.
99. Burns, *Phoenix Rising,* 164–65.
100. Ibid., 171–72.

Chapter 7. Living and Learning in Lebanon, 1920–1947

1. Cumberland School of Law Catalogue, 1915; Cumberland University Catalogue, 1914–15.
2. Cumberland University Bulletin, June 1918; Cumberland School of Law Catalogue, 1918–19.
3. Cumberland School of Law Catalogue, 1918–19.
4. Cumberland School of Law Catalogue, 1922.

5. G. Frank Burns, *Phoenix Rising: The Sesquicentennial History of Cumberland University, 1842–1992* (Lebanon, Tennessee: n.p., 1992), 160.

6. *Cumberland Alumnus* 6 (May 1927): 9 (reporting on the improvement of highway transportation into Lebanon).

7. *Cumberland Alumnus* 8 (January 1929): 9–10 (reprinting an article from the *Lebanon (Tenn.) Democrat* about the 1928 opening of a large new bus terminal in Lebanon).

8. Howard P. Walthall, "Parham H. Williams, Jr.: Showing the Way to What is Best in Our Profession," *The Alabama Lawyer* 57 (May 1996): 153.

9. Interview by Walthall with Judge Clifford E. Sanders, Cumberland School of Law class of 1933, Birmingham, Alabama, March 29, 1990 (transcript on file with Beeson Library, Samford University, Cumberland School of Law). Sanders settled in Kingsport, Tennessee, after his graduation and eventually became a member of the Tennessee Court of Appeals.

10. *Cumberland Collegian,* October 6, 1933, p. 1.

11. "The Law Schools of Tennessee: Report of the Survey Committee," *Tennessee Law Review* 15 (June 1938): 360 (hereinafter cited as "Report of Survey Committee of Law Schools").

12. *Phoenix* (1921): 87.

13. *Cumberland Collegian,* October 13, 1937, p. 1; Floyd F. Ewing, "James V. Allred," in *The Handbook of Texas: A Supplement,* ed. Eldon Stephen Branda (Austin: Texas State Historical Association, 1976), 3:21–22.

14. Interview by Walthall with Margaret Peters, Cumberland School of Law class of 1931, Birmingham, Alabama, March 31, 1990 (transcript on file with Beeson Library, Samford University, Cumberland School of Law).

15. Tom Wagy, *Governor Leroy Collins of Florida: Spokesman of the New South* (Tuscaloosa: University of Alabama Press, 1985), 14.

16. *Phoenix* (1932): 33.

17. Cumberland School of Law Catalogue, 1923.

18. J. Thomas Gurney, *Summing Up or A Walk Through a Century* (n.p., 1991), 47.

19. Wagy, *Governor Leroy Collins of Florida,* 14.

20. "Report of Survey Committee of Law Schools," 359–60 (reporting that Cumberland placed such advertisements in a number of newspapers and magazines).

21. Cumberland School of Law Catalogue, 1923; Cumberland University Catalogue, 1923–24.

22. Interview by Walthall with Judge John A. Jamison, Cumberland School of Law class of 1941, Birmingham, Alabama, March 30, 1990 (transcript on file with Beeson Library, Samford University, Cumberland School of Law).

23. Cumberland School of Law Catalogue, 1925. Figures in the remainder of this paragraph are taken from the law school catalogues for the corresponding years and the Cumberland University Catalogue, 1946–47.

24. "Report of the Survey Committee of Law Schools," 322–23.

25. *Report of the Committee on Legal Education and Admission to the Bar,* 1932 Tennessee Bar Association Proceedings 89; Lewis L. Laska, "A History of Legal Education in Tennessee, 1770–1970" (Ph.D. dissertation, Vanderbilt University, Peabody College for Teachers, 1978), 252.

26. Cumberland School of Law Catalogue, 1933–34.

27. *Cumberland Collegian,* September 21, 1934, p. 1.

28. Cumberland School of Law Catalogue, 1922.

29. Ibid., 1923.

30. Ibid., 1925. These five books all came from West's competitor, Callaghan and Company, which published the "National Textbook Series" in competition with West's "Hornbook Series."

31. "Report of the Survey Committee of Law Schools," 363, charging in 1937 that "some of the books of a former day and time are still being used as standard materials. For instance, the class in Contracts is still using the Sixth Edition of Parsons on Contracts, published in the year 1873. Students who cannot secure this edition, which is now scarce, may also use the seventh, eighth, or ninth editions, which latter brings them down to 1904."

This particular charge conveys an inaccurate picture of the currency of the materials in use at Cumberland at the time. The report implies that the continued use of Parsons was simply an example of a general use of out-of-date materials. This overstates the case. Rather than exemplifying the books in use in the Cumberland course in 1937, Parsons stands in contrast to the student-oriented blackletter texts that had come to dominate the list. As for most of the books in the one-year course, new editions were substituted as West or Callaghan brought them out.

32. Cumberland Law School Recruitment brochure, September 1938.

33. Cumberland School of Law Catalogue, 1942–43, and one-page recruitment flier for 1946–47, which lists Parsons as one of the texts for contracts.

34. Russell Grant, "Text vs. Case," *Cumberland Collegian,* May 17, 1935, p. 2.

35. "Judge Pitts Talks of Cumberland University Law School of 65 Years Ago," *Cumberland Collegian,* February 8, 1935, p. 1.

36. "Report of Survey Committee of Law Schools," 362.

37. Inferred from a note in *Cumberland Collegian,* May 18, 1934, p. 2.

38. "Report of Survey Committee of Law Schools," 362. Neil later replied to the report, stating that the committee visited his class on the first day of Torts, and that the questions were not representative. A. B. Neil, "Reply of Judge A. B. Neil . . . to the Report of Will Shafroth and H. Claud Horack," *Tennessee Law Review* 15 (December 1938): 490. At the annual meeting of the Bar Association of Tennessee, June 3, 1938, a motion to "expunge" the Survey Report from the *Tennessee Law Review* insofar as it referred to Cumberland was carried by a "small majority" (443).

39. Interview with Clifford Sanders (see note 9).

40. Record Group 490, Box 2, William R. Chambers Collection, Stockton Archives, Visc Library, Cumberland University, Lebanon, Tennessee.

41. "Report of Survey Committee of Law Schools," 363, setting forth the examination.

42. Both the exam and the question set are found in Record Group 490, Box 2, William R. Chambers Collection, Stockton Archives, Vise Library, Cumberland University, Lebanon Tennessee.

43. *Cumberland Collegian,* November 3, 1933, p. 1.

44. Ibid., September 27, 1935, p. 2.

45. Ibid., November 3, 1933, p. 1.

46. Ibid., February 3, 1933, p. 1.

47. Ibid., February 10, 1933, p. 1.

48. Ibid., February 10, 1933, p. 3.

49. Ibid., October 18, 1935, p. 2.

50. On file with the Beeson Library, Samford University, Cumberland School of Law, Birmingham, Alabama.

51. Interviews by Walthall with Margaret Peters and Clifford Sanders (see notes 9 and 14). Peters was married, and Sanders worked three jobs, which perhaps explains their lack of interest in moot court.

52. Robert W. Gordon, "The Case for (and Against) Harvard," *Michigan Law Review* 93 (May 1995): 1231 at 1241, reviewing William P. LaPiana, *Logic and Experience: The Origin of the Modern American Legal Education* (New York: Oxford University Press, 1994).

53. Collins returned to Tallahassee, passed the bar, and commenced practice. Collins recalled, "I came home, boldly hung out a shingle—and proceeded to starve." Wagy, *Governor Leroy Collins of Florida,* 14; Jamison recollected that after serving in the Navy during World War II, he found employment with a sole practitioner in Front Royal, Virginia, who paid him twenty-five dollars a week. Sanders remembers that he and a classmate decided to remain in Tennessee and start a practice together in Kingsport. They hitchhiked to Kingsport, and, after a few nights in a cheap hotel, rented a two-room office, putting their desks in the front office and, for over a year, sleeping on army cots in the back room. Finding an office that would also serve as living quarters was spurred by their discovery that the hotel in which they first stayed was actually a house in which a profession older than that of law was practiced. Some years later, after Sanders had become a judge in Kingsport, the owner of the hotel was brought before him on charges of running a house of prostitution. Remembering Sanders, the defendant pleaded, "Now, Judge, you know what kind of place I run up there; you used to stay with me." Sanders quickly agreed to accept a plea bargain in which the defendant paid a fine and agreed to cease business, rather than bind him over to the grand jury.

54. *Cumberland Collegian,* October 28, 1932, p. 1, noting that thirty-two law students were enrolled in the public speaking class.

55. *Cumberland Collegian,* October 8, 1937, p. 1; October 23, 1936, p. 2; February 26, 1937, p. 2; March 12, 1937, p. 2; March 19, 1937, p. 2; March 26, 1937, p. 2.

56. *Phoenix* (1931): 82–5; *Cumberland Collegian,* October 6, 1933, p. 2; Winstead Paine Bone, *A History of Cumberland University, 1842–1935* (Lebanon, Tennessee: n.p., 1935), 256 (noting that the membership of the Philomathean Society always came principally from the law school). The Amasagassean apparently ceased to function in 1931 but was revived by law students. *Cumberland Collegian,* January 20, 1933, p. 1.

57. *Phoenix* (1921): 76.

58. *Phoenix* (1931): 91.

59. *Phoenix* (1931): 85.

60. *Phoenix* (1939): 31–32 (unpaginated).

61. Irwin F. Gellman, *Secret Affairs: Franklin Roosevelt, Cordell Hull, and Sumner Welles* (Baltimore: Johns Hopkins University Press, 1995), 207–15; "Editorial," *Cumberland Collegian,* April 28, 1933, p. 2, going "on record" nominating Hull for the 1940 nomination.

62. *Cumberland Collegian,* February 10, 1933, p. 1.

63. Ibid., October 11, 1935, P. 2.

64. Interview with John Jamison (see note 22).

65. *Cumberland Collegian,* October 12, 1934, p. 1, provides an example: the Lambda Chi pledge class chose a junior law student from its midst as pledge class president.

66. Ibid., December 6, 1935, p. 1.

67. *Phoenix* (1932): 90.

68. Interview with Clifford Sanders (see note 9).

69. *Phoenix* (1932): 91.

70. *Phoenix* (1932): 87–89.

71. *Phoenix* (1932): 91 (listing the university Bible class as providing representatives to the student council). Brief notes pertaining to the Bible class appeared in the *Cumberland Collegian* throughout the 1930s.

72. Interview with Clifford Sanders (see note 9).

73. *Cumberland Collegian,* April 28, 1933, p. 1.

74. Albert Bramlett Neil, "My Great World or Fifty Years on the Bench," Typescript, 1964, p. 125, on deposit with Beeson Law Library, Cumberland School of Law, Samford University, Birmingham, Alabama.

75. *Cumberland Collegian,* May 14, 1937, p. 2.

76. Interviews with Peters, Jamison, and Sanders (see notes 9, 14, and 22).

77. "Presenting 'Chief Justice' Rascality," *Cumberland Collegian,* March 27, 1936, p. 1.

78. Robbie Walker, "Cumberland's Youngest Student Leads Life of a Dog," *Cumberland Collegian,* March 27, 1936, p. 1; *Cumberland Collegian,* December 10, 1937, p. 1; Charles Mooshian, "'Rascality,' Famous Lawyer Bulldog, To Receive Law Degree With Lawyers," *Cumberland Collegian,* April 5, 1935, p. 1.

79. Mooshian, "Rascality."

80. *Pathfinder* (Washington, D.C.), May 22, 1937, p. 2. It may be that Rascal received his degree more than once. The writer's letter was in 1937, in response to an announcement in the same magazine on May 1, 1937, p. 12, that plans were being made at Cumberland to award Rascality the degree in June of that year. On the other hand, *Cumberland Collegian,* April 5, 1935, states that the degree is to be conferred in 1935.

81. Josephine Murphey, "'Rascal,' A Gentleman and a Scholar, Victim of Heart Attack," *Cumberland Collegian,* October 4, 1940, p. 4.

82. Rascal, "What Law College Has Learned Me," *Cumberland Collegian,* May 7, 1937, p. 1.

Chapter 8. The Final Years in Lebanon, 1947–1961

1. Interview by authors with Arthur Weeks, former dean, Cumberland School of Law, Birmingham, Alabama, April 10, 1990 (transcript on file with Beeson Library, Samford University, Cumberland School of Law).

2. G. Frank Burns, *Phoenix Rising: The Sesquicentennial History of Cumberland University, 1842–1992* (Lebanon, Tennessee: n.p., 1992), 181.

3. Ralph Waldo Lloyd, *Maryville College: A History of 150 Years, 1819–1969* (Maryville, Tennessee: Maryville College Press, 1969), 94–108.

4. Herman A. Norton, *Religion in Tennessee, 1777–1945* (Knoxville: University of Tennessee Press, 1981), 3–9 and 117.

5. Cumberland University Catalogue, 1940–41 (Centennial Edition).

6. Burns, *Phoenix Rising,* 181–82; Cumberland University Catalogue, 1946–47.

7. Cumberland University Catalogue, 1946–47, reporting that the part-time instructors in the third-year program were Alfred Thompson Adams and Walter Raymond Denney, both Vanderbilt law graduates, along with Byrd Douglas, Alfred Towson MacFarland, and Weldon B. White, all Cumberland law graduates. Sara Hardison still served as law librarian and taught legal bibliography.

8. Interview with Arthur Weeks (see note 1).

9. Ibid.; Cumberland University Program of Centennial Celebration, October 1947.

10. Interview with Arthur Weeks (see note 1); Cumberland University Catalogue, 1947–48 (listing Gilreath as acting dean and Weeks as professor of law); and Cumberland University Catalogue, 1948–49 (listing Weeks as dean).

11. *Review of Legal Education, Law Schools and Bar Admission Requirements in the United States* (1948), 20. The American Bar Association Section of Legal Education publishes this annual review of legal education each fall. It is available at most major academic law libraries.

12. *Review of Legal Education, Law Schools and Bar Admissions Requirements in the United States* (1951), 8; *Review of Legal Education, Law Schools and Bar Admissions Requirements in the United States* (1953), 9; Robert Stevens, *Law School: Legal*

Education in America from the 1850s to the 1980s (Chapel Hill: University of North Carolina Press, 1983), 207.

13. *Review of Legal Education, Law Schools and Bar Admissions Requirements in the United States* (1948), unnumbered page following p. 26. (Effective September 1952 this would be increased to three years, and Cumberland would have to meet the increased standard when it received full approval in 1952.) *Review of Legal Education, Law Schools and Bar Admissions Requirements in the United States* (1951), unnumbered page following p. 25. References hereinafter to the ABA standards as of 1948 are from the *Review of Legal Education, Law Schools and Bar Admissions Requirements in the United States* (1948), unnumbered page following p. 26.

14. Interview with Arthur Weeks (see note 1); Cumberland University Catalogue, 1947–48. "The Report of the Survey of Law Schools in Tennessee, Conducted in November, 1937" *Tennessee Law Review* 15 (June 1938): 358, crediting the library with 7,000 volumes. (In 1948 the minimum for complying with the ABA Standard was 7,500.) Cumberland University Catalogue, 1946–47 (apparently the first one designating the law library as the Cordell Hull Library). Burns, *Phoenix Rising,* 164–65, explains that the designation of the law library as the Cordell Hull Law Library had its inception in plans undertaken by President L. L. Rice after he took office in the fall of 1941 for a fund-raising campaign to build a new law library at Cumberland honoring the then secretary of state. World War II prevented the carrying out of the campaign, and the new building never proceeded beyond an architect's sketches, but apparently as a result of this aborted initiative, the library, still housed in Caruthers Hall, came to be called the Cordell Hull Law Library. (The designation continued after the move to Birmingham until a new law library building, the Lucille Stewart Beeson Law Library, was completed in 1995. The name Cordell Hull was continued as the name for the international law collection.)

15. A. B. Neil, "Reply to the Report," *Tennessee Law Review* 15 (December 1938): 491.

16. Interview with Arthur Weeks (see note 1).

17. Cumberland School of Law Catalogue, 1947–48.

18. Interview with Arthur Weeks (see note 1). "Report of Survey Committee of Law Schools," 358, noting that in a library of approximately 7,000 volumes there were "about 30 textbooks." Probably some of those were extra copies of those used in the classroom.

19. "Report of the Survey of Law Schools," 358, observing of the library in 1937: "There are no Law Reviews and most of the standard modern texts are missing."

20. Interview with Arthur Weeks (see note 1).

21. Ibid.

22. "Report of the Survey Committee of Law Schools," 358.

23. Ibid. The report notes that the auditorium was used for examinations, in which case students had to be provided lap boards.

24. Interview with Arthur Weeks (see note 1).
25. Ibid.
26. Elliott E. Cheatham, "The Law Schools of Tennessee, 1949," *Tennessee Law Review* 21 (April 1950): 287–88.
27. Interview with Arthur Weeks (see note 1).
28. Cumberland School of Law Catalogue, 1951.
29. Minutes of the Executive Committee, Howard College Board of Trustees, September 17, 1961 (on deposit in Special Collections, Samford University, Harwell G. Davis Library, Birmingham, Alabama).
30. Cumberland University Catalogue, 1949–50; Interview with Arthur Weeks (see note 1); Burns, *Phoenix Rising,* 184.
31. Interview with Arthur Weeks (see note 1); Burns, *Phoenix Rising,* 188–89.
32. See, e.g., Cumberland University Catalogue, 1946–47 ("Special Announcement: The President's Message").
33. Interview with Arthur Weeks (see note 1); Burns, *Phoenix Rising,* 188–89.
34. Interview with Arthur Weeks (see note 1).
35. Ibid.; Burns, *Phoenix Rising,* 188–91; Cumberland School of Law Catalogue, 1955–57.
36. Interview with Arthur Weeks (see note 1); Cumberland School of Law Catalogue, 1952–53; Burns, *Phoenix Rising,* 191.
37. Interview with Arthur Weeks (see note 1); Lewis Lyman Laska, "A History of Legal Education in Tennessee, 1770–1970" (Ph.D. dissertation, Vanderbilt University, Peabody College for Teachers, 1978), 607.
38. Interview with Arthur Weeks (see note 1); Cumberland School of Law Catalogue, 1951–52; Burns, *Phoenix Rising,* 201.
39. Cumberland School of Law Catalogue, 1951–52.
40. Interview with Arthur Weeks (see note 1).
41. Cumberland School of Law Catalogue, 1951–52.
42. Interview with Arthur Weeks (see note 1); *Review of Legal Education, Law Schools and Bar Admissions Requirements in the United States* (1952), 13; Laska, "History of Legal Education in Tennessee," 606–7; Burns, *Phoenix Rising,* 201.
43. Interview with Arthur Weeks (see note 1).
44. Cumberland University Catalogue, 1946–47.
45. Ibid., 1947–48.
46. *Review of Legal Education, Law Schools and Bar Admissions Requirements in the United States* (1948), 18.
47. Ibid.; *Review of Legal Education, Law Schools and Bar Admissions Requirements in the United States* (1949), 13; *Review of Legal Education, Law Schools and Bar Admissions Requirements in the United States* (1950), 13; *Review of Legal Education, Law Schools and Bar Admissions Requirements in the United States* (1951), 13.
48. Cumberland University Catalogues, 1946–47, 1947–48, 1949–50; Cumberland School of Law Catalogue, 1951–52.

49. Cumberland School of Law Catalogue, 1951–52.

50. Interview with Arthur Weeks (see note 1); Cumberland School of Law Catalogue, 1951–52; *Review of Legal Education, Law Schools and Bar Admissions Requirements in the United States* (1951), 13.

51. Lowell S. Nicholson, *The Law Schools of the United States* (Baltimore: Lord Baltimore Press, 1958), 135–39.

52. *Review of Legal Education, Law Schools and Bar Admissions Requirements in the United States* (1951), unnumbered page following p. 25 (Interpretation of Standard 1(c), Standards of the American Bar Association).

53. Burns, *Phoenix Rising,* 181–84, 289.

54. *Phoenix* (1948): 52–62.

55. Ibid., 80–81.

56. Cumberland University Catalogues, 1949–50 and 1950–51.

57. Interview with Arthur Weeks (see note 1).

58. "Gilreath Bible Class Enjoys Annual Picnic," *Cumberland University Newsletter,* June 1956, p. 5 (unpaginated).

59. *Phoenix* (1948): 64.

60. Ibid., 50, 68, 72.

61. *Phoenix* (1953): 32.

62. "Program for Cumberland University School of Law 2nd Annual Law Day," October 30 and 31, 1959, sponsored by the Student Bar Association, located in Arthur Weeks's personal papers.

63. Cumberland School of Law Catalogue, 1950–51 (listing board of trustee members and places of residence).

64. Interview with Arthur Weeks (see note 1); Burns, *Phoenix Rising,* 191–92.

65. Interview with Arthur Weeks (see note 1); Burns, *Phoenix Rising,* 192–93.

66. Interview with Arthur Weeks (see note 1).

67. David A. Lockmiller, *Scholars on Parade: Colleges and Universities, Academic Degrees, Caps and Gowns, Hood Colors, Regalia* (Chapel Hill, North Carolina: Professional Press, 1993), jacket copy.

68. Interview with Arthur Weeks (see note 1).

69. Ibid.

70. Elmer T. Clark, *The Small Sects in America* (Nashville: Abingdon Press, 1949), 204–5; Interview with Arthur Weeks (see note 1); Letter from Weeks to unspecified addressee (probably identical copy sent to each member of the board), June 14, 1954.

71. Interview with Arthur Weeks (see note 1).

72. Ibid.; Burns, *Phoenix Rising,* 193.

73. Interview with Arthur Weeks (see note 1); Burns, *Phoenix Rising,* 193.

74. *Review of Legal Education, Law Schools and Bar Admissions Requirements in the United States* (1953), 7, 12–13.

75. *Review of Legal Education, Law Schools and Bar Admissions Requirements in the United States* for the years 1953 through 1960.

76. *Review of Legal Education, Law Schools and Bar Admissions Requirements in the United States* (1953), 7.

77. Ibid.

78. *Review of Legal Education, Law Schools and Bar Admissions Requirements in the United States* (1955), 7.

79. *Review of Legal Education, Law Schools and Bar Admissions Requirements in the United States* (1959), 7.

80. Gilbert L. Lycan, *Stetson University: The First 100 Years* (Deland, Florida: Stetson University Press, 1983), 360–69.

81. *Review of Legal Education, Law Schools and Bar Admissions Requirements in the United States* (1955), 12.

82. *Review of Legal Education, Law Schools and Bar Admissions Requirements in the United States* (1956), 12.

83. *Review of Legal Education, Law Schools and Bar Admissions Requirements in the United States* (1957), 12.

84. Interview with Arthur Weeks (see note 1).

85. Lycan, *Stetson University,* 360–63.

86. *Z. Smith Reynolds Foundation, Inc. v. Trustees of Wake Forest College,* 227 N.C. 500, 42 S.E.2d 910 (1947).

87. Burns, *Phoenix Rising,* 193.

88. Ibid., 201; Cumberland School of Law Catalogue, 1955–57.

89. Burns, *Phoenix Rising,* 196; "Havens' Address to Annual Homecoming Banquet, June 8, 1956," *Cumberland University Newsletter,* June 1956.

90. *Review of Legal Education, Law Schools and Bar Admissions Requirements in the United States* (1951), 13; *Review of Legal Education, Law Schools and Bar Admissions Requirements in the United States* (1953), 13; *Review of Legal Education, Law Schools and Bar Admissions Requirements in the United States* (1954), 14.

91. "Havens' Address to Cumberland Homecoming Banquet"; *Review of Legal Education, Law Schools and Bar Admissions Requirements in the United States* (1955), 14.

92. "Havens' Address to Homecoming Banquet."

93. Ibid.; Burns, *Phoenix Rising,* 196, 202; Cumberland School of Law Catalogue, 1955–57.

94. Cumberland School of Law Catalogues, 1955–57, 1957–58, and 1960–62.

95. *Review of Legal Education, Law Schools and Bar Admissions Requirements in the United States* (1956), 14.

96. *Review of Legal Education, Law Schools and Bar Admissions Requirements in the United States* (1957), 14.

97. *Review of Legal Education, Law Schools and Bar Admissions Requirements in the United States* (1956), 14; *Review of Legal Education, Law Schools and Bar Admissions Requirements in the United States* (1957), 14; *Review of Legal Education, Law Schools and Bar Admissions Requirements in the United States* (1958), 14; *Re-*

view of Legal Education, Law Schools and Bar Admissions Requirements in the United States (1959), 14; *Review of Legal Education, Law Schools and Bar Admissions Requirements in the United States* (1960), 15.

98. Cumberland School of Law Catalogues, 1957–58, 1960–62.

99. See generally, "Cumberland University School of Law; Minutes of Faculty Meetings, 1954–1960," on file with Beeson Law Library, Samford University, Cumberland School of Law, Birmingham, Alabama.

100. On October 11, 1957, President Havens requested the law faculty to adopt a policy concerning drinking by law students. He thought that through voluntary cooperation of the law faculty "brief comments during the lecture periods could help greatly to minimize our drinking problem." Letter from Charles B. Havens to Dean Walker, October 11, 1957, contained in "Cumberland University School of Law; Minutes of Faculty Meetings, 1954–1960." Then on November 2, 1957, an intoxicated law student broke a door of the dormitory room of another law student and had the poor grace to defend himself in part on the basis that "he had never been advised by the school of any definite policy on the use of intoxicants." Minutes of Cumberland School of Law Faculty, November 4, 1957.

101. Minutes of Cumberland School of Law Faculty, November 5, 1957, located in "Cumberland University School of Law; Minutes of Faculty Meetings, 1954–1960."

102. "Havens' Address to Annual Homecoming Banquet."

103. Laska, "History of Legal Education in Tennessee," 607–8.

104. Ibid., 608; Burns, *Phoenix Rising,* 202–3.

105. Burns, *Phoenix Rising,* 195–96.

106. Laska, "History of Legal Education in Tennessee," 609, 612; Burns, *Phoenix Rising,* 203.

107. "Proposed Plan of Campaign for the Cumberland University Development Program, January 3, 1958–December 31, 1959," 9-page typescript document and multicolor printed campaign brochure directed to Nashville alumni, both located in personal papers of Arthur Weeks.

108. Burns, *Phoenix Rising,* 205–7.

109. Ibid., 211–12.

110. Ibid., 215; Laska, "History of Legal Education in Tennessee," 610.

111. Laska, "History of Legal Education in Tennessee," 610–3; Burns, *Phoenix Rising,* 146, 215; one-page untitled typescript chronology of events involving accrediting agencies located in personal papers of Arthur Weeks.

Chapter 9. The Cumberland Phoenix Rises in Birmingham, 1961–1983

1. Circular letter from Ernest L. Stockton Jr. to Cumberland alumni, June 27, 1961, copy on file with Beeson Library, Samford University, Cumberland School of Law, Birmingham, Alabama.

2. Interview by authors with Arthur Weeks, former dean, Cumberland School of Law, Birmingham, Alabama, April 10, 1990 (transcript on file with Beeson Library, Samford University, Cumberland School of Law); Arthur Weeks, "Tennessee Roots—Tradition and Heritage," *Cumberland Lawyer* 24 (Winter 1988): 2–4.

3. Interview with Arthur Weeks (see note 2); G. Frank Burns, *Phoenix Rising: The Sesquicentennial History of Cumberland University, 1842–1992* (Lebanon, Tennessee: n.p., 1992), 213–16; Statement by Howard College President Leslie S. Wright (with reference to the acquisition of the Cumberland University Law School of Lebanon, Tennessee, by Howard College, Birmingham, Alabama; dictated July 15, 1962), reprinted in Katherine Brock Fuller, "A History of the Cumberland University School of Law From Its Beginning in 1847 to Its Acquisition by Howard College in 1961" (M.A. thesis, Birmingham Southern College, 1962), Appendix D (hereinafter, "Wright Statement"); Susan Ingram Hunt Ray, *The Major, Harwell G. Davis: Alabama Statesman and Baptist Leader* (Birmingham, Alabama: Samford University Press, 1996), 149–50.

4. "Building a Law School," *Memphis State Magazine* 6 (Spring 1987): 5–6.

5. Ibid.

6. Circular letter from Stockton to Cumberland Alumni, June 27, 1961.

7. "Building a Law School," 7, 26; Burns, *Phoenix Rising,* 213–16; Interview with Arthur Weeks (see note 2).

8. "Change of Venue," *Newsweek,* August 14, 1961, p. 68.

9. Ibid.; Interview with Arthur Weeks (see note 2).

10. "Change of Venue," 68.

11. Minutes of Annual Meeting of Howard College Board of Trustees, May 26, 1961 (on deposit in Special Collections, Samford University, Harwell G. Davis Library, Birmingham, Alabama).

12. Minutes of Executive Committee of Howard College Board of Trustees, September 17, 1961.

13. Wright Statement.

14. Ivan Swift, "Howard Acquires New Law Division," *Birmingham News,* June 27, 1961, Late Final Edition, p. 1; Frank Burns, "Cumberland Reveals Move," *Nashville Banner,* June 27, 1961, p. 1.

15. Walling Keith, "Little School Has Big Names among Its Graduates," *Birmingham News,* June 27, 1961, Late Final Edition, p. 1.

16. Circular letter from Stockton to Cumberland School of Law Alumni, June 27, 1961; Letter from Dr. Leslie S. Wright to Cumberland School of Law Alumni, June 27, 1961.

17. *Howard College Alumnus* 12 (June 1961): 16.

18. Leon Alligood, "Clause Hampers Move to Reopen Law School," *Nashville Banner,* April 30, 1993, sec. B, p. 5.

19. Civ. Act. No. 3–930409, United States District Court for the Middle District of Tennessee, Nashville Division (declaratory judgment action was originally

filed in the Circuit Court for Wilson County, Tennessee, Docket No. 8671, and removed to federal court).

20. Wright Statement; Letter from Arthur Weeks to John Hervey, June 2, 1961.

21. Burns, *Phoenix Rising,* 213; Cumberland School of Law Catalogue, 1960–62.

22. *Howard College Alumnus* 12 (Fall 1961): 11; penciled marginal notation on list of "Graduates 1960–61" in Cumberland School of Law Catalogue, 1962–63.

23. Burns, *Phoenix Rising,* 213; Cumberland School of Law Catalogue, 1960–62.

24. "Howard Names Acting Law Dean," *Birmingham News,* August 27, 1961, sec. A, p. 28; "Cumberland School of Law," *Howard College Alumnus* 12 (Fall 1961): 8–11.

25. Circular letter from Stockton to Cumberland School of Law Alumni, June 27, 1961.

26. Winstead Paine Bone, *A History of Cumberland University, 1842–1935* (Lebanon, Tennessee: n.p., 1935), 55; Burns, *Phoenix Rising,* 19; James E. Sulzby Jr., *Toward a History of Samford University* (Birmingham, Alabama: Samford University Press, 1986), 7.

27. Sulzby, *Toward a History of Samford University,* 115–16.

28. Interview with Arthur Weeks (see note 2); Cumberland School of Law Catalogue, 1962–63.

29. Interview with Arthur Weeks (see note 2); Ray, *The Major,* 149–50.

30. Ibid.

31. Minutes of Cumberland School of Law Faculty, September 7, 1961.

32. Minutes of Cumberland School of Law Faculty, October 12, 1961.

33. "Home Runs . . . 61 in '61?" *Newsweek,* August 14, 1961, p. 42.

34. Interview with Arthur Weeks (see note 2).

35. "Howard to Ask Legislative Act," *Birmingham News,* June 27, 1961, Late Final Edition, p. 1.

36. Interview with Arthur Weeks (see note 2).

37. Ivan Swift, "Howard Acquires New Law Division," *Birmingham News,* June 27, 1961, p. 1.

38. Minutes of Executive Committee of Howard College Board of Trustees, November 7, 1961.

39. Minutes of Annual Meeting of Howard College Board of Trustees, May 21, 1962.

40. Minutes of Executive Committee of Howard College Board of Trustees, April 26, 1962.

41. Minutes of Annual Meeting of Howard College Board of Trustees, May 24, 1963.

42. Minutes of Executive Committee of Howard College Board of Trustees, April 26, 1962.

43. "Law Day—Dedication at Cumberland School of Law of Howard College," *Howard College Bulletin* 123 (October 1964).

44. Arthur A. Weeks, "A Report on the Progress of the Cumberland School of

Law of Samford University (Formerly Howard College)" (undated but internal evidence indicates 1965–66; file copy bears a received stamp dated Jan. 25, 1966).

45. "Samford University President's Report to the Board of Trustees," annually for 1966–67 (May 26, 1967); 1967–68 (May 31, 1968); 1968–69 (May 30, 1969); 1969–70 (May 29, 1970); and 1970–71 (April 16, 1971).

46. *Review of Legal Education, Law Schools and Bar Admission Requirements in the United States* (1973), 47. The American Bar Association Section of Legal Education publishes this annual review of legal education each fall. It is available at most major academic law libraries.

47. Minutes of Executive Committee of Howard College Board of Trustees, January 24, 1974.

48. Peter deL. Swords and Frank K. Walwer, *The Costs and Resources of Legal Education* (New York: Oxford University Press, 1974), 6–7.

49. Interview with Arthur Weeks (see note 2); Minutes of Cumberland School of Law Faculty, August 25, 1971. Sources for the information on Corley and Bishop also include miscellaneous personal conversations of Walthall with those individuals over many years and, in the case of Bishop's selection of Cumberland rather than the University of Mississippi, the recollections of Parham Williams Jr. in addressing the Cumberland faculty in the spring 1985, when Williams interviewed for the deanship at Cumberland. Walthall was present on that occasion.

50. William A. Nunnelly, *Bull Conner* (Tuscaloosa, Alabama: University of Alabama Press, 1991), 129–64; William Warren Rogers, Robert David Ward, Leah Rawls Atkins, and Wayne Flynt, *Alabama: The History of a Deep South State* (Tuscaloosa, Alabama: University of Alabama Press, 1994), 559–61.

51. *Sweatt v. Painter,* 350 U.S. 629, 70 S. Ct. 846 (1950).

52. *American Bar Association Reports* 88 (1963): 423–24 and 614–18; American Association of Law Schools (AALS) Articles of Association, Section 6–3.

53. Minutes of Executive Committee of Samford University Board of Trustees, January 17, 1967; Minutes of Called Meeting of Samford University Board of Trustees, January 21, 1967; Interview with Arthur Weeks (see note 2); Arthur G. Gaston, *Green Power* (Birmingham, Alabama: Southern University Press, 1968), 115–36; "1970 Senior Brochure," Cumberland School of Law, Samford University.

54. Minutes of Cumberland School of Law Faculty, November 7, 1968, and attached Memorandum To: Members of the Board of Trustees, Samford University, Members of the Law School Advisory Board, Honorable Leslie S. Wright, President, Honorable James Newman, Vice President, Honorable H. Evan Zeiger; From: The Faculty; Subject: Comparison of Salaries and Fringe Benefits at Cumberland School of Law with other Church related law schools and law schools in the Southeast.

55. Minutes of Executive Committee of Samford University Board of Trustees, May 1, 1968.

56. "President's Report to the Trustees," May 29, 1970, p. 10.

57. Dean Roy L. Steinheimer Jr., "Report on Cumberland School of Law,

Samford University," March 31–April 2, 1971, p. 9, transmitted by letter from Millard H. Ruud (Consultant, American Bar Association, Section of Legal Education and Admissions to the Bar) to Dean Arthur A. Weeks, May 21, 1971.

58. Minutes of Executive Committee of Samford University Board of Trustees, August 29, 1971.

59. Minutes of Cumberland School of Law Faculty, January 12, 1972.

60. Cumberland School of Law ABA Questionnaire for Fall 1971, on file with Beeson Library, Samford University, Cumberland School of Law, Birmingham, Alabama.

61. *Review of Legal Education, Law Schools and Bar Admission Requirements in the United States* (1976), 4.

62. *Review of Legal Education, Law Schools and Bar Admission Requirements in the United States,* for applicable years.

63. David H. Vernon, "Anatomy of Legal Education (Report of the Tunks Committee): The Way We Were and the Way We Are," *Washington Law Review* 60 (June 1985): 571–72.

64. *Review of Legal Education, Law Schools and Bar Admission Requirements in the United States* (1982), 40.

65. *Review of Legal Education, Law Schools and Bar Admission Requirements in the United States* (1971), 6.

66. *Review of Legal Education, Law Schools and Bar Admission Requirements in the United States* (1980), 5.

67. Minutes of Executive Committee of Samford University Board of Trustees, March 29, 1972; Interview with Arthur Weeks (see note 2).

68. Minutes of Cumberland School of Law Faculty, August 25, 1971.

69. Interview with Arthur Weeks (see note 2); Minutes of Executive Committee of Samford University Board of Trustees, June 23, 1972, p. 9; Letter from Ruric Wheeler to Dean Donald S. Corley, June 1, 1972, attached as Appendix A to Minutes of Executive Committee of Samford University Board of Trustees, April 24, 1984; Minutes of Cumberland School of Law Faculty, May 29, 1972.

70. James Spotswood, "Law Always Was Goal of Cumberland Dean," *Birmingham News,* July 14, 1974, sec. B, p. 1.

71. Vernon, "Anatomy of Legal Education," 572.

72. Swords and Walwer, *Costs and Resources of Legal Education,* 6–25 (a study of the period from 1955 to 1974); Vernon, "Anatomy of Legal Education," 571.

73. Swords and Walwer, *Costs and Resources of Legal Education,* 276–80.

74. Minutes of Cumberland School of Law Faculty, June 7, 1972; July 13, 1972; and February 13, 1973.

75. Ibid., May 29, 1972.

76. Ibid., September 26, 1972.

77. Minutes of Executive Committee of Samford University Board of Trustees, June 23, 1972, p. 9; August 8, 1972, p. 9; December 14, 1972, p. 8; March 25, 1973, pp. 5–6.

78. Fall 1972 ABA Law School Questionnaire; Minutes of Cumberland School of Law Faculty, March 6, 1973.

79. Lindsey Cowen and Cameron H. Allen, "The Association of American Law Schools, Progress Report on The Cumberland School of Law, Samford University, Birmingham, Alabama," June 20, 1974, updated October 17, 1974.

80. Cowen and Allen, "Progress Report on the Cumberland School of Law," p. 7 (unpaginated); Minutes of Executive Committee of Samford University Board of Trustees, September 26, 1975.

81. Minutes of Called Meeting of Samford University Board of Trustees, November 7, 1974; Minutes of Executive Committee of Samford University Board of Trustees, August 15, 1974, p. 3; January 24, 1975, p. 2; March 13, 1975, p. 2; July 8, 1975, p. 3–4; September 26, 1975, p. 5; January 16, 1976, p. 9; March 31, 1976, pp. 2–3; August 13, 1976, p. 3; March 14, 1978, pp. 4, 10; "Program, Dedication of the New Memory Leake Robinson Hall," Birmingham, Alabama, November 4, 1977; Peggy Roberson, "$1 Million Gift Cheers, Challenges Samford Fund Raisers," *Birmingham News,* July 14, 1974, sec. B, p. 1.

82. Minutes of Executive Committee of Samford University Board of Trustees, January 24, 1974, p. 3; May 22, 1974, p. 2; August 15, 1974, p. 2.

83. Letter from Millard Ruud to Dr. Leslie S. Wright and Dean Donald S. Corley, June 1, 1976, on file with Beeson Library, Samford University, Cumberland School of Law, Birmingham, Alabama.

84. Letter from James P. White, Consultant on Legal Education to the American Bar Association, to Dr. Leslie S. Wright and Dean Donald S. Corley, June 2, 1978, transmitting the inspection report submitted by Dean Richard G. Huber, Professor Harry J. Haynsworth, Robert J. Kutak, and Professor Harry S. Martin, III, after their visit to the Cumberland School of Law of Samford University on October 16–19, 1977, on file with Beeson Library, Samford University, Cumberland School of Law, Birmingham, Alabama.

85. Dean Donald S. Corley, "Cumberland Law School—The Decade of the Seventies," *Cumberland Law Review* 11 (1980–81): 251, note 57; Cumberland School of Law Catalogues, 1972–73 and 1979–80.

86. Irl Marcus, "Interview with the Dean," *Pro Confesso* (Cumberland School of Law student newspaper), February 1982, p. 14 (quoting Corley as having no comment on rumors of his being considered for position of clerk of the Alabama Supreme Court).

87. Minutes of Cumberland School of Law Faculty, April 15, 1982.

88. Minutes of Cumberland School of Law Faculty, February 6, 1984 and February 8, 1984.

Chapter 10. Student Life and Accomplishments, 1961–1983

1. *Cumberland Lawyer* 6 (November 1971): 5.

2. Interview by Walthall with Judge John A. Jamison, Cumberland School of

Law class of 1941, Birmingham, Alabama, March 30, 1990 (transcript on file with Beeson Library, Samford University, Cumberland School of Law).

3. Interview by authors with Arthur Weeks, former dean, Cumberland School of Law, Birmingham, Alabama, April 10, 1990 (transcript on file with Beeson Library, Samford University, Cumberland School of Law).

4. Cumberland University School of Law Bulletin, 1960–62.

5. *Cumberland School of Law Student Lawyer,* November 1964, p. 2; p. 3; p. 4.

6. "Legal Sorority," *Cumberland School of Law Student Lawyer,* December 1965, p. 6; "Phi Delta Delta Installed," *Cumberland Lawyer* 1 (September 1966): 11.

7. "Delta Theta Phi" and "Phi Alpha Delta." *Cumberland Lawyer* 6 (November 1971): 26.

8. See, e.g., *Cumberland Lawyer* 3 (November 1968): 3–5, and 6 (November 1971): 26–27.

9. "Phi Alpha Delta's 'Speakers Programs,'" *Cumberland Lawyer* 3 (March 1969): 6; "Supreme Justice Presents Outstanding Chapter Award to Hull Chapter," *Reporter of Phi Alpha Delta,* January 1970, p. 3; "PAD Chapter at Cumberland Named Number One in the Nation," *Cumberland Lawyer* 4 (April 1970): 12.

10. "Delta Theta Phi," *Cumberland Lawyer* 4 (November 1969): 10.

11. "Delta Theta Phi Law Fraternity Wins Award," *Cumberland Lawyer* 13 (Winter 1979): 14.

12. Frank W. Donaldson and Paul D. Davis, "The Positive Image," Summer 1975, p. 4 (on file with Beeson Library, Samford University, Cumberland School of Law).

13. W. C. Lassiter and D. Bruce Mansfield, "The Duke Bar Association," *Duke Bar Association Journal* 1 (March 1933): 2–4.

14. See chapter 7, notes 62 and 63 and accompanying text.

15. *Phoenix* (1953): 32.

16. "Program for Cumberland University School of Law 2nd Annual Law Day," October 30–31, 1959, sponsored by the Student Bar Association, located in Arthur Weeks's personal papers.

17. "Law Day—Dedication at Cumberland School of Law at Howard College, April 17–18, 1964," *Howard College Bulletin* (October 1964, Special Issue): 32–33; "Current and Past Presidents of the Student Bar Association," *Cumberland Lawyer* 6 (November 1971): 16.

18. "Student Bar Plans Projects," *Cumberland School of Law Student Lawyer,* November 1964, p. 1.

19. "Senior Placement Brochure," *Cumberland School of Law Student Lawyer,* November 1964, p. 4; "Current and Past Presidents of the Student Bar Association," *Cumberland Lawyer* 6 (November 1971): 16–17.

20. "SBA Named Nation's Best," *Pro Confesso,* August 1974, p. 1; "Cumberland SBA Best in the Nation—Once Again," *Cumberland Lawyer* 10 (December 1975): 5 (unpaginated).

21. *Reports of the American Bar Association* 74 (1949): 410–11.

22. "Editor's Notes," *Student Lawyer Journal of the American Bar Association* 13 (September 1967): 2.

23. *Cumberland Lawyer* 6 (November 1971): 16–17, 20.

24. Ibid., 21; *Cumberland Lawyer* 8 (October 1973): 5; Woody Smith, "Powell Proposes Plan," *Pro Confesso,* March 2, 1976, p. 2.

25. "SBA Named Nation's Best," *Pro Confesso,* August 1974, p. 1.

26. Dennis Knizley, "Ledbetter assumes Presidency," *Pro Confesso,* September 21, 1978, p. 1; "Cumberland Student Heads American Bar Association Law Student Division," *Cumberland Lawyer* 13 (Fall 1978): 11.

27. Jack McLaughlin, "Lovelace Elected President of National Student Bar Association," *Pro Confesso,* September 1982, p. 1; "Lovelace Elected National President," *Cumberland Lawyer* 18 (Fall 1982): 1.

28. "Cumberland Captures A.B.A. National Awards," *Cumberland Lawyer* 7 (April 1973): 2.

29. Interview with Arthur Weeks (see note 3).

30. Charles L. Robinson, "Chapel Attendance and Sanctions," *Cumberland Lawyer* 1 (November 1966): 10.

31. Interview with Arthur Weeks (see note 3); Gary Pears, "SBA Gives Leadership," *Pro Confesso,* February 1974, p. 2.

32. "Cordell Hull Forum Series Brings Outstanding Speakers to Cumberland," *Cumberland Lawyer* 11 (Winter 1977): 1.

33. "Forum '74 Brings National Speakers to Cumberland," *Cumberland Lawyer* 8 (February 1974): 1–2; "Forum '74," *Cumberland Lawyer* 8 (April 1974): 7; Bob Splitt, "Journalist Speaks," *Pro Confesso,* February 1974, p. 2; Joe DePaola, "Shriver on Injustice," *Pro Confesso,* March 1974, p. 4; "Nader Calls Law 'Pivotal Profession'; Hits Law Schools," *Pro Confesso,* August 1974, p. 2.

34. "SBA Named Nation's Best"; "Cumberland SBA Best in the Nation—Once Again," *Cumberland Lawyer* 10 (December 1975): 5 (unpaginated).

35. Tim Pirtle, "Cumberland's 'Law Day 1977' best in U.S." *Pro Confesso,* September 9, 1977, pp. 1, 3; "Cumberland Student Bar Association Outstanding," *Cumberland Lawyer* 12 (Fall 1977): 10.

36. "Arkansas Governor to Address Banquet," *Pro Confesso,* April 2, 1979, p. 1; "ABA President Shepherd Tate opens Law Week '79," *Pro Confesso,* April 2, 1979; "Interesting Program for Law Week," *Pro Confesso,* April 2, 1979; "Cumberland Receives ABA-LSD Awards," *Pro Confesso,* September 18, 1979, p. 1.

37. Ferris Stephens, "Law Day Keynote," *Pro Confesso,* March 1980, p. 1; Alan Burdette, "Bob Cauthen," *Pro Confesso,* March 1980, p. 1; "Bar Notes," *Pro Confesso,* September 1980, p. 2.

38. Jack McLaughlin, "Cumberland #1 In Nation—Again," *Pro Confesso,* September 1982, p. 14.

39. Jack McLaughlin, "Lovelace Elected President of National Student Bar Association," *Pro Confesso,* September 1982, p. 1.

40. "James S. Witcher, Jr.," *Cumberland Lawyer* 6 (November 1971): 16–7;

"Cumberland Student Heads American Bar Association Law Student Division," *Cumberland Lawyer* 13 (Fall 1978): 11.

41. Michael I. Swygert and Jon W. Bruce, "The Historical Origins, Founding, and Early Development of Student-Edited Law Reviews," *Hastings Law Journal* 36 (May 1985): 739–40.

42. *Harvard Law Review* 1 (1887): 35.

43. Swygert and Bruce, "Historical Origins of Student-Edited Law Reviews," 769–71; Frank L. Ellsworth, *Law on the Midway: The Founding of the University of Chicago Law School* (Chicago: Law School of the University of Chicago, 1977), 68–77; William R. Roalfe, *John Henry Wigmore: Scholar and Reformer* (Evanston: Northwestern University Press, 1977): 35.

44. Martin H. Brinkley, "The North Carolina Law Review at Threescore and Ten," *North Carolina Law Review* 73 (1995): 773–77.

45. Swygert and Bruce, "Historical Origins of Student-Edited Law Reviews," 783–87.

46. "Dr. Cassidy Urges New Law Review," *Cumberland Collegian,* May 13, 1938, p. 1.

47. "Pledges—Phi Alpha Delta" and "Pledges—Phi Delta Phi," *Student Lawyer,* March 1966, p. 6.

48. Bill Haney, "Faculty Spotlight," *Student Lawyer,* May 1966, p. 2.

49. "Cumberland Wins First Moot Court Event," *Student Lawyer,* May 1966, p. 1.

50. "Dean Weeks Reports Plans," *Student Lawyer,* November 1964, p. 1.

51. Governor George C. Wallace, "Political Parties and Principles," *Cumberland Lawyer* 1 (September 1966): 2.

52. Richmond M. Flowers, "Civil Obedience Under Law," *Cumberland Lawyer* 1 (November 1966): 1.

53. "*Miranda v. Arizona,*" *Cumberland Lawyer* 1 (November 1966): 6.

54. Joanne Furner, "Artificial Insemination," *Cumberland Lawyer* 1 (September 1966): 14.

55. Minutes of Cumberland School of Law Faculty, September 7, 1965.

56. *Cumberland Lawyer* 6 (November 1971): 5, 25.

57. Arthur A. Weeks, "A Report on the Progress of the Cumberland School of Law of Samford University (formerly Howard College)" (undated but internal evidence indicates 1965–66; file copy bears a "received" stamp dated Jan. 25, 1966).

58. "Essay Contests," *Cumberland Student Lawyer,* October 1965, p. 2; Stephen H. Davis, "Opportunity Knocking," *Cumberland Student Lawyer,* May 1966, p. 4.

59. "Cumberland Students Win Writing Contests," *Cumberland Lawyer* 3 (November 1968): 9.

60. Joan Wood, "Walker Wins National Award," *Pro Confesso,* September 1983, p. 1.

61. O. K. Ames, "The *Cumberland-Samford Law Review,*" *Cumberland Lawyer* 3 (December 1968): 9.

62. *Cumberland-Samford Law Review* 1 (Spring 1970): 83.

63. "The Cumberland-Samford Law Review," *Cumberland Lawyer* 4 (November 1969): 12; "The Cumberland-Samford Law Review," *Cumberland Lawyer* 4 (April 1970): 21; *Cumberland-Samford Law Review* 1 (Spring 1970): 1, 35.

64. "Cumberland-Samford Law Review," *Cumberland Lawyer* 5 (November 1970): 11.

65. *Cumberland Law Review* 6 (Spring 1975): front cover.

66. "Law Review Hosts National Conference," *Cumberland Lawyer* 20 (Fall 1984): 4.

67. Ann Skipper, "Cumberland Clinical Trial Board publishes Journal," *Pro Confesso,* March 25, 1977, p. 11.

68. See chapter 7 above, notes 43–50 and accompanying text; *Cumberland University School of Law Bulletin,* 1960–62, pp. 20–21 and 30–31 (course description of moot court) describing last years in Lebanon.

69. *Catalog of Cumberland School of Law of Howard College,* 1962–63 (with the move to Howard College, the shorter spelling "catalog" was adopted).

70. "Moot Court Team Ready," *Cumberland School of Law Student Lawyer,* November 1964, p. 1.

71. "National Moot Court," *Cumberland School of Law Student Lawyer,* December 1964, p. 1.

72. Catalog of Cumberland School of Law of Howard College, 1964–66.

73. Michael Medway, "Law Day Moot Court Competition," *Cumberland Lawyer* 2 (May 1968): 7.

74. "Cumberland Wins First Moot Court Event," *Cumberland Student Lawyer,* May 1966, p. 1.

75. Medway, "Law Day Moot Court Competition."

76. Minutes, Cumberland School of Law Faculty Meeting, December 1965.

77. Medway, "Law Day Moot Court Competition."

78. "Law Day Moot Court," *Cumberland Lawyer* 4 (April 1970): 20.

79. "Moot Court Team Selected," *Cumberland Lawyer* 2 (no date; no. 1): 2.

80. "National Moot Court Contest," *Cumberland Lawyer* 2 (January 1968): 6.

81. "National Moot Court Competition," *Cumberland Lawyer* 3 (December 1968): 15.

82. "Cumberland's Nat'l Moot Court Team Victorious in Regional—Competed in Final Rounds in New York City," *Cumberland Lawyer* 5 (April 1971): 4.

83. "Moot Court Board," *Cumberland Lawyer* 5 (April 1971): 23.

84. Catalog of Cumberland School of Law of Samford University, 1981–82; "Moot Court Board Named in Honor of Henry Upson Sims," *Cumberland Lawyer* 16 (Fall 1980): 9.

85. Catalog of Cumberland School of Law of Samford University, 1981–82.

86. Ron Henry, "Henry Upson Sims Moot Court Board wins 2nd Place in Regional Competition—Nationals Coming Up Soon," *Pro Confesso,* November 1980, p. 10.

87. "Association of Student International Law Societies Philip C. Jessup International Law Moot Competition," *Cumberland Lawyer* 2 (January 1968): 13; "Jessup Moot Court Competition: 1972," *Cumberland Lawyer* 7 (April 1973): 3; "International Law Society Moot Court Team to Participate in Moot Trial Contest at the U. of Ga.," *Cumberland Lawyer* 5 (April 1971): 13.

88. "International Law Moot Court Competition Results," *Cumberland Lawyer* 2 (March 1968): 9.

89. "New International Law Society Formed," *Cumberland Lawyer* 2 (May 1968): 11.

90. "International Law Society," *Cumberland Lawyer* 3 (December 1968): 15; "Cumberland International Law Society 68–69," *Cumberland Lawyer* (May 1969): 11.

91. "International Law Moot Court Competition," *Cumberland Lawyer* 3 (May 1969): 14.

92. "International Law Society," *Cumberland Lawyer* 3 (December 1968): 15; "Cumberland International Law Society 68–69," *Cumberland Lawyer* (May 1969): 11.

93. "Cumberland Hosts Philip C. Jessup Southern Regional International Law Moot Court Competition," *Cumberland Lawyer* 4 (April 1970): 8–9; "Cumberland Hosts Most Successful International Moot Court Competition in Years," *Cumberland Lawyer* 5 (November 1970): 13; Brendan B. Brown, "The 1970 Philip C. Jessup Moot Court Competition at Cumberland Law School—An Appraisal and an Appreciation," *Cumberland Lawyer* (April 1971): 6.

94. "The Cordell Hull International Law Society," *Cumberland Lawyer* 6 (November 1971): 29; "International Law Society," Ibid. (April 1972): 10; "Jessup Moot Court Competition: 1972," Ibid. 7 (April 1973): 3.

95. "The Cordell Hull International Law Society," *Cumberland Lawyer* 6 (November 1971): 29.

96. "International Law Society," *Cumberland Lawyer* 6 (April 1972): 10.

97. "Cordell Hull Chapter International Law Society Academic Year 1972–73," *Cumberland Lawyer* 7 (November 1972): 5.

98. "Rickner Elected National President of International Law Society," *Cumberland Lawyer* 8 (February 1974): 3.

99. "Admiralty Proctor Certificates Support International Law Society," *Cumberland Lawyer* 13 (Winter 1979): 14.

100. "Cumberland Hosts Most Successful International Moot Court Competition in Years," *Cumberland Lawyer* 5 (November 1970): 13; "The Cordell Hull International Law Society," *Cumberland Lawyer* 6 (November 1971): 29; "Admiralty Proctor Certificates Support International Law Society," *Cumberland Lawyer* 13 (Winter 1979): 14.

101. "The Cordell Hull International Law Society," *Cumberland Lawyer* 6 (November 1971): 29.

102. Tony Abbott, "Cumberland wins international moot court competition," *Pro Confesso,* April 4, 1978, p. 11.

103. See chapter 7, note 44 and accompanying text; Cumberland University School of Law Bulletin, 1960–62.

104. Irl Marcus, "National Mock Trial Competition," *Pro Confesso,* November 1981, p. 8.

105. Randy Hurst, "Clinical program offers opportunity," *Pro Confesso,* April 1976, p. 13; "Clinical Trial Program," *Cumberland Lawyer* 11 (Winter 1977): 6.

106. "Trial Team Excels at Duke," *Pro Confesso,* February 10, 1977, p. 5; "Trial Team Excels at Duke," *Cumberland Lawyer* 12 (Fall 1977): 2.

107. "Mock Trial Competition," *Pro Confesso,* March 3, 1977, p. 6; "Donald E. Corley Mock Trial Competition," *Pro Confesso,* March 25, 1977, p. 5.

108. "County Judges' Mock Trial," *Pro Confesso,* March 25, 1977, p. 2.

109. Ronald David Ashby, "New Center for Advocacy and Clinical Education," *Pro Confesso,* March 25, 1977, p. 2; Mike Ingram, "Journal of Trial Advocacy Published," *Pro Confesso,* September 9, 1977, p. 5.

110. Vince Sullivan, "Two Clinical Firsts at Cumberland," *Pro Confesso,* March 1980, 3 (unpaginated).

111. "Cumberland Mock Trial and Moot Court Teams Win Honors," *Cumberland Lawyer* 16 (Spring 1981): 6 (unpaginated); "Cumberland Wins Mock Trial Competition," *Pro Confesso,* March 1981, p. 6; "Cumberland Wins National Honors," *Pro Confesso,* April 1981, cover page; Irl Marcus, "Cumberland Wins National Trial Award," *Pro Confesso,* p. 1.

112. "Roscoe Pound Foundation Gives Award to Cumberland's Prof. James O. Haley," *Cumberland Lawyer* 26 (Fall 1991): 3.

113. Sumter Camp, "Cumberland Wins Again in '82," *Pro Confesso,* March 1982 (no. 5), p. 1.

114. "ATLA Team Completes Third Leg of The Triple Crown," *Pro Confesso,* March 1982, p. 1; Bill Horne, "Peterson B'ham Best," *Pro Confesso,* May 1984, p. 1.

115. "ATLA Team Dominates Regional Competition," *Cumberland Lawyer* 18 (Spring 1983): 5; "The ATLA National Trial Team Members and Regional Champions Glenn Martin and Labella Kyle," *Pro Confesso,* May 1984, p. 8.

116. Buddy Ackers, "National Trial Teams Sweep Competition," *Pro Confesso,* February 1984, p. 1.

117. "National Champs," *Pro Confesso,* May 1984, p. 1; "Step By Step," *Pro Confesso,* May 1984, p. 6; Jeff Shuminer, "Rowe, Outstanding Oralist," *Pro Confesso,* May 1984, p. 6; "Cumberland Wins National Championship," *Cumberland Lawyer* 19 (Spring 1984): 13.

118. Recollection of author Howard P. Walthall, who was a member of the committee.

Index

Accreditation concerns, 118; Havens and, 192; at Howard College, 205, 206; indifference to, 225; Keeton report and, 203; in 1985, 248, 251; in 1959, 196–97; in 1948, 172–73; in 1970s, 219–20, 222–25, 226; in 1930s, 125, 137; in post–World War II era, 183; Preston and, 170, 171; Root committee and, 136; segregation and, 212; Shafroth-Horack report and, 140; Steinheimer report and, 215–16; Stockton and, 134, 194–95, 205; Stockton Jr. and, 194–95; at Vanderbilt, 127; Weeks and, 172, 174, 177, 178, 180–82, 194, 198

Adams, Alfred Thompson, 181, 282 (n. 7)

Aderholt, Bobby R., 27, 207–8

Administrators. *See under individual names*

Allen, George E., 95

Allred, James V., 145–46, 161, 163

Alumni notables, 81–82, 113, 161

Amar, Akhil Reed, 250

Ames, James Barr, 105, 119, 121, 126, 235

Anderson, Joseph M., 88

Anderson, T. C., 43

Arnold, Earl C., 127

Ayres, Brown, 127, 128, 135

Bailey, Bernard B., 174, 181, 190, 207

Bailey, Joseph Weldon, 81, 86

Baird, W. J., 130, 144

Baird, William D., 189–90

Bankester, Claude E., 192, 213

Bar examinations, 101–2, 125, 148–49, 171–72, 225

Bashinsky, L. E., 203

Beale, Joseph, 236

Beard, Edward E.: appointment of, 129; career of, 120; compensation for, 129; deanship of, 119; illness of, 121; library acquisitions and, 100; in moot court, 82; part-time instruction by, 78; power of, 128; professorship offered to, 116

Beard, Richard, Sr., 120

Beard, Richard, Jr., 120

Beard, W. D., 120

Beeson, Lucille Stewart, 252, 253

Biden, Joseph, 233

Bishop, Thomas B. (Brad), 79, 211, 218, 226, 247, 290 (n. 49)

Blackstone, William, 3, 5, 32, 33, 59, 187

Bone, Sam Stratton, 275 (n. 34)

Bone, Winston P., 124, 174

Boren, David, 234

Bouton, Mrs. W. P., 90

Bowers, S. C., 48

Bradford, William R., 93, 96

Brian, William G., 41

Bridges, M. L., 95

Bridges, Marvin O., 94, 95

Brown, Milton, 46

Brown, Richard, 158

Browning, G. W., 77

Buchanan, James, 45

Buildings, 43, 50; Campbell Academy, 52; Caruthers Hall ("law barn"), 56–57, 78, 80, 86, 90, 91, 92, 98, 99, 100, 134, 140, 144, 147, 156, 159, 160, 163, 167, 175, 181, 184, 191–92, 194, 204, 225, 243, 283 (n. 14); Cordell Hull Building, 192; Corona Hall, 53, 57, 67; Divinity Hall (A. Caruthers house), 51–52, 85–86, 99; dormitory, 84–85, 86, 163, 192–93, 287 (n. 100); Memorial Hall, 80, 85, 99–100, 132, 181, 184, 191, 229; Memory Leake Robinson Hall, 209, 210, 211, 215, 217, 220, 222, 223, 231, 252. *See also* Libraries
Bulloch, Loren, 213
Burns, G. Frank, 141–42, 144, 168, 260 (n. 21), 269 (n. 64), 275 (n. 34), 283 (n. 14)
Burns, John, 95

Caldwell, Waller C., 78, 82, 266 (n. 64)
Carlock, Robert L., 193
Carter, John Cartwright, 19, 46, 49
Caruthers, Abraham: "collateral course" offered by, 33; compensation for, 20; daughters of, 19, 46; death of, 27, 47; financial demands of, 10–11; former house of, 51–52, 85–86, 99; S. B. Gilreath and, 123; *History of a Lawsuit,* 27, 62, 74, 75, 123, 151, 157, 175, 208; ideas developed by, 17; inaugural address of, 1, 9, 15, 24–25, 32; initial appointment of, 9; personal qualities of, 31; political views of, 21–22; post–Civil War faculty and, 59; professorship offered to, 8; self-interest of, 12
Caruthers, Robert L.: Corona Hall purchased by, 53, 67; correspondence of, 8; death of, 77, 98; faculty recruitment by, 12, 13; full-time teaching by, 52; Greenleaf and, 12; on Harvard textbooks, 30; illness of, 77, 108; lot donated by, 56; Lurton and, 69; office of, 1, 11, 124; personal qualities of, 64; pranks and, 66; professional background of, 7; resignation of, 54, 77; salary guaranteed by, 9, 10; tribute to, 78
Caruthers, William A., 40
Cash, A. J., 132–33
Cassidy, Lewis, 126, 236, 238, 275 (n. 39)
Chambers, William R., 124, 129; classroom manner of, 155; first-day lectures of, 146; legal ethics exam of, 157; A. B. Neil and, 123; professional background of, 120–21; questions by, 156; resignation of, 125, 138; school opened by, 275 (n. 34)
Cheatham (student), 80
Cheatham, Elliott, 168, 177, 178
Childs, Edward P., 114–15, 129, 133
Civil War, 22, 43, 46, 47–48, 49–50, 51, 54, 56, 68, 98
Clapp, Laurel R., 222
Cleveland, Grover, 47, 68
Clinton, William J., 234
Coeducation. *See* Students, coeducation
Coffman, Patricia, 203–4, 208
Cole, Charles, 213
Collins, LeRoy, 112, 146–47, 163, 199, 280 (n. 53)
Connor, Eugene ("Bull"), 207
Cooper, Henry, 51
Copeland (student), 159
Corley, Donald E., 225–26; acting deanship of, 217–18; CLE and, 252; extracurricular activities and, 228, 233, 234, 244–45; Grooms on, 221; promotions/tenure committee and, 247; Ruud and, 219, 220, 222; student years of, 211; Walthall on, 290 (n. 49); J. P. White and, 224

Corts, Thomas E., 226, 246–47
Cossitt, Franceway Ranna, 6, 36–37, 43, 205
Course requirements. *See* Curriculum, course requirements
Cox, Nicholas N., 46
Cross, Joseph D., 48
Crutchfield, Charles, 88
Curriculum: continuing education, 252; course requirements, 29–30, 57–58; duration, 5, 34, 58, 59–60, 61, 102, 103–4, 118, 125, 127, 129, 135, 137, 138, 141, 148, 149, 151, 167, 171, 176, 182, 235; evening program, 210, 211–12, 214, 215; grading (*See* Grading policies); moot court, 16, 27–28, 46, 62–63, 78, 82, 157–59, 160, 175, 238–41, 243–44; postgraduate, 73, 121–22; practical, 32–33; stable, 72, 75, 83, 97, 103, 105; summer program, 73–74, 183; teaching methods, 2, 16–17, 24–25, 29–30, 35, 57, 60, 61–62, 63, 78–79, 102–3, 105–8, 122, 152, 153, 154–57, 159–60, 169–70, 173, 175, 235–36, 239; tuition (*See* Tuition)

Daniel, Sinclair, 274 (n. 23)
Davis, Harwell G., 186, 197, 198, 204, 205, 206
Davis, Jefferson, 45
Debt. *See* Finances/debt/endowment
Dees, Morris, 233
Demeree, Richard J., 181
Denney, Walter Raymond, 282 (n. 7)
Desucckes (student), 40
Discipline. *See* Students, discipline
Dodd, Annette, 213, 218
Donaldson, Frank, 213–14
Doss, Chriss, 213
Douglas, Byrd, 282 (n. 7)
Dwight, Theodore, 107

Edison, McGraw, 147
Eggleston, Katharine, 91
Ellington, Buford, 199
Elliott, Sheldon, 181
Endowment. *See* Finances/debt/endowment
Enrollment, 17, 55, 109–10, 143–45, 149–51, 182, 191–92, 210, 215–16
Entrance requirements, 25, 26–27, 77, 112–13
Eshelman, Betty Davis, 204
Extracurricular activities, 82, 162, 184, 227–45; fraternities and social clubs, 43–45, 162–63, 183, 184, 227, 229–30; literary societies, 44–45, 53, 69–70, 71, 92, 160–61, 281 (n. 56); moot court (*See* Curriculum, moot court); pranks, 43, 66–67, 86; publications (*See* Publications); social activities, 86, 90–91, 164–65, 229; sports, 93–96, 163, 183, 246, 247; student bar association, 184–85, 229, 230, 231, 232, 233–34, 244

Faculty. *See under individual names*
Fancher, Frank T., 125–26, 159
Faxon, Julian K. (Kenneth), 121–22, 123, 126, 133
Fillmore, Millard, 45
Finances/debt/endowment: ABA standards for, 172; in antebellum era, 19–21; Beard professorship and, 116; in depression era, 125, 138, 140; faculty compensation in 1920s, 9–12, 129–33; faculty compensation in 1930s, 137–38; faculty compensation in 1960s and 1970s, 214–15, 222–23; Gamble committee and, 221–22; in Havens era, 191, 193, 194; at Howard College, 205, 221; Keeton report and, 203; in late 1970s, 223–24, 225; in 1920s, 130, 131–32; from 1920 to 1947,

Finances/debt/endowment (*Continued*) 118–19; Phoenix Fund and, 220; in post–Civil War era, 50, 51–52, 53, 54, 55–56, 99; in post–World War II era, 183; Second Century Campaign and, 170, 178–79; "A Senior Lawyer" on, 166; in Stockton era, 135; at University of Tennessee, 127; at Vanderbilt, 127; World War II and, 283 (n. 14); Wright and, 214–15, 224
Fine, John, 159
Finley, Thomas B., 126, 141
Fletcher, Joseph, 233
Flowers, Richmond, 237
Ford, Gerald R., 253
Forrester, Hal, 184
Fraternities. *See* Extracurricular activities, fraternities and social clubs

Gamble, Charles, 220, 221–22
Gaston, A. G., 213
Gaston, Audrey Lattimore, 212–13
Gibbs (student), 159
Gilreath, Samuel B., 141, 181; ABA and, 174, 177; acting deanship of, 170, 171, 172, 178; Daniel and, 274 (n. 23); *History of a Lawsuit* and, 27, 123, 207–8; Howard College service of, 207; C. C. Humphreys and, 199; marriage of, 124; military service of, 126; in moot court, 158, 159, 243; Pope and, 179, 180; Sunday school of, 163–64, 167, 184, 227; University of Tennessee offer and, 201; Weeks and, 190, 197, 200
Grading policies, 75–77, 132
Grant, Russell, 154
Green, Betty M., 45
Green, Grafton, 129, 137
Green, Nathan, Sr., 19; in Civil War era, 47, 49; compensation for, 20; constitutional amendment and, 14; death of, 51; full-time instruction by, 15, 18; inaugural address of, 13–14; on H. Jackson, 46, 263 (n. 82); Lurton and, 69; part-time instruction by, 10, 13; personal qualities of, 31–32; political views of, 21–22; professorship declined by, 8, 12–13; on school policies, 24, 33; on vices, 38
Green, Nathan, Jr.: A.B. degree of, 25; affection for, 80, 268 (n. 30); alumni and, 81, 101; on antebellum students, 41, 43, 60; appearance of, 32; automobile of, 79, 91; J. W. Bailey and, 86; bar exam issue and, 101; on R. L. Caruthers, 7; Caruthers house purchase and, 52; on Civil War era, 47, 50; commencement receptions by, 80, 92; compensation for, 20, 98; deanship of, 102; death of, 114, 115, 119, 120, 129; on discipline, 38–39, 65–66, 87–88, 89; exams graded by, 77, 114; extramural changes and, 59, 108; Fancher and, 126; full-time faculty of, 78; on grading, 75–76; hall rented by, 98; initial appointment of, 18–19; last days of, 113–14; library acquisitions and, 100; longer curricula and, 104; longevity of, 108, 110, 116; Lurton and, 69; marriage of, 45–46, 79; military service of, 49; in moot court, 28–29, 62–63, 82; multiple responsibilities of, 54–55; A. B. Neil and, 123; personal qualities of, 63–64; political views of, 21–22; in post–Civil War era, 51; postgraduate program and, 73; power of, 128, 225; on recent graduates, 83; student years of, 13, 204; theological department and, 54, 72; on valedictorian selection, 70, 71
Green (student), 87
Greenleaf, Simon, 12
Greer, David B., 34
Grooms, H. H., 203, 209, 216, 217, 219, 221

Haley, James O., 244
Hardison, Sara, 122, 123, 146, 148, 155, 162–63, 183, 282 (n. 7)
Harrell, John, 213
Harris, John Royal, 128, 130–31, 132, 133
Harrison, Benjamin, 47
Haskell, Wyatt Rushton, 250
Hatch, Carl, 112
Havens, Charles B., 190–91, 192, 193, 194, 287 (n. 100)
Head, James, 207
Heisman, John W., 95
Henry, Patrick, 48
Hervey, John, 177–78, 181, 193, 203, 206, 209, 215, 219, 224
Hill, H. R. W., 34
Hooker, Amzi Waddell, 128, 130
Hooker, John J., 123, 126, 197–98, 199, 201–2
Horack, H. Claude, 127, 139, 140, 142, 167, 177
Horton, James E., 128–29
Hoskins, James, 131
Houston, Sam, 7
Huddleston, George, Sr., 81
Huddleston, George, Jr., 209
Hughes, James L. ("Commander"), 213, 242
Hull, Cordell, 72, 81–82, 92, 93, 101, 112–13, 141, 161, 166, 201, 228, 242
Humphreys, Allison B., Jr., 126, 141
Humphreys, Cecil C., 198, 199, 200
Hutchens, Raymond, 213

Indebtedness. *See* Finances/debt/endowment
Irving, Washington, 45

Jackson, Alexander, 46, 263 (n. 82)
Jackson, Andrew, 4, 91, 177
Jackson, Howell, 46–47, 81–82, 166
Jamison, John A., 148, 153, 154, 156, 157, 163, 167, 229, 280 (n. 53)
Jessup, Philip C., 241
Johnson, Andrew, 45
Johnson, Tillman Davis, 85–86

Keeton, Page, 193–94, 203
Kilpatrick, James J., 233
Kirkland, James H., 127, 128, 135
Kirkpatrick, John D., 99
Kronman, Anthony T., 250
Kuhn, Thomas, 97

Langdell, Christopher Columbus, 60, 105, 119, 135, 175
Laska, Lewis L., 97
Lebanon Law School, 57, 265 (n. 33)
Lewis, Thomas, 158
Lewis, William Draper, 138
Libraries: ABA standards for, 172, 173, 174, 183; in antebellum era, 33–34, 55; Cordell Hull Library, 283 (n. 14); Davis Library, 204; international law books in, 242; in late 1970s, 222–23, 224, 225; Lucille Stewart Beeson Law Library, 252–53, 283 (n. 14); in Memorial Hall, 99–101, 181; Memory Leake Robinson Hall, 209, 252; in 1950s, 194; in 1930s, 148; in post–Civil War era, 57, 62; "Report of the Survey of Law Schools" on, 283 (nn. 14, 18, 19); Ruud report on, 220–23
Likens, Edith, 90
Lile, W. M., 97
Lincoln, Abraham, 22, 47, 48, 69
Lindsley, J. Berrien, 64
Literary societies. *See* Extracurricular activities, literary societies
Lockmiller, David A., 186–87
Love, D. L., 66–67
Lurton, Horace, 67–69, 78, 81–82, 166

McClain, Betty, 45
McClain, Josiah S., 45–46
McDermott, Malcolm, 132

MacFarland, Alfred Towson, 159, 282 (n. 7)
Mack, Julian, 235–36
McNeilly, Edward L., 126
Manning, Kenneth R., Jr., 221–22
Martin, Andrew Bennett: compensation for, 98; death of, 119, 120, 129; extramural changes and, 108, 113; Fancher and, 126; Gilreath and, 123; on Greens, 49; Hull on, 72; library acquisitions and, 100–101; longer curricula and, 104; A. B. Neil and, 81, 120, 123; part-time instruction by, 52, 77; personal qualities of, 80–81; political economy course of, 89; power of, 128, 225; presidency of, 115; sketches attributed to, 260 (n. 21); summer program and, 73, 74, 102; tributes by, 78, 114
Michael, Van Reeves, 204
Miller, Justin, 230
Moot court. *See* Curriculum, moot court
Morgan, Charles, 233

Nader, Ralph, 233
Neil, Albert B., 124, 198; conservatism of, 118, 141; on discipline, 164; Ellington and, 199; Martin and, 81, 120, 123; resignation of, 125; return of, 121; Shafroth-Horack report on, 140; torts class of, 156, 279 (n. 38); on treatise method, 173
Neil, M. M., 266 (n. 64)
Newman, Claire B., 90

Otho, John, 158

Papale, A. E., 193
Parsons, Theophilus, 2
Patterson, Haywood, 129
Pearce, Wooten, 208
Peay, Austin, 121
Pedagogy. *See* Curriculum, teaching methods
Peters, George B., 66–67
Peters, Margaret, 146, 147, 148, 155, 162
Peters, Richard, 147, 148, 162, 280 (n. 51)
Phillips, Harry, 146, 163, 179, 209
Pitts, John A., 61, 63–64, 107, 266 (n. 64)
Pope, Charles W., 179, 180
Powell, Lewis F., 209
Pranks. *See* Extracurricular activities, pranks
Preston, Edwin, 168, 169, 170–71, 174, 177, 179
Prim, Paine P., 26
Publications: alumni publication, 101, 118, 237; literary magazine, 69; newspapers, 82, 86, 87, 93, 124, 138, 143, 145, 157–58, 159, 161–62, 164–65, 167, 227, 228, 229, 233, 234, 236, 237, 238, 239, 282 (n. 80); yearbook, 79, 80, 92–93, 94, 183, 184. *See also* Scholarly publications
Pullias, Athens Clay, 188, 198–99

Quillian, Joe, 186

Rafferty, Max, 233
Rascal (dog), 163, 166–67, 282 (n. 80)
Reed, Alfred Zantzinger, 134, 135, 272 (n. 27)
Rice, Grantland, 94, 95
Rice, Laban L., 43, 130, 141, 283 (n. 14)
Richardson, W. Edwin, 169, 179, 180
Ridley, Bromfield L., 10, 13, 15, 18, 19
Robertson, C. W., 48
Robinson, Memory Leake, 197, 198, 201–2, 203, 209, 210
Rollison, William, 213
Roosevelt, Franklin D., 81, 160, 161
Root, Elihu, 135–36
Rousseau, Mary Gregory, 160
Rushton, Ray, 250
Rusk, Dean, 232
Ruud, Millard, 219–20, 222

Samford, Frank P., 203, 209, 210, 220
Sandel, Alberta, 90
Sanders, Clifford E., 144, 146, 147, 148, 154, 155, 156, 278 (n. 9), 280 (nn. 51, 53)
Sanders, Joseph, 88, 269 (n. 64)
Scholarly publications, 173–74, 235, 236–38, 243, 247, 248, 249–50
"Senior Lawyer, A," 164–66
Seston, W. N., 41
Shafroth, Will D., 139–40, 142, 167, 177
Shannon, J. L., 91–92, 166
Sherman, Samuel Sterling, 205
Sherman (student), 158
Shores, Janie L., 213, 214
Shriver, Sargeant, 233
Sims, Henry Upson, 241
Slayden, Mary, 46
Social activities. *See* Extracurricular activities, social activities
Sowa, Walter, 213
Spencer, William F., 84, 117
Stanford, William J., 181
Steinheimer, Roy L., Jr., 215, 216, 219, 220, 222
Stephenson, T. C., 77
Sterne, Edwin, 213
Stockton, Ernest L., Sr., 133–35, 137, 194–95; on beer, 164; inaugural address of, 118, 138; M. Peters and, 162; resignation of, 141
Stockton, Ernest L., Jr., 194–95; on coincidental foundings, 205; Howard College representatives and, 198, 201; purchase approved by, 202
Story, Joseph, 3, 119, 153, 154
Student bar association. *See* Extracurricular activities, student bar association
Students: attrition, 55, 111–12; boarding, 41–42, 67, 84, 85, 86; coeducation, 45, 67, 89–90, 93, 146, 147, 165, 184, 216; composition, 56, 60, 109–12, 145; discipline, 36–41, 65–66, 87–89, 130, 164, 192–93, 287 (n. 100); extracurricular activities (*See* Extracurricular activities); minority students, 17–18; 211–13
Sumner, Charles, 45
Sykes, Columbus, 28

Taft, William Howard, 68, 136
Taney, Roger B., 45
Taylor, Henry L., 272 (n. 27)
Teaching methods. *See* Curriculum, teaching methods
Templeton (student), 158
Terrell, Glenn, 147
Themistocles, 177
Thomas, Clarence, 250
Thurman, Samuel D., 203
Totten, A. W. O., 46
Trammell, Park, 81
Tuition: in antebellum era, 12, 19–20, 34; family plan for, 147; at Howard College, 221; in 1950s, 192; in 1977, 223; in post–Civil War era, 53–54, 57; in post–World War II era, 183; stability of, 83–84, 98, 148

Vance, Currell, 125
Vaughn, Lena K., 90

Walker, Grissim H., 190–91, 192, 198
Wallace, George C., 237
Ward, W. E., 50
Weeks, Arthur A., 170–71, 225–26; AALS and, 198; ABA and, 172, 174, 177, 178, 180–82, 194, 216; acting deanship of, 204–5; alternatives favored by, 185, 201; appellate advocacy and, 239, 243; W. D. Baird and, 189–90; Catholics and, 186, 233; Corley and, 217, 218; at dedication ceremony, 207; on diploma privilege, 208–9; on enrollment growth, 210; evening division and, 211; extracurricular activities and, 228, 244, 245;

Weeks, Arthur A. (*Continued*)
faculty grievances and, 214; Free Will Baptists and, 187; Howard trustee committee and, 203; C. C. Humphreys and, 199; Keeton and, 194; law review and, 236; library inspection by, 173; Moot Court Board and, 241; Pope and, 179, 180; post-1961 faculty and, 213; Preston and, 168–69; resignations of, 188, 217, 228; return of, 195; Robinson and, 197; SBA and, 234; University of Tennessee proposal and, 200; on writing contests, 237
West, Wilson, 163
Wheeler, Joseph, 50
Wheeler, Ruric, 222
White, James P., 224
White, Weldon B., 282 (n. 7)
Wieczorowski, Alexander E., 94
Wigmore, John, 235–36
Wilburn, George, 159
Wilkerson (student), 80
Williams, Albert, 121, 122, 124, 125, 137–38, 158, 159
Williams, Parham H., Sr., 144, 246–47
Williams, Parham H., Jr., 211, 247–48, 249, 290 (n. 49)
Wilson, Mrs. Billy, 84
Wilson, Silas, 158
Women students. *See* Students, co-education
World War I, 74, 85, 93, 111, 143
World War II, 126, 141–42, 151, 205, 280 (n. 53), 283 (n. 14)
Wright, Leslie S.: ABA and, 215, 216, 224; on Corley, 219; H. G. Davis and, 206; endowment campaign of, 214; on enrollment, 208; Gamble committee and, 222; Gaston and, 212–13; Hervey and, 203; Hooker and, 202; retirement of, 226; Ruud and, 220; Samford and, 209; Stockton and, 201; Weeks and, 197, 217